Jasper County Public Library System

Overdue notices are a courtesy of
the library system.
Failure to receive an overdue notice
does not absolve the borrower of the
obligation to return materials on time.

MUSIC

Johannes Rademacher

BARRON'S

Cover photos from top to bottom and left to right: Sydney Opera House / Autograph of Maurice Ravel / Joseph Karl Stiller, Ludwig von Beethoven, painted in 1820 (Beethoven House, Bonn) / Scene from a classical opera / Louis "Satchmo" Armstrong / Renaissance illustrated diagram of a canon in the form of a riddle / French Baroque harpsichord with elaborate decoration (Museum of the History of Fabrics and Decorative Arts, Lyon) / Walther von der Vogelweide, miniature from the Manessesche Manuscript (Library of the University of Heidelberg) / The Beatles (Apple Corp.) / 19th-century violin / Elias Gottlob Hausmann, Johann Sebastian Bach, painted in 1746 (Municipal Historical Museum, Leipzig) / Richard Wagner, 19th-century cut paper silhouette / Jan Steen (1626–79), "A Young Woman Playing the Harpsichord for a Young Man," painting (The National Gallery, London)
Back cover from top to bottom: Joseph Lange, "Wolfgang Amadeus Mozart at the Piano," unfinished oil painting, 1789 (Mozart's birth house, Salzburg) / "Pythagoras Performs an Acoustical Experiment," medieval woodcut / Balinese Dancers
Frontispiece: Pablo Picasso, "La table devant la fenêtre," gouache 1919

American text version by: Editorial Office Sulzer-Reichel, Rösrath, Germany
Translated by: Ann Jeffers-Brown, Cambridge, Mass.
Edited by: Bessie Blum, Cambridge, Mass.

First edition for the United States and Canada
published by Barron's Educational Series, Inc., 1996.

First published in the Federal Republic of Germany in 1995 by
DuMont Buchverlag GmbH und Co. Kommanditgesellschaft,
Köln, Federal Republic of Germany.

Text copyright © 1995 DuMont Buchverlag GmbH und Co. Kommanditgesellschaft,
Köln, Federal Republic of Germany.

Copyright © 1996 U.S. language translation, Barron's Educational Series, Inc.

All inquiries should be addressed to:
Barron's Educational Series, Inc.
250 Wireless Boulevard
Hauppauge, New York 11788

Library of Congress Catalog Card No. 96-83723

ISBN 0-8120-9773-4

Printed in Italy by Editoriale Libraria

Contents

Preface

This book is neither a concert guide nor a musicological essay.

But if, for example, you happen to hear a sonata on the radio and find yourself wondering what, after all, a sonata is; or you're curious to know why Beethoven was such a great figure in his own time as well as for us today; or why the evening-long operas of Richard Wagner had such a powerful influence on the composers of all Europe–the answers are here, in a clear, concise format.

The facts of music history—so often the dry material of textbooks—appear not as an orderly recitation of all kinds of things supposedly worth knowing, but rather as connections between the musical events of an age and the reigning assumptions and realities from which they emerged. In such a context, against such a background, music is not only interesting, but often exciting. Through such an approach we can appreciate why, for example, Johann Sebastian Bach was considered old-fashioned and outmoded in his own time, while his son was treated essentially as a superstar; why *Le Sacre du printemps* of Igor Stravinsky unleashed such a scandal in 1913; or why the music of Arnold Schönberg seemed so strange to his contemporaries. In this manner, and so informed, we can experience the delight of music well beyond the pleasure of a single concert or visit to the opera.

Another thing this book is *not*: it is not another tribute to the ancient monuments of the history of music. No composer, or his or her works, can be explained simply as the outpouring of the individual's brilliance; we do far better to understand their contributions in relation to the impulse to further development of music.

The compact form of this book allows quick access to information, beyond a quick orientation of the basic continuity of European music history. Therefore, the Barron's Crash Course is an aid in understanding music not only as cultural history, but also as an exciting and interesting phenomenon.

Johannes Rademacher, Cologne

Between speculation and calculation

Musical activity is one of the elemental activities of life. While not everyone will feel the need to paint a picture or to write a poem (beyond the developmental scribbles and word plays of childhood), each in his or her own way has felt the need to sing—even if only in the shower or the car.

No one can say definitively how music emerged. One may assume, however, that singing is another form of speaking, and thus that it enabled communication between individuals or within a group. Other theories suggest that the making of music originated in imitation of animal sounds. In many of the world's cultures, there is a distinction between personal music making for the satisfaction of emotional needs, and the institutionalized performance of music, which requires the specialization and professionalization of musicians.

In many non-Western cultures music still serves as a way to make contact with gods or spirits, or to transmit the history and tradition of

Music is an essential part of social life in all cultures. The variety of displays in tomb paintings allows us to infer its importance in Egypt. Some of the instruments shown in these paintings are still in use today, and were common throughout the Mediterranean region. To the left of the dancers sits a woman playing a wind instrument resembling the Greek aulos; beside her a woman plays the cymbals.

the respective group with which it is closely associated. (Even in the history of Western civilization, one finds this function—Homer's *Iliad* and *Odyssey* were originally "sung," while the role of song in Western religious ritual is well known.) Music becomes thereby a religious act and occupies a central position within the society.

In Western civilization, the meaning of music has changed considerably over the course of time. The metaphysical component has almost completely disappeared. The idea that everything in life rests on an order, which music allows one to imitate and understand, was the real sense of music, and this view had never been essentially questioned until very recently.

Of intervals and planets

As for the scholars of all advanced civilizations, so for the philosophers of ancient Greece, music was included in their system of thought as a basic assumption of society. This assumption carries two strands, both of which are completely essential for the understanding of music: on the one hand are the mathematical and physical bases of music, and on the other hand are the resulting emotional effects.

In the 6th century B.C., Pythagoras calculated that vibrating strings produce pitches in certain proportions to one another. He discovered that dividing a string in the middle produces a sound exactly an octave (eight notes) higher than the whole string, and dividing a string in the relationship 2:3 produces a fifth higher, the relationship 3:4 a fourth, and so on. Pythagoras and many others believed that the ratios of the intervals correspond to the proportions of the planets, which was interpreted as the best proof that music is cosmic and has a divine source.

Medieval drawings often depicted the Greek music theoretician Pythagoras. Whether Pythagoras really experimented with water-filled glasses to demonstrate ratios in music is not certain, though it is conceivable.

Pythagoras surely used a stringed instrument to calculate the relationship between intervals.

PITAGORAS

The Dorian Mode: a scale with two four-note halves, each with identical relationships between whole and half steps.

Music moves the soul

While the mathematical calculation of the properties of vibrating strings went undebated, the discussion around the emotional effects of music was occasion for furious controversies. Some believed that certain keys exercised a negative influence on the soul or promoted lack of character and loose behavior. The Greek tonality system was set up so that an octave (eight-note scale) was divided into two equal halves, or tetrachords. The sequence of whole and half steps within the tetrachords determined the respective keys, which were named Dorian, Phrygian, and Lydian after Greek landscapes. Indian and Arabic music were similar to the Greek in that they were thought of completely linearly; that is, certain notes of a scale were especially important for melodic development. The idea that the character of a key calls forth certain emotions in the listener is central to the Greek musical aesthetic, which it shares with Arabic and Indian music.

It is impossible to say whether one key really could make people behave better, and another scale promote wantonness. It is clear, however, that music—as in the scene depicted on this Greek vase—can call forth extraordinary emotions.

Song—Wind music—Theatrical music

Displays on Greek vases and the accounts from Homer's *Iliad* and *Odyssey* suggest that the epics were recited in a kind of speech-song, or recitative, while the singers accompanied themselves on a kithara, a lyre-like instrument. It is hard to imagine that the rhythmic formation of this song exactly followed the meter of the text: the result would have been far too monotonous.

Aside from this form of recitative, known as *kitharodie*, the Greeks had an independent instrumental music, which was performed on the *aulos*. The aulos was a wind instrument with a tone like that of an oboe, on which the player tried to imitate the human voice with all its individual qualities (this was called *aulodie*).

In the Greek theater, song played a central role. In a semicircular area in front of the stage, the so-called orchestra, stood the chorus, whose task was generally to comment upon the stage action.

Cultural export

This very theoretical, carefully reasoned Greek musical system exerted a strong influence on Western musical understanding far into the Middle Ages; its influence may even be discerned to this day. Both the Greek musical outlook and Greek philosophy were primarily disseminated in the first centuries through Arabic handwriting. Meanwhile, through the Emperor

The aulos was a wind instrument with an oboe-like tone, here shown along with a drum and finger cymbals, a miniature form of the modern orchestral cymbals.

Prehistory – 1200 A.D.

Gregorian chant (plainsong): most important type of medieval church music; sung in unison; basis for further development of medieval music

Proportional intervals: relationship of the notes (pitches) to one another; the octave (eight notes apart) in the relationship 1:2, the fifth (five notes apart) 2:3, the fourth 3:4, the third 4:5, etc.; these sound as so-called overtones in each pitch and determine the sound character of tonalities (keys)

Church modes: tonalities named after the Greek keys, although containing other pitches; originally four "authentic" and four "plagal" modes—Dorian, Phrygian, Lydian, and Mixolydian—with different key notes and relationships between notes

Recitative: combination of speaking and singing; usually with a specific rhythm, which is often monotonous

Tropes: textual inserts in hymns, performed with many melodic embellishments

Troubadour, trouvère, minnesingers: noble secular poets who composed complicated rhyming poetry set to the tunes of Gregorian hymns

Musical education in ancient Greece: Students learn to play an instrument by exact observation and imitation of the teacher. This is typical of cultures where music is primarily transmitted orally.

Constantine I, the city Byzantium (present-day Istanbul), evolved into an important Christian cultural center. In this time, music received its essential impulses from both these cultures: New forms such as psalmody, with a clear system for the singing of psalm verses in an alternating manner ("antiphon"), or hymnody, antiphonal singing of religious texts on already existing melodies, show Christian influences. The formation and development of the melodies, however, including freedom of improvisation and delicacies of tuning, come from Arabic music.

Monastic musical culture—The Gregorian chant

For about a half millennium Gregorian chant, also known as plainsong, stood at the center of European music. Groups of up to seven monks (most commonly) stood in a circle and chanted hymns in unison. The designation "Gregorian" is misleading. Pope Gregory I the Great (590–604) set himself the task of centralizing the Catholic Church and standardizing its liturgy. This task was extended to include church music. First, the *Schola Cantorum* (School of Singing) was established in Rome. These singers were entrusted with the music of the church. Soon convents all over Europe set up similar singing schools in which the clerics were instructed in Gregorian plainsong style. The hymns were recorded with the help of the so-called neumes, which indicated only an approximation of the pitches and their move-ments. Only with the invention of staff lines in the 11th century was it possible to notate precise pitch (see p. 19).

The Romanesque Abbey of St. Riquier, drawn by Pettau, 1612, after an 11th-century manuscript. The music of Gregorian chants was observed strictly in the cloister.

Phrases, forms, systems

One of the essential features of plainsong is that the melody has fixed phrases made up of smaller musical parts strung together. The phrases of the melody correspond to the lines of the text. As a rule, these melodies are syllabic—that is, one note is sung on each syllable of text. The melodies formed from the phrases once again make up a regular pattern, using typical intervals and turns. First, the melodies themselves were developed in practice, and then a theoretical tonality (key) system was derived to explain and fit them.

In standardizing the liturgy, Pope Gregory I the Great also reformed church music. Thus, plainsong, or the chanting of hymns, was given his name, although the tradition was already quite old.

This system proceeds on the assumption that the phrases and melodies are built on certain pitches (notes), which indicate by their order and number a certain scale (ordered series of notes). Initially four "authentic" and four "plagal" church scales, or modes, were derived. Their number was later expanded. Whether a mode was authentic or plagal, and what its key note was, was determined by the closing pitch (*finalis*) and by often repeated pitches (*repercussa*) in the course of the melody. The church modes were named after the Greek modes: Dorian (built on D), Phrygian (built on E), Lydian (built on F), and Mixolydian (built on G). At this point, however, an error crept in: the Greek Dorian mode begins on E. The Greek and Medieval modes are not comparable on this point. However, the theorists have been very little disturbed by this. Until around 1600, when the church modes were finally displaced by the major/minor system, many drafted their own systems.

Prehistory – 1200 A.D.

The system of church modes, with authentic modes using notes 1, 3, 5, and 7 of the scale, and plagal modes using notes 2, 4, 6, and 8. From the order of the structural, repeated, and final notes emerge certain melodic phrases, which are typical for the respective mode.

Expansion of the form

This purely syllabic text setting of hymns led to a certain monotony, which was counteracted in two ways: first, by embellishing certain syllables of a word with melodic turns and runs (*melismas*) or by inserting into the hymn a completely new text (*trope*), which would be highly melismatic. From this, the "sequences" developed, which also served as forms for secular vocal and instrumental music. In the Middle Ages there were about 5,000 known sequences. The Tridentinic Council of 1545–63 decided to shrink their number to four, and these were sung on church holidays and to the requiem.

Presentation of a play in the marketplace. It is easy to imagine how spectacular shows arose out of the original intent of instructing the masses.

Religious instruction with consequences

The Gregorian plainsong style spread outside church liturgy. A trope (a small piece of interpolated text sung in highly melismatic style) from the Easter liturgy, *Quem queritis in sepulcro? (Whom do you seek in the tomb?)*, was presented with scenery and a procession. Soon these small dramas and miracle plays, which were thought of primarily as religious instruction, were parodied. The repertoire of traveling scholars and clerics included such titles as "All Fools' Day" and "Donkey's Feast" and these were presented to general hilarity in the marketplace.

The courtly music tradition: Troubadours, trouvères, and minnesingers

The music of the church and cloister once again was put to a secular purpose when toward the end of the 11th century the noble poets in France began to set their texts and poems to melodies they knew from church. Those in the south were called troubadours, and in the north trouvères (from the Provençal *trobar* and French *trouver*—to find or invent). An abundance of songs emerged; they were complicated in rhyme structure and construction, but identical in musical style with liturgical songs, and musically offered nothing new. Almost as abundant as the constructions of these songs was their subject matter. A specific song form was used for each occasion—for example, the *Chanson de Croisade* (Crusade Song) set to the music of "The Outcry from the Cross," or the *Lamentation*, for the death of the master of servants. One subject, however, towered above all others: not surprisingly, that one subject was love.

In the French Anjou a miniaturist painted music as an allegory. Pictured are the typical instruments used by troubadours, trouvères, and minnesingers. The idea that the organ takes a central position among the instruments is already very old.

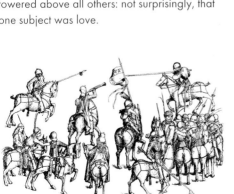

The modern mind often associates the Middle Ages with the Age of Chivalry. This scene shows the preparations for a German joust, announced with a trumpet fanfare.

Walther von der Vogelweide (around 1170–1228 A.D.), the most famous minnesinger. His songs describe not only high courtly love, but also "ebene minne," a form of requited love between equals.

Oswald von Wolkenstein (1377–1445 A.D.) is known not only for his eye trouble, but because his songs spoke very realistically and occasionally crudely about "niedere minne"—earthly love.

With this idea the medieval poets bound together all the merits and virtues that they sought in the ideals of chivalry. Their songs glorified the theme of "high love," the holy, unconsummated love for a virtuous and unattainable woman, as opposed to "earthly love," which was generally presented more coarsely and graphically. In Germany, these poets were called *Minnesänger,* (derived from the medieval German "minne," love). They were mostly nobles or courtiers, and their names are documented in contemporary writings. The composers themselves are rarely mentioned. Walther von der Vogelweide was, and still is, the most famous minnesinger. His poem, "Unter der Linden" ("Under the Linden Tree") is perhaps the most famous lyric in medieval German. In fact, it was set to music again in 1960 by the Swiss composer Frank Martin. Another famous minnesinger was Oswald von Wolkenstein, whose lyrics speak realistically of earthly, one might even say carnal, love. Heinrich von Meissen was given the honorific surname *Frauenlob* because he reput-

edly handled the theme of high love with particular sensitivity.

Unlike singers in the church, troubadours, trouvères, and minnesingers were accompanied by instruments. Either the poet himself played the lute or the fiddle

Everywhere in Europe music was associated with the followers of courtly festivals. Pictured here in the *Book of Hours*, the Duke de Berry participates in a country outing of noble ladies and gentlemen with a group of instrumentalists who accompany the excursion musically. The troubadours, trouvères, and minnesingers often did not belong to a particular court, but traveled from castle to castle. They thereby fulfilled an extremely important function: In a time without telecommunication, the so-called "traveling people" were some of the most important conveyors of news.

while he sang, or he was accompanied by minstrels called *jongleurs*. The instruments imitated the vocal line with variations and ornamentation (an influence from Arabian music). This style was called *heterophony*.

Brief blooming—Great meaning

Parallel with the decline of chivalry was a waning of interest in courtly song. In the course of the history of European music, this form of the song was the peak of a long development that had prevailed for over a millennium. As courtly song experienced its last blossoming in the mid–1500s, polyphony (multivoiced music) was already 200 years old in Europe.

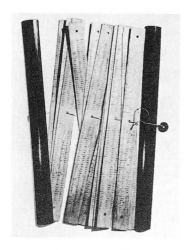

As varied as music itself is its notation. In the different ages of European music and in the musical cultures outside Europe, countless different forms of notation exist, which can be organized by two different points of view.

1. Notation as an aid to memory

In cultures where music is passed orally—and this is worldwide by far the largest number—pitches and durations are notated only for pedagogical use. The student

of music has a long apprenticeship with a master in which he or she learns music in all details. For performance of music these notes serve only as mnemonic aids.

The same is true of orally transmitted music in Europe and the West. For a folksinger, written notes serve only as a resource for the realization of what the performer has conceived.

European art music as well sometimes uses certain notation forms that are designed to provide the performer only certain indispensible information and leave open possibilities for improvisation.

2. Notation as specification for performance

In the course of the history of music, notation that gives the performer exact instructions as to pitch and duration developed relatively late. It came to assume great importance, however, as performers proceeded on the assumption that a composer was not merely making a record of a work, but was also trying to convey its entire meaning.

The exact observance of notational instructions leads to a standardization of interpretation, which pushes the individual character of a composition to the background. Only when a musician is in the position of taking instruction at the time can he or

she produce an interesting interpretation for the listener.

Early traditions

For a long time, music was hand-notated and indeed indicated neither pitch nor duration exactly, but only an approximate reference point for execution. These notes traditionally are chiefly in theoretical writings, where they function as examples, rather than as independent pieces of music.

Increasing precision

From the 9th century people used *neumes* (pronounced "nooms") to

make a record of music (from the Greek *neuma*, meaning appearance, sign, or pointer). Neumes were usually handwritten by the performers and indicated only the direction of the melody, not its precise pitches. In the 11th century, Guido of Arezzo introduced a line system which allowed musicians to determine pitches exactly. The notes are ordered on and between the individual lines to indicate an

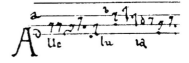

order of thirds. Precise rhythm was not yet given; it followed the flow of speech and was not notated at all.

Square (Roman) notation

This form of notation, which had already developed by the 12th century in France, is still in use today in the Catholic Church. This so-called Roman or square notation indicates the melody exactly, but notates the rhythm using rules that show patterns and are obviously not absolute from the notation. Every convent or church singing group therefore has a leader, who is responsible for regulating with inconspicuous gestures the music's rhythmic course.

Musica mensurabilis— Precise and calculated

In 1280 A.D., Franco of Cologne developed a system that determined the duration of the notes in a certain ratio. In numerous modifications these mensural notations were used until about 1600. The system

rests on the subdivision of a beat into three values, which according to their position relative to one another can cause a shortening or lengthening of a main note. Franco saw the rhythmic division by three (triple meter) as a representation of the Holy Trinity and called it *Perfectio*. The division by two (duple meter) stood, by contrast, for imperfection, and was accordingly called *Imperfectio*.

This notation was thought-out to the extent that it could be used to represent very complicated rhythms. At the same time, however, it considerably constrained the freedom of improvisation which had heretofore been an important element in medieval music.

Different notation for different instruments

The *Mensuralis* was a system that raised the standard not only of representation of music but of music itself, and demanded a considerable capacity for abstraction on the part of the musician. It determined specifically only which notes in which duration are to be produced, but it did not offer a concrete guide to interpretation.

On a completely different principle rests the *tablature* system, which was developed for keyboard and string instruments,

and is still used today. Tablature proceeds on the assumption that a musical symbol is associated with a certain note on the instrument. This allows the player

to go ahead completely mechanically, playing his or her part without reference to other written parts. For string instruments, tablature indicates which finger to place on which string. For keyboard instruments, the symbols indicate a specific key, but leave fingering decisions to the player. In both cases, phrasing is left up to the performer. The tablature system's greatest advantage was that it was very space-saving.

Full-score notation

Polyphony (musical thinking in several individual voices) lent itself to horizontal notation of

each voice. However, it was very difficult to have an overview of a piece of music if the voices (or instrumental parts) that sound together were separated from

one another in the written music. In the 17th century people began to notate voice lines that happen at the same time one on top of each other. This full-score notation, which is so practical for ensemble playing, was also common for keyboard instruments. For example, J. S. Bach notated the "Ricercare" in his *Musical Offering* on six systems even though it is performed on one harpsichord (see illustration).

Printed and engraved music
With the invention of the printing press, the appearance of musical output also changed. Like Gutenberg's movable letter-type, people developed movable note-type. This latter, however, proved increasingly unsatisfactory because it could not handle important musical elements such

as exact articulation of the tone or phrasing of a melody. This was accomplished, and still is some-times today, by hand engraving, by which all elements important for the reproduction of a piece are noted after exactly determined rules. Today most publishers produce much printed music using computer software and laser printers.

The notation of contemporary music

The complexity of contemporary music necessitated new forms of musical notation. Composers have invented new kinds of sounds and rhythms, and new ways of producing them, and the old symbols have proved inadequate to represent them. The new notation provides additional signs to indicate playing technique—for example, for the exact use of piano pedals or of a violin bow. It also departs from traditional

rhythmic notation, for example, sometimes indicating time in seconds rather than by note value. Composers have felt free to invent their own graphic symbols to indicate an exact score for performance. The result is a more authentic mental impression of the music for both the composer and the performer. Often, contemporary music parts are really records of a musical experiment and do not necessarily correspond to the purpose of recreating the same music; rather, they may enable musicians to repeat the same experiment on the basis of the record. (Of course, some contemporary composers write traditionally and tonally, using standard score notation.)

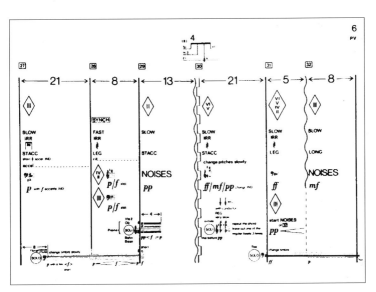

The people of the Middle Ages believed that music sprang from a divine source and—this seemed self-explanatory—was made by angels. In addition to the four wind instruments in the center (three trumpets and a shawm), the three angels on the left play psaltery, "Trumscheid," and lute, while the two on the far right play fiddle and harp ...

No other change in the orientation of European music has been as earthshaking as the transition from plainsong (a melody sung in unison) to polyphony (more than one different melody happening together). This change occurred between the 9th and 12th centuries.

The beginning of parallel fifths

Certainly the idea of adding another voice to an already existing voice, which doubles it at the distance of an octave (i.e., eight notes apart, lower C with middle C, etc.) or a fifth (five notes apart, i.e., C below G, D below A, etc.), was not in itself particularly ingenious. Nevertheless, this idea produced a fundamental rethinking of the supposition that the melody is always the most important voice, putting it in context with other voices as only one part of an entire composition.

Even if parallel fifths and fourths sound very hollow, they were considered the perfect reflection of consonance because when they are combined with each other, they yield the octave.

... The angel to their left plays a portativ, a small organ, whose wind source is a hand-bellows. Almost all medieval instruments are represented in these two pictures, except the small drum and kettledrums. Drums were considered earthly, or even the work of the devil.

1200 – 1600

Medieval books were often lavishly produced and thus very expensive. In a monastery or cloister, if one could not sing from memory, one could use a book for help. The painter of this initial "C" on the title of the piece *Cantate Domino* would have thought of himself as more erudite than the monks, if they had to rely on books.

At first the blended sounds that resulted from the simultaneous performance of different voices were passed through very quickly. Only very much later did these combinations of notes become emphasized, and did the concept of harmony emerge. Much later still came the notion of a primary melody to which one

Age of Notre Dame: Important period of the medieval music. Leading composers were Leonin and Perotin (around 1200).

Conductus: along with the motet, the principal musical form of the Age of Notre Dame

Descant: treble voice

Fauxbourdon: 15th-century style of composition where the melody is doubled by another part a sixth lower

Isometric: Division of the tenor (melody line) into identical phrases

Isorhythm: Repetition of a rhythmic pattern, usually in the tenor part

Mass: one of the main forms of sacred music, set in five parts: Kyrie, Gloria, Credo, Sanctus, and Agnus Dei

Motet: one of the principal forms in the Middle Ages and the Renaissance; at first secular, later as musical setting of sacred and scriptural texts

Organum: Musical style in which the voices proceed primarily in parallel fifths and fourths, the overriding medieval conception of composition

Tenor: until about 1600 the main melodic voice of a composition

(Vocal) Polyphony: composition syle with contrapuntal (simultaneous) treatment of separate voices; prevailed until around 1600

King Alfons the Wise, of Castile (1254-84) had a richly illustrated book of over 400 songs dedicated to the Virgin Mary. Normally the songs were accompanied by an instrument, which either doubled the vocal part or improvised its own part.

In the Middle Ages, dance festivals and even dance "epidemics" were reported. The civil authorities and the Church tried to stop these excesses by all means in their power. There was even occasionally dancing in the monasteries and cloisters. Why should a monk or a nun, who spent his or her whole life behind a desk writing books or notes, not adopt this fashion?

added—as we often do today—an accompanying harmonic framework.

Organum—Organized relationships

Almost all the innovations of medieval music (primarily the developments of polyphony) also quickly appeared in the convents and churches. Initially the new arts of musical performance appeared and were practiced only at certain convents and schools of singing, but they then gradually spread through all Europe. These new polyphonic sacred songs, which were sometimes accompanied by the organ, were called *organum*. They began with a melody and another lower voice a fifth lower in pitch. Because strict observance of the interval of a fifth between voices tended to produce monotony, people began to add other intervals; for example, a voice singing fourths from the melody was called a descant, and had a very enlivening effect. Originally this descant was written with longer note values (slower notes) under the primary voice and sung by the tenor. Two

26

important changes occurred now, which could transform a comparatively simple organum into an artistically commendable composition. First, the descant was placed over the principal melodic voice and the note values were shortened (made faster) so that over a single note of the melody, the descant would add embellishments (*melismas*). Second, another different voice was added to the principal voice and thus expanded the possibilities of combinations of sound even further. Throughout the Middle Ages this three-voice pattern was the rule, reflecting the popular idea that the number three was a symbol of the Holy Trinity and therefore of perfection.

The worship of woman as pure and unattainable in secular courtly music and as the Virgin Mary in sacred music was sometimes taken to absurd extremes.

Because the tenor voice of organum was a Gregorian hymn melody, it was common for the descant and the other voice to use the same text. The texts of the other voices, however, were not always strictly liturgical, which facilitated the transfer away from the convents and churches into secular music.

For composers, the Virgin Mary was the center of reverence. The motet texts are often metaphoric and describe Mary as a star above the sea or a rose without thorns. In this painting, Geertjen tot Sint Jans presented Mary as Queen of Heaven, surrounded by angels playing music.

The Motet—The text determines the melody

Besides organum, another vocal form soon developed that gave the text greater meaning in relationship to the melody, which spurred the increasing individuality of the other voices. These first truly multivoiced compositions were called *motetus* (from the French "mot" [word] or "motet" [rhyme, verse]). From this came the name "motets."

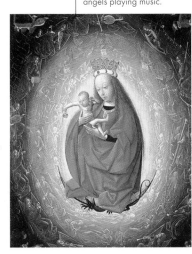

Excerpt from the manuscript of the Füssener Osterspiel (Easter Play) from the late 14th century.

The strict rules, which determined the exact course of a motet, were also applied to another important form, the *conductus*. This form differed from the motet in that the tenor is not a hymn tune, but a song melody. In addition, the conductus included an introductory piece, a middle piece, and an after piece, the *sine littera*, which were sung without words. The form of the conductus was thus better suited to festive occasions than was the more severe motet.

Besides these two musical forms, it has been reported that the monks and students also knew rondelli, or circle music, to which they danced and sang.

Rosette window in the south wing of Notre Dame Cathedral in Paris. Here Leonin and Perotin worked. Around 1200 they helped establish Paris as an important musical center.

Notre Dame

Around 1200 A.D. polyphony reached a peak, which is associated especially with two only vaguely known composers from Paris: Leonin and his pupil Perotin. In church music, composers

Three-part organum. Only the underlying voice is furnished with the text "Alleluia" which is sung in long syllables.

as a rule remained anonymous. That an unnamed author, known in musicology as Anony-mous IV, calls them by name is a sign of their importance. Leonin and Perotin were members of the musical school of the Cathedral of Notre Dame, whose construction began in 1163 and ended in the 13th century. It is not inappropriate that their age had been called the Age of Notre Dame: they and their unnamed colleagues, with their new organum compositions, laid the groundwork for about 400 years of European music history.

Ars antiqua—Ars nova

By 1320 the music theorist Jacobus of Lüttich developed the twin ideas of Ars antiqua and Ars nova ("old art–new art"). As a follower of the old art, Jacobus tried to stem the tide of the ubiquitous new currents, as propagated by Philippe de Vitry in his 1322 treatise *Ars nova*. Political disputes during this time weakened the church influence on general cultural and musical developments, which had in the centuries before been determined almost exclusively by the clerics. Secular music gained more importance relative to church music. With this development, the old forms of organum and conductus also disappeared entirely, and the form, content, and

1200 – 1600

Music was one of the seven lively arts and belonged thus to the subject canon of the universities. The theoretical connections were interesting for the scholars, because they could join it effortlessly with the general Christian world view, according to which everything rests on a divine plan.

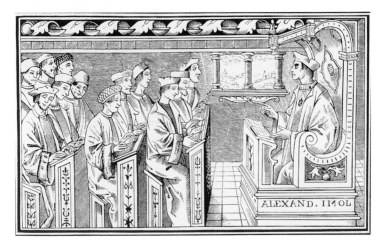

ALEXAND. IIMOL

The musical picnic is not just a modern invention. Many contemporary displays show that playing music outdoors was very popular already in the Middle Ages and the Renaissance.

function of the motet changed completely. The church in Rome took these developments very seriously and in 1325 forbade the performance of the new music in the church.

This did not stop the innovations, however, especially since they not only enriched the relationship of musical parts but changed the entire musical understanding of the time.

Musical precision

The most important innovation affected the rhythmic structure of the compositions. In the year 1280 Franco of Cologne invented a system to denote exact durations (note values) (see p. 20). This system was expanded and refined to include very small divisions of the beat. Now musicians could record and precisely reproduce very complicated rhythms. The descant voices were especially lively, with rhythmic as well as melodic invention. The tenor usually proceeded more quietly against it in relatively longer note values.

Equal construction, equal rhythm

To unify all voices and to tie together their individual structure, musicians developed a simple method: they divided the tenor into equal repeating segments (*isometers*). The additional voices were adjusted to these periods so that pauses and caesuras (breaking points) always appeared at the same place. These periodic divisions did not depend upon the melody or the text. Also the rhythm within the periods was uniform (*isorhythmy*). Even though the strict application of the model is quite simple, it can result in highly complex structures, which can be understood only after intense study of the compositional style. Performance of this music was therefore reserved for professional musicians, who were employed as a rule in the choirs (*cappella*) of the large churches and cathedrals.

Universally applicable

The composers of the Ars nova were so drawn to isometers and isorhythmy that they utilized these processes in almost every form. First the motet, common since the Notre Dame period, became the primary form. Its text, however, was no longer strictly spiritual, but had worldly contents with love as the prevailing theme. That the composers of these secular motets were priests or low clerics apparently did not faze the people of the Middle Ages.

At the courts and in the palaces of the aristocrats these demanding works of art were well known and well loved. The music was suited to pageantry as well as to intellectual enjoyment.

Although the church had initially spoken out against the new art, in time it relented, especially since those composers who understood the Ars nova could effectively use it on the five Ordinaries, or traditional parts of the Mass, which, in the course of the following centuries, helped this innovation develop into the central form of church music.

A quarrel between the church and composers might have developed had not the most important Ars nova composers been influential in the church. For example, Philippe

1200 – 1600

Guillaume de Machaut (1300–77) was so highly regarded that even the high-born paid him their respects.

1200 – 1600

Performers had to master the rhythmically complicated music of a Trecento-madrigal. Of course, an occasional peek at the notes couldn't hurt.

Music flowered in the Italian Renaissance somewhat later than in art and literature. The Trecento is one of the golden ages of Italy, full of personalities like the Medici, Pope Alexander VI, Macchiavelli, and also Alighieri (pictured below).

de Vitry was a politician and bishop of Meaux, and Guillaume de Machaut, the most important composer of that age, traveled in civil service throughout Europe and finally became canon at the Cathedral of Reims.

Trecento

Almost contemporaneously with the French Ars nova, a form of secular polyphonic music developed in northern Italy that found favor in aristocratic circles. It is known as *Trecento* music (from the Italian "Trecento," or 14th century). Though it shared many characteristics with the French Ars nova, Trecento had a certain style found only in Italy. The melodies are generally more spirited, the harmony more straightforward. Its form is less structured and its rhythm is simpler. The Italian spirit spoke through such forms as the *madrigal*, which treats love as part of a pastoral idyll. Madrigals are replete with depictions of nature and imitations of animal sounds, like the bleating of sheep or the song of a bird. Francesco Landini, the most important composer of the Trecento, composed madrigals as well as another form called *ballata*. These follow a clear pattern comparable to the French *virelai* and the barform of the German minnesingers. These pieces were sung by high male voices with instrumental accompaniment. Lutes, harps, and small portable organs (portativs) were especially popular.

The renaissance of music is Franco-Flemish

If an abstract idea was central to the musical outlook of the Middle Ages, the individual with spiritual needs was increasingly central to the vision of artistic and musical aesthetics in the 15th and 16th centuries. The new ideas of the

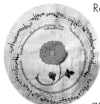

Renaissance came later to music than to the fine arts. The striving for naturalness changed all aspects of music. Melodies lost their often bizarre sequence and assumed more and more simple forms, often influenced by human breathing. The complicated rhythmic patterns of medieval music were pared back to simple proportions. Thirds and sixths, intervals that had been heard before as discord, were preferred for their unified, smooth, pleasant sound. This practically complete change in musical understanding developed over a period of 150 years up until 1600. The impetus for these sweeping changes came from composers almost without exception from northern France and present-day Belgium, and so this period of the history of music is called *Franco-Flemish* or the Time of the Low Countries.

The people of the Renaissance thought in visual terms with a penchant for speculation. In this canon the musicians are given a puzzle, to find the entry of the second voice in the fourth (diatesseron).

1200 – 1600

The Burgundian Court attracts the best musicians

If the essential musical impulses were coming from Paris, the main activities now increasingly shifted to the politically important noble manor houses in the country. To this group belonged Philippe the Good, and music and art came to be used consciously as a means of representation of his power at the Burgundian Court in Dijon. Gilles Binchois, one of the period's leading composers, stood in service to this prince. He turned the *chanson*, usually a love song, into the most important musical form of the time, which is now known as the Burgundian Age.

The two most important composers of the Burgundian Court in Dijon were Guillaume Dufay (1400–74) and Gilles Binchois (1400–60). One might think they were both priests because the majority of their works were masses and motets. That is by no means the case. They both also wrote chansons, and of course chiefly love songs. The Burgundian chanson could be considered the central form of an entire era.

The beginning of the *Ave Maris Stella* Mass of Josquin des Prez (ca. 1450–1521). Often masses were named after the first lines of the chansons or motets on which they were based.

The motif of the angel playing music is omnipresent in Renaissance art.

Guillaume Dufay belongs to this same generation of composers, and was probably the best-known musician of the period. Dufay incorporated into his works musical stimuli from all over Europe. He introduced essential innovations, such as the Fauxbourdon style from England, into the various forms of French music (masses, songs, etc.).

Vocal polyphony through the generations

The Mass (a musical setting of the parts of the Catholic liturgy) was a form that offered the composer a chance to use voices independently as well as to combine them in relationship with each other. But these new polyphonic methods were also used in many other forms: in motets, which had returned in this era to sacred texts; in Italian madrigals, with their idyllic depictions of nature; and in love songs.

Clearly one can perceive a development by the respective generations of composers in the use of vocal polyphony, which expanded from its Franco-Flemish roots throughout Germany and Italy. Almost all composers traveled and worked in different European countries and therefore were in a position to influence the next generation of composers. In addition to Dufay, whose influence was strong over two generations, Jan Ockeghem became particularly well known because of his expressive music.

The works of Josquin des Prez had an especially clear, transparent style, and gained him the reputation as the most important composer of his time. The fourth generation, through composers such as Nicolas Gombert, Clemens non Papa, and Adrian Willaert, brought for the first time free-standing instrumental compositions. Still, Mass settings based on popular chansons, madrigals, or other tunes—the so-called parody masses—continued to be very popular. In this way, secular songs arrived in the church, and the clergy were not on the whole pleased.

With Orlando di Lasso, the fifth generation reached the absolute high point of the Franco-Flemish vocal polyphonic style. Di Lasso also composed in all forms. His works distinguished themselves through a particular liveliness, as well as occasionally through wit.

Orlando di Lasso, here before the Munich Royal Chapel Choir, was, along with Josquin des Prez, one of the most important Renaissance composers. He came from Mons in present-day Belgium, lived for many years in Italy, and for over 20 years conducted the Royal Chapel Choir in Munich. With him, European vocal polyphony came to an end.

Palestrina in Rome

Giovanni Pierluigi da Palestrina, whose highly perfected style may be considered the embodiment of the composer's art, is also seen as the pinnacle of vocal polyphony. Palestrina sought to express the inner meaning of a text by using four voices simultaneously singing

different syllables. In the compositions of his colleagues, this was not always the case. His masses and motets convey a clear impression of tonality, which around 1600 became the basis of the new music.

Orlando di Lasso (1532–94)

Giovanni Pierluigi da Palestrina (ca. 1525–94)

1200 – 1600

35

Form and Genre

The different musical genres, which have developed in the course of the history of Western music, evolved from a comparatively small number of musical forms that essentially determine the organization and structure of later forms. Simple patterns—for example, three sections with the repetition of one section—are dispersed like the more complex forms, which can combine different elements to consolidate a piece of music into an intellectually demanding whole. Some of these forms were only important in a certain period, destined thereafter to become mere footnotes in music history.

Simple forms

A B A: This formula can be used to explain clearly and simply the structure of a large proportion of Western music. A B A diagrams a typical structure for a piece of music in three sections: section A, section B which is noticeably different from A, and then a repeat of section A. This structure implies one of the most important features of musical forms: repetition.

Understanding and recognition of these simple forms and features make it easier to recognize the structure of a musical composition.

This schema can be expanded in many ways; for example, one of the repeated sections may be changed slightly (A B A'), or the order of parts and repeats may be altered (A A B). It is also possible to arrange repeated parts with varied interpolations possible (A B A C A D A E, etc.). With even such simple variations one arrives at a multitude of different forms, which then constitute a basis for the emergence of different styles and formats.

The song

The most important class of composition based on the simple A B A form is the song. Both the folk song, whose compositional process remains unknown and which is passed on orally, as well as the so-called art song, which seeks through features such as the

Des Knaben Wunderhorn, a collection of old German songs assembled by Achim von Arnim and Clemens Brentano, served as inspiration for songs by Romantic composers, including Gustav Mahler.

relationship between words and notes to wed melody and expression of the text's poetic meaning, have essentially the same basic structure. Hence, the medieval minnesong, the simple hymns sung by German men's choirs, the chanson, the communally sung protest song of the 1960s, and the art songs of

The public expects opera singers to have special roles and operas in which they sing particularly beautifully. The Swedish singer Jenni Lind completely enthralled 1846 Vienna.

Schubert, Schumann, Brahms, and other "classical" composers are all structurally comparable.

The aria

Only the aria, a particular shaping of the song, is an important form unto itself. It has also essentially determined other forms, which over the centuries have come to be overarching musical genres: ora-

torio and opera. With an especially artful melodic setting, and through many embellishments and "coloratura" (ornamental runs), the aria is the most important element of oratorio and opera. In the *oratorio*, which is usually biblical in content, the purpose of the aria is to comment upon the narrative as presented in recitative (a spoken style of singing over a minimal accompaniment). The oratorio is as a rule presented as a concert piece. The *passion* is a special class of oratorio, which narrates the story of the death of Christ.

In opera the aria serves still a further task, which depends heavily on the personality of the singer: many opera arias, especially from the Italian and French Romantic repertoire, were conceived less to elucidate the action than to display the vocal art and emotional range of the performers.

Theme with variations

Another important elementary musical form is variation on a given theme. The theme is usually a song melody or harmonic pattern that can be elaborated and changed in many different ways. The methods of variation are inexhaustible. Some comparatively simple methods of variations are instrumental techniques such as runs, arpeggios, and other ornamental figures. These methods were particularly popular in the English instrumental music of

Title page of J.S. Bach's *Goldberg Variations*, which Bach composed for his student Goldberg, who had to play them as lullabies for his employer.

Dance forms were assembled into suites and stylized so that they were no longer suitable for dancing.

the Baroque period. It was not uncommon to have variation cycles with up to 60 variations. These methods of variation became increasingly interesting as musicians tried to combine other musical methods with them in the course of variation cycles. Besides using many technical instrumental subtleties in his *Goldberg Variations*, Johann Sebastian Bach works out the theme contrapuntally. In the Classical and Romantic eras the theme-and-variation genre was carried over to solo orchestral instruments, which had a great appeal.

The rhythm determines the form

The *suite*, a series of dances, was the leading form of European instrumental music from the 16th to the 18th centuries. The 16th-century suite was composed on the basis of certain rhythmic models, each of which was marked by a certain character: the *Pavane*, a walking dance; the *Courante*, a measured

dance; and the *Gaillarde*, a jumping dance, the most animated. In the 17th century the dances were modernized, which lengthened suites and tended to standardize their sequences. Johann Sebastian Bach composed suites on the A C S O G scheme: *Allemande, Courante, Sarabande, (Optional), and Gigue*. The optional movement between sarabande and gigue was usually one of several other dances (minuet, bourrée, etc.), which broke up the monotony of the form. Originally this music was suitable for dancing, but increasing stylization eventually made dancing impossible. The suite was a very important form during the Baroque period, but lost its meaning in the Classical and Romantic periods. Of course, Romantic composers wrote many stylized dances, such as waltzes, Ländler, mazurkas, and Hungarian and Bohemian dances. However, such compositions were almost exclusively intended to portray supposedly independent national characteristics.

More complex forms

In contrast to songs and arias, variations and dances, the form of many musical genres does not emerge through the application of simple repetitions or orderings, but through analysis of the compositional methods. In both instrumental as well as vocal music, the polyphonic composition style exerted the greatest influence on the development of music from the 15th century on.

imitation (delayed repetition of a theme) through all voices. This was also true of motets and madrigals.

The fugue

In the fugue, the possibilities of polyphony are all brought intimately together. The fugue adds to the strict application of the rules of counterpoint highly artful variations of the individual voices by rhythmic augmentation or diminution (lengthening or shortening of the note values of the original theme). The voices are worked out further, by changing the direction of intervals (reversal), playing the theme backwards

Masses, motets, madrigals

Until the stylistic changes around 1600, musical setting of the Ordinaries of the Roman Catholic Mass, with its parts *Kyrie*, *Gloria*, *Credo*, *Sanctus*, and *Agnus Dei*, was a preeminent musical genre. The structure of the Mass was not only determined through the points of its text, but also through the rules of polyphony—for example,

Beginning of the *Fugue in C Major* from J.S. Bach's *Well-Tempered Clavier*.

(crab), etc. These technical features complicate the fugue in different ways, so that a quick and easy understanding of the form is not possible. With the shift in musical consciousness toward harmony beginning in the middle of the 18th century, people began to take an

Form and Genre

Sonatas belonged to the standard repertoire of the Classical period.

interest in polyphony in general and in the fugue in particular. Polyphonic composition was fairly isolated, and usually had a historical connotation.

The sonata form as the basis of many others

The sonata form was the basis for a multitude of important musical genres in the Classical era. The sequence of thematic exposition, development, and recapitulation (see p. 79) offered many possibilities for variation and expansion. Besides the sonata—as both a structural and a generic term—by far the most important form is the *symphony*, which follows the principles of the sonata form. Likewise, the first movements of string quartets and concertos (virtuosic works for a solo instrument with orchestral accompaniment) of the Classical period and, in expanded form, also those of the Romantics, are marked by the features of sonata form. The middle movements of these works often

Ludwig van Beethoven's *Symphony No. 9* marks the end of the Classical symphony.

Fantasia

BWV 903

1.

In the *Chromatic Fantasy*, Bach unites instrumental difficulties with free musical ideas.

hark back to a simple song form. Even though the sonata form is an idealization of the aesthetics of the Classical period, its influence was felt well into the 20th century.

Free forms

Relatively few musical forms do not follow a set pattern or schema, but are determined solely by a musical idea or mood. The *fantasia*—which originated in the Baroque period and then spread—not only breaks compositional rules, but directly combines musical ideas, without necessarily following a set form. Likewise, the free forms that were popular in the Romantic period— such as the *rhapsody, impromptu,*

Impromptus, the name Schubert on a whim gave his miniatures, are today known by almost all advanced piano students.

or *nocturne*—circulated widely. Dance forms such as the *mazurka*, the *polonaise*, and the *waltz* also vary in their form.

In a survey of the development of musical forms, it becomes clear that the tendency toward strict forms is more prevalent than free, unstructured fantasias. The strict forms offer the composer the possibility to integrate free elements. For example, free melodic phrases (*tropes*) were inserted into the standard Gregorian hymn melodies. In the Classical sonata form, both the structures of polyphonic counterpoint as well as the limit to two opposing themes force the composer into creativity through dialogue with the given strict form. The appeal of varying a form, expanding it, and by changing it renewing it, is for most composers greater than that of the pure expression of fantasy.

VIER IMPROMPTUS

Komponiert 1827

Opus posth. 142 · Deutsch-Verz. 935

Allegro moderato

1.

1600 – 1750

Music around 1600

The turn of the 16th to the 17th century brought basic innovations to the music of Europe that revolutionized the entire understanding of what music is, and of the purposes it should serve. Vocal polyphony, which the Franco-Flemish and Palestrina (see p. 34) had led to a golden age, was considered by the musicians and theorists of the early Baroque period to be decidedly defective in one respect: the imbalance of text and music.

The new practice

Renaissance music had been extremely skillfully laid out, especially in the highly formal polyphonic compositions such as masses and motets, so that the expression of the text was often relegated to acoustic unintelligibility in the background. Aside from overcoming this problem, the efforts toward innovation had still a further, much more fundamental dimension. The composers, musicians, and listeners of the time desired most of all that music grasp and convey the inner meaning and emotional content of the text. First in Italy arose a musical style that was diametrically opposed to polyphonic writing: the

Musical scene at the beginning of the 17th century. A Baroque palace garden had a place for almost every kind of art. The instrumentalists accompany the singer on typical basso continuo instruments, a viola da gamba, and a lute.

monody. It did not suit the aesthetic ideas of the period at all to leave the exceedingly important expression of the text to an unaccompanied solo voice. An instrumental line was added to the song, the so-called *figured bass* or *thoroughbass*. The thoroughbass dictated the bass note and its accompanying harmony, but left the filling in of details to the player's discretion, thereby functioning as a sort of scaffolding for the song.

This new or—as the Italians called it—*second practice* (*seconda pratica*, in contrast to the *prima pratica*, the outdated polyphony) decisively set the future course of Western music.

The monody—Music as affect

The most striking characteristic of monody was that the rhythm and pitches of the melody were set according to the natural patterns of speech. The declamatory principle led to a stylized recitative with relatively quick tempo, which gave the music a wonderful liveliness. Especially important words were sung where the naturally emphasized beats fell, and were marked

The *Lamento d'Arianna* (Ariadne's Lament) by Claudio Monteverdi. This piece epitomizes the art of the new music around 1600: The declamation of the text had absolute precedence. The piece begins with a sighing figure on the text "Lasciate mi morire" ("Let me die"). The signs and numerals under the bass indicate the harmony to be filled in by the accompanying instrument. A sharp sign means to add a major third above the bass—in other words, a major chord is played; a flat sign indicates a minor third from the bass, and thus a minor chord.

Vincenzo Galilei, father of physicist Galileo Galilei, wrote this theoretical essay on the new music.

The opening of the oldest preserved opera, *Eurydice*, by Giulio Caccini (ca. 1545 – 1618).

additionally through certain musical phrases. The monody was also characterized by numerous ornamentations. The dramatic effects of monody song were also intensified by corresponding gestures.

The figured bass—Omnipresent and unquestionable

The new art of song (*nuova maniera di cantar*) unfolded over a bass, a figured or thoroughbass, on which the entire composition was hung. Figured bass became prevalent at this time for essentially two reasons: on the one hand it provided a grounding point for the voice to follow, and on the other hand it manifested the new understanding of harmony, which began to depart in this time from the modal system of church tonalities, and it strengthened the new major–minor system.

The still simple harmonic structures of this time were indicated through a number system, which indicated to the player of the accompanying harmonic instrument (organ, harpsichord, lute) which notes to play.

Not only did the figured bass system determine the formal-technical structure of the music, but also, because its figures referred to notes of the scale and the chords to be built over them, it clarified the theoretical basis of the new major–minor

Figuration: also *Doctrine of the Affections*; formula that dictates which harmonic and melodic figures are used to accompany which kinds of text

Figured bass: fundamental bass voice with added harmony indicated by numbers and symbols, played on harpsichord, organ, or lute

Monody: declamatory style of vocal music in which melody and rhythm follow speech patterns, supposedly a revival of ancient Greek techniques

Opera: developed from madrigal comedies, intermedium, and the *dramma per musica*; the first notable example was *Orfeo* by Claudio Monteverdi (1607).

Seconda pratica: designation for the new vocal music, ca. 1600, consisting of a solo melody line accompanied by instrumental chords

tonality system. Accepted all through Europe, this system sustained its importance well into the 18th century.

From the scholarly chamber to the stage

In their contemplation of the antique, especially Greek culture, the scholars of the late Renaissance and early Baroque eras believed that with monody they had rediscovered the presentational method of ancient Greek drama. Now popular, this kind of performance lacked any real models to suggest how it might be transferred into the present and adjusted to the needs of an audience always hungry for innovations. To this end, musicians, poets, artists, and theorists met in small circles, the so-called *chambers*, where they discussed and experimented musically. Especially important impulses came out of one circle that met in the Tuscan capital: the *Florentine Camerata*.

Naturally, the aesthetic advances and experiments of this new music did not remain within the circle of the Camerata, but gained immediate entrée to the stages of the high Italian aristocracy.

1607—A year of change

The musical and dramatic developments emerging around 1600 in widely different manifestations not only resulted in and affected

How the poets of the early Baroque liked to imagine themselves: in Greek robes, adorned with laurel crowns, standing before ancient temples. It was not long before the attempts of the Florentine scholars to translate Greek poetry into Italian were imitated in other languages. Martin Opitz wrote the libretto to the opera *Daphne*, which was set to music by many contemporary composers in the new monody style.

1600 – 1750

Noblemen all over Europe used pageantry-filled festivals and processions to demonstrate their status, power, and wealth.

Claudio Monteverdi (1567–1643)

It was a sign of status to employ the best composers as court musicians. The royal family Gonzaga in Mantua managed to hold Monteverdi in their service for ten years.

Monteverdi labeled his *Orfeo* a "musical fable."

the figured-bass-accompanied monody, but also initiated widespread innovations to the genre that can be considered one of the most important musical forms of the time: the *opera*. Especially popular were *madrigal comedies*. These were usually stylized shepherd idylls that were built around a stereotypic treatment of the love theme.

The so-called *Intermezzi* or *Entr'actes* can be seen as direct precursors of the opera. These were sometimes presented between the acts of longer stage productions. Often the Intermezzi were allegorical in content, though material from ancient Greek and Roman mythology was also very popular.

The composers of these pieces—such as Giulio Caccini or Emilio de Cavalieri—who presented them as "favola pastorale" or "dramma per musica," by no means claimed to be presenting a wide range of emotional expression.

That changed in the year 1607 with the opera *Orfeo*, by Claudio Monteverdi. In this work, commissioned by Prince Gonzaga of Mantua, Monteverdi attempted, for the first time, to compose music that represented an entire spectrum of action, emotion, and character. He designated solo instruments or groups of instruments to represent certain characters or situations. For example, he

City map of Mantua

1600 – 1750

used the regal (a small organ with nasal-sounding reed pipes) for the death of boatman Charon, and light-sounding string instruments in sleeping scenes.

This early example shows that Monteverdi already knew how to handle almost all the musical methods for a major opera in extremely subtle ways. With the composition of *Orfeo*, he formulated the features that determined the essential structure of opera in varying degrees over the following centuries.

From Italy to the world

Like other cultural renewals, the new opera style spread quickly throughout Italy and the entire continent of Europe. Soon the various lands stamped their own characters on the medium (see pp. 52). The Italian model, however, dominated for about two centuries.

Considering the contemporary interest in Italian opera, one might easily infer that it pushed other musical forms completely to the background. Rather, other musical genres besides opera experienced new growth, a revival, and/or a final flourish before they finally lost their meaning.

Music in the church

Parallel to the explosive development of opera—every city in Italy, with any kind of civic pride, had an opera house, Venice up to eight at a time—emerged a multitude of sacred works, composed either for liturgical use or for general edifi-

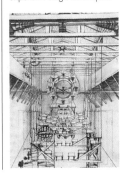

Operatic scenery required expensive stage techniques.

The Dome of St. Mark's Cathedral in Venice. Here composer Giovanni Gabrieli and his pupils tested the double chorus, or antiphonal method, where they placed two or more ensembles in each gallery. The acoustic effect is just as amazing today as it was then.

A typical house music ensemble.

cation. Masses and motets in the old style once again found listeners. Again, it was Monteverdi who delivered the most important contributions to the genre. In the *Marienvespers* (1610), his most important sacred work, he cleverly mixed elements of the old polyphonic style with the innovations he had introduced in the landmark opera *Orfeo* three years before. Like his landmark opera, the *Marienvespers* employs singers and instrumentalists in constantly changing ensembles. Though set to a sacred text, the virtuosity of the vocal and instrumental lines often eclipses the piety of the words. Some of the ensemble pieces are reminiscent of lively dances, and the soprano aria "Pulchra es," on a text from the Song of Solomon, is lush and sensual. The overtures of both *Orfeo* and the *Marienvespers* contain brilliant cornetto cascades as opulent as the interior of St. Mark's itself.

In the first thirty years of the 17th century emerged the first oratorios—large works for chorus, soloist, and orchestra. Though the texts were chiefly biblical, oratorios borrowed from the stylistic devices of opera, including virtuosic arias that expressed the characters and their emotions. Oratorio reached its summit about one hundred years later with the works of George Frideric Handel and Johann Sebastian Bach. Handel's *Messiah*, written in 1741 and premiered in Dublin in 1742, uses Old and New Testament texts from the King James English translation. It is without a doubt the most widely performed oratorio today, though it is still sometimes heard in an inflated Victorian interpretation. Some of the choruses are based on earlier secular compositions of Handel's, but that does not diminish the overall brilliance of the work. Bach's *St. John Passion* (1723) and *St. Matthew Passion* (1729), though written for church performance, carry over well to the modern concert hall. They employ large forces: double orchestra, double chorus, and soloists. The choruses are exemplars of Baroque polyphony, and the solo arias, often with solo instrument obligatos, are deeply touching. Mendelssohn chose the *St. Matthew Passion* to launch the Bach revival of 1829.

House music

Today, house music tends to have a negative connotation: one thinks of amateurishness and dilettantism. In the 17th century this was by no means the case. The European aristocracy took it for granted that in addition to the study of classical languages, philosophy, and natural science, they would have a musical education sufficient to play an instrument competently or to sing well. There was a rich repertoire for this kind of civic music making. It consisted primarily of polyphonic vocal music to be sung either a *capella* or with accompaniment. The madrigal was dominant, a music form elevated to supreme complexity and expressiveness, set to the love poetry of prominent contemporary poets.

Title page of the *Marienvespers*, the religious masterpiece of Claudio Monteverdi.

1600 – 1750

Heinrich Schütz (1585–1672) was a pupil of Gabrieli (1557–1612) in Venice. In Schütz's works the Italian antiphonal style joins with Protestant rigor.

49

It is particularly easy to imagine splendor and "joi de vivre" in Venice.

Once again, Monteverdi produced important contributions to this form, with his eight *Madrigal Books* (1587–1638), establishing him as one of the greatest figures of the 17th century.

Music as theology

A parallel development sprang from the same musical source as the art of Monteverdi and is closely associated with the name Heinrich Schütz. The groundbreaking theological changes that came with the Reformation also influenced musical outlook, including the understanding of biblical texts and their high value, attributed to Martin Luther.

During this time, the borders of Europe expanded north of the Alps (the Thirty Years' War), although Italy was little affected by this conflict. Artists and musicians thought of the countryside merely as the subject matter of artistic thought and culture. For this reason, it was evident for many of them that they should seek fulfillment of artistic development in Italy. Schütz also spent nineteen years in Italy on a stipend, to study with Giovanni Gabrieli who was organist at San Marco in Venice. The organ of the Cathedral of San Marco in Venice stood on the left and right galleries in the sanctuary. From this physical arrangement, Gabrieli developed the technique of a double chorus, one ensemble in each gallery. In the large domed room, the action of echo effects and augmented

Composers outside of Italy also adopted the antiphonal choral method, including Michael Praetorius in his *Musae Sionae* of 1607.

resonance were so amazing and overwhelming that every composer who studied there endeavored to integrate this double ensemble technique into his own style. Schütz also arranged many of his works in double chorus, but his purpose in doing so went beyond its spectacular effect. The Protestant Schütz was interested in formulating theological expression by musical means. In later years, he was aghast that he had allowed himself to compose a book of madrigals (in no way inferior in quality to those of Monteverdi), which he also allowed to be printed, likely as final examination work for his studies with Gabrieli.

In the course of his sixty-year musical career, Schütz exclusively composed sacred works. Along with the monodic principles of text declamation and the double choir technique, Schütz employed a consistent, sometimes stereotypical application of the Baroque figured bass, according to which only specific musical phrases and turns are used to represent certain content.

Monteverdi used methods that were quite similar to those of Schütz, but produced wholly contrary musical statements. Monteverdi and Schütz stand together, though as opposing forces, at the pinnacle of musical development of the second half of the century.

At the beginning of the 17th century the organ was the standard instrument of church music.

1600 – 1750

The holy Cecilia is honored by the Catholic Church as patron saint of church music.

The History of Opera

In the medieval theater, the personification of death played an important role. The mystery plays, for example, were commonly allegorical displays of virtues or vices, which were often characterized in part musically.

Music set to a story: The history of opera

Opera is a musical form that fascinates composers, writers, musicians, producers, directors, and designers. By telling a story through the cooperation of many art forms, an opera can become an event that is celebrated by the public and by the entire musical world. Opera offers a place for everything: for literary statement, for psychological character development, for theatrical effects, for the demanding concept of a certain musical framework, or for the star quality of exalted singers. This breadth of possibilities has inspired people since the form's beginnings.

The beginnings of opera

As an independent musical form, opera first established itself in the 17th century. The medieval mystery plays, in which certain scenes were presented against a musical background or selected texts were set to music, are precursors of opera. Musical interludes, called *intermezzi* or *entr'actes*, which were originally used as fillers between changes of scene in larger theatrical works, increasingly came into their own as independent pieces. The *intermezzi* were particularly favored at the courts of the Italian nobility during the Renaissance.

Claudio Monteverdi, who worked at the court in Mantua, although not the first, was surely the most important 17th-century composer to set a dramatic text completely to music. His *Orfeo*, first performed in 1607, already displays all the defining features of the opera. Individual characters are associated with specific music that describes them, and illustrates or comments on the action. In other words, the music serves a larger purpose than mere stereotypical stage trimming, as it often does, for instance, in operettas.

Innovation versus tradition
With the innovations introduced by Monteverdi, which continued to develop over the next century and a half, it became harder for the ordinary public to follow opera, with its complex connections between ancient themes and the motivations of characters. In France, in particular, which like Italy had a long operatic tradition, resistance stirred against this learned and more realistic form of opera.

"Quarrel of the Buffoons"
A performance of Pergolesi's *La serva padrona* by an Italian opera troupe in 1752 was the occasion of the so-called "Quarrel of the Buffoons." Opera buffa, the Italian

The production of a Haydn opera in the Eszterházy castle. Operas would not have been performed daily, but alternated with chamber music and orchestral concerts. Operatic evenings, however, were the high points of musical life.

The Italian influence spread quickly throughout Europe, but in England the traditional Masque, a theater piece with musical interpolations, endured. Henry Purcell (1659–95) composed innovative music in many other musical forms, which set the style. Only one Purcell opera was ever produced onstage, *Dido and Aeneas*, but it is so convincing and engaging that it remains in the repertoire of many opera houses.

53

Opera productions became increasingly costly. This production in 1675 at the Teatro San Geminiano sul Reno in Venice included choreography for people and horses. Productions also often used theatrical fog.

form of comic opera, provoked the displeasure of the French followers of the traditional style, who were influential enough to have the Italian buffo performers banned from the Parisian operatic scene. The sanction, however, may well have prompted a backlash among the public, as the popularity of *Opera buffa*, or *Opéra comique*, immediately spread.

Gluck and Calzabigi look for a way out

The easy lightheartedness of opéra comique was naturally not an acceptable alternative for connoisseurs of grand opera. But serious opera had to be drastically reformed if it was to have any broad public appeal. All the superfluous embellishments and mannerisms had to be removed to create a simpler, more natural mode of expression. Instead of the Baroque da capo arias (long, florid pieces in A B A form) came simple, through-composed songs (songs without major repeats). False pathos was brushed away. The singers were required to put their voices at the service of the music and were not given a vehicle merely to showcase their own abilities. The most important advocate of these new demands was Christoph Willibald Gluck (1714– 87), who first incorporated them into his works. The writer Ranieri de' Calzabigi delivered operatic texts, or *libretti*, on ancient materials, which were largely free of gratuitous emotionalism, though this by no means suggests that they did not evoke deep feeling. Gluck further demanded that the music must become international. Therefore in his operas he mixed Italian elements, such as *accompagnato* (accompanied recitative) and *arioso* (a style between recitative and aria), with French elements such as the *chanson*

Christoph Willibald Gluck (1714–87) was Austrian, but his reformed style of opera met with great success in Paris.

Wolfgang Amadeus Mozart

(polyphonic song) and the *vaudeville* (simple song with chordal accompaniment) to create a new artistic whole.

Far-reaching influence

The newly created opera aesthetic, which spread out in many different directions, was enthusiastically accepted by European composers, and grew rapidly. Meanwhile, opera had traveled beyond the exclusive stages of royal courts and had become accessible to everyone. A striking example of the growing popularity of this form is the sensation stirred by the premieres of operas by Wolfgang Amadeus Mozart (1756–91). It rarely took

Three years after Mozart's death, this flyer for *The Magic Flute* appeared. A certain "Vulpius" is listed as "arranger." It was possible to earn a fair amount of money from the popularity of *The Magic Flute*'s melodies.

long after a premiere for the entire city to be heard singing and whistling Mozart's melodies. Still, many of his operas express a classical humanistic attitude, which fitted with the dominant mood of the late 18th century. Gluck's reform ideas and Mozart's influence transformed the opera in the 18th century into a popular and widespread musical form. Many composers devoted themselves almost exclusively to writing operas. The best known was Johann Adolf Hasse, who spent most of his life in Italy, where his treatment was akin to that of our own pop superstars.

Wagner and his "Gesamtkunstwerk"

The composer of an opera seeks to express in music a

Richard Wagner

text, with its particularities of action, character, and philosophical background, as exactly as possible. The ideal opera then becomes a copy of life in art (or "holds a mirror up to nature"). For Richard Wagner (1813–83), the opposite was true: music and opera were life itself. In this extreme view he understood the opera as a work that not only contained all art forms within it, but also should affect human existence (*Gesamtkunstwerk*). His operas and music dramas always deal with questions of human thought in

Wagner had an opera house built in Bayreuth specifically for the production of his large music dramas. The annual Wagner Festival still takes place there today, making the provincial town an international attraction.

connection with dependence on fate or other larger forces. Sometimes the intellectual background is difficult to decode. Although they contain much that is typical of their time, Wagner's works also have a particularly timeless dimension. They are still performed at major opera houses and each generation seems to discover new meanings in them.

The opera as artistic center

For many composers of the late 19th and the early 20th century, Wagner's operas retain a central position in their creative endeavors.

Some opera composers, however, have consciously tried to resist Wagner's influence on their work. Their model, instead, is Giuseppe Verdi (1813–1901). Verdi's works are the standard for all Italian opera. The literary style of *verismo*, a mixture of naturalism and realism, was taken up by Puccini, Leoncavallo, and Mascagni, among others, as a starting point for a new musical opera aesthetic.

Opera is also well suited to identification with national identity, which was a particularly strong impulse at the turn of the century. Many different countries poured forth operas drawing on stories and heroes from their own mythology, or glorifying national characters (for example, the Russian Mussorgsky and Bohemian Leoš Janáček.

Further development

As with other musical forms, the 20th century brought many new developments for the opera. Because operas often constitute a composer's central musical statement, however, they are generally well formulated. One of the key works of our century is Alban Berg's (1885–1935) opera *Wozzek*, based on a text by Georg Büchner. Berg's masterpiece is about an exploited, suppressed man, a victim of his environment and

A production in Verona of *Aida*, by Giuseppe Verdi (1813–1901), one of his most popular operas.

his own psyche, who murders his lover: it is a prime example of opera as social criticism.

Contemporary opera composers often choose materials that are disturbing and/or provocative. It is not uncommon, therefore, for their works to present a disproportionate and extravagant current of political statement. As is true for most new music, it is difficult to offer qualitative judgments, since the composers themselves determine the aesthetic criteria for their works, leaving the critic, or the listener, with no standard basis for comparison.

A scene from the opera *Lulu* by Alban Berg.

American music wielded a noticeable influence in Europe in the 20th century. George Gershwin (1898–1937) especially impressed European composers with his opera *Porgy and Bess*. Composers such as Debussy and Ravel incorporated jazz elements in their music, although Gershwin remains alone in his convincing melding of jazz into symphonic music.

Just as vocal music underwent a transformation around 1600, a new era for instrumental music began half a century later and extended until about 1750 (with the death of Johann Sebastian Bach). The period is characterized by a wealth of developments originating in northern Italy and spreading over the Continent and to Great Britain. The creation of new musical forms was closely allied with an expansion in the range of Baroque instruments as well as with refinements in playing technique. Combined, these developments greatly increased the creative possibilities for both musicians and composers.

Music as the image of divine order

These changes took place within a philosophical framework that defined the entire intellectual outlook of the period. Basic to this philosophy was the assumption that the universe and its workings were organized according to a divine plan. Human thoughts and actions were meant to correspond to this divine order. In particular, a work of art as an *opus perfectum*—a complete and perfect whole—was to reflect the perfection of this plan.

The image of the divine order was especially manifest in organ music. Registers, or sets of pipes, offer a rich variety of pitches and timbres (tone colors). Multiple keyboards arranged before, behind, and to the side of the organist, in addition to the pedals, enable the organist to combine many different sounds and melodic lines to produce extremely complex effects.

Most of the Baroque composers not only sought to represent this order in their works, but also regarded their own creative activity as an act of homage to the divine plan. This connection becomes especially clear if one considers the new forms of music that were either created or further developed during this period.

New forms of music

The *ricercare* of the Renaissance was expanded into the *fugue*, one of the most important musical developments of the period. Both forms involve the repetition at spaced intervals of several (usually up to four) nearly identical musical themes. The complex interplay of the theme against itself is the defining characteristic of the form. The fugue (from the Latin *fugere*, to flee) differs from the ricercare (Italian *ri + cercare*, to seek out) in that the individual voices or themes of the fugue are treated at once more distinctly and more economically. At the same time, the harmonies created by the chords of the interwoven themes are more tonally varied. In the construction of a fugue, the precise proportions of its temporal and tonal elements carry great symbolic importance: the length of the theme, the number of theme entrances, and the harmonic relation of the themes to each other manifest the divine proportions of form and number.

Music—represented here by the horn—in the early Baroque period was a symbol for the transitory nature of life—a reminder that all moral actions and efforts were in essence futile. The skull, the most important symbol of life's evanescence, wears a wreath of withered leaves. Warnings to meditate on one's own death were omnipresent.

The *toccata* (from the Italian *toccare*, to strike) developed in the course of the 17th century into a musical form that far transcended its initial function. Originally the tocatta was supposed to allow the musician to demonstrate his or her technical and interpretational virtuosity, as well as

Concerto grosso: musical form in four movements (slow–fast–slow–fast) for a small orchestra with several instrumental solos
Fugue: polyphonic composition in which the voices closely resemble each other; a short melodic theme is presented by one part and varied by the following parts according to a strict set of rules of counterpoint; double and triple fugues are very sophisticated forms in which several different themes are interwoven and put in relation to each other
Ricercare: polyphonic organ piece, predecessor of the fugue
Sonata a tre: piece for three instruments, usually two violins and a continuo

Playing music at home was a favorite hobby of the educated classes. Part books for the singers normally contained the music for only one part. Bass accompaniment was typically provided by a lute or viola da gamba.

to present the full tonal possibilities of the instrument. As the dimensions of the toccata grew, however, its original role as a vehicle for technical virtuosity also expanded to incorporate greater expression of musical thought. Its initial function as a demonstration piece for finger dexterity gave way to more serious musical tasks and by midcentury the toccata was almost without exception incorporated as a part of a fugue.

New forms also arose in the realm of instrumental music. The *concerto grosso* developed from the exchanges between the full orchestra and a group of soloists, the so-called *concertino*. A further form of concerto, the *solo*

concerto, involved the musical exchanges between a single instrument and the answering *tutti* orchestra.

Characteristic of the Baroque concerto in general is exact observance of prescribed harmonic schemes, proportions, and other musical principles. The rigidity of the requirements, however, often led to a certain stereotyping of the form that was detrimental to the composers of the period. Hence, Igor Stravinsky's charge against Antonio Vivaldi, the most productive solo concerto composer of the period: "In reality he wrote only one concerto, but he did it 500 times."

The *trio sonata* similarly acquired a standard form. Two instruments, normally violins, play interwoven, often polyphonic melodies over a figured bass, or *basso continuo*. Throughout the whole, the listener is expected to be aware of the symbolism of the number 3, standing for the

Manuscripts, usually dedicated to noble patrons, were lavishly adorned. The imagery used was very similar to the imagery in art: an hour-glass (left) represents the transitory nature of life; in contrast, a rising music scale leads into a luminous heaven (right).

1600 – 1750

1600 – 1750

Girolamo Frescobaldi (1583-1643), the most important organist of his time.

Jan Pieterszoon Sweelinck (1562-1621), composer and organist.

A program from Buxtehude's *Evening Music*. Buxtehude was one of the first to organize public evening presentations of his own as well as other composers' works.

Christian trinity. The trio sonata occurs in two distinct forms: the *sonata da camera* (chamber sonata), which includes a prelude and a series of dance movements, and the *sonata da chiesa* (liturgical, or church sonata), which is characterized by a standard movement series of fast-slow-fast. An instrument capable of producing chords (harpsichord, organ, or lute) provides the harmonic accompaniment according to a numerical script written over the bass (figured bass or basso continuo).

New musical impulses throughout Europe

Italy

As often in the history of music, so in the Baroque period, the dissemination of new musical forms and possibilities of expression grew out of individual musical personalities whose students—often numerous—carried the innovations of their masters throughout Europe. In Rome the organist Girolamo Frescobaldi elevated not only the ricercare but all the other significant contemporary forms of organ music—the toccata, the capriccio, and the fantasia—to their first musical zenith. Frescobaldi's most important student was Johann Jakob Froberger, a decidedly cosmopolitan musician, who introduced the achievements of his teacher to Europe's other metropolitan centers—Vienna, Paris, and London.

The Netherlands, northern Germany

Rome was not the only source of innovation. The Netherlands and northern Germany provided further impulse to the development of organ music. In Amsterdam, the composer and organist Jan Pieterszoon Sweelinck attracted so many distinguished students that he earned a reputation as a regular "organist maker." Far from being a quiet pedagogue, working modestly in the background to produce brilliant students, Sweelinck was himself a star of European eminence.

In northern Germany, his students, particularly Samuel Scheidt and Heinrich Scheidemann, in turn influenced the succeeding generation of composers, of whom the most important was Dietrich Buxtehude, whose influence on J.S. Bach is not to be underestimated.

England, France

Between 1600 and 1750, England and France successively take their places in Baroque music history as centers of composition and musicianship. During the reign of Elizabeth I (1558–1603) and into the 17th century, England witnessed a musical blossoming initiated by the *virginalists*. A rectangular form of the harpsichord, the virginal was a favorite instrument in England for which William Byrd, John Bull, and Orlando Gibbons composed significant works. Their keyboard music was later gathered into the *Lady Neville Virginal Book* (1591) and the *Fitzwilliam Virginal Book* (1613–19). All three composers wrote for other instruments as well; in particular, William Byrd left behind significant liturgical pieces.

John Bull's achievements with the virginal were replicated by John Dowland with the lute. Music for the lute alone or for a small vocal/instrumental ensemble, the *consort*, was enormously important for noble and bourgeois musicians of the Elizabethan era.

Alongside virginal and consort music developed a distinctly English form of stage music that defined the British music scene for 30 years: the *masque*. Noble lay people, called *masquers*, performed masked plays complemented by pantomimes.

Pictures of women at the virginal were very popular. There are many stories about the meaning of the name of this keyboard instrument, but in fact the origin of the word is *virga* (from the Latin for "rod" or "staff"), referring to the instrument's design, rather than the commonly assumed *virgo* (Latin, virgin).

Parthenia, the first printed book of virginal music.

1600 – 1750

Jean-Baptiste Lully (1632–87). Born in Florence, Lully crowned his exemplary career as court composer to the Sun King, Louis XIV. As one of the most important figures of the 17th-century music world, he was highly regarded everywhere in Europe, and influenced the development of musical culture at many royal courts, which competed with each other to imitate Louis XIV's lifestyle at Versailles.

In France music reached its high point, a style blended from many other European influences, at approximately the middle of the 17th century. The Court of Louis XIV was a particular sphere of activity for composers. (The French king's penchant for pageantry to signify the extent of his power did not limit itself to the architecture of the Palace at Versailles.) Louis maintained a large orchestra, for which all important French composers of the day wrote pieces. The viola da gamba, predecessor to the modern-day cello, was Louis XIV's favorite instrument, and thus a popular favorite. Composers including Marin Marais and Sainte Colombe wrote gamba music almost exclusively. The palace orchestra in Versailles, the *Violons du Roi*, commanded forces of 24 strings and 12 winds. The style that traveled and grew from Paris to become *the* European style owes almost everything to Jean-Baptiste Lully (1632–87). Lully was born in Italy, and enriched French music with stylistic innovations in his operas, ballets, and orchestral suites.

The French musical scene of the time also boasted composers who wrote predominantly

Opera and ballet in the court of Versailles of Louis XIV around 1745.

The Palace of Versailles, where Lully worked, was the center and inspiration of French musical life.

1600 – 1750

keyboard music. Known as *Claveci-nistes*, these composers placed heavy emphasis on finger technique for the harpsichord as well as on the extremely refined art of musical ornamentation. Beside Jacques Champion de Chambonnières and Jean Henri d'Anglebert, especially notable were Louis Couperin and his nephew François; the younger Couperin's music is still widely performed, and he was dubbed by his contemporaries "le Grand" (the Great).

This example from François Couperin's pedagogical work *L'Art de Toucher le Clavecin* (The Art of Playing the Harpsichord) illustrates the diversity of improvisatory musical ornamentation expected of players of the time.

New sounds, new possibilities
Along with compositional innovation came enlargements and improvements of instruments, which thereby gained new functions and a much greater rank.

King Louis XIV, employer of J.B. Lully and model for all European princes of his time.

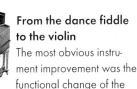

From the dance fiddle to the violin
The most obvious instrument improvement was the functional change of the

French harpsichords of this time generally had two manuals (keyboards) and were sumptuously trimmed and painted.

65

The violin assumed its final form late in the Baroque period. Cat-gut strings produced a considerably softer sound than do modern steel strings.

violin. Originally used only to accompany dances, it became a concert solo instrument during the first decades of the 17th century, and soon came to dominate. Until that time, the cornetto, a wooden wind instrument with a cupped mouthpiece, had dominated Baroque instrumental music.

Straight and crooked cornetti (wind instruments) in the *Syntagma musicum* of Michael Praetorius, a standard work on music from 1619.

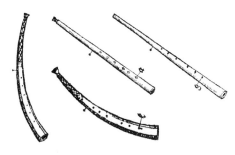

The organ: Queen of the instruments?

The organ has been apostrophized as "queen of instruments" because of its unusually rich and powerful tone, which has almost unlimited possibilities through combinations of its different pipe registers. Along with its characteristic sonorities, the organ can imitate the sound of other instruments. The history of organ building is reflected, like the history of music, in the names of important organ builders and organ families. Two names are of particular importance: Silbermann and Schnitger.

Organs of the north German type differ from organs of Italian construction in several respects, including the expansion of the pedals to play not

Flue pipes of an organ: Designed like a whistle, the airstream meets a flat opening. In reed pipes, a small metal plate moves and displaces the air in oscillation.

only bass notes but an independent melody as well, and the combination of many different sounding registers, or groups of pipes.

The gamba: Instrument for citizens and kings

Before the violin finally prevailed, the viola da gamba, along with the cornetto, was a premier solo instrument, because it offered many different possibilities. On the one hand, as a solo instrument, it can play chords; on the other hand it is a good ensemble instrument, with a whole family (treble, alto, tenor, and bass gambas) able to reproduce complex musical structures. It also serves well as a basso-continuo instrument, reinforcing the important bass line and holding an ensemble together rhythmically. For a long time, the gamba was an indispensable part of Baroque instrumental ensembles, and was displaced from the string instrument family relatively late by the younger violoncello (the modern cello).

House organ from Southern Germany.

1600 – 1750

Prince Emanuel Franz Joseph of Bavaria playing the gamba. The order of the strings and the construction of the bow made it possible to play chords.

Johann Sebastian Bach (1685–1750) at the age of 30.
That he actually looked like this is doubtful. This portrait dates from the 19th century, when it seemed suitable to present the most important Baroque composer as a sympathetic, even-tempered man.

There is surely no other composer whose work was labeled by his contemporaries as backward and outmoded, whose name was forgotten soon after his death, whose personality was so in-effective at generating publicity, who is so fascinating to musicians and concert-goers today as Johann Sebastian Bach.

Unlike Ludwig van Beethoven, who shocked his public with unconventional innovations, Bach irritated his listeners and critics all the more because he composed in a time in which the entire musical world—led by his own son Carl Philipp Emanuel—was possessed by *Sturm und Drang*, while he persisted in old, traditional forms and techniques. Very few of his colleagues comprehended that Bach's work was the culmination point of an age. Bach himself was comparatively untouched by the reproach that he was out-moded. On the one hand, he was well aware of the quality of his music, even if it was not fashion-able. On the other hand, he con-sidered it his task to create music to the glory of God. Therefore he did not feel terribly dependent on the judgment and goodwill of the public. In the course of his pro-fessional career, which led him to many small places in Thuringia, Saxony, and to the Saxon metro-polis of Leipzig, he often met with lack of understanding from his listen-ers and, more often still, was in con-flict with his superiors. The whole meaning of his work, which emerged over a period of almost fifty years and includes at present count over one thousand com-positions, becomes clear, if one realizes that he reached, with "old" means, a pinnacle of musical perfection. Though his methods were in application certainly out-moded, in substance they were universal. Calculation and pro-portionality, clear organization and construction are the hallmarks of Bach's works, which even today inspire musicians and composers. The agreement of content and form, particularly in the vocal works, is the most impressive characteristic of Bach's compositions.

The origin of a many-layered musical output

If one considers the life and career of Bach, it becomes clear that his in every respect extraordinary work emerged under relatively unfavorable conditions. Throughout his creative life, Bach worked in the service of different employers, for whom he had to produce compositions on demand. And produce them he did, on the one hand to act as a tool of God, and on the other hand with the desire to express his personal musical convictions clearly. More than once this attitude led to extreme conflicts.

The first position

At eighteen years of age (1703) Bach already had a place as a fiddler at the Court in Weimar. He then spent three years at the

Bach's life in the small town of Arnstadt was marked by vexations. He was reproached for playing too long during church services, and for "mixing in fantastical variations." In musical questions, however, Bach always remained adamant, convinced of his own righteousness in the face of his employers.

Michaelisschule in Lüneburg. He soon moved on to the post of organist in Arnstadt, where he accompanied the community singing so imaginatively that nobody could follow along. After he spent nearly half a year on vacation—indeed, because of an educational trip—his job was abruptly terminated. For a year (1707) he held the post of organist in Mühlhausen, but he lost this job because of religious differences between the Pietists and orthodoxy.

Organist in Weimar

For the next nine years (1708–17) Bach returned to the Court in Weimar, where he was employed as court organist and chamber musician. During this time he composed many organ works and cantatas, for services and special occasions. He quit this position, however, because he was not promoted to the position of Hofkapellmeister (court conductor).

Bach's first wife was his cousin, Maria Barbara, who was mother of four of his twenty children. She tried, as did his second wife Anna Magdalena, to give Bach the privacy he needed for his work despite their many children.

In 1708 Bach returned to Weimar, where he had worked for six months in 1703. He remained there for almost ten years serving as court organist and chamber musician. In the conflict around his termination, Bach was taken into custody for almost a month because of "obstinacy."

Hofkapellmeister in the province

Bach worked for six years (1717–23) at the Court of Prince Leopold in the backward provincial town of Köthen—"by which also may be supposed," he wrote, "that my life is over." Actually Bach felt rather good here, because he could rely on his employer's musical expertise and he was allowed more artistic freedom. It was during this period that he wrote a large part of his keyboard and chamber music, including the first volume of *The Well-Tempered Clavier* and the *Brandenburg Concertos*. Upon Prince Leopold's second marriage, to a woman who was not particularly musically inclined, Bach applied for the positions of cantor at the Thomasschule and music director of the city church in Leipzig.

Bach spent six relatively unencumbered years working at the Court in Köthen. A large number of instrumental works date from this period, including the famous *Brandenburg Concertos*. The musicians in the court orchestra in Köthen were skilled enough to undertake the technically difficult parts he composed for them.

Johann Sebastian Bach

The Thomaschurch in Leipzig. This was the center of the German music world. Through Bach, who wrote his great cantatas and passions during his time here, the church and its still-famous choir became a center for European musical excellence.

The Leipzig years

Although it seemed to Bach "to begin with, not respectable from a Capellmeister to become a Cantor," he saw the possibilities of this position. Here, beside the weekly composition of cantatas that was one of his duties, he could try out other forms and styles. With the *Passions of St. John* and *St. Matthew*, Bach made his most important contribution to the oratorio form. He also composed a considerable body of instrumental music during his twenty-seven years in Leipzig, even though this was not directly among his duties.

During these years he produced the cycle of the *Goldberg Variations*, the second volume of *The Well-Tempered Clavier*, and the *Musical Offering*, which Bach dedicated to the Prussian King Frederick II. In the *Art of the Fugue*, his last work, Bach once more seized upon the wide range of possibilities of polyphony. This work moves on so high a spiritual and speculative level that an exact specification of instrumentation appears to have meant little to the composer. The *Art of the Fugue* remained unfinished. After Bach's death in 1750, somebody added the printed draft of works based on the chorale, "Before your throne here I stand," which was invoked as evidence, particularly in the 19th century, that Bach was indeed attempting to fulfill a divine plan through music.

Johann Sebastian Bach at the age of 61.
His work was the apogee of Baroque music. In all important forms—with the exception of the opera—his contributions stand out. He holds in his hand a notation of a triple canon in six voices. In 1747, when this picture was made, this kind of polyphonic composition was considered outmoded.

Bach's best-known, though not most important piece, is the *Prelude in C Major*, which opens the cycle of *The Well-Tempered Clavier*. The new voicing of keyboard instruments, which was developed in the 1720s, allowed composition in all 24 major and minor keys.

1600 – 1750

Johann Sebastian Bach, absorbed completely in the Baroque way of thinking of order in proportion and number, was born into a time when the necessity and validity of such strict standards had already begun to be questioned. The body of work he left behind, however, suggests that his purpose in the process of musical composition was not to pander to current taste but to honor God with his music.

Like Heinrich Schütz (see p. 49), Bach saw himself as a servant of God, who works to elucidate the divine order on earth. Despite such philosophic underpinnings, his work is also characterized by qualities commonly associated with the idea of the Baroque—namely, festivity, splendor, liveliness, learning, as well as the completely ordinary joy of making music.

The importance of Bach's work rests primarily on two bases: first, he expanded the boundaries of many contemporary musical forms: for example, the fugue with his *Well-Tempered Clavier*, and the oratorio with his *St. John* and *St. Matthew Passions*; second, his works act in the context of musical history as a sort of conclusion, a summary of everything that came before. This is true not only of the fugue and the oratorio, but of other forms as well, including the instrumental concerto, the solo or figured-bass-accompanied sonata, and the suite. It is generally fair to say that Bach's compositions

mark the end of the line for several forms, but certainly also the peak. His mastery of strict contrapuntal composition using old forms is the basis for the disinterest and misunderstanding of his contemporaries toward his work.

From the town of Halle into the world

George Frideric Handel, a worldly man from Halle, represents an opposite position from that of Bach. Handel found his primary musical

In 1747 the Prussian king, Frederick II the Great, invited Bach to Potsdam. Frederick gave Bach a theme on which to improvise a fugue, which gave Bach no difficulty. After his return to Leipzig, Bach used the "king's theme" as a foundation for his *Musical Offering*, which he dedicated to Frederick. Therein unfolded for Bach all conceivable possibilities of contrapuntal art, which, however, no longer caught the public imagination. In a sonata for flute, violin, and continuo bass, Bach did make one concession to the new musical taste, influenced by the king himself, an accomplished flute player, as well as by Frederick's court composers Johann Joachim Quantz and Bach's son Carl Philipp Emanuel.

1600 – 1750

inspiration in Italy, where he lingered several years (1707–09). After a short stay in Hanover, he came eventually in 1711–12 to England, where he had a decisive impact on that country's musical development. As his course of travels makes clear, composing music was something altogether different for Handel than it was for Bach. Of course, religion played a role in some of his writing—the most obvious example is his famous *Messiah*—however, sacred works by no means stood in the foreground of his composing career.

Handel composed a large body of operas and oratorios using chiefly biblical or ancient materials, and he assumed direct responsibility for the promotion of his work. He proceeded in much the same manner with his instrumental music, his concerti grossi and his chamber ensemble pieces. The commercial prospects for

George Frideric Handel (1685–1759).

George Frideric Handel's birthplace in Halle, the German city he soon left for ...

his work were ever in his mind. The place he holds today in the history of music is largely due to the consistently high quality of his prolific output.

Like Johann Sebastian Bach, George Frideric Handel was not a great innovator, but he raised existing musical forms to a higher level. At the latest, around the middle of the 18th century, the forms he used were considered obsolete.

... Hamburg, Italy, Hanover. and ultimately England, where he became world-famous.

Handel knew well how to use his talents. He produced and marketed himself the many operas he composed.

However, his life was not without setbacks. His model career developed a chink when it turned out that nobody wanted to hear more of the operas he wrote based mainly on ancient materials: His opera production company went broke. With his oratorios, like *Messiah*, he steered his career back on course.

But Handel's focus was not purely on worldly success. When asked, what he intended with his art, he is supposed to have answered: "To make people better."

Rameau synthesizes the musical thinking of his time

France's musical development was quite unlike that in Germany, Italy, or England. The French music scene was in part occupied with perfecting traditional forms and more or less preserving the musical status quo. But it was also an environment populated by people who were open toward the new ideas brewing in the general atmosphere of European intellectual life. Jean-Philippe Rameau brought together in his compositions and his theoretical work (for example, *Traité de l'harmonie*, 1722) different compositional lines that establish it as a culmination point of Baroque music.

Jean-Philippe Rameau (1683-1764), contemporary of Handel and Bach, who summarized the music theory of his time. Through Rameau's influence, European music was given an essentially French stamp.

The new style: Sentimentality and *Sturm und Drang*

The demands of the Enlightenment for naturalness and immediacy were rife also in the musical aesthetic discussion of the 1720s. The overriding question was how to bring this naturalness and simplicity to music. The polyphonic compositional methods of composers such as Johann Sebastian Bach were rejected, and the new composers sought new forms of expression that might adequately mediate the general ideas of the time.

Contrast as structural principle

In keyboard music the search for new forms was particularly far-reaching. First of all, composers attempted to change the character of the melodies and themes. The idea of the "speaking principle" emerged, as musicians strove to give every musical idea an individual character. In his keyboard works, for example in his free *Fantasies*, Carl Philipp Emanuel Bach (the second surviving son of Johann Sebastian Bach) reached a high degree of personal expression. The ideal instrument for this music was the clavichord, an extremely sweet-sounding keyboard instrument whose

Carl Philipp Emanuel Bach (1714-88) was employed 28 years at the Prussian Court. Here he had to accompany as harpsichordist the works of Frederick the Great and his colleague Johann Joachim Quantz, which seemed to Bach simple-minded and conventional. In Sanssouci he scarcely had the chance to realize his progressive, sometimes bold, musical ideas. Later, as chief musician in Hamburg, he found all the musical freedom he had lacked in Potsdam. This position counted among the most important in Europe, not least because G.P. Telemann had preceded him in this post, and had composed many long and good works during his tenure.

Georg Philipp Telemann (1681–1767), the godfather of C.P.E. Bach, was one of the integrating figures of European music between the Baroque and the Rococo. As music director in Hamburg, he was predecessor to his godchild.

1600 – 1750

dynamic range lies between soft and extremely soft. The dangers, however, of exaggeration and excessive pathos that one often encounters in the Rococo period were manifest in the younger Bach's work.

First attempts at a formal structuring, which became standards for the next two hundred years, again, came mainly from C.P.E. Bach, who set contrasting themes in relationship to one another and no longer only strung them together. Still without strict standardization, he transferred this contrast principle to other instrumental genres.

Carl Philipp Emanuel Bach, who had for decades served in Prussia where he had been obliged to conform to the musical tastes of his king, Frederick the Great, clearly articulated his musical aesthetic positions in the essay, *Attempt at the True Art of Playing the Clavier* (1752/62). In 1768 he went to Hamburg and took over from Georg Philipp Telemann as music director of the five main churches. This professional success was instrumental in the dissemination of his musical ideas.

Gallant style, new sounds

The departure from the strict polyphonic style to a freer art of composition was not confined to Germany, but occurred throughout Europe. The same development of style may be discerned through the progress of many individual composers. Especially important in this is Georg Philipp Telemann (1681–1767), the transitional figure between the Bachs (father and son), on the one hand, and Italian and French music, on the other.

New sounds from Mannheim

It did not take long for the "free writing style" to spread—at times with typical regional characteristics—and become obligatory in all Europe.

Johann Christian Bach (1735–82), J.S. Bach's *enfant terrible* son, brought the new gallant style to England. In London he organized concerts, ...

... in the open air of Vauxhall Gardens ...

Johann Stamitz, from 1741 head of the Mann-heim Court Chapel, especially enjoyed experi-mentation. He promoted the so-called *terraced dynamics*—alternating soft and loud phrases without gradation, also known as the Mannheim rocket—in the orchestra, which was later modu-lated into a more subtle stylistic device. Georg Mathias Monn and Christoph Wagenseil in Vienna joined the gallant style with lighthearted-ness, which granted the early Classical music a rococoish-sweetish flavor.

1600 – 1750

... and not quite so publicly, in the houses of the bourgeoisie and palaces of the aristocracy.

1750 – 1830

If lightness, naturalness, and immediacy expressed in music were the central concern for the Rococo composers, the Classical composers increasingly sought musical modes of expression that would reflect one of the central themes of the Enlightenment—the freedom of the individual and his or her position within the world. This new conception of the self was particularly well suited to the already developed sonata form, which evolved into a universal structural principal in almost all classical musical forms. The new understanding of self and the insistence with which the musicians conveyed it to the public established a completely new role for music in general and for composers in the social life of the time.

From experiment to standard form: The sonata

The setting of contrasting themes, as developed by C.P.E. Bach, was the starting point for the development of sonata movements as a standard form. One essential innovation came when the number of the themes was reduced, as a rule to two; these at first opposed each other, then they were interwoven, and finally they were summed up in a synthesis. This formal structure comprises three parts: (1) exposition, in which the first

The new sonata form developed primarily through piano music. Though the Hammerklavier of this period may sound mediocre today, they offered the Classical composer an advantage over the harpsichord: the volume could be varied by adjusting the amount of pressure used to strike the key.

Sonata form

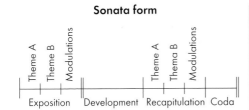

Theme A · Theme B · Modulations | Theme A · Thema B · Modulations

Exposition · Development · Recapitulation · Coda

Even though sonatas had different lengths—from short sonatinas to powerful piano works of up to a half hour duration—common to all was the basic three-part structure.

theme appears in the tonic key, and the second theme appears in the dominant; (2) development, in which the previously presented material is worked out (more and more freely in late Classical and early Romantic works); and (3) recapitulation, which repeats the exposition, but with the second theme also now in the tonic. The exposition usually ends with a coda, which by the time of Beethoven could be quite extended.

In musical academies, a mixture of public and private concerts offered contemporary music in what were often quite colorful sequences: an aria might follow a symphony, then a piano quintet, then again a solo, and so on.

1750 – 1830

The development of the clear tripartite structure of the sonata form allowed the composer to draw complex musical connections within a relatively simple structure. Throughout Europe, sonatas of this new form emerged, especially for the piano, which during this period evolved gradually out of its experimental form into a usable instrument. Only one decisive feature of what we today think of as the sonata form was still missing in the early piano sonatas, or, at most, was introduced only incidentally—namely, the real processing of the themes in the development section.

Concerto: musical form in which a soloist and the orchestra are equally involved
Sonata form: musical form in which two opposing themes are processed in exposition, development, and recapitulation
String quartet: musical composition for two violins, a viola, and a violoncello in sonata form
Symphony: main form of classical orchestra music, first developed using sonata form
Thematic work: fragmenting of a theme, with new combinations of individual parts within a sonata development section

Joseph Haydn (1732–1809) at the age of 60. After 21 years as court musician to Prince Eszterházy, he started a second career, which brought him, among other things, to London, where his works were played with great success. No longer the court musician wearing livery, Haydn was now a worldly figure whose works were known throughout Europe.

1750 – 1830

Joseph Haydn sets the standard

Joseph Haydn (1732–1809) set out to combine the two main themes with each other so that individual motives and theme fragments always appear in new combinations. This splitting up of the material, to be perceived from different aspects, was exciting for both composers and listeners. The possibilities of this thematic work, as this method is called, are virtually inexhaustible. Surely this is a major main reason why composers continue to be interested in the sonata form.

Haydn was himself aware that with the technique of thematic work he had found the means to add decisive impulses to the music of his time. His application and refinement of this technique are particularly evident in his piano works. In the early phase, dating from about 1750, his compositions retain a strong Rococo flavor, which might strike one as somewhat superficial. This disappeared in time as Haydn brought to the foreground of his compositions the formal aspects of the sonata. However, Haydn was not only a paragon of Enlightenment rationality, as expressed in his absolute mastery of sonata form. He was also famous for his sense of humor, especially in symphonies, with nicknames like "The Surprise" and "The Toy." Though rarely performed today, Haydn's operas were popular in his time.

A street scene in Vienna in the late 18th century.

The early Classical symphonies did not yet have the extensive instrumentation of the Romantic orchestras. As a rule, they contained two violin parts, viola, cello, two oboes, and two flutes, strengthened by the contrabass (string bass).

1750 – 1830

The symphony

The entire field of "absolute" music—contrasted with program music which follows a narrative or scene—came to be dominated by the sonata form. Its principles of composition were universally and almost exclusively applied. The symphony, which held until now a relatively subordinate position in musical performance and composition, stepped in as the orchestral counterpart to the piano sonata.

Originally, symphonies functioned as a prelude before a cantata, an opera, or a ballet. In Italy, *sinfonia* were pieces for a string ensemble with wind instruments. They were chiefly operatic pieces, produced with modest claim and in enormous number—there were about twenty thousand sinfonia. The appeal of combining the possibilities of varied instrumentation with the dynamics of the sonata form seems natural enough to us today. The instrumentation allowed the composer to strengthen the thematic contrasts effectively, while the varied thematic work using different instruments came through clearly and naturally.

With its growing potential and appeal, the symphony form evolved away from a kind of mass production into a more individualistic work of art. Joseph Haydn composed altogether one hundred and four, Wolfgang Amadeus Mozart fifty-one, and Ludwig van Beethoven nine symphonies. The outer form of the symphony also became standardized. As a rule, it had four sections or movements, described through Italian tempo and expression markings. The usual order of the movements was *allegro* (fast), *andante* (a slower but flowing tempo), *tempo di minuetto* (a 3:4 dance tempo), and back to *allegro*. Over time, the third movement was often dispensed with, as a too lightly and shallowly felt minuet, so that the three-movement form became standard.

1750 – 1830

The score of piano sonatas of Wolfgang Amadeus Mozart. Though considerably more difficult to play than the concertos of Haydn, they still lack the virtuosity found in the piano works of Beethoven.

The concerto

The concerto was a different story. As the concerto grosso and solo instrumental concerto, it was a mainstay of Baroque composition, but it now underwent a radical change. The growing dominance of the sonata style not only energized and transformed the outward form of the concerto, which was marked by its exchanges and recurring themes, but also reinforced the conviction that the solo instrument is entitled to equal partnership in musical presentation. Moreover, the soloist came to see the concerto as an opportunity to express his or her individual artistic personality. This figured strongly in the

discussions, so rabid and portentous during the 18th and 19th centuries, of the position of the artist in society.

The string quartet

The string quartet was rife with the possibilities of developing into an ideal Classical form. On the one hand, the setting with four instruments seemed to offer a well-balanced sound, while on the other hand, despite their strong inter-dependence, the instruments could speak individually. The violoncello no longer served only as a continuo bass, but assumed as great a part as the three higher voices. The viola, meanwhile, which had long been considered a mere filler instrument, necessary to complete the harmony, was accorded a stronger role in the late Classical period—a role that was to be further expanded in the Romantic period.

Destination: Vienna

As it grew in political influence, the Austrian capital

The string quartet is more or less the premier musical form of the Classical period. It may be thought of as a "musical conversation between four intelligent people" in which all voices carry equal weight.

1750 – 1830

Vienna, the metropolis on the Danube, developed into a musical center of world renown.

The relationship between Haydn and Mozart was built upon mutual admiration. Haydn recognized the tremendous talent of his young colleague, while Mozart always recognized his debt to Haydn. By no means a revolutionary composer, Mozart was able to extend Haydn's musical vision.

city developed into an unusually magnetic cultural center. An Italian influence prevailed in the musical life of the city. Operas were sung in Italian, and Italian composers and conductors were a mainstay in Vienna. As these Italian traditions became mixed with the innovations in instrumental music, a new music emerged, ultimately associated most closely with three names: Haydn, Mozart, and Beethoven. From the Burgenland, near the Hungarian border, came Joseph Haydn, destined soon to create a stir in Vienna with his compositions, even though his earliest attempts were rather conventional. Haydn was employed for 21 years as composer to Prince Eszterházy, who gave him free reign to employ musical experiments of many kinds with his court orchestra. Not least because of this freedom, Haydn kept to the court, where he was rather cut off from Viennese life. In 1790, after the closing of Eszterházy's court chapel, Haydn settled in Vienna. In the following years he pursued his career, which brought him renown in the other major European musical centers, London (where he traveled twice) and Paris.

Wolfgang Amadeus Mozart did not stay long in his native town of Salzburg. The idea of service to the local church went against his personality and sense of himself as an artist. So Mozart centered his activities in Vienna, though his career led him on numerous journeys all over Europe. Mozart's work reflects the entire range of changing influences that were rampant in the second half of the 18th century. His operas are pervaded by Italian influences; his instrumental works combine the search for the Classical form,

Many portraits of Mozart convey a sweet and sentimental image of the child prodigy. This portrait from 1789 (*W.A. Mozart at the Piano*, unfinished oil painting by Joseph Lange) shows the composer in a more contemplative pose.

which he inherited from Haydn, with an extraordinary genius for melodic invention. Despite the effortlessness with which he appeared to compose (his manuscripts contain very few corrections), his music always sounds like the result of well-reasoned planning. Mozart's methods and process of composition have fascinated not only musicians but psychologists as well.

In 1792, Ludwig van Beethoven came from the provincial Rhine town of Bonn to the Austrian metropolis. It quickly became clear to him that his studies with Johann Georg Albrechtsberger and Antonio Salieri would offer him no insights into the new music, for which he was hungry. He was pleased to be a personal pupil of Haydn, though their meetings were to be sporadic. In place of lessons, Beethoven studied Haydn's works so intensely that in the notes to his *Piano Sonata Op. 2*, he wrote, "dedicated to my teacher Joseph Haydn." Beethoven's sonatas opened a cycle of 32 works, with which Beethoven not only changed the course of contemporary music, but through them set the standard for piano music for the next 50 years. Beethoven planned his compositions very carefully and rejected many ideas or improved them in several drafts that are nearly illegible to laypeople; experts, however, have come to recognize them as extremely informative sketchbooks.

Wolfgang Amadeus Mozart (1756–91) was a child prodigy who was heavily promoted by his father Leopold, a famous violinist. His relationship to his father was never completely free of strain. Wolfgang, who called himself Amadeus, felt very close to his sister Maria Anna, called Nannerl.

Ludwig van Beethoven (1770–1827), with his wild hair, met the classic 19th-century image of the wild genius.

1750 – 1830

The burial of Beethoven. Reports estimated that 20,000 people attended.

Over a period of 24 years Beethoven extended his symphonic works, in which—especially in the last works—he expanded, indeed exploded, the framework of the sonata movement form. The particularity of his work, but also his personal circumstances—his choleric character and the onset of his deafness in 1795—somewhat justifiably earned Beethoven the image as the archtypical creative genius that emerged in the Classical period, only to become even more rampant during the Romantic.

The rest of Europe sets other priorities

From the development of the sonata form, with its consequences for orchestral and piano music stretching well into the 19th century, the musical centers of the remaining European countries remained more or less untouched.

Catchy operas—great virtuosi

In Italy in particular, musical development proceeded without the shock waves Beethoven had triggered in the Germanic musical world. His revolutionary innovations were not especially discussed here. Composers continued to dedicate themselves to the opera. After the turn of the century, this genre was to be changed

1750 – 1830

The Barber of Seville by Gioacchino Rossini was the most performed opera of the 19th century. Rossini was so popular that he could afford a luxurious lifestyle. He stopped composing almost completely in 1829, at the age of 37. He dedicated the rest of his life more to cuisine than to music.

dramatically through the work of one Italian composer, and the impulses of his influence would be felt throughout Europe. Gioacchino Rossini (1792–1868) set himself the goal of freeing opera buffa (the comic opera style dating from the Baroque era) from its cliché settings and to build from the simple farces an opera with real independent characters. The melodies of Rossini's operas are catchy, the rhythms clearly and firmly outlined. Of his 39 operas, only a few are still produced today, although certainly the delightful *Barber of Seville* is as appealing as ever. In his time, however, Rossini's popularity was without equal.

Gioacchino Antonio Rossini (1792–1868)

The operas of Gaetano Donizetti (1797–1848) unite all the features of opera popular at the time: simple buffo elements of somewhat stereotyped plots and foolish overdrawn characters as dramatic materials, which anticipate future operatic developments. Vincenzo Bellini (1801–35), influenced by Mozart, tried with the style of *bel canto* (literally, "beautiful singing") through simple orchestral accompaniments to keep the vocal line prominent.

Meanwhile, the first instrumental virtuosi stepped before the public. The Italian fiddlers, in particular, caused a furor in Europe. For about 100 years the general standards of instrumental technique had been in continual development. From a beginning made by Giuseppe Tartini, Francesco Geminiani, in his School for Fiddlers (London, 1751), systematized the string techniques that are so important for good playing. From this tradition came Niccolò Paganini, whose name even today is synonymous with the high art of violin playing. Paganini astounded his listeners with his playing technique. He was to

1750 – 1830

Niccolò Paganini (1782–1840) was seen as a somewhat demonic figure. His nickname "Devil's Fiddler" was due to his phenomenal skill as a violinist.

1750 – 1830

become the quintessential virtuoso, and introduced this musical specialization in actual playing technique, which in the following years, especially in the salons and concert halls of the Romantic period, was in great demand.

Music and politics

The reaction in France toward the developments emanating from Vienna was strongly antipathetic. Although Beethoven's French contemporaries also turned to the sonata form in their symphonies, with Etienne Nicolas Mehul one of the few successful French symphonists from this period, the French public was scarcely interested in the resolution of formal music problems. Rather, the

Eugène Delacroix, *Liberty Leading the People* (July 28, 1830). This most famous painting on the theme of a French revolution—though *not* the famous Revolution of 1789—reflects more than any other work of art the attitude of the French artists, who took issue intensely with their country's political situation.

stage was the avenue through which the French preferred to experience topical events. The French Revolution of 1789 changed public thinking to such an extent that opera and art in general became highly politicized. In Paris, Grétry composed "revolutionary operas" with direct reference to current political and social events.

It was not until a generation later that composers appeared on the French opera scene whose works encompassed the revolutionary theme of the "grande nation": Auber, Boieldieu, and especially Meyerbeer, whose operas particularly focused on the relationship between the individual and society.

Private initiatives

In the 100 years after Händel's death in 1759 in England, the already entrenched vocal tradition marched on almost exclusively via oratorios and anthems, the English equivalent of motets. Otherwise, there is hardly a composer from this period in England whose name is remembered. That London retained its status as a musical center is due in large part to the engagement of two composers, both of German origin. Carl Friedrich Abel and Johann Christian Bach (yet another son of Johann Sebastian) not only contributed their own compositions but also devoted their energies to creating a public concert life that kept the English capital attractive. Once Abel and Bach died, London's musical life was dependent on imports from the Continent. Still, when the concert agent Salomon hired Joseph Haydn for two tours, the Classical tradition was partially established in England.

Giacomo Meyerbeer (1791–1864) came from Berlin, Italianized his first name, and built his career in France. His operas perfectly suited the spirit of the times: their melodies were sung everywhere.

English musical life lay stagnant in the 18th century, though the same cannot be said of other arts. This century produced such moralistic, though also ironic, pictures as William Hogarth's portrayals of life and customs. Below: *Shortly After the Wedding* from Hogarth's sequence of pictures, *Marriage à la mode.*

1750 – 1830

On the other side of reality, another world: The early Romantic

For almost half a century Vienna was the home of the new music of Europe. The sonata form had become a musical *idée fixe*. Other forms with less popular philosophical claims were eclipsed and if they were to develop, they would have to do so outside the mainstream.

Already, in the 1820s, a new idea washed over musicians and composers, in much the same way that it had already spread in European literature and other arts. At the heart of this new direction was a focus on the fantastical, the irrational, the magical. Reason, that pillar of the Enlightenment, no longer held center court; there was, many began to assert, more to life than empirical logic—there was an unseen source for thoughts, and art would tap this source.

In music, this Romantic concept, a counterweight to Classical rationality and perfection of form, called for a complete reorientation. Such a reorientation, however, was not to be easy. Beethoven loomed like a giant in the eyes of all Ro-

Caspar David Friedrich (1774–1840), *Das Eismeer* (The Ice Sea). Friedrich captures with this painting the Romantic sentiment. In nature, the Romantics saw a reality in which their soul was reflected.

mantic composers. While they measured themselves against his work, they were not sure they could understand it. It gradually became clear to them that their own, new work had its own, new quality, and Beethoven's achievements were not the sole measure of their success.

On Sunday, May 23, 1824, Beethoven's *Symphony No. 9* was heard for the first time. The composer—already completely deaf—sat beside the conductor, to take "entire part" as the concert program explains. It was only with great difficulty that he was restrained from conducting himself. He was unable to perceive the audience's frenetic applause. This symphony not only marked the high point of Beethoven's achievement, but also became the model and scale by which the early and high Romantic composers would all measure themselves, and be measured.

Franz Schubert

Five years after Beethoven had finally settled in Vienna, Franz Schubert was born in the village of Liechtenthal near Vienna. Schubert in particular personifies the inner conflict of the first generation of composers after Beethoven. Plagued by feelings of inferiority, he saw himself all of his life in the shadow of Beethoven, whom he idolized and honored. His symphonic work is dependent in details on Beethoven, but it expands the form with a particular artfulness.

Schubert's extraordinary gift for inventing melodies which on the one hand are suitable to

1820 – 1850

Lieder (songs): Most Romantic songs were written on poetry cycles by contemporary authors. They stand as great works of chamber music, with beautiful melodies and an independent piano part that no longer serves merely as accompaniment for the vocal part. The music does not simply illustrate or paint a tone for the text, but interprets it in some psychological depth.

Piano works: mostly short pieces, grouped in cycles, often with poetic titles.

Cult of virtuosity: With increasingly skillful instrumental techniques, the interpretative demands of music also increased, but few performers were able to meet these demands. Pure technical prowess often overshadowed the actual quality of the music.

By the age of 19, Franz Schubert (1797–1828) had composed a large part of his works, which show the influence of Beethoven. Schubert was recognized less for his large symphonies and pianos sonatas than for his small *Ländler* (country waltzes) and other dances.

1820 – 1850

Although Schubert ignored public recognition, he had a large circle of friends. In the later so-called "Schubertiads," he played his own piano pieces or accompanied singers performing his own songs, for which he drew on the texts of poets such as Goethe, Eichendorff, and Heine. He set text by a contemporary favorite, Wilhelm Müller. Two of his song cycles, *Die Winterreise* and *Die schöne Müllerin*, are still widely performed today. Schubert's songs are the most famous in the entire genre of German song known to concertgoers as lieder.

symphonic development and on the other hand in their originality have remained fresh, gave not only his orchestral works but also the quartets and piano works in which he expounded the sonata form a dimension beyond even Beethoven.

Schubert departed from Beethoven in that he turned toward musical miniatures, which became increasingly important in the early Romantic era. He called these pieces "impromptus" (as in improvised music) or *moments musicaux* (musical moments). Far from musical trifles, as their titles might suggest, these pieces are so extraordinary that they have become a necessary foundation of the repertoire for piano students everywhere.

Another lesser form elevated to an entirely new plane by Schubert is the song. His immense (far more than 500 pieces) lieder (the German word for "songs" has been adopted by the English language in this context) output makes it clear how strongly Schubert felt that he was an artist, and an outsider, against the world. One of his prevailing themes is failure, with its attendant disappointment and consequences. One of his central figures is the wanderer who leaves the place of his failure to look elsewhere for his fortune, which he ultimately can only find in death. With Schubert, the idea of "Todessehnsucht" (longing for death), which became even

stronger later in the Romantic era, is already prominent. In his two song cycles, *Die Winterreise* (Winter Journey) and *Die schöne Müllerin* (The Beautiful Miller's Wife), this becomes especially clear: in the 19th century, a winter journey was doomed from the start and could only end in a disaster. The miller also was compelled to wander—also even then— certainly not just for pleasure or because he heard the murmur

Schubert was dependent on his friends for support. He lived extremely unpretentiously in modest circumstances. As a rule, when he was able to find a publisher willing to buy his compositions, he received very little money for them.

A Viennese street scene of the 1820s.

of a brook, but because of the hopelessness of his love for a miller's wife.

In Schubert's songs, the piano no longer has only the function of supporting the vocal melody, but becomes an equal partner, often with the task of describing an alternate, better world.

There was only one public concert of Franz Schubert's works.

Romanticism captures Europe

If indeed the clear shift of epoch from the Classical to the Romantic was so marked by two individuals who lived in one city, music after the death of Beethoven and Schubert took its impulses not from Vienna outward, but from the Romantic aesthetics that arose in the various European nations, each bringing its own character and forms.

1820 – 1850

Robert (1810-56) and Clara (1819-96) Schumann in 1850. Clara, the composer's wife, was a celebrated pianist who worked tirelessly to promote her husband's music. Early in his career, Robert Schumann developed a mechanical device to improve his piano technique, but it injured his hand and ended his career as a performer. Many of his piano works have poetic titles such as *Vogel als Prophet* (Bird as Prophet).

The early 1800s were a banner era for the births of composers. Within the span of a few short years, Robert Schumann (b. 1810), Frédéric Chopin (b. 1810), Felix Mendelssohn Bartholdy (b. 1809), Franz Liszt (b. 1811), Richard Wagner (b. 1813), and Giuseppe Verdi (b. 1813) were born. Héctor Berlioz, the most important French composer of his time, came into the world just three years after the turn of the century. Beethoven died in 1827, just as this new generation was reaching puberty, and within three years, by around 1830, the transformation from the Classical to the Romantic period was essentially complete.

Schumann—Between literature and music

No other composer adopted the ideas of literary Romanticism and assimilated them into his musical compositions so thoroughly as Robert Schumann. The influence of the novels of Jean Paul (the pseudonym for the German-born Johann Paul Friedrich Richter) and the poetry of Novalis (the pseudonym for the German poet, Friedrich von Hardenberg) may be traced in Schumann's cycles of piano music (for example, *Kinderszenen, Kreisleriana, Davidsbündler-Tänze, Carnaval, Bunte Blätter*), which are full of miniatures with highly romantic-poetic titles.

After Schumann composed the bulk of his piano works, in the year 1840 alone, he wrote 126 songs, expanding and modifying the groundwork laid by Schubert when he redefined the song.

In addition to composing, Schumann was an author. In the *Zeitschrift für Musik* (Magazine for Music), he published numerous essays, and also contributed the column "Neue Bahnen" (New Paths) in which he proclaimed Johannes Brahms the new "star" of the music world.

Among his other apparent similarities to Schubert, Schumann, too, considered Beethoven a central force in his creative career. He composed four expanded symphonies, which reveal just how well Schumann understood the symphonic form and how independently and self-confidently he was able to use Beethoven's model as a jumping-off point.

Frédéric Chopin—The man at the piano

Frédéric Chopin left behind a body of work that is remarkable in many ways. For one thing, it consists almost exclusively of piano music of a consistently high level of technical difficulty, which considerably expanded the art of the piano. On the other hand, Chopin's oeuvre contains folkloric elements (among other things); though, of course, using such elements was not unique to Chopin, he made use of an unusual variety and with uncommon frequency. His *polonaises, mazurkas, waltzes,* and other pieces were primarily heard in French salons, where he was celebrated with justifiable enthusiasm.

Franz Liszt—From salon lion to abbé

The Hungarian-born Franz Liszt led an eventful life. Just as Paganini had earlier revolutionized the technical virtuosity of the violinist, so Liszt was known, and famed, throughout Europe for his highly skilled, but also deeply expressive and dramatic playing. Like Chopin, he composed music for the salons, though he later turned increasingly to symphonic music, to which he, as well as his son-in-law Richard Wagner, made great contributions. Liszt turned to religion; in 1866 he was made an abbé by Pope Pius IX. Thereafter, his works took on an increasingly religious character.

Just how cutting disputes over aesthetic positions within the music world were during this

Frédéric Chopin, born in 1810 near Warsaw, conquered the Parisian salons of the 1830s. He lived in France until his death in 1849.

Chopin almost exclusively composed piano works, all of which are technically difficult to play. In keeping with the Romantic ideal of genius, his hands were an object of veneration.

1820 – 1850

Franz Liszt (1811–86) was a sensation in the concert halls and salons of Europe as a piano virtuoso. Occasionally his listeners (especially women) reportedly fainted from excitement. This is consistent with the Romantic cult of virtuosity, as well as with the reality of Liszt's extraordinarily vivid personality.

Felix Mendelssohn Bartholdy (1809–47)

era is demonstrated by the curt dismissal of Liszt's piano music by the more refined and restrained Felix Mendelssohn: "Many fingers, little brain."

Felix Mendelssohn Bartholdy—The favored son

Felix Mendelssohn Bartholdy began his career as a child prodigy; through diverse influences in his family—his grandfather was the philosopher Moses Mendelssohn—he was familiar with all the important contemporary intellectual currents in Europe. Aside from his symphonies and over-tures, which are in general program music (that is, inspired by nonmusical ideas, such as his Overture to *A Midsummer Night's Dream*), his *Songs without Words* for piano were influential.

In 1829 Mendelssohn conducted the first 19th-century, thoroughly romantically conceived revival of J. S. Bach's *St. Matthew Passion*, which had more or less fallen into obscurity for nearly a century. Mendelssohn was intensely preoccupied with Baroque music in general, and with Bach's music in particular. This consciousness of the past stirred many furious disputes over the study and application of old compositional techniques (such as fugal techniques). Some saw it as a misguided orientation that would impede the progress of music (see p. 105).

Héctor Berlioz—The *enfant terrible*

"Familiarity with his music gives anyone the right to break off all contact with him," averred Frédéric Chopin about his colleague Héctor Berlioz. In debates over musical aesthetic positions, sensitivity and choler transcended

Berlioz's revolutionary music, when it was noticed at all, was frequently misunderstood. He was often the target of personal attacks and hostilities, reflected in numerous caricatures.

issues surrounding the music of the preceding century. Indeed, Chopin's remark suggests that he simply did not recognize the significance of Berlioz's music.

Berlioz's *Symphonie fantastique* premiered in 1830. In it, Berlioz repeatedly brings back a musical idea in continually changing forms. With this *idée fixe* at the heart of the entire piece, Berlioz anticipated techniques such as the leitmotif, which Wagner would later use to great effect. In the *Symphonie fantastique*, Berlioz so convincingly expressed non-musical, narrative content—in this case, the life of an artist dreaming of his own execution—that this kind of program music set the standard for the next fifty years (see p. 105).

Héctor Berlioz (1803–69) was the first French composer to realize the Romantic ideal in music.

(see p. 105)

1820 – 1850

97

Hear music—Make music—Understand music

There are three different ways to experience music: One can hear it—as background "muzak" in elevators, department stores, and restaurants, in the concert hall and on the radio or television, or in one's living room on the stereo. One can make it, as a singer or instrumentalist, alone or in a group. And one can wrestle with it intellectually, by trying to understand its internal connections, the conditions under which it was composed, and its connections to those conditions.

The theoretical-philosophical study of music has a central place in the intellectual history of many cultures. One reason for this is that in ancient high cultures (Greece, India, and China), as well as in medieval Christian culture, music was thought to spring from a divine source. European music theory, as a consequence, evolved almost entirely out of a Christian-religious background. This theory, however, is not free of contradictions and unresolved problems, which offered plenty of possibilities for intellectual speculation and reflection. For centuries, intellectual discourse over music rested almost exclusively on this theoretical plane. The Enlightenment (late 17th, early 18th centuries) brought out other aspects that diverged from the arena of pure theory. For example, some questioned whether music might serve purposes other than the glorification of God. The arousal of emotions was suggested as a goal of music. For the first time, the musical-emotional needs of the listener took center stage.

Musicology

Until the first half of the 19th century, musical life was dominated by production and performance of contemporary works. But since around 1850, interest increased in the music of past ages. Students of old music depended on scholarly methods, as they had been developed in philology. Historical documents—musical manuscripts and prints—as well as theoretical essays from earlier centuries (so-called sources) became almost the sole object of musicological study. These sources were analyzed with great care. Musicians then generally accepted the notion that once

Greek theorist Pythagoras founded a musical system which, down to the Middle Ages, remained the foundation of all considerations and discussions of music theory.

In the mid–18th century, English scholar Charles Burney undertook an extensive tour of the continent. During his tour he interviewed composers about their aesthetic positions and also asked about the effect of contemporary music on its listeners. In literary essays, he summed up his research and articulated a musicological approach whereby musical art is not alone at the center.

one has recorded the nature of a work, described it, and analyzed it, one could summarily decide which works are masterpieces and which composers are geniuses. Although this positivist approach has long been obsolete, one can still find pockets of it in practice today. It has, unfortunately, resulted in the accumulation of myriad individual facts, with little organizing structure or principle. More recently, however, musicological studies have served to promote a revival in the popularity of Renaissance and Baroque music. Though some squabbles over the authenticity of performance practices such as ornamentation have broken out, in general both musicians and audiences alike have benefited from a plethora of lively performances.

Composition and reception

It took a long time for musicologists to realize that the music produced by composers of different ages was not some self-contained, analyzable entity, but was received and processed by different listeners in completely different ways. The public that heard Beethoven's late symphonies, for example, reacted with confusion because they did not understand or perceive the innovations Beethoven introduced. It was not until the following generation that composers and listeners found their own entry to his music. Today we are more accustomed to consider the works of past epochs against the background of their entire development. This branch of musicology, called "reception research," can help separate the essence of a work from the interpretations and extra baggage the course of history has attached to it. Observation of newer developments can also be meaningful in this way, since it allows the musicologist to detect which music is

In 1750, Carl Philipp Emanuel Bach, son of Johann Sebastian, published his *Study of the True Art of Piano Playing*. Despite the title, it dealt with far more than piano study. Bach described his view of music and with it began an open debate and discussion.

Eduard Hanslick (1825–1904) landed himself smack in the middle of a real musical controversy with his essay *On Musical Beauty* (1856), in which he clearly took up the position of Johannes Brahms.

Hugo Riemann (1849–1919) is considered the founder of the academic field of musicology.

wielding an influence, as well as which music meets public acceptance.

Music in the realm of culture

Sociological methods came comparatively late to musicology. Interest in who played music, with whom, for whom, and under what conditions, increased first with the advent of the mass media, which also help to determine these very conditions. By means of empirical investigation, musicology tries to determine which elements determine the musical culture.

The realm of the personal

People have always understood, even if only intuitively, the psychic effects of music. In the Old Testament, King Saul called for David and his harp to soothe the king's melancholy. In the 18th and 19th centuries, African–American slaves sang rhythmic call–and–response songs to lighten their labor. Liturgical music, such as mass settings, can evoke feelings of awe even in nonbelievers. The protest songs of the 1960s spurred young listeners to march against the Vietnam War. And film scores, such as Sergei Prokofiev's stirring music for *Alexander Nevsky*, can evoke deep emotion with or without being wedded to the visual. It was not until the turn of the century, however, that psychology addressed musical questions. With acoustic experiments, scientists attempted to formulate objective measures for the perception and assessment of keys and sounds. Today the methods of musical psychology have naturally considerably expanded. Out of research into the sensations and emotions that emerge when a person hears or plays music have come frequent attempts to derive some universal theory—though this has, generally, proven quite problematic.

From the exotic to the global

There is one branch of musicology that made early use of the different

Erich Moritz von Hornbostel (1877–1935) was one of the first academicians to recognize the individuality of non-European musical cultures. He formulated the essential principles of modern ethnomusicology.

knowledge drawn from other disciplines: ethnomusicology. Ethnomusicology starts from the question of whether there are any musical constants in all cultures of the world. Starting with this line of inquiry, ethnomusicologists sought the source of music. The question itself, however, remains unanswered. Research into the tonality systems of non-European musical cultures, often using the simplest of physical methods, came in time, and with it evolved the field of historical musicology, the evaluation of historical documents of non-European music theories. The resulting aggregation of facts, however, is of little use without a concomitant exploration of the function of music within a society. An understanding of such contextual connections in a wide spectrum of world cultures acts as an overview that makes it less plausible to value certain musical trends based solely on their inherent exoticism or on their national origin.

Synthesizing disciplines

Although there are certainly connections between the various individual branches of musicology, the field tends to lack a much needed interdisciplinary approach. Ethnomusicologists bemoan the exclusion of non-European music from traditional music history, while the historians tend to regard ethnomusicologists as overly eclectic and exotic. Meanwhile, music pedagogues often regard both with academic disdain, and dispute their stature as scholarly disciplines. Understanding of the value of a society's cultural self-image, thus, is blunted rather than supported by the lack of interdisciplinary cooperation among the different fields.

1850 – 1900

Brahms versus Wagner: The quarrel of the century

At the beginning of the 19th century, music was dominated by the individual composer, who sought to step out of the shadow of Beethoven and to develop his (or her) own mode of expression. Around mid-century, the whole musical world seemed to split into two camps, all focused around one central question: Should a composer try to express something nonmusical—like a literary work or a programmatic idea—by musical means, or does music have its own internal meaning and no need for an extramusical impulse?

This question was debated so furiously that the argument, which normally would have been confined to theoretical essays and argumentative papers, grew into a regular fight, waged publicly in the literary sections of major newspapers, or as an out-and-out campaign exploiting lampoons and pamphlets riddled with personal hostilities. Against this background, European music thenceforward developed along individually distinctive styles, but always on one or the other side of this aesthetic dialectic.

Like a defendant, Richard Wagner stands before Eduard Hanslick, the advocate of absolute music and spokesman for the Brahmsians.

Johannes Brahms

For Johannes Brahms, grappling with Beethoven's legacy in his symphonies as well as in his entire oeuvre of chamber and piano music, the working out and completion of form were central. When he published his first piano sonata, in 1856, opening it with a motif that closely resembles a theme of Beethoven's *Hammerklavier Sonata*, Brahms faced criticism for this imitation of his predecessor. When the resemblance was pointed out to him, in a critical vein, he responded, "Any ass can see that!" For Brahms, the struggle with Beethoven had nothing to do with such superficialities as imitation of motifs. Rather, he sought to bring into his work the principle of moderation with which Beethoven had reached a perfection of form. That Brahms inscribed his *First Symphony*, composed in 1868,

Wagnerians come to the defense!

Johannes Brahms (1833–97)

1850 – 1900

Chromaticism: literally, melodic writing in half-steps (as opposed to the major-minor system which is composed largely of whole steps). In the late 19th century, chromaticism of melody and chords gradually led to the dissolution of harmony.
Tonal color: the tonal characteristics of an instrument. Generally, this came to mean new effects achieved through certain combinations of different instruments. An important stylistic device, especially for Wagner and Liszt and other later composers.
National color: a musical mood typical of a region or a nation, achieved through application of certain melodic embellishments, rhythms, and instrumental colors.
Nationalization: current in different countries of Europe, especially Eastern Europe, to create or to protect the supposedly independent music tradition of a country or region.

Johannes Brahms at the age of 20. By this time he had already composed major piano works. In this introverted, sensible composer, Robert Schumann saw the renewer of music.

1850 – 1900

Autograph of Johannes Brahms's *Fourth Symphony*. Brahms struggled, especially in his orchestral works, with the legacy of Beethoven. His critics mocked him by singing to the introduction of this symphony the text: "Mir fällt nichts ein, mir fällt nichts ein" ("I can think of nothing").

as "Beethoven's Tenth" underscores his particular debt to Beethoven especially clearly. Brahms was firmly convinced that the content and statement of a composition are to be comprehended with purely musical means.

This point of view had clear consequences for the nature of his work. Symphonic and chamber music stand in the center of his compositions, dedicated on the one hand to the Classical ideal of perfection of form, and on the other hand to certain musical innovations, whose groundbreaking nature was neither recognized nor understood until the beginning of the 20th century. Brahms sought to develop all possible paths out of a single musical thought, to consider a theme in all its details, to create new combinations, and to vary them. Arnold Schönberg called these techniques "evolutionary variation," and seized upon the process of concentrating on only one idea and working it through totally in his own twelve-tone theory (see p. 143). This is also the basis upon which Schönberg considered Brahms a "modern"—an assessment that Brahms's contemporaries would have found just as absurd as if he had, for example, vehemently proposed that they study the works of Renaissance and

Baroque composers and employ their techniques. To fashion a whole movement of a symphony in the form of a Baroque chaconne, as Brahms did in the final movement of his *Fourth Symphony*, earned him not simply no public understanding, but mockery by his contemporaries in the other camp.

An idea in the background: Program music

Unlike Brahms, who did not articulate his views theoretically, the partisans of the opposing musical camp developed their musical aesthetic not only in their compositions, but also in their attempts to locate their music in the context of a philosophical world view common, or universal, to all art. The poetic idea on which each musical work is grounded determines both the outer form as well as the content of a composition. Two different forms of music developed out of this basic assumption: the symphonic (or tone) poem, a programmatic orchestral work; and the music drama, which clearly distinguished itself from the traditional form of opera. The protagonists of this "New German School" were Franz Liszt and his son-in-law, Richard Wagner.

1850 – 1900

Richard Wagner

Richard Wagner saw himself as a musical revolutionary and though such a self-image suggests a degree of arrogance, it is not without some support from fact. His importance to the further development of

Richard Wagner (1813–83)

Brahms was a brilliant pianist and a good conductor, but apparently lacked charisma.

Héctor Berlioz spread the idea of program music in France.

music rests on two factors, which changed musical understanding completely, from the ground up.

From opera to the "Gesamtkunstwerk"

Wagner's idea, to expand the progression of an opera from a rigid series of recitatives and arias (see p. 55) so that the musical, poetic, scenic, and, not least, philosophical components work together into an organic whole, was not only new, but introduced many possibilities to consider operatic production from many perspectives. Characters, as well as inanimate objects and feelings, were designated by a specific "motif," or brief musical pattern, that returns in constantly new connections, opening a view of the psyche of the respective characters, whose acts are chiefly predetermined by fate. Wagner

himself called this method the "ground theme" or "foreboding motif." Later, Wagner's friend Hans von Wolzogen coined the term "leitmotif." Wagner himself no longer called such compositions, which as a rule lasted an entire evening, "operas," but

The path to recognition was by no means straight for Richard Wagner. He almost always had financial worries. In 1848 or 1849, he had to flee from Germany because of his political convictions. He received assistance from prominent sponsors like King Ludwig II of Bavaria, who already had an almost pathological attachment to Wagner's music, and Franz Liszt, whose daughter he married.

1850 – 1900

Absolute music: instrumental music that is not based on any extramusical idea (e.g., a story or poem)

Leitmotif: the assignment of a certain musical fragment to a certain person, situation, or scene

Music drama: the name given by Wagner to his expanded operas, examples of "Gesamtkunstwerk"

Program music: compositions that derive their form and content from an extramusical idea, usually a literary work

Symphonic poem (or tone poem): primary form of instrumental program music; most important composer is Franz Liszt

instead "music dramas," and envisioned them as "Gesamtkunstwerke," or "unified works of art."

The expansion of harmony

In order to include the multiple layers he perceived in the progress of the drama's action, Wagner not only loosened up the internal and outer frame of the opera, but also considerably expanded the harmony. He took Romantic harmony, which was firmly fixed in specific keys, or tonal centers, and stretched it into ambiguity. One chord from his opera *Tristan and Isolde* (1859) has become famous because it is so ambiguous that it could lead to almost any other chord. Wagner's work is a harbinger of the complete dissolution of harmony that would come later in the work of Schönberg and others (see p. 138).

(see p. 138)

Only a few composers have dared to structure their works without a foundation of harmonic and tonal relationships; Wagner's techniques, however, persisted, most notably with Schönberg. In Schönberg's work, the opposing concepts of the Brahmsians and the Wagnerians, which had formed the basis for the major musical controversy of the second half of the 19th century, converge.

Magic Lantern Projection by Carl Emil Doepler for the premiere of Wagner's chief work, *Ring of the Nibelung.*

1850 – 1900

Contemporary costume designs for leading characters in Wagner's *Ring of the Nibelung.*

107

Brahms was astounded by this ceiling fresco, which he saw at the opening of the Zurich Concert Hall. Wagner no doubt would also have surely wondered how he came to be immortalized in a painting with his rival, though the two are separated (or one might say joined) by Beethoven.

Wagner surprised the public with completely new combinations of sound. Together with his increasingly ambiguous harmony, many listeners have a moving musical experience which speaks to all the senses. *Lohengrin* is the last work Wagner designated as an "opera," before he began his cycles of "music dramas." This picture shows a scene from *Lohengrin*—the arrival of the Swan Knight.

Between Wagner-fever and the large symphonic—Music of the late Romantic

The opposing musical aesthetic positions, reflected in the work of Brahms and Wagner, soon traveled beyond the narrow frame of their personal followers to assume a European dimension. Any composer who wanted to be taken seriously felt pushed into one camp or the other. This did not mean that the Brahmsians composed only symphonies and chamber music while the "New German School," the Wagnerians, only wrote music dramas and symphonic poems. Rather, the individual composer reflected on the foundations of his or her own particular outlook to develop a distinctive profile that would then be expressed via various musical forms.

Another factor that wielded a decisive influence on music up to the turn of the century was nationalism. In the midst of general discussions of traditions and values, of philosophy and economics, the countries of Europe were developing a more or less distinctive national consciousness, which became a strong undercurrent in the music world. More and more composers tried to create music that reflected pride of national identity. Operas and symphonic poems often drew on

1850 – 1900

historical material and national heroes and composers employed folk tunes to give their music the desired national color.

These two quite different impulses—absolute versus program music, on the one hand, and nationalistic impulses on the other—delineated the picture of the music up to the turn of the century.

Convoluted sound with a plan— Anton Bruckner

Wagner's influence on his contemporaries was by no means limited to the understanding of the opera as *Gesamtkunstwerk*. His harmonic changes, which fundamentally changed the use of melody and instrumentation, were equally important to his contemporaries and successors. Other composers of his time adopted Wagner's often bold innovations in their works. Anton Bruckner, a great admirer of Wagner, composed no operas, but he understood how to use Wagner's musical elements on the basis of solid musical workmanship, and fused them into his sometimes grandiose, but always impressive symphonies. Bruckner's symphonies introduced tonal effects that had never been heard before. One of his particular innovations was to put the brass players (trumpets, horns, trombones) in the foreground, utterly altering the overall impression of the symphony.

Bruckner subsequently reworked and revised many of his symphonies. Originally, the individual instrumental groups tended to sound very separately,

The extraordinary sound of Wagner's music was not everyone's cup of tea. A five-hour operatic evening can sometimes produce the sensation of damaged ear-drums, as this contemporary caricature suggests.

1850 – 1900

In an important musical journal, *Neue Zeit-schrift für Musik*, in which Schumann had spoken of Brahms as the "Messiah" of new music, Wagner also took the opportunity to promote his pseudo-philosophical and anti-Semitic ideas.

Anton Bruckner (1824–96) as conductor.

The symphonies of Anton Bruckner, like the works of Richard Wagner, distinguish themselves through an especially large and forceful sound. With orchestration in which the brass players are very dominant, he succeeds in creating a veritable sound picture.

1850 – 1900

or to act as contrasting elements. In the later versions, the instruments increasingly blend into different tonal colors. Despite the great Wagnerian influence, apparent everywhere in Bruckner's symphonies, he also, like Brahms before him, reached back to the old pattern of sonata movement form, which he modified and expanded for his own purposes. The discrepancy between Bruckner's personality—he tended to be modest and to suffer feelings of inferiority—and the dimension of his work has led to speculation over what motivated him to create this sweeping body of work. One explanation is as unspectacular as it is clear: As a religious Catholic, Bruckner saw himself in the more Baroque tradition of a divine tool, through whom music is created.

New from the East

From the countries of central and eastern Europe, which were clearly Western-oriented in their cultural heritage, Bohemia, Hungary, and not least Russia stepped to the foreground of the musical world.

Silhouettes were a popular method of caricature in the 19th century. Here, Bruckner is seen at Heaven's door, where he is welcomed by Liszt and Wagner. At the far right Johann Sebastian Bach sits at the organ.

Bohemia (a former kingdom now engulfed within the Czech Republic) had always produced many musicians. But dominated as the region was by the influence of Austria, the individuality, and even "national" character, of Bohemian musicians were limited. They nonetheless often had a considerable influence on the music of the countries in which they worked. In the second half of the 19th century, their own cultural background was redefined in the face of political demands for autonomy.

The Bolshoi Theater in Moscow.

Among the Bohemian composers, Bedřich Smetana consciously tried to incorporate national materials into his symphonic poems, and especially the cycle *Má Vlast* (My Country), in

left: Bedřich Smetana (1824–84)

right: Antonín Dvořák (1841–1904)

1850 – 1900

which he vividly depicts the flowing of the Moldau River. He also incorporated national materials in his operas, thereby strengthening the sense of cultural independence.

The most important Bohemian composer of this time was Antonín Dvořák, who forged a synthesis between a deep working through of symphonic techniques and the flavor of Bohemian folk music. Dvořák's *New World Symphony* is, in fact, thoroughly Bohemian in melody and rhythm,

Modest Mussorgsky (1839–81), one of the world's greatest musical geniuses, was unfortunately ravaged by alcoholism.

Pyotr Ilyich Tchaikovsky (1840–93)

Giuseppe Verdi (1813–1901)

with only a minor influence from the African-American spiritual.

In Russia, as well, music revealed the flavors of nationalism. Though only comparatively few composers were active in Moscow and St. Petersburg, they sought above all to create specifically Russian music.

In his piano music, Modest Mussorgsky, including the famous "Pictures at an Exhibition," produced a "color" that we have come to hear as typically Russian. His operas, most notably *Boris Godunov*, draw heavily on historic Russian themes. Mussorgsky belonged to a group of five, the so-called "Mighty Little Band," which wanted to define one Russian national music.

Pyotr Ilyich Tchaikovsky was another exponent of Russian music, who wrote what is now some of the most popular 19th-century music still in the repertoire. His music abounds in lovely melodies, tinged with Eastern exoticism. He did add elements of national color to his music, but in its internationalism it also reflects his deep love for Mozart and Bizet. Most famous for his ballet scores (including *Swan Lake* and *The Nutcracker*), Tchaikovsky also wrote six symphonies and two piano concertos that are favorites of pianists with large tones and hearts. Though unsuccessful at their premieres, his operas *Eugene Onegin* and *Queen of Spades* are staples of the international operatic repertoire.

Italian music goes its own way

Italian music development in this time followed a remarkably narrow track. The great operatic tradition, which had continued south of the Alps from the Baroque until the mid-19th century in the

1850 – 1900

works of Rossini, Donizetti, and Bellini, reached a peak in the work of Verdi, which at the end of the 19th century was displaced by the new naturalistic current, the so-called *verismo*.

Though Verdi's operas, like Wagner's, describe individual characters with psychological subtlety, Wagner's musical influence is very slight. The emphasis lies rather on clearly articulated melodies, which Verdi composed with a ticking metronome. The exaggerated chromaticism (used to express emotion and producing harmonic ambiguity) that marks Wagner's late works as well as the work of succeeding generations of Wagnerians (particularly Richard Strauss) is missing. The imperviousness to Wag-

At La Scala in Milan, one of the greatest opera houses in the world, programs are posted permanently on the outside wall.

The orchestra of the Milanese opera, the "Professori."

A scene from the opera *I Lombardi* by Guiseppe Verdi in a production at La Scala in Milan.

1850 – 1900

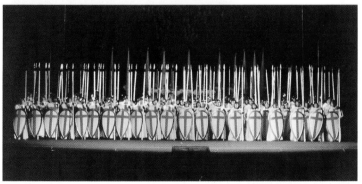

ner's aesthetic was especially manifest in the Romance countries. It is interesting that Verdi, who like Wagner almost exclusively composed operas, remains so essentially untouched by Wagner's aesthetic influence.

In France, music plays on all stages

French composers in the second half of the 19th century, like it or not, were heavily exposed to the influence of Wagner, and many tried very hard to escape it. Unlike in Italy, the French musical scene was not fixed only on the opera. It is in fact characteristic of the French composers that they wrote program music and operas on the one hand, but on the other hand they did not renounce large symphonies. The influences of Berlioz, from the preceding generation, continued to be felt in the composition of French program music.

The public, however, mainly had ears for opera. Georges Bizet's *Carmen* was a smashing success, and is still a mainstay of opera houses everywhere. Gia-

When Jules Massenet's opera *Thaïs* premiered in 1894 in Paris, art nouveau was in style in the visual arts. Massenet, like Giacomo Puccini an exponent of the naturalistic style *verismo*, tried to depict psychological realities in his works.

como Meyerbeer and Jacques Offenbach were also successful. Primarily opera composers, they seemed little affected by questions of Wagnerian influence; their symphonic music stands largely in the tradition of Camille Saint-Saëns, César Franck, and Vincent d'Indy, while their program music draws on the ideas of Berlioz, Liszt, and Wagner.

Saint-Saëns renders the programmatic content in his symphonic poems completely realistically. For example, chimes sound midnight and the band of the skeletons in the *Dance of Death* play on a xylophone. Paul Dukas proceeds similarly. His orchestral composition *The Sorceror's Apprentice*, based on a poem by Goethe, follows the text quite literally.

Toward the end of the 19th century, the musical world had become oversaturated by this style, especially by the extremes reached by harmony. Calls for a fundamental reorientation grew loud, especially and importantly emanating from Claude Debussy. Debussy's brand of musical impressionism would become one of the most important stylistic movements of the early 20th century.

Georges Bizet (1838–75) became especially famous for his opera *Carmen*.

Edouard Manet, *Concert in the Tuileries*. By the turn of the century, musical style had changed. As with the paintings of the Impressionists, composers backed away from realistic description and instead sought expressive impression through many-faceted sounds.

1850 – 1900

Most of the larger cities of Europe, the United States, and Canada have a symphony orchestra. Essentially the instruments have not changed since the Classical era, except in their seating arrangement. Earlier, the first violins sat on the left, the second violins on the right of the conductor. Today, a "modified American" order is common, with violins on the left, and cellos, violas, and basses on the right. The remaining instruments—woodwinds, brass and percussion—are arranged behind the strings.

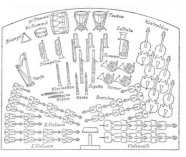

From the musical bow to the synthesizer

Almost as diverse as the many languages of the world are the musical instruments of different cultures. It has fallen to the lot of musicologists in the 20th century to classify instruments by uniform criteria, though this has meant that they must first develop a system for cataloging all the instruments of the world according to common attributes. Musicologists now try—beginning with ancient cultures up to the modern world—to organize instruments according to distinctions important to the specific culture. For example, in ancient China, instruments were distinguished by whether their strings were made of animal gut or of silk, or by whether they were constructed out of wood, animal hide, or stone. Function is an important classification feature for musical instruments in all cultures. For example, if an instrument is attributed with a healing effect that can only be achieved in a certain ritual connection, or an instrument is reserved for only a certain person to play to complete a sacred ritual, function can become a classification principle for different instruments across cultures.

Another classification criterion is the method of playing. Thus, the stringed instruments violin and guitar may be identified as bowed and plucked, and trumpets and flutes, though both wind instruments, may be differentiated by means of their different blowing techniques.

At the beginning of the 20th century, German ethnomusicologists Erich Moritz von Hornbostel and Curt Sachs developed a classification system of musical instruments based on a single organizing criterion: the generation of tone. This criterion—how an instrument actually sends vibrations into the air—allows comparison of all instruments in the world. Hornbostel and Sachs distinguished four basic ways in which instruments generate tone: self-sounding, hide (or skin or membrane)-sounding, string-sounding, and air-sounding. As is common in academic disciplines, these were quickly given Greek designations, by which most ethnomusicologists now recognize them: idiophone, membranophone, chordophone, and aerophone.

Idiophone

A marimba or a xylophone, such as may be found in many schools, a baby's rattle or Spanish castanets, Chinese jade bells or European church bells, the tubular chimes of a modern orchestra or the glockenspiel of a high school marching band, all produce sound when they are struck in some way, or shaken.

Membranophone

The tympanist of a symphony orchestra, the Siberian shaman, the African drummer who imbues his instrument with living language, the Indian tabla player who can beat the most complicated rhythms, all have one thing in common:

Bells are closely associated with religion in many cultures. This bell is from China.

Xylophones, such as these made of wood, are common in Africa. The playing technique is virtuosic. The music is based on different scales played in combination to create haunting effects.

The baya and the tabla, the two drums of classical north Indian music.

they displace the air with a vibrating, taut skin.

Chordophone

The Bavarian zither player at a house concert, the celebrated violin virtuoso in the concert hall, the

fingers down upon the string, thus shortening its vibrating length. Sometimes, "harmonics" are produced by following Pythagoras's rules—by lightly pressing the string exactly in the middle, for example, it vibrates in two equal sections and produces a pitch an octave higher than the string's fundamental.

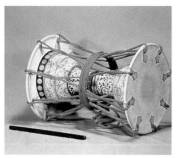

The Japanese drum *san no tzusumi*. The pitch can be changed by regulating the tension of the cords.

Zithers are found throughout the world.

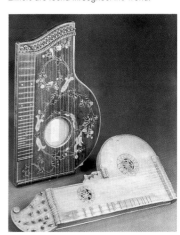

Indian sitar player, the fiddlers and banjo pickers in a blue-grass band all pluck or stroke their instruments so that a tight string vibrates over a resonating chamber. In the case of orchestral string instruments, players all change pitches by pressing their

Aerophone

The alphorn player, the Scottish bagpiper, the jazz trumpeter, the wind players of a Baroque orchestra, and young children playing pennywhistles all make music by setting a column of air in motion. Changing the length, shape, or speed of the vibrating column of air changes the pitch. For example, the valves on a trumpet open and shut sections of the instrument's brass tubing. On a transverse flute, the type played in modern orchestras, padded "keys" perform this purpose, but the performer may also make a pitch sound an octave higher or lower by changing the force with which he or she blows across the flute's opening.

While Hornbostel and Sachs' classification system has its uses, it leaves out essential details in under-

Baroque recorders (or block flutes) were often decorated with rings of ivory. Today, recorders are widely used in music education, and by Baroque music performers.

standing instruments. It cannot describe tone character or color, nor can it describe the repertoire of specific instruments, or their historical development.

To remedy this, for about the last 20 years, musicologists have begun to assemble "instrument monographs" describing all aspects of a single instrument. They have also undertaken studies of the hierarchy of orchestral instruments and the social status of their players. The psychological changes and demands of playing an instrument are also being studied. Such questions are particularly suggested by new music, because it does not follow traditional ground rules, but on the contrary seeks new effects directly through unusual combinations of instruments, often played in nontraditional ways.

The larger the pipe of a wind instrument, the deeper its tone. This flute from Slovakia is called the fujara.

1900 – today

The other music of the 20th century

Every style of music, every trend, whether a classical symphony or a passion by J. S. Bach, or a Haydn string quartet, reflects and expresses the self-image of a group, a particular social stratum, or the sensibility of a particular time. For the social meaning of the music within a culture, whether the music is accorded "artistic" merit is insignificant, as is Classical Western music, or whether—often unjustly—it is not, as in jazz and pop.

Traditions in contrast

Over many centuries, slave traders carried people from the west coast of Africa to become

The slave trade was a booming business.

slave labor in the New World. In 1786 alone, over 4 million Africans were forced into slavery in America, bringing no more with them from Africa than their language, their music, and their history.

Although African musical styles are very different from each other, these individual styles have not survived in the United States. Instead, a new African-American style developed. In the course of time, African-American musicians also incorporated elements of European-American music, especially as Christianity was imposed on them. They borrowed from European harmony; they seized on instruments that seemed suited to their nuance-rich melodies. The first of these were the

wind instruments (trumpets, clarinets) used in American military bands. From this mixture of two musical traditions—evident in ensembles that combine rhythm instruments with more melodic instruments—emerged jazz.

Improvisation and "passing along"

Two qualities define jazz in all its forms and styles to the present day. Jazz is essentially improvised music; it gives the individual musician a chance to bring to his or her playing both personal experiences and emotions. Much of jazz is based on "call and response" (common to traditional

African-Americans were often stereotyped in a racist climate as slow, lazy, happy-go-lucky, and naturally musical. This print shows the "fire brigade" of "Darktown."

African-American music tradition: original music, brought by the slaves from Africa and mingled with European-American styles.
Blues progression: Typical harmonic pattern of the Blues: 4 measures of I (tonic), 2 of IV (subdominant), 2 of I, 2 of V (dominant), and 2 of I. Used frequently as a groundwork for jazz improvisation.
Call-and-response: Originally a vocal tradition common to gospel music in which a solo voice is answered by a group, transformed in jazz into the interplay between soloist and ensemble.
Improvisation: the most important element in jazz; improvisations develop over determined harmony schemata.
Sound: The characteristic collective sound of a group or style.

1900 – today

Eubie Blake (1883–1983, above) and Scott Joplin (1868–1917) were virtuoso pianists and composers of ragtime, an early and very popular form of jazz.

American gospel music) between a soloist and an ensemble. Since jazz is usually not precisely notated, a piece is always played fresh, and is continually passed along with additions and variations. This is one of the reasons for the diversity of jazz, which seemed to generate a new style almost every ten years over the last century.

Blues

Almost no other concept in jazz has as many different meanings as "the Blues." On the one hand, this means a simple harmonic pattern over which a melody is improvised; on the other hand, it is infused with the idea of feeling, reflecting the social and emotional reality of African-Americans. Another facet of the blues, often misunderstood by listeners, is that it does not necessarily imply a melancholy state of mind, despite the slow tempos and so-called "blue notes" (lowered third, fifth, and seventh notes within the blues scale).

Many musical characteristics of the Blues are found in other jazz styles, especially in the traditions of spiritual and gospel songs.

New Orleans

While it may be misguided to try to specify a single "birthplace" of jazz, New

Bessie Smith (1894–1937), the queen of the Blues.

Orleans, the city at the mouth of the Mississippi, was full of music toward the end of the 19th century. It was also full of peoples, and their cultures, from a variety of backgrounds—from the French and Spanish to the German, African, and Native American—so that the mixing of African and European styles—the Creole and the Cajun—was inevitable.

Many of the Blues greats lived adventurous lives. Legend has it that Robert Johnson (1911–38, shown at left), one of the greatest Blues singers, sold his soul to the devil in return for his talent. (The same was said of the great violinist Paganini.) Johnson was poisoned by a jealous husband.

One of Robert Johnson's record labels.

Dixieland and ragtime

Around the turn of the century, the New Orleans style became established in the southern states, and was increasingly imitated by white musicians. They called this new music Dixieland, after the nickname for the South. Dixieland jazz jumped on features of music made popular around 30 years before by black musicians such as Scott Joplin. They wrote stylish piano pieces called "rags," based on European dance forms updated by syncopated American rhythms. Joplin was the first African-American composer to become popular all over the country and across the color line. His music enjoyed a renaissance in the 1970s that continues to this day.

New Orleans, circa 1870.

1900 – today

Louis Armstrong, called "Satchmo" (1900–71), was one of the greatest figures of jazz. Over the years, he performed almost everywhere.

A typical Dixieland band.

1900 – today

The paddle-wheeled riverboat still symbolizes the relaxed life of New Orleans, also known as "The Big Easy."

From New Orleans to Chicago

The closing of the New Orleans entertainment district Storyville in 1917 was only one reason why many musicians left to go to Chicago. Despite the generally bad state of the economy, Chicago in the 1920s offered musicians a place to earn money with their jazz, a place where they did not have to make artistic compromises.

The strangely respectable jazz of New Orleans was changing. Through "dirty notes" (intentionally bent out of intonation), accented heavy pauses, vibrato, etc., New Orleans jazz transported to

Chicago reached a greater level of expressivity. The musicians, among them the already famous Louis Armstrong, Jelly Roll Morton, and King Oliver, called this kind of playing "hot"—and their

bands the Hot Five, Hot Seven, or Hot Peppers.

Originally played by only a few musicians in a few bands, hot jazz spread out to other instruments, as often happened in New Orleans. Soon the tuba, bass, banjo, guitar, piano, trombone, and saxophone were playing "hot," too.

Swing—From the origins of jazz to commercial success

In the 1930s, the Chicago-style jazz bands developed into real orchestras, with more than one instrument playing the same parts, and divided into two

Chicago in the 1920s.

sections: brass (trumpets, trombones) and reeds (sax, clarinets). This expansion required the re-distribution of solo parts, which were now less im-provised and occasionally, like symphonic orches-tral parts, completely arranged (written out). These changes were accompanied by a smoothing out of the melodies, which were played over a rela-tively strict rhythmic pattern. The essence of swing lies in its rhythm: the accent is just slightly displaced from the basic beat, to give a hovering feeling, which became known as the "swinging sound."

The popularity of this sound grew through the 1930s, and was coopted by other styles, especial-ly dance music. The new phenomenon of the Big

1900 – today

Ferdinand "Jelly Roll" Morton (1885–1941), self-appoint-ed "inventor of Jazz" and his Red Hot Peppers.

Benny Goodman (1909–86) was one of the first successful "Big Band" leaders. With his legendary 1938 concert in New York's Carnegie Hall, the American temple of classical music, he brought new respect and recognition to jazz.

Bands was led by individuals who introduced more showmanship—dressing their players in flashy costumes, choreographing their movements—and became more commercially successful. Some of the band leaders, like Duke Ellington, Count Basie, or Benny Goodman, were already outstanding musicians; commercialization, however, tended to produce a homogeneity of sound, like Glenn Miller's. The style became exhausted, and after its huge popularity, disappeared, except in obscure pockets where it is revived for ballroom dancing and other nostalgic trends.

Musical high pressure: Bebop

By the 1940s, many jazz musicians had had enough of Swing and again gathered in small groups, seeking new modes of expression. Their experimentation led to rapidly played, very chromatic melodies interspersed with pauses, giving a somewhat ragged overall effect. The improvisations of Charlie Parker and Dizzy Gillespie—the lat-

William "Count" Basie (1904–84) and his orchestra, circa 1941.

ter a trumpet player, the former a saxophone player—perhaps bebop's most famous practitioners, did not follow traditional rules of tonality and harmony, but unfolded over series of atonal chords.

Since bebop developed on a somewhat esoteric level, it was not immediately popular. Only in retrospect did musicians and the public understand the impulse behind "bop," as it became known. It was only after his death in 1955 that Charlie Parker attained the status he keeps to this day. Dizzy Gillespie, on the other hand, lived long enough to achieve considerable popularity. He died in 1993.

The heat cools down

Around 1950, a countermovement to bebop emerged. Dubbed "cool jazz," it kept bebop's freely atonal harmonic groundwork as the basis for improvisation, but used slower, more reflective melodic lines. The cool jazz musicians incorporated European techniques such as melodic imitation between voices, and revived Baroque counterpoint. (Some popularizers of cool jazz performed actual Baroque pieces by J. S. Bach and others, adding a percussion part and jazzing up the rhythm a little. It is not surprising that younger-generation jazz artists like Keith Jarrett have turned in recent years to interpretation of Bach's concertos.) Lester Young, Gerry Mulligan, and also Miles Davis, who in the following decades would lead jazz in still other directions, are the best-known exponents of cool jazz.

Jukebox from the 1930s. Records were an important medium for the dissemination of jazz. The first examples date from the beginning of the century.

Charlie "Bird" Parker (1920–55) played in Swing orchestras before he blazed the trail of Bebop.

Charlie Parker's alto sax.

Thelonious Monk (1917–84), individualist of the piano. His bebop style is still revered.

John Birks "Dizzy" Gillespie (1917–93) influenced jazz since the 1940s.

Parker was so respected that he received a Grammy Award nineteen years after his death.

Gerry Mulligan (1927–96), leading exponent of cool jazz, looking not so cool here.

Free jazz

At the beginning of the 1960s, musicians for the first time altered one of the basic elements of jazz, by questioning the harmonic background upon which they improvised. Ornette Coleman demanded that all the music should be played, not just serve as background. Along with John Coltrane, he liberated jazz so that yet another new style could emerge: free jazz.

Stylistic plurality

From the 1970s until today, jazz has evolved along several stylistic lines, combining diverse elements. Unbound by rigid rules or categorization, mixtures like jazz-rock or jazz-pop have developed, though these designations are in most cases inexact, and generally only the product of record marketers' (including music reviewers as well as radio producers) attempts to define a niche.

Rock 'n' roll is here to stay

After the Second World War, all art forms began to react critically to (and against) the trappings and conditions of mass culture and the affluent

society. Artists often walked a narrow line between criticism and denial on the one hand, and acceptance and use of popular culture on the other hand. So-called serious or classical music, especially by 20th-century composers, and also the later styles of jazz have tended to be appreciated by a small group that is particularly educated or informed about their purposes, rather than by the general public. Pop music, by definition, is aimed at the masses.

The MJQ (Modern Jazz Quartet), with its cool jazz style influenced by classical chamber music, was popular with aficionados as well as with the uninitiated.

The 1950s brought a new kind of music that strove for commercial success via rebellion. Overtly at times, but more often implicitly, young musicians looked for their own voice in their culture, rejecting the artificiality and stilted complacency (as the Cold War raged) of the decade. Music embodied social protest. Rock'n'roll drew on Blues, gospel, and spirituals, and added the fast, driving beat of jazz. Jerry Lee Lewis, Little Richard, and Fats Domino defined rock's wild, percussive piano style, while groups like the Platters sang in falsetto, using smooth harmonies and tight vocal ensemble, and the strong foundation of gospel and blues is unmistakable in the

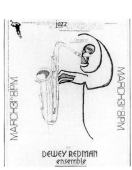

A poster for a jazz concert.

Ornette Coleman (1930–)

Miles Davis (1926–91) made over 50 years of jazz history.

By the 1950s, jukeboxes were sleek, modern, and hi-fi.

songs of Ray Charles. Rock's inherent (though some might say dubious) "dance-ability" increased its popularity and record sales—though the style of dancing, like the music, was a rebellion against the formal structures of the older generation.

Now known by admirers and detractors alike as "the King," Elvis Presley exemplified rock 'n' roll. Considered by many a white man with a black voice, his bluesy Memphis singing style combined with his rollicking physical and sexual energy to establish him as an adored performer, sex symbol, and icon of youthful rebellion. Though controversial with the older generation, Presley enjoyed wild success, first as a recording artist making TV appearances, and later as a movie star.

Later in his career, however, Presley toned down both his music and his body language to accommodate somewhat more conventional standards, though with little diminution in his massive commercial success.

Since his death in 1977, Elvis's cult status has only increased. Elvis

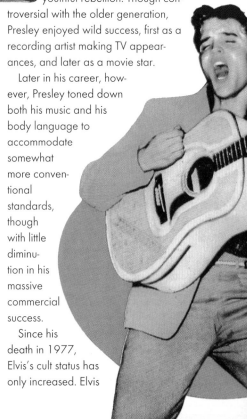

1900 – today

130

impersonators thrive and his image adorns the pages of tabloids, oil paintings on velvet, whiskey bottles, and even, as of 1995, a U.S. postage stamp (where he is joined, it should be added, by jazz greats like Charlie Parker and Dizzy Gillespie).

And in Europe, the beat goes on

In Great Britain, a genuine, individual kind of music answered the spirit of working-class youths in their own quest for the voice of their generation. The Mersey Beat, named after the river Mersey in Liverpool and after the beat at the heart of the music, emerged as more than just an answer to the pop music coming out of America. Its characteristic rhythm is repetitive and steady, with strong accents. Harmonically and melodically, the Mersey Beat was more European and intentionally simple and spread rapidly out of England as rock 'n' roll had out of America.

The "Cuba Imperial Comet" of 1954—television, radio, record player, and stylish furniture, all rolled into one.

Elvis Presley (1935–77), the first superstar of rock 'n' roll.

Starting as just another group of Merseyside Liverpudlians moved by the music of Chuck Berry and the disenchantment of their generation, the Beatles became international idols. Their style encompassed hard-driving rock and sensitive ballads, performed with unerring technique and charm. Perhaps the greatest pop composers and performers of all, their music has remained popular, some of it crossing

George Harrison, Ringo Starr, Paul McCartney, and John Lennon—the Beatles—came from Liverpool and took their name from the new style they helped to shape: the Beat. They were influenced by the music of Chuck Berry (1931–), and forged a link between American and British pop music.

over into the standard repertoire of musicians from other genres.

What is the purpose of pop?

Pop musicians have never been known to care about critics. They simply experiment until they find something they like, something that appeals to them and to the public. Pop "democratized" music—in a way classical music never could. Long years of study and conservatory training weren't necessary. Pop musicians and bands have flooded the music scene since the 1960s—some seeking artistic fulfillment, some seeking glamour, some achieving both.

By the late 1970s, "rock 'n' roll" had come to mean the music of the fifties and early sixties, while the word "rock" has come to encompass many strands of pop music and is today a more generic label for the music of the past three decades. Rock music, in its early years, created a certain social awareness, and musicians began to comment upon and argue with not just the culture, but their own artistic medium. For example, J. Cale, a student of the successful "serious" composers John Cage and Aaron Copland and formerly a member of the avant-garde band Velvet Underground, released an album in 1972 called *Academy in Peril*, in which he argues intensely with the art music canon of the 18th and 19th centuries. The Beatles' *White Album* (1968) offers a kind of sketch of rock music since the fifties, but it can also be compared with the program music of the 19th century in its use of recurring motifs and sound painting.

From folk songs to protest songs

In Europe as well as in the United States, the sixties was a decade of political and social turmoil, most of it felt by the younger (rock-listening) generation.

College students, mostly middle class, re-belled against the narrow-mindedness and conformity of the fifties. In the United States, more and more young people joined the Civil Rights Movement, and pro-tested their country's growing involvement in Vietnam. Vietnam, in fact, came to crystallize what young people saw as the false values and oppression of the so-called establishment, and this kind of disenchantment spread well beyond the coasts and borders of the United States. Young people were ready and eager to respond to a popular music that spoke for them not only in its musical form but in its expression of political and social protest. The Blues, rock 'n' roll, bluegrass and country and western, and an entire canon of traditional folk material from around the world were melded into a musical style giving voice to protests for peace and freedom.

Joan Baez (1941–), one of the best-known folk singers of the sixties and seventies, wrote and performed songs with political themes that made her unpopular with conservative Americans.

Bob Dylan and Joan Baez

Although their lyrics expressed rebellion against the establishment and called for change, folk songs were not merely intended to arouse anger. Rather, they mixed protest with an often romantic longing for self-expression. The early songs of Bob Dylan were deliberately simple, often derivative melodies through which he was able to give voice to the sentiments of his age. Many of his songs could just as easily have been writ-ten as poems, with equally enduring effect, but clearly, as songs, they found a wider audience. Dylan first achieved recognition on the folk song circuit of the early sixties when Joan

Bob Dylan (born Robert Zim-merman, 1941–). Dylan's songs were often highly political. A versatile artist, he has never limited himself to a single style. He has had many fans over the years, but also many critics.

1900 – today

Baez, by then a moderately successful folk singer known for her clear soprano purity of voice ("success" for folk singers must, of course, be considered a relative entity). Baez brought Dylan on tour with her, introducing him and his songs to an audience that would carry him far beyond the folk music revival of that time. Baez herself sang traditional folk ballads as well as new music—often by Dylan himself—and steadfastly maintained her position as an anti-war activist and protest leader, even when doing so put her at odds with the record producers and concert promoters. Still, in the early years, there was financial potential in protest music and Dylan and Baez became idols, after a fashion, of their generation. Of course, both Dylan and Baez owed a considerable debt to the revival of interest in an older generation of folk musicians, including Woody Guthrie, Leadbelly, Pete Seeger, and the Weavers, and both were joined in their popularity by contemporaries such as Judy Collins, Tom Paxton, Phil Ochs, and Joni Mitchell.

Another side of rock

Rock, which assumed many features of rock 'n' roll and of the Mersey Beat, sought in many ways to establish a distance from the kind of mainstreaming of the counterculture and commercialization. The Rolling Stones, with Mick Jagger and Keith Richard, The Who, Cream, and Led Zeppelin all used exaggerated musical means, such as harsh electric guitar sounds and pounding bass and rhythm as an alternative to established pop music. With the Stones, Jagger represented a consciously opposing concept to the Beatles. He rejected their metaphorical use of language and attacked his enemies and excited his fans through direct and provocative lyrics. Of course, we ought to remember that whereas the Beatles shocked their fans with their decision to disband in 1969, opting out of the commercial pressures that were affecting

The high point of early rock and folk-rock, and in many ways the culmination of the sixties, was the musical event of the decade—the "three days of peace and music" in White Lake, New York, in August 1969. As a gigantic protest for peace and the ultimate expression of the "hippie" era, Woodstock offered a platform for numerous musicians who dominated American pop music. The dream of a golden moment, of a lost youth, the Woodstock Festival was recorded, filmed, immortalized, remembered, and often imitated. Exploited by the media and the record industry, it is an example of how the commercial forces of pop culture were ready to exploit even the radical politics of the sixties.

their personal lives, the Rolling Stones remained together as a band, continuing to record and to tour, even into the eighties and nineties when rock tours were often sponsored by private corporations for commercial purposes.

Jimi Hendrix, one of the greatest virtuoso guitarists and still adored today by teenagers around the world, influenced the style of seventies and eighties rock through his revolutionary handling of electric guitar. At Woodstock, he stopped the show with his interpretation of the American national anthem. It was both political statement and musical experiment, with distortion, feedback, and "wah-wah" sounds.

Mick Jagger (1943–) thought of himself and his group, the Rolling Stones, as polar opposites to the Beatles. Still in the business, he is less controversial now but his tours still draw fans.

Marketing pop music

The pop music of the sixties and seventies was perhaps destined to move away from expressing the convictions and feelings of an entire generation and toward whatever the market would bear. This trend continues in the eighties and nineties—it may even have become more exacerbated by the growing role of music video, with its television-commercial-like style and appeal. Producers consciously manufacture pop music as a product with a short shelf-life with mass appeal, leading to a homogenized sound for the mass market.

Janis Joplin (1943–70), brought her expressive Blues singing to a rock repertoire. In keeping with one of her songs, "Get It While You Can," Joplin lived a fast life and died of a drug overdose at the age of 26.

1900 – today

135

James Marshal "Jimi" Hendrix (1942–70) was famous for setting his guitar on fire. He was also famous as a great guitar virtuoso who evoked entirely new sounds from his instrument.

Punk rock is both a music and a lifestyle, which includes outrageous hair styles and body piercing as a protest against convention.

1900 – today

Again, some musicians reacted against this and developed a new protest music. "Hard rock" and "heavy metal" express alienation through their increasingly extreme music, which to the uninitiated can sound like people screaming to an accompaniment of chain saws and oil drums. Punk rock, which began as an underground music movement in Britain in the mid-seventies, with groups like the Sex Pistols, employed extreme musical and extramusical means. With hair streaked with neon colors and cut in mohawks, wild and sometimes violent behavior onstage and off, punk rockers protested cultural norms and declining economic conditions.

Today's pop music continues to develop into diverse styles, sometimes as young people seek to differentiate themselves from a passing generation, sometimes as they are manipulated by producers and promoters. Rap music, which expresses the anger of alienated urban youth—mostly of African-Americans, though it has been coopted by the white mainstream—consists of rhythmic, rhyming lyrics spoken over a scratchy background and heavy beat. Folk styles are still popular, though certainly on a smaller scale than rock, rap, and other kinds of pop music. And the electronic age has arrived on the music scene with a vengeance: pop and rock lean increasingly on synthesizers for effects, and live tours rely on lasers, lighting and sound reinforcement for enhanced spectacle. The last few years have witnessed a revival movement of the music of the fifties and sixties—cult bands like Pink Floyd have re-grouped, Woodstock II (a bland attempt to give a new generation a taste of the past) was held in 1994, even the remaining three Beatles reissued their music and collaborated on some "new" songs based on fragments recorded before Lennon's death.

Rock music is always loud. Groups use huge stacks of speakers in order to fill a concert hall or football stadium with sound.

Idols, superstars, and fans

More than any other genre—fanned by the media and music industry—pop music inspires a near-religious devotion to its idols. The Beatlemania of the early sixties actually pales in comparison to the devotion and idolatry focused on more recent pop phenomena. There is the mainstream (MTV) marketing of Michael Jackson and Madonna, both of whom seem ready to use the media as readily as the media are eager to use them, the less glamorous but equally successful Bruce Springsteen whose capacity for energetic touring seemed until recently superhuman, and there is the phenomenon of Dead Heads—the fanatically devoted followers of the Grateful Dead (until the recent death of its leader, Jerry Garcia)—which as a social phenomenon (and perhaps a sociological case study) far outstrips the merits of the music itself.

1900 – today

137

1900 – 1950

Gustav Klimt, *Death and Life or Death and Love,* ca. 1908. The stylistic exaggeration and high emotionalism characteristic of the music of the turn of the century finds its counterpart in the paintings of Gustav Klimt.

The beginning of the 20th century

Unlike such transitions in music history as the Classical into Romantic, where one epoch ends and a dominant new style emerges fairly fluidly out of the old one, the turn of the 19th into the 20th century witnessed radical upheaval which resulted in many new currents that were similar in some ways but in other ways were totally distinct.

Many of the most important musicians of the first half of the century did not consider themselves in relation to the past; rather, they saw themselves as revolutionaries who were destined to break with it. Driven not only by musical history, but also by social and economic conditions, they felt that the traditional fundamentals of European music, such as major–minor tonality-based harmony, had been exhausted by

The "Tristan chord" permits harmonic movement in almost any direction.

the late Romantic composers, and they also felt that changes in society demanded new forms of expression.

In the mid-1800s, Richard Wagner in his music dramas, beginning with *Tristan and Isolde* in 1859, developed a musical language that rested on a more ambiguous harmony (see p. 107). Many theoreticians and music historians see *Tristan* as a sharp turning point, although clearly Liszt had employed similar harmonies at least 20 years earlier.

Gustav Mahler

In his nine monumental symphonies, as well as an unfinished tenth and several symphonic song cycles, Gustav Mahler strove to express the scope and contradictions of the human psyche. Mahler employed both distinct, "high art" methods and simple folk music melodies to evoke powerful emotions in his listeners. His works reflect moods ranging from sunny cheerfulness to shock to deep reflection on mortality. His music reflects to some extent the psychic situation of the end of a bourgeois epoch emerging into the new century.

Richard Strauss

Richard Strauss continued the 19th-century strain of programmatic music in his large symphonic poems (*Thus Spoke Zarathustra, Till Eulenspiegel*)

Gustav Mahler (1860–1911). Mahler's work forms the conclusion of the late Romantic symphonic.

1900 – 1950

Atonality: compositional method that dispenses with a tonal center so that the harmonic movement of the music hovers freely and allows new chord progressions.
Impressionism: designation of the music of Debussy in accordance with the French Impressionist painter; Debussy works with shimmering surfaces of sound and tries for impressions without the overloaded emotionalism of the late Romantic period.
Twelve-tone music: compositional principle resting on the equality of all 12 chromatic pitches, from which a tone row is derived, transformed, and used in various combinations and fragments. The hierarchy of notes in traditional major–minor tonality systems is deconstructed.

Mahler often conducted his works himself. The balance between large symphonic sound on the one hand and finely colored nuance on the other is especially distinctive in his works.

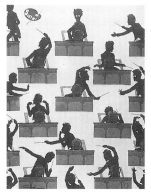

and many operas and songs. In his operas *Salome* (1905) and *Elektra* (1909), he reached a peak of harmonic tension primarily through the extensive use of discords. These works are still challenging audiences today. Strauss, however, did not continue in this revolutionary vein, but increasingly wrote with a nostalgia for both the music and social arrangements of the latter part of the previous century. Though critics and musicologists question his importance as a first-rank composer, the public continues to love his music, especially the 1910 opera *Der Rosen-kavalier*.

Richard Strauss (1864 – 1949)

A Strauss Festival was held in Munich in 1910. At this time, the composer was still considered avant-garde.

Impressionism as an opposing force

When a newspaper critic described Claude Debussy's work *Printemps* as "impressionistic," he was using the term disparagingly. But this term, imported from the late 19th-century painting of Monet, Renoir, Manet, and others, characterizes the peculiarities of Debussy's style quite accurately. Debussy was a passionate anti-Wagnerian, whose style he opposed with his concept of *clarté* (clarity), which rejects the overblown emotionalism of the late Romantic era. Debussy's music shows clear form and shimmering sequences of parallel chords. Like Wagner, Debussy was a key figure in the breakdown of traditional harmony, but instead of Wagner's over-heated chromaticism, Debussy's harmony is more diatonic, with occasional Oriental influences.

In similar ways, Maurice Ravel created in his piano and orchestral works iridescently colored but formally structured music. Debussy and Ravel prepared the way for the so-called neoclassical style, which was conceived as a counter to the twelve-tone music of Schönberg and his followers.

Claude Debussy (1862–1918) incorporated widely different influences in his work. At the World's Fair in Paris he heard an Indonesian Gamelan orchestra, which piqued his interest in still more unusual tonal colors.

Design for Debussy's ballet *Prélude à l'après-midi d'un faune*, featuring Vaslav Nijinsky. In this work, written in 1892–94, the composer experimented with sounds that became characteristic of his later work.

Maurice Ravel (1875–1937) was influenced by Debussy, but soon developed his own expressionistic tone language, unrelated to Schönberg and his followers.

1900 – 1950

Arnold Schönberg: An unorthodox, but traditional beginning

Like most other composers of his generation, Arnold Schönberg began his musical career under the influence of the late Romantic Wagnerian ideals. Since he had studied instrumental and compositional technique only a little, he was largely self-educated in music theory. Schönberg's irregular and unacademic musical educa-

Self-portrait by Arnold Schönberg (1874–1951).

tion was very important to him, because he thought it afforded him the possibility, through solitary reflection and constant self-control, to make his work truly original and not to have to fall back on stale received wisdom.

Schönberg's earliest works from 1898 to 1903 already showed him to be a highly skilled composer who understood how to push the late Romantic idiom to its boundaries, and occasionally to overstep them. In addition to songs, his early works include the string sextet *Verklärte Nacht* (Transfigured Night) and from 1900 the *Gurre-Lieder*, a monumental work of Wagnerian dimensions, in which Wagner's influence is clear.

Gradually overcoming tonality

After Schönberg reached the boundary of traditional Western harmony, he thought the only consistent way forward could be to abolish it completely, a feat which he accomplished gradually.

In his *Second String Quartet*, Schönberg quoted (strange to say) the first line of the folksong "O du lieber Augustin," but did not continue the song. This eclecticism helped him break with musical tradition.

Naturally this renunciation did not mean simply throwing out the total tonal-harmonic structure of music, as many of his ignorant and mocking contemporaries contended. Rather, it meant that music would no longer have a single fixed tonal center, as it had since about 1600 when the major–minor system developed. Then, as today, most Western listeners expected to hear typical chord progressions, based on I-V-I (where I is the chord on the tonic or key note, and V is the chord on the dominant or 5th tone of the scale), or some expansion and variation on that basis. In order to break through these expectations and create new, surprising sound possibilities, Schönberg and contemporaneously with him the Russian Alexander Scriabin experimented with chords built upon intervals of a fourth instead of the traditional thirds. Like Wagner's "Tristan chord," this chord built on fourths (which Scriabin called the "mystical chord") sounded as if it could move to almost any other chord, and so widened harmonic possibilities considerably. (Scriabin was a religious as well as a musical visionary—he believed his music was a preparation for a "supreme ecstatic mystery" that would accompany the imminent end of the world.) Because these new harmonies did not clearly lead to another specific chord, tonality—the notion of a single key note as tonal center—was broken down. This style is known as "atonal" music, and most listeners still find it very challenging.

The "mystical chord" of Alexander Scriabin (1872–1915) opened even more harmonic possibilities than Wagner's "Tristan chord."

The final step: Twelve-tone music

If atonality destroyed the hierarchy of chords, Schönberg's next step was to break down the hierarchy of the twelve individual pitches of the chromatic scale (A, A#, B, C, C#, D, D#, E, F, F#, G, G#). Schönberg's revolutionary idea, to make all twelve pitches equally important in a composition, is considered one of the most important musical innovations of the 20th century. "Composition with twelve tones only arranged one after another," as Schönberg called the process, rests on "row technique." From the supply of twelve tones, a chromatic "ladder" or series is built, which contains all notes with the greatest possible intervals between them. This foundation, or "tone row," in which no single note is repeated, can now be repeated in many different transformations: forward, backward

1900 – 1950

143

(retrograde), with intervals that previously went up now going down, and vice versa (inversion), and retrograde inversion. Further, the row can be transposed to begin on a different pitch, but keeping the relationship of the tones the same, so that altogether the composer has fourty-eight different possible arrangements of a single row.

Although this technique seems mathematical and calculated, in practice it proves extremely flexible. Schönberg did not think about these series and their transformations as coming rigidly one after another, or sounding exactly simultaneously. Rather, he combined fragments from different transformations of the series with each

Schönberg's aesthetics compared with the paintings of Wassily Kandinsky (*Composition X*, 1939). The two carried on an intense correspondence over artistic issues.

other, and achieved a very lively musical language.

The twelve-tone system, or dodecaphony, which Schönberg used for the first time in his *Piano Pieces, Op. 23* (1923), broke with all traditional musical habits, with all rules determined through convention, and with all supposedly natural musical rules, and set a new norm of their own, which gave Schönberg his own artistic voice.

This musical system, which is to some extent also a system of thought, found enthusiastic followers. Schönberg's pupils, in particular,

Alban Berg and Anton Webern, expanded the twelve-tone system of their teacher and thus created the basis for most European music until after the Second World War.

Alban Berg

The work of Alban Berg, which employs both atonal and twelve-tone compositional techniques, is structured on severe, almost classical forms. Berg attempted to bring the compactness and precision of twelve-tone music to larger musical forms in his two operas (*Lulu* and *Wozzeck*) and in many cycles. Berg, however, was by no means strictly guided by the rules of twelve-tone writing. His works have extraordinarily natural melodies and phrasing, which is difficult to achieve in twelve-tone music.

Anton Webern

Anton Webern's compositional methods were, by contrast with those of Alban Berg, extreme. Webern followed twelve-tone theory religiously, which led to produce short compositions in which he made precise musical statements. The clarity of his music, which proceeds with hardly a superfluous note, made Webern in particular a model for postwar composers who hoped to find yet more new directions of twelve-tone music through serial techniques.

Schönberg and his students. His instructional technique was not traditionally academic. Schönberg attempted to use conversations to nurture the particular talents of his pupils, and not fill them with knowledge of the musical past.

Alban Berg (1885–1935)

Anton Webern (1883–1945) was uncompromising in his use of twelve-tone technique. Many of his works are unusually short. In this condensing of musical ideas to the essential, his teacher Schönberg saw the particular quality of Webern's music.

1900 – 1950

Otto Dix (1891–1969), *Grosstadt* (triptych), 1927/28 (detail). The 1920s were a time of contradictions. They ended in a global economic crisis, which intensified social unrest. The conduct of people at the time is sometimes described as dancing on a volcano. Whoever could, danced.

1904–05	Russo–Japanese War
1917	October Revolution in Russia
1922	Mussolini comes to power in Italy
1929	Crash at the New York Stock Exchange
1930	Clyde Tombaugh discovers Pluto
1944	Death of Antoine de Saint-Exupéry
1952	Eisenhower elected president of the U.S.

1900 – 1950

Music as contrast—
Music from all directions

Schönberg and his pupils broke radically with European musical traditions and developed their concept of twelve-tone music based on rationality and structure. Many of their contemporaries, however, could not or did not want to follow in Schönberg's footsteps. Instead, they looked for other ways to renew music, and to establish different musical traditions. Harmony, as it had been broadened by Wagner, and carried to chromatic extremes by the late Romantics, could be changed thoroughly to serve an aesthetic that was aligned with the numerous social, political, and psychological contradictions within Europe's current intellectual and cultural situation. The expansion of harmony meant not only using new chords with chromatic alterations, or adding additional tonalities, but redefining the relationship of individual chords with each other. Each chord should reasonably follow the previous one and the harmony overall should be logical in terms of a tonal language.

The perceived contradictions of the times were expressed by some composers using bitonality or polytonality. In these styles, individual melodies and harmonies make sense (in terms of traditional Western tonality) within themselves, but confront other melodies and harmonies with totally different internal logic. In bitonality, two distinct tonalities are used simultaneously: for example, a melody might be written in E major, with harmony in C major. Polytonality is similar, with more than two tonalities in use at one time.

Darius Milhaud (1892–1974), *First Piano Sonata*: The upper voice is in E-flat minor, while the lower voice is in G major—an example of bitonality, which sounded much more shocking then than it does now.

Bitonality, polytonality: simultaneous combination of two or more keys (tonalities), which produces clashing harmonies especially in keys harmonically far removed from each other (such as C major and F-sharp major)

Folkloric style: the incorporation of traditional regional folkloric melodies and characteristics into art and music

Modal melody: Return to the use of church modes (see p. 13) in melody writing of composers like Bartók and Stravinsky

Neoclassicism: return to classical forms and means of expression, which are changed with contemporary techniques, most famously by Igor Stravinsky

Polyrhythm, polymeters: combination of several rhythms or meters to create asymmetrical accents

Autograph of *Allegro Barbaro* by Béla Bartók (1881–1945). Signed on the right. This was a flashy pianistic showpiece that challenged contemporary pianists and audiences alike.

1900 – 1950

Sergei Diaghilev (1872–1929) and Igor Stravinsky (1882–1971) worked together on notable ballet productions.

Rhythm as a driving force

Just as suddenly as bitonality and polytonality appeared, rhythm also changed. Previously in European music, rhythmic structure played a somewhat subordinate role. Now, rhythm no longer served only as structure for a melody, but often as the overall driving impulse for a composition. Especially suitable to this purpose were rhythms outside the traditional three- or four-beat pattern. Composers were especially attracted to compound meters such as 3+3+2, which produced naturally asymmetrical accents. They also used frequent changes of meter within a piece to produce a similar effect.

Constantly repeated rhythmic patterns in unusual meters soon became a fashionable feature of the music of the first decade of the 20th century (exemplified by Igor Stravinsky's *Le Sacre du printemps*). Another rhythmic trend developed at the same time through the influence of American jazz on European composers (notably on Ravel, Poulenc, and later Stravinsky). These influences, however, were basically limited to the application of syncopation, which causes a simple shift of accent, and some melodic turns containing so-called blue notes (see p. 122).

Elementary structures

Some composers sought the supposed basic roots of music in the orally transmitted musical traditions of their own and other cultures. They then hoped to transform music from the foundation up, using their own individual creativity. The results ranged from the adaptation and reworking of the simplest folk melodies to the full permeation of the material, often with challenging results. Hungarian composer Béla Bartók (see p. 151) is probably the most famous of this school.

Until the 1950s, the music scene in Europe was dominated by the contrast between Schönberg's followers with their rigid theoretical concepts and the proponents of different styles who were alike in only one respect: the rejection of twelve-tone theory.

Igor Stravinsky

In 1913, the premiere of Stravinsky's ballet *Le Sacre du printemps* (The Rite of Spring) caused perhaps the most famous music-inspired riot of all time. Two previous Stravinsky ballets, *The Firebird* in 1910 and *Petruschka* in 1911, had been presented, so the Parisian public already knew the work of this young Russian composer. Sergei Diaghilev, director of the Ballet Russe, had commissioned Stravinsky to write them. In both the earlier works, Stravinsky had employed unusual effects with discords and asymmetrical rhythms, among other innovations. But, in *Le Sacre*, he drove these elements to the limit. Hammering rhythms, played by the entire orchestra

Choreographic sketches by Valentine Hugo for Stravinsky's *Le Sacre du printemps*.

1900 – 1950

149

The original costumes for *Le Sacre du printemps* were very folkloric. The ballet's scandalous impact was primarily due to its music.

over long stretches, seemed to have a physical effect on listeners, especially those seated in the front rows. The music is so loud and dissonant that it is still challenging for some audiences.

What especially irritated the Parisian public in 1913, however, was the ballet's subject. *Le Sacre du printemps* enacts a pagan ritual—the adoration of the earth, culminating in human sacrifice. For the 31-year-old Stravinsky, it was appropriately provocative. In the following years he experimented with widely different stylistic elements. In his theory, art is "freer, the more it is controlled, bounded and worked at." From the 1920s on, Stravinsky developed a neoclassical style that he founded on the demands of well-balanced form, and with which he consciously opposed the "turmoil and noise" of Wagner's expressionistic aesthetic.

For over half a century, Stravinsky represented an opposing standpoint to Schönberg. In his seventies, however, he experimented with serial techniques, as they had been further developed by the composers of the first generation after twelve-tone theory.

Igor Stravinsky (1882–1971) later in his life.

1900 – 1950

Folklore into art

As a music student in Budapest, Béla Bartók learned to compose in the style of Brahms. But for his life's work he moved into a totally different field. Bartók traveled extensively and on expeditions through Hungary, Rumania, Turkey, and North Africa, he listened to local music, and transcribed and analyzed it thoroughly. He noticed that the melodies of Arabic music were built on the same modes as early European music. This knowledge set Bartók on a completely different path in his work. Besides arranging such melodies for one or more instruments, he integrated these archaic melodies

Béla Bartók (1881–1945) in 1905.

Announcement of the premiere of Bartók's pantomime *The Miraculous Mandarin* in Cologne 1926.
Because the piece takes place in a bordello, it was closed by then mayor of the city, Konrad Adenauer (later first West-German chancellor).

into his own compositions. In a further step, he then wrote works that combined these elements in new, extremely subtle ways. In this way, these modal melodies and—or so Western ears might find them—unusual rhythms occur in his large orchestral works, operas, and string quartets, as well as in his piano works, not just as simple folklore.

Béla Bartók listened to his collected folk melodies on a phonograph, and transcribed them. He then worked them into his highly original compositions.

Zóltan Kodály (1882–1967) was a colleague of Bartók's and also a composer. In Kodály's works, folkloric elements sometimes held the upper hand.

A scene from the opera *Mathis der Maler*, which Hindemith also set in a symphony. The Mathis of the title is the painter Matthias Grünewald (ca. 1480–1528).

Paul Hindemith (1895–1963), misunderstood in his time, well respected today.

Bourgeois-phobia to musical conservative: Paul Hindemith

Paul Hindemith started his career with a provocation: in 1919 his one-act play *Murder, Hope of Women*, after a text by the painter Oskar Kokoschka, was produced. The years following the First World War were characterized by a pervasive feeling of uncertainty, and artists and composers found themselves (or placed themselves) at the center of the search for new modes of expression that would reflect ideological and political reality. Schönberg's twelve-tone theory emerged in this time, and Stravinsky and Bartók oriented themselves to older and/or traditional models.

Hindemith not only sought to provoke and rejected the traditional, but wanted particularly to show that music followed basic humanistic norms. For example, the

theme of his opera *Mathis der Maler* (Mathis the Painter) is the role of artists in society.

In his book *Unterweisung im Tonsatz* (Instruction in Composing), he set out to demonstrate that music rests on a natural order in which harmony is derived directly from the system of overtones (see p. 11, "Proportional intervals"). Thus, he set himself up in opposition to Schönberg, who considered the demands of the individual composer's aesthetic to be the first principle of music.

International music styles

For the music of the first half of the 20th century, the Western world could no longer be said to be dominated—as it had been previously—by one style with various regional variations. Out of the discussion of different theories and streams emerged a pluralism of style, that in reciprocal definitions or in partial mixtures offers a diversified picture of music.

France

During the Classical period, French music stood in the shadow of Mozart and Beethoven. Then, at the turn of this century, Paris again became an important musical center. Almost all of French cultural life was concentrated in the capital. Claude Debussy and Maurice Ravel, leading impressionists, exercised a strong influence on the younger generation. Stravinsky was also a major influence in Paris.

"Les Six"—the composers Auric, Durey, Honegger, Milhaud, Poulenc, and Taillefferre— joined together around a common musical aesthetic, though each expressed it quite individually. Playfulness and wry humor mark the music of Poulenc and Milhaud, the best-known members of the group.

Les Six were strongly influenced by the poet Jean Cocteau and composer Erik Satie, who was as famous for his personal eccentricity as for his music. Satie's early piano compositions, with pseudo-Greek titles such as *Gymnopédie* and

Les Six: The poet Jean Cocteau, sitting at the piano, wrote literary propaganda for the group's music aesthetic.

1900 – 1950

Gnossiennes, were a reaction to Wagnerian harmony. Satie's later pieces, more aggressive and lacking the wistful melodies of his early works, are even more clearly anti-Wagnerian.

Satie followed no formal musical principles, but often organized his compositions around literary or architectural themes. In his 1917 ballet *Parade*, he included pistol shots and typewriters in the score. Satie was an important influence on Debussy and Les Six, as well as on composers of the next generation, including John Cage.

Erik Satie (1866–1925) composed pieces with strange titles like *Three Pear-Shaped Pieces* or *Dessicated Embryos*. He was far more concerned with pleasing himself than with pleasing his audience with his music.

Spain and Italy

The music of the Iberian peninsula was heavily influenced by folklore. Spanish composers were less successful than Bartók in molding folk elements into an independent art music. Manuel de Falla and Isaac Albéniz tended to set flourishes of national color against a conventional "serious music" background.

In Italy, where the opera tradition thrived, Ottorino Respighi composed orchestral nature paintings. His only bow to nationalism was in his titles, such as *The Fountains of Rome* and *The Pines of Rome*.

Britain and Scandinavia

The 19th century marks a clear break in English musical history. The choral tradition of Händel and Purcell continued, but on a considerably diminished level. Not until Edward Elgar (1857–1934) did an English composer again become well known outside the British Isles. Elgar's popularity has waned, but the march from

1900 – 1950

Pomp and Circumstance has become a staple of school graduations, and his *Cello Concerto* is often programmed.

In Elgar's shadow, Frederick Delius and Ralph Vaughan Williams tried to create a uniquely British style, exemplified by Vaughan Williams' programmatic symphonies.

The classical music tradition of Scandinavia is tied primarily to one name: Jean Sibelius. Late Romantic in form and style, Sibelius's symphonies are part of standard orchestral repertoires.

Russia

As in other countries, Russian music in the early 20th century was based on the late Romantic tradition using folkloric elements. However, the works of the most important composers of this time soon distinguished themselves. Sergei Rachmaninoff's piano concertos stand as a pinnacle of late Romantic virtuosity. His contemporary Sergei Prokofiev joined neoclassical techniques with motor rhythms in his highly animated works. Dmitri Shostakovich continued the symphonic tradition, sometimes in agreement, sometimes in conflict with the Soviet government. His music continues to gain popularity.

Manuel Maria de Falla y Matheu (1876–1946)

1900 – 1950

Edward Elgar (1857–1934). After Purcell and Händel, there was a gap of over 100 years before a British composer came to European prominence. First Elgar and then Benjamin Britten broke the drought.

Jean Sibelius (1865–1957) lived to be 92, but stopped composing in 1929 at the age of 64.

The United States

While jazz both dominated the American popular music scene and influenced "art music" composers in Europe, American academic musicians plodded on in the tradition of the European Romantics. None of these composers wrote truly memorable works, but from their ranks emerged a true musical genius.

Charles Ives (1874–1954) was a New Englander, who broke from the stuffy traditionalists to follow his own off-beat drummer. Ives' father was an eccentric mid-19th-century band master who had experimented with some of the same techniques (polytonality, tone clusters, polyrhythms) that the young Turks of Europe would employ more than 50 years later.

Because Ives' music was unacceptable to the American classical musical establishment of the day, he wrote in seclusion, and only late in life heard a few of his compositions performed. Besides his near-obsessive composing, Ives started a New York insurance agency that made millions. He financed the publication of some of his own works, and gave them away by mail order to anyone who asked. (Imagine the surprise of a genteel lady opening his *114 Songs* at her parlor piano, only to

Sergei Rachmaninoff (1873–1943) enjoyed his greatest successes in the United States, probably because his music seemed "typically Russian."

The Kremlin.

find tone clusters, polytonality, and mocking quotes from religious and patriotic songs.)

Ives sprinkled his symphonies, chamber works, and songs with familiar musical quotes, but always integrated them into his own complex sound world. He was fascinated not just by polytonality as a theory, but by the actual sound experience of hearing different pieces of music performed simultaneously and moving through space (like hearing two marching bands, one approaching and one departing, in a parade). He experimented with twelve-tone techniques before Schönberg. His rhythm is much more complex than Stravinsky's. He used what would later be called aleatory methods which involve random chance in performance. After his death, Ives' orchestral music was championed by Leonard Bernstein, among other conductors, and his *Concord Sonata* for piano, and some of his *114 Songs* are often performed today.

Sergei Prokofiev (1891–1953, *left*) and Dmitri Shostakovich (1906–75, *center*), beside Aram Khachaturian (1903–78), were closely monitored by and often in conflict with the Soviet government. Prokofiev was reproached as "bourgeois," while Shostakovich sometimes aligned himself with the communists.

1900 – 1950

Sacred Music, Secular Music

Since the 18th century, the contrast between spiritual and worldly (or sacred and secular) music has been a determining element of music history. Not surprisingly, the reasons lie in the different conditions and motivations for the two kinds of compositions. Until the Enlightenment, the authority of the church in matters of philosophy and understanding of the world was unquestioned. This meant that music was often judged on theoretical grounds by musicians who were often priests or monks, or at least actively religious. For these theorists, unequivocally, all music not expressly made for the glory of God came from the devil. With such a pronouncement, they denied both the quality and the theoretical bases of secular music. Meanwhile, musical reality was completely different. Each musician made music according to his or her personal needs and worried little about the theoretical background of his or her works. Dance music in particular devel-

Musical angels. For hundreds of years, people believed that music was made in heaven.

oped independently of the church. Often, though, the differences between sacred and secular music were not so clear-cut. The entire courtly tradition (see pp. 15–17) is based on forms that were developed in religious music. Only the poetry was worldly and new, while the tunes were straight out of the liturgy. The reverse was also true: Händel set several of his most famous choruses from *Messiah* to Italian love duets he had written earlier.

St. Peter's Church in Rome. The Catholic Church was a great influence on sacred music. At the Council of Trent in 1545–63, it demanded that the texts of masses and motets be set to music so that the words were more intelligible.

Mutual influences

The process of using church melodies for love poetry could also be reversed. Composers often borrowed secular tunes—in particular love songs—to set spiritual texts. In one famous example, the chorale "O Haupt voll Blut und Wunden" (O Sacred Head Now Wounded) from J.S. Bach's *St. Matthew Passion* is based on the melody of a love song, "Mein G'müt ist mir verwirret" (My Mind Is Bewildered) by Hans Leo Hassler.

Some composers borrowed back and forth quite often and carelessly, not because they were ignorant or lacked their own ideas, but sometimes simply only from deadline pressure. So Bach took several parts of his Christmas *Oratorio* from a cantata he had composed in homage to the son of August the Strong. Handel based some of his most famous choruses in *Messiah* on some Italian love duets he had written earlier in his career.

The different functions of sacred music

Mass and requiem

Both the Mass as well as the requiem are compositional forms with unchangeable Latin texts dictated by the church. The performance of the individual movements of a Mass is a means of expression of worship in the context of ritual liturgy. The listener is not addressed

Songbooks with uplifting Christian texts brought the scriptures to the common people.

by the music, but can participate in the worship.

Cantatas, motets, oratorios

In contrast, cantatas, motets, and oratorios were directed toward the listener. The texts of these compositions—a mixture of biblical texts and religious poetry—were meant to educate the listener, and to encourage meditation over an individual's own faith.

Sacred works as a high point of creation

In the Middle Ages, the primary forms of secular music came out of the sacred. By the mid-18th century secular music had an important place, and this situation changed gradually and ultimately reversed itself. None of the important composers of the 19th and 20th centuries has written exclusively or even predominantly sacred works. In the catalog of many composers

who have composed primarily secular works, however, sacred music often is important, or even marks a kind of climax. Joseph Haydn composed the oratorio *Die Schöpfung* (The Creation) near the end of his career, marking a high point not only for his career but for the whole genre. Mass settings also permeate the work of Mozart. He composed his breathtaking *Requiem* shortly before his death, dictating it to his pupil Süssmayr, who completed the orchestration. The Requiem, or Mass for the Dead, begins with the words, "Requiem aeternam" (Rest eternal) and has inspired profoundly

moving music. Brahms, Berlioz, Fauré, and Verdi each also wrote a single, intensely beautiful Requiem. In our era, Benjamin Britten wrote his *War Requiem*, an antiwar as well as a religious statement. Krzysztof Penderecki carried on Bach's tradition with his 1966 *St. Luke Passion*. It stands at a central place within his work, but, like the spiritual compositions of other 20th-century composers, represents only a small part of his output.

The functions of secular music

Secular music fulfills far more and different functions than sacred music. It can entertain and heal, as in dance and cabaret music. It can evoke various kinds of group pride, as in national anthems and schools' "fight" songs. It can unite a group around work, as in sea shanties. It can menace and alienate, as in heavy metal or punk styles. In its more demanding forms, it is often an expression of a particular philosophical outlook, as in complex forms like symphonies and sonatas. In its commercialized forms, secular music is also a means to trade in current clichés or to elicit cheap sentiment. Pop "hits" often do both.

Music as status symbol

One of the few functional commonalities of sacred and secular music

At this summery garden party around the fountain of youth, the music must surely have been very worldly.

is their suitability for display and pageantry. Commissions by the church for 40-voice masses were of course the exception, with a commemorative motet for the opening of a local church more like the rule. In either case the work reflected well upon the commissioning organization.

A scene from a production of Verdi's *Falstaff* in Verona, home of the most visited opera festival in the world.

The nobility and prosperous middle class have always used music as a means of self-promotion. So, for example, for the high noble Italian families of the 17th century, no expense was too great to produce a splendid opera with elaborate stage machinery. Even today, cities establish cultural affairs offices funded by local taxes for no other purpose than to raise their cultural standards and reputations. These efforts benefit all of music by supporting musical experiments outside the commercial/pop realm. Some currently argue that such government subsidies to artists, including musicians, are unnecessary; that if an artist's work is worthy, it will succeed in the marketplace. The lessons of history and the avalanche of low-quality "popular culture," however, prove the weakness of this argument.

Music was an important part of many kinds of public display. In this imperial army, the musicians are splendidly attired.

Heinrich Strobel. For decades Strobel promoted composers of new music. As coordinator of various festivals and a broadcaster, he used his influence to publicize many new composers.

From stylistic pluralism to internationalism

Music at the beginning of the 20th century followed many different directions, in part as a rejection of Schönberg's theory. Through Neoclassicism and folkloric styles, composers tried to continue and to expand traditional lines of musical development. From about 1950, this situation changed fundamentally, as many composers tried logically to continue Schönberg's ideas. This was a jumping-off point for many different musical results, but is based on an aesthetic that is still followed by some today: that each individual composer develops the rules for his or her own compositions.

Darmstadt, Donaueschingen, Paris …

Only very rarely does contemporary music reach a large public (other than "pop" music, of course). Now and then a work of new music

Pierre Boulez (*center*) and Hans Werners Henze (*right*) in 1955, with the son of conductor Schmidt Isserstedt. Henze made his mark especially with settings of literary texts and operas. Since the 1970s he has combined music with political activism.

1950 – today

arouses interest, but usually only when it is scandalous enough to be covered by the media. Most people are oblivious to the continuing development of music over the last 40 years.

This continuity is chiefly carried out in Europe by regular festivals where new works are performed and musical aesthetics discussed. After World War II, such festivals sprang up in Darmstadt, Donaueschingen, Paris, Metz, and then many other places. In the United States, the development of tradition takes place in academic music departments at universities such as Princeton, Yale, Julliard, Indiana, and others. In both systems, older and younger composers meet, work, and put forth their works and strong individual opinions.

Before electronic music, composers experimented with all conceivable acoustic instruments.

Serialism

The controversy over serialism came to the fore around 1950. Composers endeavored to apply the row techniques of Schönberg and Webern consistently to all musical parameters. That is, not only pitch but also duration (rhythm) and tonal volume (dynamics) were organized in row techniques.

With mathematical precision, Karlheinz Stockhausen, Pierre Boulez, and György Ligeti in their early works sought to express serial thought, which was soon understood to be not for the benefit of performers or listeners. Boulez and Stockhausen took this notion much further than their teacher Olivier Messiaen, who projected

Anton Webern, the great model of the serialists.

Aleatory: inclusion of chance (from the Latin, "alea," meaning cubes) as an essential musical element
Electronic music: result of experimentation with synthesizers and computers; through the application of technical means, the aesthetics of new music changed fundamentally
Serialism: further development of twelve-tone theory through the consistent application of the row technique to all musical parameters

1950 – today

György Ligeti (1923–)

serial ideas only as a model, not as an all-encompassing duty.

Music with the help of technology
Musique concrète

In 1948–49 the Frenchman Pierre Schaeffer broke a convention that had apparently remained

Pierre Boulez (1925–)

intact over many centuries: Music is either sung, or made by playing instruments especially constructed for the purpose. This convention proved to be less than self-evident, as Schaeffer collected tape recordings of not only tones, rustlings, and noises, but also birdsong, among other things, and assembled them in an acoustic collage. For the first time in the history of music, he used acoustic phenomena from the natural environment for another purpose, and transformed the ordinary into art. Although the tonal results of what he dubbed *musique concrète*, because of their arbitrariness quickly became monotonous and ultimately tedious, this experiment excited the serialist composers, because now really everything had become material for music.

Pierre Schaeffer (1910–84)

Electronic music

Schaeffer had worked with concrete sound materials and reproduced sound solely with the help of a tape recorder. Going a step further, composers produced

the sounds themselves electronically, and combined them. Their goal was to use all acoustic phenomena, natural and synthetic, to order them and to make a musical statement, which could now be realized with the help of electronics.

Musical interaction

In the Studio for Electronic Music in West Germany, which was set up in 1953, Karlheinz Stockhausen first began to experiment with electronic sounds, which he sought to order with serial methods. He structured pitch, duration, loudness, and timbre (tone quality) as a combination of different fundamental pitches (pure pitches without overtones), which he stored on a tape. For the realization of his composition, neither an interpreter nor a score was necessary. The tape *is* the composition. Its unvarying nature precluded any further artistic activity. Stockhausen solved this problem by giving musicians the possibility to influence the electronic sound outcome either personally or through the use of electronic influences.

Karlheinz Stockhausen (1928–). In 1963 Stockhausen assumed the direction of the Herbert Eimert's Studio for Electronic Music in Cologne.

Many electronic compositions use this method. Pierre Boulez, president of the Institute for Research and Coordination of Acoustic Music, with Stockhausen a central figure of mid-century music, takes off from the interaction between technique and music. Boulez's works rely more upon conventional instruments than Stockhausen's, but demand highly unorthodox techniques from the performers. The decades of collaboration between these two composers were responsible for many essential impulses of new music since the 1950s.

The computer

What is now obvious was once shattering—one could program a computer so that it chose musical segments, and so assemble whole pieces

I

TACET

II

TACET

III

TACET

With the piece *4′ 33″*, John Cage (1912–94) questions the sense of all music. All movements have the direction "tacet" (the player is silent). Does the audience make its own music?

of music. The coincidences that occurred through a program were based on prior calculation. The proponents of this style, Milton Babbitt, Gottfried Michael Koenig, Janis Xenakis, among others, used the possibilities of computers to structure musical form and thereby to realize new sounds and whole "sound clouds," as Xenakis describes them. Their results were spectacular and extraordinary, but offered no basic challenge to the foundations of music.

John Cage, on the other hand, certainly did, as he declared himself to work against all previous formal ground rules. In the 1950s and 1960s, he caused far more irritation than the computer-composers. He not only modified existing instruments by "preparing" them with such objects as rubber bands and hatpins, he included environmental noise and silence in his compositional materials. In one outdoor experiment, a student asked him, "But what if a truck goes by?" Cage replied, "Then I would listen." Cage did not consider his compositions as finished works, but as musical "works in progress" whose results cannot be predicted. In his works, chance plays a determining role. This style is called *aleatory*.

For the composer to surrender control over exactly how a certain composition will play out over time not only represents a radical change in the self-image of the composer and a break with Western musical traditions, but also threatens to carry musical activity and music itself into absurdity.

Musical individualism

As at the beginning of the century, when reactions against twelve-tone theory fostered diverse stylistic directions, mid-century composers reacted similarly to the dominant idea of serialism. They searched for a middle ground between tradition and strict row technique. However, unlike in the 1920s, no particular stylistic directions emerged in the traditional sense. Rather, each composer developed a personal style, which expressed his or her personality through the application of more typical, sometimes even stereotyped musical methods.

By 1938 Cage was working with the prepared piano, for which he (and it) became known in musical circles.

Leonard Bernstein almost always used typical jazz elements, which he worked out symphonically. The creations of György Ligeti have a very individual character, which originally came from the same field as Boulez and Stockhausen. His compositions are often set up on microtones. Many voices produce tones very close in pitch, and produce tonal clusters, which otherwise can only be produced electronically. (One of his ethereal pieces was featured—along with Johann Strauss's *Blue Danube* waltz—in the soundtrack of Stanley Kubrick's film *2001: A Space Odyssey*.)

Monotony as artistic device—Minimalism

Influenced by musical practices from Africa and Asia, Americans La Monte Young, Terry Riley, Steve Reich, and Philip Glass in the mid-1960s began to experiment with a totally new restructuring of Western music. Constantly repeating tone rows are gradually and slightly changed over time. New pitch combinations emerge in the course of a piece, which can have a very moving effect. Even limited to only one musical parameter, as in Reich's *Drumming*, in which he used the process of minimal change only on the rhythm, this technique can be very effective.

Once again: Grand opera

In opera, composers have always seen the possibility of presenting all facets of their art in especially vivid ways. The idea of a work in

1950 – today

167

Benjamin Britten (1913–76) was not among the new music revolutionaries. He created new tonal colors using traditional means, sprinkled with English folk and church music influences.

In his opera *Die Soldaten* (shown here in a Berlin performance), Bernd Alois Zimmerman bound different times together. He called his method the "spherical shape of time."

which all arts are involved has lost nothing of its fascination since Wagner. The great British composer Benjamin Britten employs traditional but also novel sounds in his operas, whose characters are often tragic figures. His *Peter Grimes* is especially evocative, both musically and dramatically, of its seaside setting and tangled human relationships. Carl Orff, who provoked such excitement in 1937 with his *Carmina Burana*, did not change his style even in his later operas.

Bernd Alois Zimmermann captured the limelight in 1965 with his opera *Die Soldaten*, based on Jakob Michael Reinhold Lenz. Past, present, and future, which melt into a point of consciousness, are reflected in the score as different strata of music.

Hans Werner Henze had already cut himself loose from the general developments coming out of the summer festivals in Darmstadt and Donaueschingen. Instead he sought his own way, which he found especially in "Literature Opera." From a collaboration with Ingeborg Bachmann in 1960 came *Der Prinz von Homburg* (from the German Romantic play by Heinrich von Kleist).

1950 – today

Henze's style is especially marked by a balanced tension between rhythm and melody.

Mauricio Kagel not only engages the audience's imagination, but also provokes, frightens, and amuses them. His experimental musical theater pieces are carefully thought out, but employ unorthodox means such as screaming, or bouncing tennis balls against kettledrums.

American John Adams has emerged as an opera composer in the 1990s with his politico-historical works *Nixon in China* and *The Death of Klinghoffer*. Both received critical acclaim and were successfully produced for television. Adams uses minimalist techniques, especially in ensembles, but also more traditional recitative and aria-style set pieces.

Bernd Alois Zimmerman (1918–70) at the Cologne premiere of *Die Soldaten*.

Today: Anything goes

All contemporary composers face the profusion of stylistic possibilities, attempting the near-impossible task of not only expressing their own musical ideas, but also developing an individual, singular aesthetic, that may spark a discussion among professionals and may even be recognized by the public. Therefore, they look to any and all possible means. Some return to simple, traditional stylistic materials, like Arvo Paart, whose sacred vocal works use slow-moving, open harmonies to create a medieval effect. Some commune with the cosmos, as Stockhausen did in his early works. Others may plan to be scandalous, but then enjoy their fifteen minutes of fame and disappear without a trace in the daily flood of information.

It is difficult to predict the future of music. If not determined by a commercial mainstream, highly personalized musical methods and styles may continue to develop, or they may develop alongside a more common aesthetic.

Wolfgang Rihm (1953–). No longer are Schönberg, Stockhausen, and Boulez the models, but Beethoven and Liszt. Rihm values the engagement with tradition.

1950 – today

Glossary

Glossary

Alteration: raising or lowering a pitch by a half-step

Atonality: musical organizing principle not based on major-minor or modal scales, i.e., without a hierarchy of pitches centered around a single pitch

Barform: song form with parts A A B, commonly used in medieval courtly song

Basso continuo: ongoing bass voice, over which harmonies are elaborated (chiefly Baroque)

Bel canto: singing style with a beautiful tone, great flexibility, and text projection, usually associated with 19th-century Italian opera

Bourdon: ongoing pitch, or pair of pitches in the bass (see **Pedal point**)

Cadence: Chord sequence of tonic-subdominant-dominant-tonic, or some variation on that progression; also, a virtuosic unaccompanied section in solo concerto or aria, originally improvised

Cantus firmus: leading voice of a polyphonic composition

Chaconne: Variations over a repeated, usually descending bass line, often in triple meter

Chord: simultaneous sounding of at least three different pitches

Chromaticism: use of half-steps, which do not belong to the 7-note diatonic (major/minor) scale

Circle of fifths: a clockwise arrangement of the twelve major keys in an order of ascending fifths (C, G, D, A, etc.); after all twelve fifths, the first key is reached again

Cluster: bunched tones, which are no longer perceived individually

Diatonic scale: the seven pitches of the scale of the major-minor system (do, re, mi, fa, sol, la, ti)

Dodecaphony: The 12-tone system developed by Arnold Schönberg using all twelve chromatic pitches equally

Dominant: chord on the fifth note of a diatonic scale

Finale: final movement of an instrumental work

Function: designation of certain chords within traditional Western harmony, for example, the chords on scale pitches 1, 4 and 5 as tonic, subdominant, and dominant

Gebrauchsmusic: music with a purpose or utility, for example, liturgical music

Gesamtkunstwerk: ideally, the synthesis of different arts to an overall impression, concept important in the music of Wagner

Hymn: originally, unaccompanied liturgical song of the Catholic Church; since the 16th century, designation for Protestant church song

Intermezzo: brief musical theater piece, usually between the acts of a longer play, often on an allegorical topic

Interval: distance between two pitches

Libretto: script of an opera

Major: 7-note scale made up of whole steps, with a half step between 3 and 4, and 7 and 8

Modulation: passage of one key (tonality) to another

Minor: 7-note scales made up of whole steps, with a half-step between 2 and 3 and 5 and 6 in natural minor. In harmonic minor, the 7th tone is raised. In an ascending melody, the 6th tone may be raised, in descending, it is natural

Opera buffa: Italian for comic opera, counterpart to **opera seria**

Pedal point: a single bass note of long duration, originally in organ music but also in orchestral or ensemble pieces, which continues even as the harmonies of upper voices change. Also known as drone or bourdon

Pentatonic: 5-note scale, usually made up of whole steps

Recitative: A vocal style that imitates natural speech inflections. In opera, carries the plot forward and prepares for arias. Developed out of monody.

Score: written record of orchestral or choral work

Sonata form: form principle from the Classical era, in which two themes are contrasted and processed together. Usually consists of exposition, development, and recapitulation

Glossary ... A brief chronology of the history of music

Subdominant: chord on the 4th note of a major or minor scale

Suite: In Middle Ages and Renaissance, a pair of dance movements (usually pavane and gaillarde); in the Baroque, the standard form allemande-courante-sarabande-gigue develops, occasionally with extra movements inserted before the gigue

Symphony: primary classical form of orchestral work, with three or four movements, the first in sonata form

Tempo: the speed at which a piece or section moves

Tonic: chord on the first note of a major or minor scale

A brief chronology of the history of music

600 B.C. Development of Greek notation

200 A.D. Seikilos: Greek drinking song in the Phrygian mode

Late 600s A.D. Pope Gregory I reforms liturgy; Gregorian Chant named after him

Late 900s A.D. *Musica enchiriadis*; description of Organum style

1050 Death of Guido of Arezzo, who developed the first notation system with horizontal lines

1071–1126 William of Aquitaine, first known troubadour

1163–ca. 1250 Age of Notre Dame; Leonin and Perotin; Organum compositions

1228 *Palästinalied*. Walther von der Vogelweide calls up the crusade

1280 Franco of Cologne develops mensural notation

1284 Alfons X, Cantigas de Santa Maria

1300–77 Guillaume de Machaut; isorhythmic motets

1320 Jacobus of Lüttich coins term "Ars Nova"

1365–1445 Oswald von Wolkenstein, last Minnesänger

1400–70 Guillaume Dufay, first Franco-Flemish and most important composer of the Burgundian age

1417–80 *Codex Squarcialupi*: contains over 350 compositions of the Trecento

1450–1521 Josquin des Prez; Franco-Flemish vocal polyphony

1562–63 *Missa Papae Marcelli*: Giovanni Pierluigi da Palestrina fulfills the demands of the Tridentinum for clearer text setting in church music

1580–92 Florentine Camerata: Learned Circle in Florence orients itself to Greek aesthetics and tries to transfer them to music

From 1600 Major-minor tonalities gradually replace the church modes. Monody and general bass develop

1600 *La rappresentatione di anima e di corpo* by Emilio de Cavalieri: first oratorio

1607 *Orfeo* of Claudio Monteverdi sets standards for operatic style

1619 *Syntagma Musicum*, musical text by Michael Praetorius

1621 Death of Jan Pieterszoon Sweelinck, teacher of important North German organists

1646 Jean-Baptiste Lully leaves Italy for France, becomes court composer of Louis XIV

1648 Sacred choral music; Heinrich Schütz develops Protestant liturgical music

1678 Opening of the first public opera house in Hamburg

1681–94 *Trio Sonatas op. 1–4*: Antonio Corelli publishes 48 sonatas with general bass or thoroughbass, which become the model for the form

1721 *Brandenburg Concerti*, group and solo concertos by Johann Sebastian Bach

1722 *Well-Tempered Clavier I*, preludes and fugues through 24 keys by J.S. Bach

Ca. 1725 *The Four Seasons*, Antonio Vivaldi defines the concerto form

1742–43 *Messiah*, George Frideric Handel's most

A brief chronology of the history of music

important contribution to the oratorio

1745–50 *Art of the Fugue*, Johann Sebastian Bach sums up counterpoint technique

1752 *The True Art of Playing the Clavier*, Carl Philipp Emanuel Bach sums up the musical aesthetic of his time

1752 *Querelle des Buffons* (Quarrel of the Buffoons) stimulates opera reforms of Christoph Willibald Gluck

1755 *String Quartet Op. 1* by Joseph Haydn, establishment of the sonata form

1759 Joseph Haydn's *First Symphony*: transfer of sonata form to orchestral music

1763–66 Wolfgang Amadeus Mozart tours Europe as child prodigy

1791 W.A. Mozart's opera *The Magic Flute* makes him famous in Vienna

1816 *The Barber of Seville*, Gioacchino Rossini becomes an important opera composer in France and Italy

1821 *Der Freischütz*, Carl Maria von Weber founds the German Romantic opera

1824 *Ninth Symphony* of Ludwig van Beethoven; end of the Classical era

1827 *Die Winterreise*, Franz Schubert's song cycle, a pinnacle of lieder form

1829–32 *Etudes Op. 10, Op. 25*, Frédéric Chopin establishes virtuoso piano style

1829 Revival of J.S. Bach's *St. Matthew Passion*, Felix Mendelssohn Bartholdy introduces with it the Bach renaissance

1830 *Symphony Fantastique*, Hector Berlioz composes some of the first program music

1842 *Nabucco*, Giuseppe Verdi develops his serious, dramatic operatic style

1859 *Tristan and Isolde*, Richard Wagner expands harmony

1876 *The Ring of the Nibelung*, Richard Wagner develops the music drama as "Gesamtkunstwerk"

1876 *First Symphony*, Johannes Brahms composes "absolute music" in reaction to Wagner

1883 Anton Bruckner, *Seventh Symphony*, peak of late Romantic orchestra music

1890 *Suite Bergamasque*, Claude Debussy founds musical impressionism

1902 *Peléas et Mélisande*, Debussy's impressionism becomes the most important French style of the time

1905 *Salome*, Richard Strauss composes in the late Romantic idiom

1910 Gustav Mahler's *Tenth Symphony* marks the end of late Romantic symphonies

1913 *Le Sacre du printemps*, Igor Stravinsky creates a new sound aesthetic

1922 Arnold Schönberg, *Suite Op. 25*, first completely twelve-tone work

1925 *Wozzeck*, Alban Berg's opera becomes a key work of the 20th-century opera

Ca. 1930 American jazz influences European art music

1938 John Cage experiments with his prepared piano

From 1946 Darmstadt Ferienkurse; New Music becomes the object of the discussion

1948 Olivier Messiaën's *Turangalila Symphony* influences young generation of European composers

1956 *Song of the Youths in the Fiery Furnace*, K. Stockhausen makes electronics an artistic medium

1961 *Atmosphères*, György Ligeti constructs sound planes in orchestral music

1964 The Beatles appear on the Ed Sullivan Show, their first appearance in the U.S.

1969 Woodstock Festival, peak of early Rock era

Since 1977 Karlheinz Stockhausen, *Licht*, 7-part cycle, after the days of the week: the 5th day should be pre-

A brief chronology ... List of important composers

miered in Leipzig in 1996

1980 Mauricio Kagel, *Die Erschöpfung der Welt*

1987 Wolfgang Rihm, *Die Hamletmaschine*, after Heiner Müller

List of important composers

Abel, Carl Friedrich (1723–87): symphonies, sonatas for viola da gamba and basso continuo

Albéniz, Isaac (1860–1909): piano pieces, *Iberia Suite*

Albrechtsberger, Johann Georg (1736–1809): masses, oratorios, symphonies, chamber music

Alfons the Sage (1221–84): songs, *Cantigas de Santa Maria*

Anglebert, Jean Henri d' (1628–91): harpsichord works

Auber, Daniel François Esprit (1782–1871): operas, including *La muette de Portici*, which triggered the 1830 Belgian revolution

Babbit, Milton (b. 1916): chamber, computer music

Bach, Carl Philipp Emanuel (1714–88): symphonies, oratorios, concertos, chamber music, harpsichord and piano pieces, sonatas

Bach, Johann Christian (1735–82): harpsichord and piano pieces, operas, cantatas, arias

Bach, Johann Sebastian (1685–1750): oratorios, masses, cantatas, organ pieces, sonatas for various instruments with and without basso continuo accompaniment, concertos, including the *Brandenburg Concertos*

Bartók, Béla (1881–1945): piano pieces, concertos, operas, string quartets, songs

Beethoven, Ludwig van (1770–1827): 32 piano sonatas, variations for piano, 9 symphonies, 6 string quartets, songs, an opera (*Fidelio*)

Bellini, Vincenzo (1801–35): operas, *Norma*, *La Sonnambula*

Berg, Alban (1885–1935): chamber music, songs, piano sonatas, operas (*Wozzeck*, *Lulu*)

Berlioz, Héctor (1803–69): symphonies, including *Symphonie fantastique*, overtures, Requiem

Bernstein, Leonard (1918–90): musicals, including *West Side Story*, symphonies; important conductor

Binchois, Gilles (ca. 1400–60): masses, motets, songs

Bizet, Georges (1838–75): operas, including *Carmen*, orchestral suite *L'Arlésienne*, piano pieces

Boieldieu, François-Adrien (1775–1834): operas, piano pieces

Boulez, Pierre (b. 1925), piano pieces, chamber music, electronic music

Brahms, Johannes (1833–97): symphonies, piano pieces, Requiem, songs, chamber music

Britten, Benjamin (1913–76): operas, *War Requiem*, chamber music, songs

Bruckner, Anton (1824–96): symphonies, masses, choral works

Bull, John (ca. 1563–1628): masses, harpsichord works

Buxtehude, Dietrich (1673–1707): organ pieces, harpsichord works, cantatas, trio sonatas

Byrd, William (1543–1623): masses, motets, anthems, harpsichord works

Caccini, Giulio (ca. 1550–1618): operas, intermezzi

Cage, John (1913–94): pieces for prepared piano, music for variable groups of instruments, electronic music

Cavalieri, Emilio de (ca. 1550–1602): oratorios, including *Rappresentatione di anima e di corpo*

Chambonnières, Jacques Champion de (ca. 1601–72): harpsichord works

Chopin, Frédéric (1810–49): piano concertos, piano pieces including waltzes, mazurkas, ballades, polonaises

Clemens non Papa (ca. 1510–ca.1555): masses, motets, psalm chants

Corelli, Archangelo (1653–1707): trio sonatas, violin sonatas, concerti grossi

Couperin, François (1668–1733): masses, organ pieces, harpsichord works

Couperin, Louis (1626–61): organ pieces, harpsichord works

List of important composers

Debussy, Claude (1862–1918): piano pieces, préludes, suites, études, orchestra works, including *La Mer*, stage works, including *Peléas et Mélisande*

Delius, Frederick (1862–1934): operas, orchestral rhapsodies, songs

Donizetti, Gaetano (1797–1848): operas, oratorios, string quartets

Dowland, John (ca. 1563–1626): lute works, songs, dances, including *Lacrimae*

Dufay, Guillaume (ca. 1400–74): masses, motets, songs

Dukas, Paul (1865–1935): symphonic scherzo *The Sorceror's Apprentice*, piano music

Dvořak, Antonin (1841–1904): symphonies, Requiem, operas, chamber music, string quartets

Elgar, Edward (1857–1934): symphonies, concertos, orchestra variations, choral works, songs

Falla, Manuel de (1876–1946): Symphonic *Nights in the Gardens of Spain*, opera *La vida breve* (The Short Life), ballets

Fauré, Gabriel (1845–1924): Requiem, orchestra works, piano music, songs

Franck, César (1822–90): symphonic poems, masses, organ pieces, chamber music

Frescobaldi, Girolamo (1583–1643): organ pieces, harpsichord works, madrigals, instrumental canzoni

Froberger, Johann Jakob (1616–67): organ pieces, harpsichord works

Gabrieli, Giovanni (ca. 1557–1612): organ pieces, choral works, madrigals

Galilei, Vincenzo (1520–91): lute works, madrigals

Geminiani, Francesco (1680–1762): violin sonatas, concerti grossi, violin pedagogy

Gershwin, George (1898–1937): piano pieces, including *Rhapsody in Blue*, *Concerto in F*, opera *Porgy and Bess*, symphonic jazz, songs

Gibbons, Orlando (1583–1625): vocal works, anthems, harpsichord works

Glass, Philip (b. 1937): minimalist music, opera (*Einstein on the Beach*)

Gluck, Christoph Willibald (1714–87): symphonies, sonatas, operas

Goldberg, Johann Gottlieb (1727–56): harpsichord works, cantatas, trio sonatas, pupil of J.S. Bach (*Goldberg Variations*)

Gombert, Nicolas (ca. 1500–56): masses, motets, songs

Grétry, André Ernest Modeste (1741–1813): operas, piano music

Grieg, Edvard Hagerup (1843–1907): piano pieces, including *Lyric Pieces*, piano concerto, stage music, including the *Peer Gynt Suite*

Group of Five: Mili Balakierev, Cesar Cui, Modest Mussorgsky, Nikolai Rimsky-Korsakov, Alexander Borodin

Handel, George Frideric (1685–1759): oratorios, including *Messiah*, operas, concerti grossi, sonatas, harpsichord works

Hasse, Johann Adolf (1699–1783): operas, sonatas, harpsichord works

Hassler, Hans Leo (1546–1612): masses, liturgical music, madrigals, dances

Haydn, Franz Joseph (1732–1809): symphonies, string quartets, sonatas, operas, oratorios, masses

Heinrich von Meissen, called Frauenlob (1250–1318): Minnelieder

Henze, Hans Werner (b. 1926): operas, choral music, piano pieces, chamber music

Hindemith, Paul (1895–1963): symphonies, operas, oratorio, piano pieces, chamber music

Honegger, Arthur (1892–1955): symphonic works, string quartets, chamber music

d'Indy, Vincent (1851–1931): operas, choral works, string quartets, chamber music

Ives, Charles (1874–1954): symphonies, songs, violin, piano, and organ works

Jakobus von Lüttich (1260–1330): music theoretician, Ars antiqua–Ars nova

Janáček, Leoš (1854–1928): operas, string quartets, piano music, sonatas

Kagel, Mauricio Raúl (b. 1931): stage works, chamber music, radio plays

List of important composers

Khachaturian, Aram (1903–78): ballets, symphony, choral works

Kodály, Zóltan (1882–1967): choral works, symphonies, string quartets, orchestra works, folk song settings

Koenig, Gottfried Michael (b. 1926): electronic music

Landini, Francesco (ca. 1335–97): ballads, madrigals

Leoncavallo, Ruggiero (1857–1919): operas, including *Pagliacci*, operettas, ballets

Leoninus (2nd half 12th century): organum, manuscripts in the Magnus Library

Les Six: Darius Milhaud, Arthur Honegger, Francis Poulenc, Georges Auric, Louis Durey, Germaine Tailleferre

Ligeti, György (b. 1923): stage, orchestra, and choral works, Requiem, string quartets, instrumental works

Liszt, Franz (1811–86): piano pieces, symphonic poems, symphony, choral works, songs

Lully, Jean-Baptiste (1632–87): operas, ballets

Machaut, Guillaume de (ca. 1300–77): *Notre Dame Mass*, ballads, Virelais

Mahler, Gustav (1860–1911): 10 symphonies, orchestral songs, including *Lieder eines fahrenden Gesellen, Kindertotenlieder*

Marais, Marin (1656–1728): gamba works, operas

Mascagni, Pietro (1863–1945): operas, including *Cavalleria Rusticana*, symphony, chamber music

Massenet, Jules Emile Frédéric (1842–1912): operas, oratorios, songs

Mehul, Etienne Nicolas (1763–1817): operas, symphonies

Mendelssohn Bartholdy, Felix (1809–47): symphonies, concertos, piano music, including *Songs without Words*, choral music

Messiaëns, Olivier (1908–92): *Turangalila Symphony*, orchestral works, *Quartet pour la fin du temps*, organ pieces, piano pieces

Meyerbeer, Giacomo (1791–1864): operas, choral works

Milhaud, Darius (1892–1974): symphonies, orchestral and choral works, chamber music

Monn, Georg Matthias (1717–50): symphonies, concertos, masses

Monteverdi, Claudio (1567–1643): operas, including *Orfeo*, choral works, including *1610 Marienvespers*, madrigals

Mozart, Wolfgang Amadeus (1756–91): symphonies, operas, concertos, sonatas, masses, requiem, songs

Mussorgsky, Modest (1839–81): operas, piano pieces, including *Pictures at an Exhibition*, songs

Ockeghem, Johann (ca. 1425–97): masses, motets, songs

Offenbach, Jacques (1819–80): operas, operettas, ballets

Orff, Carl (1895–1982): stage works, including *Carmina Burana, Catulli Carmina*, cantatas, music method for children

Oswald von Wolkenstein (ca. 1377–1445): songs

Paganini, Niccolò (1782–1840): violin music, including *24 Caprices*

Palestrina, Giovanni Pierluigi da (1526–94): masses, including *Missa Papae Marcelli*, madrigals

Penderecki, Krzysztof (b. 1933): *St. Luke Passion*, choral works, chamber music

Pergolesi, Giovanni Battista (1710–36): operas, *Stabat Mater*, masses

Perotinus (ca. 1155–ca. 1225): organum

Poulenc, Francis (1899–1963): choral works, operas, concertos, piano pieces, songs

Praetorius, Michael (1577–1621): choral music, dances, music theory: *Syntagma Musicum*

Prez, Josquin des (ca. 1440–1524): masses, motets, songs

Prokofiev, Sergei (1891–1953): symphonies, including *Classical Symphony*, concertos, chamber music, piano pieces

Puccini, Giacomo (1858–1924): operas, including *La Bohème, Madame Butterfly*

Purcell, Henry (1659–95): cantatas, masques, opera *Dido and Aeneas*, chamber music, trio sonatas

List of important composers

Quantz, Johann Joachim (1698–1773): sonatas for flute and basso continuo

Rachmaninoff, Sergei (1873–1943): piano concertos, symphonies, songs

Rameau, Jean Philippe (1683–1764): operas, chamber music, harpsichord works

Ravel, Maurice (1875–1937): piano pieces, concertos, ballets, orchestra works, including *Boléro*, chamber music

Reger, Max (1873–1916): organ, piano, choral, orchestral works, chamber music

Reich, Steve (b. 1936): minimalist piano pieces, chamber music

Respighi, Ottorino (1879–1936): orchestral works, operas, chamber music

Rihm, Wolfgang (b. 1953): symphonies, operas, ballet, string quartets, chamber music

Riley, Terry (b. 1935): minimalist piano pieces, chamber music

Rossini, Gioacchino (1792–1868): operas including *The Barber of Seville*, orchestra works, masses, songs

Sainte Colombe (2nd half 17th century): gamba works

Saint-Saëns, Camille (1835–1921): operas, orchestra works, including *Carnival of the Animals*, masses, piano pieces

Salieri, Antonio (1750–1825): operas, choral works, chamber music

Satie, Erik (1866–1925): orchestra, piano pieces, songs

Schaeffer, Pierre (1910–84): chamber music, musique concrète

Scheidemann, Heinrich (1596–1663): organ, harpsichord works

Scheidt, Samuel (1587–1654): organ pieces, including *Tabulatura nova*, choral music

Schein, Johann Hermann (1586–1630): choral music, dances, including *Banchetto Musicale*

Schönberg, Arnold (1874–1951): musical dramas, orchestra works, chamber symphonies, piano pieces, concertos, chamber music, songs

Schubert, Franz (1797–1828): songs, symphonies, piano pieces, string quartets, chamber music

Schumann, Clara (1819–96): piano pieces, concerto, chamber music

Schumann, Robert (1810–56): symphonies, concertos, piano music, songs, chamber music

Schütz, Heinrich (1585–1672): choral works, including *Geistliche Chormusik, Psalmen Davids*

Scriabin, Alexander (1872–1915): piano pieces, symphonies

Shostakovich, Dmitri (1906–75): symphonies, chamber music

Sibelius, Jean (1865–1957): symphonies, chamber music

Smetana, Bedřich (1824–84): symphonic poems, including *The Moldau*, chamber music

Stamitz, Johann (1717–57): symphonies, chamber music

Stockhausen, Karlheinz (1928): operas, *Licht*, piano pieces, chamber music, electronic music

Strauss, Richard (1864–1949): operas, symphonies, chamber music

Stravinsky, Igor (1882–1971): ballets, including *Le sacre du printemps*, concertos, operas, chamber music

Sweelinck, Jan Pieterszoon (1562–1621): organ, harpsichord, choral works

Tartini, Giuseppe (1692–1770): violin concertos and sonatas

Tchaikovsky, Pyotr Ilyitch (1840–93): symphonies, concertos, ballets, operas

Telemann, Georg Philipp (1681–1767): chamber music, concertos, operas, cantatas

Vaughan Williams, Ralph (1872–1958): symphonies, concertos, chamber music, songs

Verdi, Giuseppe (1813–1901): operas, including *La Traviata*, choral works, songs

Vitry, Philippe de (1291–1361): motets

Vivaldi, Antonio (1678–1741): concertos, chamber music, operas

Wagenseil, Georg Christoph (1715–77): operas, oratorios, chamber music

Wagner, Richard (1813–83): operas, music dramas, including *The Ring of the Nibelung*

Important composers ... Interpreters of classical music

Walter von der Vogelweide (ca. 1170-ca.1230): Minnelieder

Weber, Carl Maria von (1786-1826): operas, including *Der Freischütz*, symphonies, concertos

Webern, Anton (1883-1945): orchestral and piano pieces, songs

Weill, Kurt (1900-50): operas, including *The Threepenny Opera*, songs

Willaert, Adrian (ca. 1490-1562): masses, motets, madrigals

Xenakis, Jannis (b. 1922): orchestral, chamber music

Young, La Monte (1935): chamber music, electronic music

Zimmerman, Bernd Alois (1918-70): opera *Die Soldaten*, piano music, chamber music, cantatas

Important interpreters of classical music

Conductors:
Abbado, Claudio (b. 1933)
Askenazy, Vladimir (b. 1937)
Barbirolli, Sir John (1899-1970)
Barenboim, Daniel (b. 1942)
Bernstein, Leonard (1918-90)
Bertini, Gary (b. 1927)
Böhm, Karl (1894-1981)
Boulez, Pierre (b. 1925)
Celibidache, Sergiu (b. 1912)
Furtwängler, Wilhelm (1886-1954)

Gardiner, John Eliot (b. 1943)
Harnoncourt, Nikolaus (b. 1929)
Karajan, Herbert von (1908-89)
Klemperer, Otto (1885-1973)
Kubelik, Rafael (b. 1914)
Mazur, Kurt (b. 1927)
Mehta, Zubin (b. 1936)
Ozawa, Seiji (b. 1935)
Schmidt Isserstedt, Hans (1900-73)
Sinopoli, Giuseppe (b. 1946)
Solti, Georg (b. 1912)
Walter, Bruno (1876-1962)

Singers:
Adams, Theo (b. 1926, bass)
Altmeyer, Theo (b. 1931, tenor)
Ameling, Elly (b. 1932, soprano)
Augér, Arlène (b. 1939, soprano)
Baker, Janet (b. 1933, mezzo-soprano)
Berganza, Theresa (b. 1935, soprano)
Bowman, James (b. 1941, counter-tenor)
Caballé, Monserrat (b. 1933, soprano)
Callas, Maria (1923-77, soprano)
Carreras, Jose (b. 1946, tenor)
Cordier, David (b. 1958, counter-tenor)
Domingo, Placido (b. 1934, tenor)
Donath, Helen (b. 1940, soprano)
Fassbaender, Brigitte (b. 1939, soprano)
Fischer-Dieskau, Dietrich (b. 1925, baritone)
Gruberova, Edita (b. 1946, soprano)

Hamari, Julia (b. 1942, alto)
Hendricks, Barbara (b. 1948, soprano)
Jacobs, René (b. 1946, counter-tenor)
Krause, Tom (b. 1934, bass-baritone)
Mathis, Edith (b. 1936, soprano)
Norman, Jessye (b. 1945, soprano)
Otter, Anne Sophie von (b. 1955, alto)
Pavarotti, Luciano (b. 1935, tenor)
Ridderbusch, Karl (b. 1932, bass)
Schreier, Peter (b.1935, tenor)
Schwarzkopf, Elisabeth (b. 1915, soprano)
Sutherland, Joan (b. 1926, soprano)
Talvela, Marti (1935-89, bass)
Te Kanawa, Kiri (b. 1944, soprano)

Piano:
Argerich, Martha (b. 1941)
Arrau, Claudio (1902-91)
Askenazy, Vladimir (b. 1937)
Barenboim, Daniel (b. 1942)
Benedetti-Michelangeli, Arturo (b. 1920)
Brendel, Alfred (b. 1931)
Ciccolini, Aldo (b. 1925)
Cortot, Alfred (1877-1962)
Demus, Jörg (b. 1928)
Eschenbach, Christoph (b. 1940)
Franz, Justus (b. 1945)
Gawrilow, Andrej (b. 1955)
Gelber, Bruno Leonardo (b. 1941)
Gieseking, Walter (1895-1956)
Gould, Glenn (1932-82)
Gulda, Friedrich (b. 1930)
Horowitz, Vladimir (1904-89)

Kempf, Wilhelm (1895–1991)
Ousset, Cecile (b. 1936)
Pollini, Maurizio (b. 1942)
Richter, Sviatoslav (b. 1915)
Rubinstein, Arthur (1887–1982)
Serkin, Peter (b. 1947)
Serkin, Rudolf (1903–91)
Zacharias, Christian (b. 1950)

Organ:
Alain, Marie-Claire (b. 1926)
Heiler, Anton (1923–79)
Hochreither, Karl (b. 1933)
Radulescu, Michael (b. 1943)
Stockmeier, Wolfgang (b. 1930)
Zacher, Gerd (b. 1929)

Harpsichord:
Asperen, Bob van (b. 1944)
Gilbert, Kenneth (b. 1931)
Koopmann, Ton (b. 1944)
Landowska, Wanda (1879–1959)
Leonhard, Gustav (b. 1928)
Pinnock, Trevor (b. 1946)
Staier, Andreas (b. 1955)

Violin:
Accardo, Salvatore (b. 1941)
Gawriloff, Saschko (b. 1929)
Goebel, Reinhard (b. 1952)
Heifetz, Jascha (1901–87)
Kogan, Leonid (1924–82)
Kremer, Gidon (b. 1947)
Menuhin, Yehudi (b. 1916)
Milstein, Nathan (b. 1904)
Mutter, Anne-Sophie (b. 1963)
Oistrach, David (1908–74)
Perlman, Itzak (b. 1945)
Szeryung, Henryk (1918–88)
Zehetmair, Thomas (b. 1961)
Zimmerman, Frank-Peter (b. 1965)
Zukerman, Pinchas (b. 1948)

Viola:
Kashkashian, Kim (b. 1952)
Pasquier, Bruno (b. 1943)
Zimmerman, Tabea (b. 1966)

Cello:
Bylsma, Anner (b. 1935)
Casals, Pablo (1876–1973)
du Pré, Jaqueline (1945–87)
Fournier, Pierre (1906–86)
Geringas, David (b. 1946)
Harrell, Lynn (b. 1944)
Ma, Yo-Yo (b. 1955)
Palm, Siegfried (b. 1927)
Pergamenschikow, Boris (b. 1948)
Rostropovitsch, Mstislaw (b. 1927)
Schiff, Heinrich (b. 1952)
Tortelier, Paul (1914–90)

Flute:
Brüggen, Frans (b. 1934)
Galway, James (b. 1939)
Graf, Peter-Lukas (b. 1929)
Kuijken, Barthold (b. 1949)
Larrieu, Maxence (b. 1934)
Nicolet, Aurèle (b. 1926)
Rampal, Jean-Pierre (b. 1922)

Trumpet:
André, Maurice, (b. 1933)
Güttler, Ludwig (b. 1943)
Immer, Friedemann (b. 1951)
Tarr, Edward (b. 1936)
Touvron, Guy (b. 1950)

Oboe:
Holliger, Heinz (b. 1939)
Schellenberger, Hansjörg (b. 1948)

Clarinet:
Leister, Karl (b. 1937)
Meyer, Sabine (b. 1959)

Bibliography

Abbate, Carolyn. *Unsung Voices: Opera & Musical Narrative in the Nineteenth Century.* Princeton: Princeton University Press, 1991.

Abraham, Gerald E. *The Concise Oxford History of Music.* New York: Oxford University Press, 1985.

Adorno, Theodor W. et al. *German Essays on Music.* New York: Continuum Publishing Co., 1993.

Anderson, Warren D. *Music & Musicians in Ancient Greece.* Ithaca: Cornell University Press, 1995.

Antokoletz, Elliott. *Twentieth Century Music.* Englewood Cliffs: Prentice Hall, 1991.

Apel, Willi. *The History of Keyboard Music to 1700.* Bloomington: Indiana University Press 1972.

Arnold, John. *Medieval Music.* New York: Oxford University Press, 1985.

Arom, Simha. *African Polyphony & Polyrhythm: Musical Structure & Methodology.* New York: Cambridge University Press, 1991.

Ashbee, Andrew. *Records of English Court Music. Vol. 6, 1558–1603.* Brookfield: Ashgate Publishing Co., 1992.

Atlas, Allan A., ed. *Music in the Classic Period: Essays in Honor of Barry S. Brook.* Stuyvesant: Pendragon Press, 1985.

Bibliography

Austin, William W. *Music in the 20th Century.* New York: W.W. Norton & Co, Inc., 1966

Avenary, Hanoch. *Encounters of East & West in Music.* Van Nuys: Theodore Front Musical Literature, 1979.

Baez, Joan. *And A Voice to Sing With: A Memoir.* New York: Summit, 1987.

Baraka, Imamu. *Black Music.* Westport: Greenwood Press, 1980.

Barzun, Jacques, ed. *Pleasures of Music: An Anthology of Writings About Music & Musicians from Cellini to Bernard Shaw.* Chicago: University of Chicago Press, 1977.

Beethoven, Ludwig van. *Beethoven: Symphony No. Five in C Minor.* Edited by Elliot Forbes. New York: W.W. Norton & Co, Inc., 1971.

Bekker, Paul. *Story of Music: An Historical Sketch of the Changes in Musical Form.* New York: AMS Press, Inc., 1970.

Bent, Ian D. *Music Analysis in the Nineteenth Century.* Vol 1. New York: Cambridge University Press, 1994.

Bent, Ian, ed. *Music Analysis in the Nineteenth Century. Vol. 2, Hermeneutic Approaches.* New York: Cambridge University Press, 1994.

Born, Georgina. *Rationalizing Culture: IRCAM, Boulez, & the Institutionalization of the Avant-Garde.* Berkeley: University of California Press, 1995.

Borroff, Edith. *Music Melting Round: A History of Music in the United States.* New York: Ardsley House Publishers, Inc., 1995.

Brindle, Reginald S. *The New Music: The Avant-Garde since 1945.* New York: Oxford University Press, 1987.

Brown, Howard M. *Music in the Renaissance.* Englewood Cliffs: Prentice Hall, 1976.

Bukofzer, Manfred F. *Music in the Baroque Era.* New York: W.W. Norton & Co, Inc., 1947.

Bunconi, Lorenzo. *Music in the Seventeenth Century.* New York: Cambridge University Press, 1987.

Burbank, Richard & Nicholas Slonimsky. *Twentieth Century Music.* New York: Facts on File, Inc., 1984.

Burney, Charles. *Music, Men & Manners in France & Italy in 1770.* New York: Da Capo Press, Inc., 1982.

Busby, Thomas. *A General History of Music From the Earliest Times,* 2 vols. New York: Da Capo Press, Inc., 1968.

Caldwell, John. *The Oxford History of English Music. Vol. 1, From the Beginnings to c. 1715.* New York: Oxford University Press, 1992.

Caldwell, John, et al., eds. *The Well-Enchanting Skill: Music, Poetry, & Drama in the Culture of the Renaissance.* New York: Oxford University Press, 1990.

Campbell. *And the Beat Goes On.* New York: Schirmer Books, 1996.

Carlin, Richard. *Classical Music: An Informal Guide.* Chicago: A cappella Books, 1992.

Carpenter, Nan Cooke. *Music in the Medieval & Renaissance Universities.* New York: Da Capo Press, Inc., 1972.

Carr, Joe & Alan Munde. *Prairie Nights to Neon Lights. The Story of Country Music in West Texas.* Lubbock: Texas Tech University Press, 1995.

Carter, Tim. *Music in Late Renaissance & Early Baroque Italy.* Portland: Timber Press, Inc., 1992.

Cattin, Giulio. *Music of the Middle Ages I.* Trans. Steven Botterill. New York: Cambridge University Press, 1985.

Chailley, Jacques. *Forty Thousand Years of Music: Man in Search of Music.* New York: Da Capo Press, Inc., 1975.

Chanan, Michael. *Musica Practica: The Social Practice of Western Music from Gregorian Chant to Postmodernism.* New York: Routledge, Chapman & Hall, Inc., 1994.

Christofferson, Peter W. *French Music in the Early Sixteenth Century.* Concord: Paul & Co. Publishers Consortium, Inc., 1994.

Cohen, Albert. *Music in the French Royal Academy of Sciences: A Study in the Evolution of Musical Thought.* Princeton:

Bibliography

Princeton University Press, 1981.

Cohn, Arthur. *Twentieth Century Music in Western Europe: The Compositions & Recordings.* New York: Da Capo Press, Inc., 1972.

Comberiati, Carmelo P. *Late Renaissance Music at the Habsburg Court.* Newark: Gordon Breach Science Publishers, Inc., 1987.

Comotti, Giovanni. *Music in Greek & Roman Culture.* Baltimore: Johns Hopkins University Press, 1991.

Cooke, J.F. *Standard History of Music.* New York: Gordon Press Publishers, 1972.

Coplan, David B. *In the Time of Cannibals: The Word Music of South Africa's Basotho Migrants.* Chicago: University of Chicago Press, 1994.

Copland, Aaron. *Music & Imagination.* Cambridge: Harvard University Press, 1952

---. *New Music: 1900–1960.* New York: W.W. Norton & Co, Inc., 1969.

Cowart, Georgia & George J. Buelow, eds. *French Musical Thought, 1600–1800.* Rochester: University of Rochester Press, 1991.

Cowdery, James. *The Melodic Tradition of Ireland.* Kent: Kent State University Press, 1990.

Crabtree, Phillip D. & Donald H. Foster. *Sourcebook for Research in Music.* Bloomington: Indiana University Press, 1993.

Crocker, Richard & David Hiley, eds. *The New Oxford History of Music, 2d ed. Vol.2, The Early Middle Ages to 1300.* New York: Oxford University Press, 1990.

Cummings, Anthony M. *The Politicized Muse: Medici Festivals, 1512–1537.* Princeton: Princeton University Press, 1992.

Dachs, David. *Anything Goes: The World of Popular Music.* Indianapolis: Bobbs Merrill, 1964.

Dahlhaus, Carl. *Between Romanticism & Modernism: Four Studies in the Music of the Later Nineteenth Century.* Berkeley: University of California Press, 1980.

---. *Foundations of Music History.* New York: Cambridge University Press, 1983.

---. *Nineteenth-Century Music.* Berkeley: University of California Press, 1991.

Davenport, Marcia. *Mozart.* New York: Charles Scribners Sons, 1932.

Dorian, Frederick. *The History of Music in Performance: The Art of Musical Interpretation from the Renaissance to Our Day.* Westport: Greenwood Press, 1981.

Duffin, Ross. *Performer's Guide to Medieval Music.* New York: Schirmer Books, 1995.

Dunsby, Jonathan, ed. *Early Twentieth-Century Music.* Cambridge: Blackwell Publishers, 1993.

Dyson, George. *New Music.* Temecula: Reprint Services Corp., 1990.

Engel, Carl. *The Music of the Most Ancient Nations, Particularly of the Assyrians, Egyptians, Hebrews.* Temecula: Reprint Services Corp., 1990.

Evans, Edwin. *Historical, Descriptive & Analytical Account of the Entire Works of Johannes Brahms.* Temecula: Reprint Services Corp., 1991.

Everist, Mark. *French Motets in the 13th Century: Music, Poetry, & Genre.* New York: Cambridge University Press, 1994.

Farmer, Henry G. *Historical Facts for the Arabian Musical Influence.* Temecula: Reprint Services Corp., 1991.

Fenlon, Iain, ed. *Music in Medieval & Early Modern Europe: Patronage, Sources & Texts.* New York: Cambridge University Press, 1981.

Ferguson, Donald N. *A Short History of Music.* Westport: Greenwood Press, 1974.

Floyd, Samuel A., Jr., ed. *Black Music in the Harlem Renaissance: A Collection of Essays.* Knoxville: University of Tennessee Press, 1993.

Ford, Andrew. *Composer to Composer: Conversations about Contemporary Music.* Chicago: Independent Publishers Group, 1994.

Gagne, Cole. *Sonic Transports: New Frontiers in Our Music.* New York: de Falco Books, 1990.

Galpin, Francis W. *Music of the Sumerians & Their Immediate Successors, the*

Bibliography

Babylonians-Assyrians. Westport: Greenwood Press, 1970.

Gammond, Peter, ed. *The Harmony Illustrated Encyclopedia of Classical Music.* New York: Crown Publishing Group, 1989.

Gangwere, Blanche M. *Music History During the Renaissance Period, 1425–1580: A Documented Chronology.* Westport: Greenwood Publishing Group, 1991.

– – –. *Music History from the Late Roman Through the Gothic Periods, 313–1425: A Documented Chronology.* Westport: Greenwood Publishing Group, 1991.

Gart, Galen, ed. *First Pressings: The History of Rhythm & Blues.* Vol. 6. Milford: Big Nickel Publications, 1991.

Gilliam, Bryan. *Music & Performance During the Weimar Republic.* New York: Cambridge University Press, 1994.

Gleason, Harold & Warren Becker. *Chamber Music: Haydn to Bartok.* 2d ed. Van Nuys: Alfred Publishing Co., Inc., 1988.

– – –. *Early American Music.* 2nd. ed. Van Nuys: Alfred Publishing Co., Inc., 1988.

Goldman, Albert & Evert Sprinchorn, eds. *Wagner on Music & Drama.* New York: Da Capo Press, Inc., 1988.

Graf, Max. *Modern Music: Composers & Music of Our Time.* Westport: Greenwood Press, 1978.

Gray, Cecil. *The History of Music.* Westport: Greenwood Press, 1979.

Green, Robert A. *The Hurdy-Gurdy in 18th Century France.* Bloomington: Indiana University Press, 1995.

Greenberg, Noah & Paul Maynard, eds. *Anthology of Early Renaissance Music.* New York: W.W. Norton & Co, Inc., 1975.

Griffiths, Paul. *Modern Music: The Avant-Garde Since 1945.* New York: George Braziller, Inc., 1981.

– – –. *Modern Music.* New York: Thames & Hudson, 1994.

Grout, Donald J. & Palisca, Claude V. *A History of Western Music.* 5th ed. New York: W.W. Norton & Co, Inc., 1996.

Hall, Charles J., comp. *A Nineteenth-Century Musical Chronicle: Events 1800–1899.* Westport: Greenwood Press, 1989.

– – –. *A Twentieth-Century Musical Chronicle: Events, 1900–1988.* Westport: Greenwood Press, 1989.

– – –. *An Eighteenth-Century Musical Chronicle: Events 1750–1799.* Westport: Greenwood Publishing Group, 1990.

Hammond, Frederick. *Music & Spectacle in Baroque Rome: Barberini Patronage Under Urban VIII.* New Haven: Yale University Press, 1995.

Harnoncourt, Nikolaus. *Musical Dialogue: Thoughts on Monteverdi, Bach, & Mozart.* Portland: Timber Press, Inc., 1989.

Hayes, Gerald R. *Musical Instruments & Their Music: 1500–1750.* 2 vols. New York: AMS Press, Inc., 1974.

Hefling, Stephen E. *Rhythmic Alteration in 17th & 18th Century Music: Notes Inegales Overdotting.* New York: Schirmer Books, 1993.

Heintze, James R. *American Music Before 1865 in Print & on Records: A Biblio-Discography.* Brooklyn: Institute for Studies in American Music, 1990.

Heintze, James R., ed. *Heritage of Music: The Romantic Era.* Vol 2. New York: Oxford University Press, 1992.

– – –. *American Musical Life in Context & Practice to 1865.* New York: Garland Publishing, Inc., 1994.

Hildesheimer, Wolfgang. *Mozart.* Translated by Marion Faber. New York: Vintage, 1983.

Hodeir, Andre. *Since Debussy: A View of Contemporary Music.* New York: Da Capo Press, Inc., 1975.

Holmes, John L. *Conductors on Composers.* Westport: Greenwood Publishing Group, 1993.

Hoppin, Richard H. *Medieval Music.* New York: W.W. Norton & Co, Inc., 1978.

Horowitz, J. *Understanding Toscanini: A Social History of American Concert Life.* Berkeley: University of California Press.

Horowitz, Joseph. *The Post-Classical Predicament: Essays on Music & Society.*

Bibliography

Boston: Northeastern University Press, 1995.

Jensen, Eric F. *The Walls of Circumstance: Studies in Nineteenth-Century Music.* Metuchen: Scarecrow Press, Inc., 1992.

Kaplan, Lloyd & Nancy Carroll. *Twentieth Century. An Introduction.* West Greenwich: Consortium Publishing, 1991.

Kelly, Michael Bryan. *The Beatle Myth: The British Invasion of American Popular Music, 1956–1969.* Jefferson: McFarland, 1991.

Kendall, Alan. *The Chronicle of Classical Music.* New York: Thames & Hudson, 1994.

Kenyon, Nicholas, ed. *Authenticity & Early Music.* New York: Oxford University Press, 1989.

Kerman, Joseph, ed. *Music at the Turn of the Century: A "Nineteenth-Century Music" Reader.* Berkeley: University of California Press, 1990.

Kiesewetter, Raphael G. *History of the Modern Music of Western Europe: From the First Century of the Christian Era to Present Day.* New York: Da Capo Press, Inc., 1973.

Kinderman, William. *Beethoven.* Berkeley: University of California Press, 1995.

Kirby, F.E., ed. *Music in the Romantic Period: An Anthology with Commentary.* New York: Schirmer Books, 1986.

Kirby, F.E. *Music in the Classic Period: An Anthology with Commentary.* New York: Schirmer Books, 1979.

Kmen, Henry A. *Music in New Orleans: The Formative Years, 1791–1841.* Ann Arbor: Books on Demand, 1966.

Kmetz, John, ed. *Music in the German Renaissance: Sources, Styles, & Contexts.* New York: Cambridge University Press, 1995.

Knighton, Tess & David Fallows, eds. *Companion to Medieval and Renaissance Music.* New York: Schirmer Books, 1992.

Kostelanetz, Richard. *On Innovative Music.* New York: Limelight Editions, 1989.

Kraehenbuehl, David & Richard Chronister, eds. *Exploring the Masters.* New York: Carl Fischer, Inc., 1980.

Kramer, Lawrence. *Music As Cultural Practice, 1800–1900.* Berkeley: University of California Press, 1993.

Krohn, Ernst C. *The History of Music.* New York: Da Capo Press, Inc., 1973.

Lahee, Henry C. *Annals of Music in America: A Chronological Record of Significant Musical Events.* Temecula: Reprint Services Corp., 1990.

Landon, H.C. & John J. Norwich. *Five Centuries of Music in Venice.* New York: Schirmer Books, 1991.

Lasocki, David & Roger Prior. *The Bassanos: Venetian Musicians & Instrument Makers in England, 1531–1665.* Brookfield: Ashgate Publishing Co., 1995.

Lee, Vernon, *Studies of the 18th Century in Italy.* New York: Da Capo Press, Inc., 1978.

Little, Meredith & Natalie Jenne. *Dance & the Music of J. S. Bach.* Bloomington: Indiana University Press, 1991.

Longyear, Rey M. *Nineteenth Century Romanticism in Music.* 3d ed. Englewood Cliffs: Prentice Hall, 1987.

Lowe, Charles E. A *Chronological Encyclopedia of Musicians & Musical Events from A.D. 320 to 1896.* New York: Gordon Press Publishers, 1976.

Lowinsky, Edward E. *Music in the Culture of the Renaissance and Other Essays.* 2 vols. Chicago: University of Chicago Press, 1989.

Loza, Steven. *Barrio Rhythm: Mexican American Music in Los Angeles.* Champaign: University of Illinois Press, 1993.

Lulu Huang Chang. *From Confucius to Kublai Khan: Music & Poets Through the Centuries.* Henryville: Institute of Mediaeval Music, Ltd., 1992.

Mache, François-Bernard. *Music, Myth, & Nature, or, the Dolphins of Arion.* Newark: Gordon & Breach Science Publishers, Inc., 1993.

Malone, Bill C. *Singing Cowboys, Musical Mountaineers: Southern Culture &*

Bibliography

Roots of Country Music. Athens: University of Georgia Press, 1994.

Mann, William. *James Galway's Music in Time.* Englewood Cliffs: Prentice Hall, 1983.

Marvin, Elizabeth W. and Richard Hermann, eds. *Concert Music, Rock, & Jazz since 1945: Essays & Analytical Studies.* Rochester: University of Rochester Press, 1996.

Mason, Daniel G. *Beethoven & His Forerunners.* New York: AMS Press, Inc., 1971.

– – –. *Great Modern Composers: Biographical Sections by M.L. Mason, Appreciation of Music, Vol. 2.* North Stratford: Ayer Co. Publishers, Inc., 1977.

– – –. *From Grieg to Brahms.* New York: AMS Press, Inc., 1979.

Mason, Dorothy E. *Music in Elizabethan England.* Cranbury: Folger Books, 1958.

McCalla. *Twentieth Century Music.* Old Tappan: Macmillan Publishing Co., 1995.

McGee, Timothy J. *Medieval & Renaissance Music: A Performer's Guide.* Cheektowaga: University of Toronto Press, 1988.

McKinnon, James. *Antiquity & the Middle Ages: From Ancient Greece to the Middle Ages.* Englewood Cliffs: Prentice Hall, 1990.

Meister, Barbara. *Art Song: The Marriage of Music & Poetry.* Durango: Hollowbrook Publishing, 1992.

Merkley, Paul. *Italian Tonaries.* Henryville: Institute of Mediaeval Music, Ltd., 1988.

Meyer, Ernst. *English Chamber Music.* New York: Da Capo Press, Inc., 1971.

Meyer, Michael. *The Politics of Music in the Third Reich.* New York: Peter Lang Publishing, Inc., 1989.

Millard, Andre. *America on Record: A History of Recorded Sound.* New York: Cambridge University Press, 1995.

Miller, Hugh M. & Cockerell, Dale. *History of Western Music.* New York: HarperCollins Publishers, Inc., 1991.

Mitchell, Donald. *The Language of Modern Music.* Philadelphia: University of Pennsylvania Press, 1994.

Moore, MacDonald S. *Yankee Blues: Musical Culture & American Identity.* Ann Arbor: Books on Demand.

Morse, Jim. *Big Band Era.* Hopkins: Hiawatha Publishers, 1992.

Mozart, Wolfgang Amadeus. *Letters of Wolfgang Amadeus Mozart.* Sel. and ed. by Hans Mersmann, trans. by M.M. Bozman. London: Dutton, 1928.

Mueller, John H. *The American Symphony Orchestra: A Social History of Musical Taste.* Westport: Greenwood Press, 1976.

Neumann, Frederick. *Ornamentation in Baroque & Post-Baroque Music.* Princeton: Princeton University Press, 1978.

New York University Society Staff. *Modern Music & Musicians.* Temecula: Reprint Services Corp., 1991.

New Oxford History of Music. 4 vols. Temecula: Reprint Services Corp., 1990.

Nicholls, David. *American Experimental Music, 1890–1940.* New York: Cambridge University Press, 1991.

Niecks, Frederick. *Programme Music in the Last Four Centuries: A Contribution to the History of Musical Expression.* Temecula: Reprint Services Corp., 1990.

Niedt, Friederich E. *The Musical Guide, Pts I–III: 1700–1721.* New York: Oxford University Press, 1989.

O'Brien, Lucy. *She Bop: The Definitive History of Woman in Rock, Pop, and Soul.* New York: Penguin, 1996.

Off the Record: An Oral History of Popular Music. New York: Warner Books, 1988.

Oliphant, Dave, ed. *The Bebop Revolution in Words & Music.* Austin: University of Texas, Harry Ransom Humanities Research Center, 1994.

Oliver, Paul. *Screening the Blues: Aspects of the Blues Tradition.* New York: Da Capo Press, Inc., 1989.

Paine, John K. *The History of Music to the Death of Schubert.* New York: Da Capo Press, Inc., 1971.

Palisca, Claude V. *Baroque Music.* 3d ed. Englewood Cliffs: Prentice Hall, 1990.

– – –. *Humanism in Italian Renaissance Musical*

Bibliography

Thought. New Haven: Yale University Press, 1990.

– – –. *Studies in the History of Italian Music & Music Theory.* New York: Oxford University Press, 1994.

Palmer, Robert. *A Tale of Two Cities: Memphis Rock, New Orleans Roll.* Brooklyn: Institute for Studies in American Music, 1979.

Pannain, Guido. *Modern Composers.* North Stratford: Ayer Co. Publishers, Inc., 1977.

Parry, Charles H. *The Evolution of Music.* Temecula: Reprint Services Corp., 1990.

Pauly, Reinhard G. *Music in the Classic Period.* 3d ed. Englewood Cliffs: Prentice Hall, 1987.

Pendle, Karin, ed. *Women and Music: A History.* Bloomington: Indiana University Press, 1991.

Potter, S.B. *A Survey of Western Music to 1750.* Dedham: Gamut Music Co., 1993.

Raeburn, Michael & Alan Kendall, eds. *Heritage of Music: Classical Music & Its Origins.* Vol. 1. New York: Oxford University Press, 1992.

– – –. *Heritage of Music: The Nineteenth Century Legacy.* Vol. 3. New York: Oxford University Press, 1992.

– – –. *Heritage of Music: Music in the Twentieth Century.* Vol. 4. New York: Oxford University Press, 1992.

Rankin, Susan & David Hiley, eds. *Music in the Medieval English Liturgy: Plainsong & Medieval.* Music Society Centennial Essays. New York: Oxford University Press, 1993.

Rimbault, Edward F., ed. *The Old Cheque-Book: or Book of Remembrance of the Chapel Royal from 1561 to 1744.* New York: Da Capo Press, Inc., 1966.

Robertson, Carol E., ed. *Musical Repercussions of Fourteen Ninety-Two: Encounters in Text & Performance.* Washington: Smithsonian Institution Press, 1993.

Rolland, Romain. *Musical Tour Through the Land of the Past.* North Stratford: Ayer Co. Publishers, Inc., 1977.

Rosenstiel, Leonie et al. *Schirmer History of Music.* New York: Schirmer Books, 1982.

Rostand, Claude. *French Music Today.* New York: Da Capo Press, Inc., 1973.

Rothschild, Fritz. *The Lost Tradition in Music: Rhythm & Tempo in J.S. Bach's Time.* Westport: Hyperion Press, Inc., 1986.

Rushton, Julian. *Classical Music: A Concise History from Gluck to Beethoven.* New York: Thames & Hudson, 1986.

Sadie, Julie A., ed. *Companion to Baroque Music: A Biographical Dictionary & Guide to National Traditions.* New York: Schirmer Books, 1991.

Schuller, Gunther. *The Swing Era: The Development of Jazz, 1930–1945.* New York: Oxford University Press, 1989.

Schwartz, Elliot & Daniel Godfrey. *Music Since 1945.* New York: Schirmer Books, 1993.

Schwartz, Elliot & Barney Childs, eds. *Contemporary Composers on Contemporary Music.* New York: Da Capo Press, Inc., 1978.

Selfridge-Field, Eleanor. *Venetian Instumental Music: From Gabrieli to Vivaldi.* New York: Dover Publications, Inc., 1994.

Shaw, Arnold. *The Jazz Age: Popular Music in the 1920s.* New York: Oxford University Press, 1989.

Shelton, Robert. *No Direction Home: The Life and Music of Bob Dylan.* New York: Ballantine, 1987.

Sitsky, Larry. *Music of the Repressed Russian Avant-Garde, 1900–1929.* Westport: Greenwood Publishing Group, 1994.

Slonimsky, Nicolas. *Music Since 1900.* 5th ed. New York: Schirmer Books, 1994.

Sparks, Edgar H. *Cantus Firmus in Mass & Motet Fourteen Twenty to Fifteen Twenty.* New York: Da Capo Press, Inc., 1975.

Stanley, John. *Classical Music: An Introduction to Classical Music Through the Great Composers & Their Masterworks.* New York: Reader's Digest Association, Inc., 1994.

Straus, Joseph N. *Remaking the Past: Musical Modern-*

Bibliography ... Index

ism & Influence of the Tonal Tradition. Cambridge: Harvard University Press, 1990.

Streatfield, Richard A. Masters of Italian Music. North Stratford: Ayer Co. Publishers, Inc., 1977.

Strohm, Reinhard. The Rise of European Music, 1380–1500. New York: Cambridge University Press, 1994.

Taruskin, Richard. Music in the Western World. New York: Schirmer Books, 1996.

– – –. Stravinsky & the Russian Traditions: A Biography of the Works Through "Mavra". 2 vols. Berkeley: University of California Press, 1995.

The Oxford History of Music. 8 vols. Temecula: Reprint Services Corp.

Toop, David. RAP Attack, No. 2: African Rap to Global Hip Hop. New York: Serpents Tail, 1992.

Turbet, Richard. Tudor Music: A Research & Information Guide. Vol. 18. New York: Garland Publishing, Inc., 1994.

Turek, Ralph. Analytical Anthology of Music. New York: The McGraw-Hill Companies, 1983.

Ulanov, Barry. A History of Jazz in America. New York: Da Capo Press, Inc., 1972.

VanDeusen, Nancy. The Harp & the Soul: Studies in Medieval Music. Lewiston: The Edwin Mellen Press, 1989.

Waddell, Helen. The Wandering Scholars. Ann Arbor: University of Michigan Press, 1990.

Watkins, Glenn. Soundings: Music in the Twentieth Century. New York: Schirmer Books, 1987.

Whitburn, Joel. Pop Memories, 1890–1954. Menomonee Falls: Record Research, Inc., 1992.

Whittall, Arnold. Romantic Music: A Concise History from Schubert to Sibelius. New York: Thames & Hudson, 1987.

Wilkins, Nigel. Music in the Age of Chaucer. 2d rev ed. Rochester: Boydell & Brewer, Inc., 1995.

Wilson, David F. Music of the Middle Ages: Style & Structure. New York: Schirmer Books, 1990.

Woliver, R. Hoot! A 25-Year History of the Greenwich Village Music Scene. New York: St. Martin's Press, Inc., 1994.

Wright, Craig. Music at the Court of Burgundy: 1364–1419. Henryville: Institute of Medieval Music, Ltd., 1979.

Yates, Peter. Twentieth Century Music: Its Evolution from the End of the Harmonic Era into the Present Era of Sound. Westport: Greenwood Publishing Group, 1981.

Yudkin, Jeremy. Music in Medieval Europe. Englewood Cliffs: Prentice Hall, 1989.

– – –. Music Past, Music Present. Cd-rom, audio cassette, and pap. text eds. Englewood Cliffs: Prentice Hall, 1995.

Index

Index

Index

Index

Index

Index

Picture credits

JEDEDIAH PURDY

A Tolerable Anarchy

Jedediah Purdy teaches law at Duke University and has also taught at Yale and Harvard. Purdy is the author of *For Common Things: Irony, Trust, and Commitment in America Today* and *Being America: Liberty, Commerce, and Violence in an American World*, and has written for *The Atlantic Monthly*, *The New York Times*, *Democracy*, and other publications.

ALSO BY JEDEDIAH PURDY

Being America

For Common Things

A Tolerable Anarchy

A TOLERABLE ANARCHY

*Rebels, Reactionaries, and the
Making of American Freedom*

JEDEDIAH PURDY

Vintage Books
A Division of Random House, Inc.
New York

FIRST VINTAGE BOOKS EDITION, MARCH 2010

Copyright © 2009 by Jedediah Purdy

The Library of Congress has cataloged the Knopf edition as follows:
Purdy, Jedediah.
A tolerable anarchy : rebels, reactionaries, and the making of American freedom /
by Jedediah Purdy.—1st ed.
p. cm.
Includes bibliographical references.
1. Liberty—Political aspects—United States—History. 2. Liberty—Social aspects—United States—History. 3. Liberty—Philosophy. 4. National charac-teristics, American. 5. United States—Politics and government. I. Title.
JC599.U5P87 2009
320.97301—dc22
2008049552

Vintage ISBN: 978-1-4000-9584-1

Book design by Virginia Tan

www.vintagebooks.com

Printed in the United States of America
10 9 8 7 6 5 4 3 2 1

Contents

A Tolerable Anarchy

The Sensations of Freedom

As LONDON'S WINTER ENDED IN 1775, two great minds clashed over the American crisis. Samuel Johnson, the reigning literary lion of the age, labored on a pamphlet titled *Taxation No Tyranny*. It was an ironic and disdainful attack on the American colonists' demands for "liberty." The Americans were rebelling in the name of freedom, and Johnson believed their idea of freedom was incoherent, their vision of politics impossible, their theories the rude blurts of aroused yokels. He called the restive colonials "zealots of anarchy" and sneered at "these lords of themselves, these kings of ME, these demigods of independence." Johnson's was no light judgment. Today we call his lifetime the Age of Johnson, and he is the English language's second-most-quoted author, after Shakespeare. He sat at the center of an Olympian circle, "The Club," which included economist and philosopher Adam Smith, historian Edward Gibbon, and parliamentary leader Charles James Fox. He made and ruined reputations with a word. He meant to give the American doctrine of freedom a career-ending review.

Near the heart of Johnson's circle was Edmund Burke,

the Irish-born political genius and the only living person who put Johnson in awe. Burke had just been reelected to Parliament from Bristol and belonged to the highest echelon of the governing Whig Party. The son of a Catholic mother in a time when Catholics were shut out of politics, Burke lived and acted at the center of British power, but all his life seemed compelled to imagine the lives of power's victims and speak where they could not. Later he would wage a heroic campaign against British abuses in India, once writing to a skeptical correspondent that he would fight the British East India Company "whether the white people like it or not." He dedicated the late winter of 1774–75 to a set of resolutions calling for a rapid and respectful peace with the colonists. Burke delivered the speech introducing the resolutions, now widely called "On Conciliation with America," on March 22, very soon after Johnson's pamphlet appeared. It was a showcase of Burke's powers at their peak. Declaring, "I do not know the method of drawing up an indictment against a whole people," he tried instead to give sympathetic voice to the idea of freedom that had brought the Americans to the brink of revolution. He agreed with Johnson that the Americans' theories were reckless, but their spirit moved him to admiration as well as alarm, and he suspected the future might belong to them.

The battles of Lexington and Concord came less than a month after Burke's speech, Bunker Hill two months after that. In some respects, the winter of 1775 was a moment of tense calm. In others, it was part of a continuing crisis. For more than a decade, England and America had struggled over Parliament's power to regulate and tax North American trade, restrict self-government in the colonies, and

quarter British soldiers in American homes. In 1765, an American boycott brought England's western ports to a deathly standstill and forced repeal of the Stamp Act. In 1773, Samuel Adams staged the act of antitax theater that became known as the Boston Tea Party. The Americans' pronouncements against British rule asserted natural rights in "life, liberty, and property" (not yet the pursuit of happiness), which government could not restrict without the people's "consent." They accused London of "making slaves of us" and claimed a right of rebellion that entitled them to defend their freedom by armed resistance.

Burke and Johnson were both skeptical of the nascent American Revolution, and for the same reasons. Johnson called the Americans' concept of natural rights "wild, indefinite, and obscure," and Burke basically agreed. He thought trying to settle concrete disputes by abstract principles was always dangerous, because ideas such as "liberty" could mean nearly anything, depending on who was interpreting them. (Today, consider the dispute over whether the word *liberty* in the Fourteenth Amendment of the United States Constitution protects rights to abortion and same-sex intimacy.) Similarly, *consent*, as the Americans used it, seemed to mean a right to withdraw from government and law whenever they became inconvenient. It was a general-purpose license for rebellion, indeed a principle for "zealots of anarchy."

Both men also hated slavery, which English law did not recognize and the colonists notoriously practiced. Their hypocrisy brought an exasperated Johnson to ask toward the close of his pamphlet, perhaps thinking of the vociferous Virginians, "Why is it that we hear the loudest yelps for

liberty from the drivers of negroes?" To him it seemed an unanswerable question. The Americans' theories were meaningless. Their practice was the furthest imaginable reach of hypocrisy. Their case wavered between inane and insane. Viewed cynically, it was so much special pleading, with no principle at all. Taken seriously, it was a charter of anarchy, which, as a later English critic wrote of the Declaration of Independence, would "put the axe to the root of all government." Either way, it was not serious politics but self-serving nonsense. The answer it deserved was satire.

Johnson delivered. In his pamphlet, he gleefully imagined the colonists pursuing their anarchic principles into the forested hinterlands of North America, far from any superior power. Somewhere beyond the Allegheny Mountains, a lonely rebel and his dog would collapse near starvation. The man would give some sensible order, which the cur would defiantly refuse, and the pair would congratulate each other on their sublime liberty.

Why did Burke react so differently, with respectful attention, to the American case? He shared Johnson's contempt for the abstract political ideals of natural rights that the Americans called on to justify their rebellion. If anything, he was the stronger enemy of slavery. Moreover, he sympathized with oppressed Catholics—he was, after all, the son of one—and the American rebels were often fanatically anti-Catholic. In October 1774, the Continental Congress denounced Catholicism as a religion that had "disbursed impiety, bigotry, persecution, murder and rebellion through every part of the world."

Burke and Johnson didn't only share enemies; they had much the same vision of the good society. Johnson believed

the great gift that political life gave its members was order. He told James Boswell, "Sir, I am a friend to subordination, as most conducive to the happiness of society. There is a reciprocal pleasure in governing and being governed." Whatever rights men had, they took from the custom of their government, not any natural law: "All government is absolutely and essentially absolute." Burke, too, believed that "the rights of man" could only mean the right to live by the laws and customs of one's own people, not the higher law the Americans called on. Rather than any abstract principle of legitimacy, he held that political society rested on authority and trust: "unsuspecting confidence is the true center of gravity amongst mankind." Living undisturbed in a familiar order was the heart of political freedom.

Yet Burke defended the Americans, with their wild and hypocritical doctrines of freedom. Throughout the war, he privately expressed regret at American defeats and publicly continued to call for peace on favorable terms—so favorable that his opponents claimed they would amount to American independence. He warned the Crown that its soldiers might lose an American war, an idea self-confident Englishmen such as Johnson thought preposterous. As early as August 1775, Burke reacted to the American war in the eerie, prophetic tone that would mark his last great works, writing to his patron, Lord Rockingham, "The Spirit of America is incredible. God knows they are very inferior in all human resources. But in a remote and difficult Country . . . such a Spirit as now animates them may do strange things. Our Victories can only complete our ruin."

The key to the difference between Burke and Johnson was how each man understood the "Spirit" that had brought

the Americans to rebellion. Johnson's attitude was half debating society, half satirical screed. He took on the Americans' principles of consent and inalienable rights and argued that they were philosophically incoherent, "the delirious dream of republican fanaticism." From this he concluded that the colonists were either lunatics, if they meant what they said, or criminals, if they did not. He grouped their British defenders into the same camps, the infatuated and the corrupt.

Burke believed that treating the Americans' principles as theoretical axioms, like parts of an attempted geometric proof, only confused the matter. One who believed—as Burke and Johnson did—that politics was not geometry but the subtle interplay of interest and passion, reason and imagination, should assume that American radicalism had the same ingredients. What, then, was the worldview behind the Americans' wild doctrines? This question was cultural and psychological, not philosophical. In his speech on conciliation, Burke set down this axiom for understanding political cultures: "Abstract liberty, like other abstractions, is not to be found. Liberty inheres in some sensible object; and every nation has formed to itself some favorite point which . . . becomes the criterion of their happiness." The quarry was not explicit ideas but beliefs so basic that they shaped the Americans' vision and experience, creating an implicit map of liberty and tyranny. To understand the Americans, their critics should try to grasp what they envisioned and felt when they spoke of freedom, what the revolutionary John Adams had recently called "the sensations of freedom."

To understand the "sensible object" of the Americans'

political imagination, Burke asked in seriousness what Johnson had in derision: Why did American slaveholders call so loudly for freedom? Instead of a damning paradox, Burke found here a key to the American rebellion. The slaveholders' special passion for freedom was not despite their owning slaves but exactly because they were masters in a slave society. Slavery gave shape and power to the American idea of freedom. Wherever slavery was widespread, Burke insisted, "those who are free are by far the most proud and jealous of rank and privilege." For the freemen of a slaveholding country, freedom was the root of identity and dignity. Freedom gave men's lives value in their own eyes and honor in others'. In the South, Burke argued, "the haughtiness of domination combines with the spirit of freedom, fortifies it, and renders it invincible." Slavery made masters uniquely sensitive to any invasion of their independence: in their minds, answering to another's power smacked of the ultimate and so-familiar debasement of the slave. Freedom meant independence from such power, being the one whose will commanded, not the one who cowered before a willful commander.

Burke found a similar insight in another of the Americans' most vexing qualities, their militant anti-Catholicism. The New England colonies formed an overwhelmingly and radically Protestant society. Burke instructed his fellow parliamentarians that the dissenting churches "have sprung up in direct opposition to all the ordinary powers of the world." The religious spirit of New England intensified that opposition; it was "a refinement on the principle of resistance . . . the dissidence of dissent and the Protestantism of the Protestant religion." Amid their many doctrinal disputes,

the Americans' churches agreed on "the communion of the spirit of liberty." The bigoted and paranoid side of this spirit was John Adams's attack on Catholicism for reducing believers' "minds to a state of sordid ignorance and staring timidity." In this anti-Catholic vision of liberty, priests and kings formed an "infernal confederacy," two faces of a single pattern of oppression over the free mind. The same vision, however, also drove a sensitivity about freedom akin to that of the South. Radical New Englanders guarded their authority of conscience as jealously as white Southerners did the authority of command. Slaveholders insisted on their mastery, sovereignty over a piece of the earth and the men on it, as key to their freedom and the dignity that freedom brought. Radical New Englanders, too, insisted on a kind of sovereignty, the authority of each man's conscience and judgment, which meant he could be governed only by his own consent. Thus John Adams called British encroachment on American self-rule "civil and political slavery."

The image of royal power as slavery was everywhere in the language of the American Revolution. Americans used it to refer to any act of Parliament or the king that changed the settled laws and charters—royally granted constitutions—of the colonies or interfered with such established rights of Englishmen as habeas corpus, jury trial, and the principle that only legitimate representatives could impose taxes. Opponents such as Johnson called the Americans "zealots of anarchy," but what the colonists opposed was not political power as such. Rather, they called "civil slavery" any arrangement in which rulers could (1) act on their own discretion, outside the law; (2) change the law without going through the requisite constitutional channels, or, worse,

change the constitution itself; or (3) interfere with sacrosanct personal rights. As the Americans saw it, the basic condition of a slave was dependence: another man's will was his law. The image of personal freedom that Burke discerned in American ideas was the opposite of slavery: a kind of personal sovereignty, the authority of one's own will and conscience. The Americans' ideal of political freedom, too, meant being immune to arbitrary power and answering to one's own law: rulers must be closely bound by constitutional limits, and legitimate authority ultimately arose from popular consent, at least that of property-holding men.

The Americans' images of freedom drew them at once in curiously opposite directions. On one hand, as Johnson observed, they spoke in what later became the language of the Declaration of Independence, of inalienable rights and political consent. These abstract and radical principles, which potentially threatened all settled government, drew Johnson's accusations of fanaticism, zealotry, and anarchism. The appeal of these ideas is easy to see: natural rights and the power of consent are the armor of a man who can never become a slave in either the personal or the political sense; conversely, they are exactly what a slave can never have. On the other hand, as Burke saw more clearly than Johnson, the Americans' concrete political ideas were deeply conservative. The bill of particulars of the Declaration of Independence, the list of the king's abuses, is as traditional as the opening passages are radical. It draws insistently on precedent from seventeenth-century English struggles between Parliament and the Crown. Here, the Americans tied their vision of liberty to the personal rights and forms of govern-

ment that they inherited from earlier generations of Englishmen. Indeed, even the colonists' decision to ascribe their list of abuses to the king was willful traditionalism: by the 1770s, most interference with colonial privileges came from acts of Parliament, but the familiar language of constitutional complaint asserted the rights of Englishmen against the prerogatives of the king, and the colonists hewed to the custom.

Even when the Americans voiced their "wild" and "obscure" ideas of liberty, then, they were not tradition-shattering fanatics. Instead, they were part of English traditions of personal and political freedom, which had grown more intense on the new continent. The Americans were creating a "sensation of freedom," a vision of personal liberty and political legitimacy, out of inherited elements and new experience. That was why Johnson and others like him went so far wrong when they dismissed the Americans as jejune political theorists, rather than recognize them as members of a nascent tradition, one with both radical and conservative chords. This was the deep thought behind Burke's remark that he did not know how to indict a whole people: to be involved in governing a people, one must understand and engage their idea of legitimate government, their "sensible object" of freedom. Trying to impose British rule otherwise could only inspire more outrage against "tyranny." Hence Burke's prophecy that military victories would prepare Britain's political ruin in North America.

As Burke spent the London winter musing on the American crisis, then, he reinterpreted the Americans' actions, contrary to Johnson and to much of the colonists' own rhetoric, as part of a living tradition with deep English

roots. That is not to say that Burke was sanguine about the Americans' prospects. The colonists' image of freedom was a new and radical thing. Its most explosive element was the doctrine that people were naturally free, formed governments to protect their inborn rights and interests, and could take down and rebuild those governments as they saw fit. It was the heart of Burke's thought, like Johnson's, that freedom was an achievement of culture and government, which had to be tended reverently to keep it vital. Society and government came first, and individual freedom was their finest fruit. By imagining freedom as a natural fact, existing outside and independent of government, the colonists reversed this relationship. They held that humans could envision and create governments that suited the demands of freedom. For Burke, this ambition courted anarchy: a people who have torn down a government may find that their rights are rags, their law in shreds, and that they have no power to re-create what they have destroyed. In this respect, he and Johnson shared the suspicion of other critics that American doctrines would "put the axe to the root of all government."

American success might be no less alarming than failure. Burke found himself forced to consider that the Americans might have discovered new and hazardous truths. He reported in his speech on conciliation that a strange and unsettling thing had happened in Massachusetts. The first British tactic against the rebels was to withdraw the Bay Colony's government, "confident that the first feeling, if not the very prospect of anarchy, would instantly enforce a complete submission." London threatened the Americans with loss of the greatest Burkean right of all, living under settled law. This measure was meant to induce, in the phrase of

another time, shock and awe, followed by obedience and proper gratitude to authority. Instead,

> A new, strange, and unexpected face of things appeared. Anarchy is found tolerable. A vast province has now subsisted, and subsisted in a considerable degree of health and vigor, for near a twelvemonth, without governor, without public council, without judges, without executive magistrates.

This experience shook Burke's premise that people who claimed natural freedom, and tried to remake their governments accordingly, would fall into anarchy:

> Our late experience has taught us, that many of those fundamental principles formerly deemed infallible, are either not of the importance they were imagined to be, or that we have not at all adverted to some other far more important, and far more powerful principles, which entirely overrule those we had considered as important.

The Americans' inadvertent experiment suggested that a people could break away from tradition and authority without destroying social order. Perhaps "anarchy" was not the inevitable graveyard of radical theories of freedom, after all. If so, then it might be possible to remake society along new lines. This seemed to Burke an extremely dangerous idea, one freighted with as much threat as hope. For all his sympathetic defense of the Americans, he offered as a major reason for peace in the colonies that war would only encour-

age more experiments in tolerable anarchy, and "I am much against any further experiments." Burke might have suspected that he could not stem the tide of visionary reform, but he urged his government not to engorge it.

In the eyes of one of their most acute British defenders, then, the Americans were attempting something new, which they likely could only halfway understand, and which would turn out to be either revelatory or ruinous. They were shaping a vision of authority on antinomian premises and a language of legitimacy based on dangerously open-ended ideas of freedom, consent, and legitimate rebellion. They were creating, that is, a tradition out of repudiation and insurrection. There was no knowing in advance whether such unstable materials could form a viable tradition— yet the American experiment had to become that tradition, or fail.

Who was the better prophet, the scornful Johnson or Burke, the Americans' ambivalent defender? The question may seem loaded: American stories are cast in the hindsight of American success, with naysayers set up to lose. But consider the story a skeptic like Johnson might tell. The Civil War, which broke out a lifetime after the United States Constitution came into being, might seem to prove both sides of Johnson's argument that American freedom was a doctrine for either fanatics or criminal hypocrites. On the fanatical side, both abolitionists and secessionists invoked the Declaration of Independence, with its principle of inviolable rights and government by consent. That might seem the strongest possible proof that those principles really were "wild, indefinite, and obscure," stimulants for the imagination more than rules for the intellect. On the hypocritical

side, the Constitution that the newly independent colonists made was such a thoroughgoing compromise with slavery that the Supreme Court in 1856 could pronounce white supremacy a founding principle of the country. Yelps of liberty, indeed.

The case for Johnson does not stop there. Distressed observers of the American misadventure in Iraq might conclude that this country, in the grips of "the delirious dream of republican fanaticism," still trusts in personal freedom and self-government magically to overcome the forces of anarchy. Nor is Iraq the first foreign slaughterhouse of American visions of freedom: a century ago, similar self-trusting promises accompanied the American conquest of the Philippines, which then sank into a bloody civil war and prolonged and costly reconstruction. The visionary arrogance that Johnson saw in the colonists' pronouncements may have claimed more victims abroad than at home.

There are plenty, too, who would say that Johnson's parable of the American and his dog holds today: that we deny one another respect and care while congratulating ourselves on our freedom. For the left, this is the mark of the winner-takes-all, loser-pays American economy, where the unchecked market drives out fairness and compassion and, as one liberal commentator remarked after President George W. Bush vetoed a children's health bill, people are free to die of whatever disease they choose. From the right, the problem lies more in a culture that prizes self-expression above all, makes abortion and same-sex intercourse constitutional rights, and neglects fidelity, integrity, and the other virtues that preserve families and communities.

There is, however, another way to see the issue. Maybe

the power of American freedom arises from the same qualities that inspired Johnson to attack it as hypocrisy on the one hand, anarchism on the other. Start with hypocrisy. The way American colonists lived could not, indeed, be reconciled with the principles they called on to justify their rebellion. A doctrine of universal and inalienable rights could not easily uphold an order of hierarchy and oppression. From the beginning, the American language of freedom gave heart and authority to those who defied the existing order. It made the prophets of a possible America seem more American, sometimes, than the defenders of the country that actually existed.

American revolutionary principles were also, as Johnson charged, a charter of anarchy. Taken seriously, they invited Americans to tear down their inherited orders, throwing open the way to reform or chaos. Some, such as the former slave Frederick Douglass, broadened the principles, demanding that the founders' liberty extend to all. Others, prophets of conscience from Ralph Waldo Emerson onward, deepened that idea of freedom, demanding recognition for personality, imagination, and intimacy. A doctrine first expressed to protect the inherited rights of landed white men contained, from the start, the potential to extend to all and grow into a rich and changing sensation of freedom.

None of this means that the history of American freedom became inevitable when the first slaveholder proclaimed universal liberty. Political orders do not grow, like trees, from patterns encoded in their seeds. But the founding principles gave ironic authority to those whom American society put down and kept out. As early as the first years of independence, blacks unnerved the white majority in

New England by petitioning for political rights, appealing to the principles of the Revolution. Soon after, Massachusetts courts abolished slavery, citing a provision of the state constitution. John Adams was a principal author of that constitution, and the key clause echoed the phrases with which his sometime friend Thomas Jefferson had opened the Declaration: "All men are born free and equal, and have certain natural, essential, and unalienable rights; among which may be reckoned the right of enjoying and defending their lives and liberties; that of acquiring, possessing, and protecting property; in fine, that of seeking and obtaining their safety and happiness." When Haitian slaves rose in revolt in 1791 and expelled their French masters, they issued a declaration of independence modeled on the American document.

It was not despite but because of its flaws, its fanaticism and hypocrisy, that the American sensation of freedom grew to anchor the tradition that Burke uncertainly foresaw. Because the Declaration of Independence was absurdly remote from the practices of its author and many of its signatories, because its theory of government threatened perennial revolution, it became the touchstone of a constitutional tradition of freedom, called on by slaves, women, racial minorities, and gay people to redeem their dignity as Americans. This half-broken legacy enabled Abraham Lincoln, Martin Luther King Jr., and millions of others to remake a tradition of hierarchy as one of equal dignity. If the Americans had succeeded as political philosophers and satisfied Johnson, they would never have created the living tradition that Burke glimpsed in its infancy.

This book is an account of that tradition, how it has

grown, and where it stands today. It is part scholarship, part narrative, and an attempt throughout to make sense of one strand of American tradition. That may seem too ambitious. Today the American creed is one of individuality and diversity, much of our search for meaning is private, and the dominance of economics over politics is almost an article of faith. Does an "American tradition," especially one grounded in politics, have much to offer now? Yes. Indeed, we can understand these antipolitical and antitraditional features of American life only by seeing how they arose from the very tradition whose beginning Burke and Johnson debated. We are more individual, fragmented, private, and self-involved than ever, but that is not a refutation of shared experience. It is our latest defining paradox, in which the drive to uniqueness and authenticity is what we have in common. We are now a country defined by the widest scope of individual ambition, the greatest freedom for the play of personality, and the vastest potential for disappointment and loneliness. We all remain, to different degrees and in various ways, deeply involved in the American sensation of freedom that Johnson denounced and Burke labored to understand. It shapes us, giving form to our pursuits of dignity and meaning, and we shape it in those pursuits. That is the condition in which we make sense of life in a nation of halfway strangers, who are both driven by the impulse to freedom and also hungry for a vision of national community that speaks to us as we are and does not neglect who we hope to become.

The tradition that this book traces begins in the "spirit" that Burke warned might do strange things in a faraway land, the way of insisting on oneself that anchored the

American sensation of freedom. This sensation began in the deep belief that freedom meant the opposite of slavery and was no mere convenience but the basis of identity and honor. It held a special sensitivity to any intimation of domination or dependence, insisting on each man's free judgment and mastery of his own life. This sensitivity bridged personal and political freedom, coloring many forms of government power as "civil and political slavery." Of course, American attitudes today are not in any simple way the consequences of the colonists' revolutionary ideas; but the tradition in which we learn to be ourselves, in which we find our measures of dignity and our visions of community, has grown from those ideas and bears their shape.

As Samuel Johnson insisted, a national community built on the freedom of all its members is no simple thing. We have already seen, briefly, that the very incoherence and excess of the American idea of freedom contributed to the vitality of the tradition it shaped. Yet freedom's grip on American imagination also imparts problems and confusions. American visions of nationhood and citizenship have sometimes been heroic and inspired, particularly when at grips with the legacies of slavery and other oppression. But Americans have also struggled, with special difficulty and often disappointing results, to create an idea of the country that can encompass the paradox of freedom-seeking people in a complex and interdependent world. We seek mastery of our own lives and find ourselves thwarted by the impersonal forces of economics, limited education or opportunity, or whatever else stands in the way of self-authorship. To overcome these barriers, we would first have to acknowledge

them; but acknowledging them seems to jeopardize the keystone of personal dignity, the power to shape one's own life free of dependence and domination. Much of political life in the last century has been a struggle with this paradox: it has, at best, produced only partial resolution. Dedication to our sensation of freedom can draw people into the crippling American myth that we have limitless power to change our private lives, none to change our politics and economics. Because politics and economics shape and constrain private lives, the myth often leaves us unable to change either.

The vision of free conscience, too, produces its confusions. On one hand, it has become the ideal of authenticity, which has driven revolutions in personality, sexuality, and constitutional law. Being true to oneself, a radical Romantic ideal with roots in the arch-Protestant "communion of the spirit of liberty" that Burke described, is now a touchstone of dignity and close to the American definition of personal freedom. On the other hand, being true to oneself can mean not looking beyond oneself, falling into solipsism that is often as banal and derivative as it is self-impressed. For some, the model of this failing is the supreme self-trust of George W. Bush, a president reportedly swaddled in an echo chamber of his own instincts and prejudices, the "gut" in which he places unswerving faith. For others, the exemplary solipsist is the rebel consumer whose up-to-date purchases show his uniqueness, just like that of everyone else in his marketing demographic, or the self-seeker whose quest for happiness leads him into trivial but self-important dalliances, and who neglects lasting commitments or never forms them in the first place. Whatever the preferred exam-

ple, it is hard not to wonder whether the spirit of conscience that Burke called "the dissidence of dissent" has arrived at the end of history as full-blown narcissism.

For all that, the tradition this book describes has always been an attempt to take a radical idea of freedom seriously and to ask how people who feel called to it—as many of us do—can live up to it and live together in dignity with others who feel the same. It has also been a series of efforts to make that ideal real. This book aims to understand those efforts and ask where they might go now.

This ideal begins in belief that the demand for dignity is deep and permanent. Dignity includes being recognized for who we are and being able to follow the precious demands of conscience and the purpose we sense in our lives. When we make this sensation of freedom the center of our lives, insisting on it against all denial and constraint, we may tear down parts of the social lives we share and give up parts of who we have believed ourselves to be and how others have known us. Here is the most radical element of faith in the American sensation of freedom: belief in something we cannot know—that our demands for dignity and individuality are not charters of anarchy, but the first signs of new forms of order. This is a faith that each act of rebellion and repudiation opens the way to fuller versions of ourselves and the country: that more choice and deeper individuality can be the roots of stronger bonds and a greater nation, if we have the discernment to find the way and the courage to follow it through.

Calling on a tradition is always, also, a way of creating it. Nowhere is this more so than among Americans. It is nearly true, today, that in this country there is no such thing as a

mandatory identity, nothing a person has to be by virtue of where or how she was born: religion, ethnicity, sexuality, sex itself, the meaning of race if not the sometimes brutal social fact of it, are compounds of what we are born into and what we decide. In the phrase of one observer, we choose our inheritances. Our foremost inheritance, perhaps, is the choosing itself: the many ways we have learned to move in the subtle middle ground between fixed custom and arbitrary will. Because this book is no exception to any of this, it is not an attempt to tell any reader what being American must mean for him or her. It is, though, a try at casting light on common, important, and difficult parts of the American experience, past and present. It will succeed if it gives readers ways to understand both their inheritance and their choices.

CHAPTER I

Declarations of
Independence

FOURTEEN MONTHS after Burke and Johnson
clashed, the Declaration of Independence seemed to
confirm Johnson's bleak estimate of the Americans.
The Declaration asserted natural rights in their vaguest
and strongest form: life, liberty, and that wide-open phrase,
the pursuit of happiness. The colonists used these indefinite
and "unalienable" principles to justify a right of rebellion as
open war took hold between American subjects and their
faraway rulers. Surely this was the "republican fanaticism"
and "anarchy" that Johnson detected in the colonists' earlier
pronouncements.

The Americans' hypocrisy was also on display. After
proclaiming human equality and the right to resist tyrannical force, they listed this among the king's offenses: "He has
excited domestic insurrections among us." That is, the
British government had promised freedom to slaves who
abandoned their masters and staked their loyalty to London. It was one degree of hypocrisy for slaveholders to
talk of liberty, another for them to base their theory of liberty on universal human equality, and still a third to claim

that the king's freeing their slaves breached their inviolable freedom. And what was their rebellion, after all, other than a "domestic insurrection"? For that matter, the Americans' anti-Catholic bigotry also carried forward into the Declaration, as they complained that London's toleration of Catholics in Quebec violated British constitutional principles and laid the groundwork for "arbitrary . . . absolute rule."

If Johnson had penned a satirical declaration of American rights, crafted to illustrate his case against the colonists, his text would not have departed far from Thomas Jefferson's. Yet the Declaration, for all its extraordinary flaws, became an anchor of the tradition Burke foresaw, an inheritance of repudiation and rebellion, which took force from its anarchic impulses and form from its hypocritical compromises. This was, of course, no automatic evolution but a political achievement. It depended on Americans' honoring their past, but only on condition that it become a better future. Later generations made their own declarations of independence, breaking with a flawed present and, in those breaks, broadening and deepening the American vision of freedom.

Slave Revolt as Constitutional Interpretation

IN 1852, Frederick Douglass addressed an Independence Day gathering in Rochester, New York. A powerfully built man in his midthirties, Douglass was a famous opponent of slavery. His eloquence and intensity had already put a scar on the world, and they seemed to stir whoever met him. He had spent two years lecturing in Britain and Ireland, founded and run an abolitionist paper, the *North Star*, and

published a successful short autobiography. His celebrity had grown large enough that, a year earlier, when he merged the *North Star* with another abolitionist journal, the editors named their new broadsheet *Frederick Douglass' Paper*. Douglass met Lincoln during the Civil War, and a few weeks after the president's assassination, Mary Todd Lincoln wrote to Douglass, "[M]y husband considered you a special friend."

Fourteen years earlier, Douglass had been property, the human chattel of a Marylander named Thomas Auld. He escaped, fleeing to New York City in 1838. An earlier escape attempt had failed. Around age sixteen, Douglass was sent to the plantation of Edward Covey, known for his skill at breaking the spirit of rebellious slaves. Douglass ran to the woods but returned after a miserable night spent shivering in the cold damp. Even reaching New York after his successful flight assured the runaway of nothing. The Constitution was as reverent toward property as the Declaration of Independence was extravagant about freedom. It obliged the courts and governments of Free States to return escaped slaves, and they did, sometimes over the resistance of abolitionist mobs. Douglass was not legally free until 1847, when British abolitionists paid Auld his value, buying their budding ally to release him.

The irony of inviting the former slave to mark the anniversary of a slaveholding country was lost on no one, least of all Douglass. He asked his listeners, "What have I, or those I represent, to do with your national independence?" He answered his own question: "This Fourth of July is yours, not mine." Independence Day celebrations mocked him, he said, revealing that "for revolting barbarity and

shameless hypocrisy, America reigns without a rival." From the point of view of a slave, "your celebration is a sham; your boasted liberty an unholy license." What the country needed was not praise but "scorching irony . . . biting ridicule" and "the storm, the whirlwind, and the earthquake."

The Rochester abolitionists knew just what they were getting when they invited Frederick Douglass to lecture. Though his personal history and muscular language gave special power to the performance, Douglass's vituperation sounded familiar abolitionist themes. As early as 1829, William Lloyd Garrison, a pioneering American abolitionist and later a mentor to Douglass, had said much the same in his own July 4 address. When other Americans praised the Declaration, Garrison declared, "I am ashamed of my country. I am sick of our unmeaning declamation in praise of liberty and equality; of our hypocritical cant about the unalienable rights of man." Garrison saw the American constitutional order as complicit in a crime against humanity, famously denouncing the Constitution as "a covenant with death and an agreement with hell." He urged his followers not even to vote, the better to protect their consciences from a corrupt system. Douglass's attacks on American hypocrisy were in this tradition.

Douglass's July Fourth speech, however, took a turn that would have been heresy to his mentor, the purist Garrison. Hypocrisy could be damning, or it could be hopeful proof that the country had not yet taken its final shape. Alongside his conventional denunciations, Douglass praised the Declaration, calling it "the ring-bolt," the anchor, of "your yet undeveloped destiny." Its sweeping claims for liberty, equal-

ity, and rebellion "are all saving principles" that the country could still live up to. On this basis, Douglass made an outrageous claim: the Constitution, "interpreted as it ought to be interpreted . . . is a glorious liberty document" with no space for slavery. This was the same Constitution that would have obliged New York to return the escaped Douglass to Maryland until his British associates bought his freedom. When Douglass was a slave, it counted him as three-fifths of a person in setting the size of Maryland's congressional delegation, a principle meant to ensure the political power of the slave states. The Constitution forbade Congress to block the import of new slaves until 1808, about twenty years after its adoption. And it protected ownership of property, a legal status Douglass had recently occupied. The Constitution fairly pulsated with slavery. About all the abolitionist lawyers had to go on was that its authors never used the word, substituting euphemisms such as "importation of persons," "person held to service or labour," and "three fifths of all other persons." Reading it as a document untouched by slavery was like concluding that Godot has no part in Samuel Beckett's most famous play because he never appears.

Douglass seized on the document's silence, not to argue that it simply outlawed slavery, but to show how it might come to have that meaning. Like some other constitutionalists, Douglass expanded the sources of interpretation beyond the document of 1787 to include the Declaration. Just as important, he expanded the community of interpreters to include each new generation of citizens, not just courts and scholars. "I hold," said Douglass, "that every American citizen has a right to form an opinion of the con-

stitution . . . and to use all honorable means to make his opinion the prevailing one." The best way to understand the Constitution, in Douglass's vision, was in the spirit of the Declaration. His highest praise of the founders was for declining to give a final answer to the question of slavery, instead naming broad principles that later generations could use in shaping the eventual resolution: "With them," Douglass told the Rochester abolitionists, "nothing was 'settled' that was not right. With them, justice, liberty, and humanity were 'final,' not slavery and oppression."

Douglass's version of constitutionalism confronted American injustice by asking the country not to surrender itself but to become itself. Both he and Garrison demanded the same justice: abolition of slavery and establishment of equal citizenship. But Douglass, for all his anger, did not treat abolitionism as the antithesis of the Constitution, Garrison's "covenant with death and . . . agreement with hell." Instead, he offered it as a way to reinterpret the Constitution to make good on the Declaration's promise.

Douglass had every reason to reject the past, throw out the Constitution along with all its compromises with slavery, and call for a *new* birth of freedom based on the natural rights of men. That path was clear: Garrison and others had laid it out. Douglass was certainly angry enough to take it. Instead, with his anger and intelligence, he reinterpreted the past in a way that made it not just the prelude to the present but a prophecy of a different future. Why?

A contrast is helpful here. Douglass's way of understanding the Declaration and the Constitution was nearly opposite that of the chief justice of the United States, Roger Brooke Taney. Four years after Douglass's Rochester address,

Taney wrote an opinion in *Dred Scott v. Sandford*, one the most notorious decisions in American law, that seemed to annul each of Douglass's sources of hope. *Dred Scott* declared what Douglass had denied: that slavery was a settled part of the constitutional order. The Supreme Court ruled that slave masters kept their rights to their slaves even when they traveled to Free States and that the Constitution forbade Congress from outlawing slavery in western territories. Taney went further, arguing that white supremacy was a constitutional principle. Free blacks could not become citizens of the United States, according to Taney, because at the time of the founding they were "regarded as beings of an inferior order, and altogether unfit to associate with the white race, either in social or political relations; and so far inferior, that they had no rights which the white man was bound to respect." Showing a keen eye for the working of caste, Taney named two examples of colonial laws that degraded blacks: bans on racial intermarriage and criminal laws setting special penalties for blacks who struck whites.

Douglass declared the Constitution an antislavery document. The Supreme Court ruled the opposite. Douglass insisted that ordinary citizens could interpret the Constitution. Taney held that the Constitution's role was to settle certain questions permanently, making the racism of the founding generation binding on everyone after. Douglass found his source of hope, the Constitution's "ring-bolt," in the Declaration. Taney's answer was relentless. True, he conceded, Jefferson had written "all men are created equal." But when a slaveholder wrote those words, a reader could make sense of the contradiction in only one of two ways. Either Jefferson meant "all white men," or he and the other

slave owners who signed the Declaration were hypocrites. And it was unacceptable to imagine them as hypocrites: "[T]he men who framed this declaration were great men— high in literary acquirements—high in their sense of honor, and incapable of asserting principles inconsistent with those on which they were acting."

On its face, this was praise of Jefferson and his allies. But the praise was a trap. It made moral imbeciles of the founders by denying that they could have held any principle higher than those that they themselves lived by in their most disappointing moments. More important, it treated living Americans as constitutional serfs, bound by the limits of earlier generations. Principles of equality that Jefferson and others had failed to make real, their descendants would now be prohibited from pursuing. Taney wrote, with exaggerated regret, that these prohibitions were the price of a constitution, which secured political order by erecting permanent principles. That was how a country achieved integrity and stability.

Douglass believed the opposite: integrity was a quality Americans might achieve by repudiating some of their principles—slavery, white supremacy—and deepening others, such as liberty and equality. Maybe he could understand repudiation as a national ideal because it had been near the heart of his own experience. In a memoir published in 1858, Douglass recalled being sent to Edward Covey's plantation, where severe treatment was expected to break the young slave's rebellious will. When Douglass's flight into the woods led nowhere, he slunk back to his quarters knowing he could expect a whipping. On the next workday (his master declined to beat slaves on the Sabbath), Covey

approached Douglass with a horsewhip. As Douglass told the story, they fought for two hours, he drew the white man's blood, and the whip never touched him. Other slaves died for less defiance, and their masters were seldom punished. For whatever reason, Douglass's resistance had a different result. Covey never mentioned the incident and never tried to touch Douglass again.

Douglass called his fight with Covey "the turning point of my life as a slave," second in importance only to his later escape from slavery. He explained his choice to resist as an act of self-preservation, even though it put his life at risk. His wish for freedom had become intolerable in the humiliation and helplessness of slave life. If he had not asserted that wish against Covey, it would have gone extinct. The story expressed Douglass's idea of the kind of integrity that freedom required: not custom, obedience, or even simple consistency, but willingness to insist on what seemed overwhelmingly right, especially in defending oneself. Assuming that a larger coherence would grow out of that concentrated, sometimes desperate point of resistance was an act of faith. It resembled the choice of slaveholders to sign a document that others denounced as a charter of anarchy, pledging to it their lives and fortune "and our sacred honor." It took the thing many of them most feared, a rebel slave, to understand that wildest part of their spirit, extended to everyone, as a permanent part of American freedom.

"Our soul-destroying slavery to habit"

EIGHTEEN THIRTY-EIGHT, the year Frederick Douglass escaped to New York City, brought an unusually cold

and dreary summer across much of the Northern Hemisphere. London shivered under unseasonable fog and a killing frost destroyed Scottish crops in August. In New England, temperatures were even farther below normal. Yet on July 15, Ralph Waldo Emerson, who was not always an optimist about the world as he found it, opened his address to the graduating class at Harvard Divinity School with extravagant praise of the summer weather. In that season, the young minister told the graduates, just to breathe was a luxury. "The grass grows, the buds burst, the meadow is spotted with fire and gold in the tint of flowers." By day the sound of birds mingled with the scent of hay, and darkness was a cleansing, gentle movement, like bathing in a cool river. The world yielded corn and wine, proof that it existed to comfort men, and for men to master.

But the perfection of nature paled beside a different perfection that Emerson had come to foretell, a spiritual perfection as harmonious as a mild New England summer. As the world was made to feed and house human beings, the mind was formed to love virtue and goodness, to be moved by them and to find beauty in them. When men saw goodness clearly and served it out of love, Emerson said, "then is the end of the creation answered, and God is well pleased." The image of Creation completed by divine love and human faith was conventional so far, but Emerson aimed at something more radical. In traditional Christianity, sin deformed humans and sundered them from God, and only the sacrifice of Christ restored the relationship, enabling sinners to rejoin the lost communion. In a world of sin, the human heart was bent and stunted by pride and lust. As Saint Paul had cried out in dismay, man unaided would do the things

he hated and could not do the things he loved. Saint Augustine put it more exactly four hundred years later, explaining that the sinful heart loved, but loved confusedly, seeking rest and completion in a flawed and fleeting world that could never give back the perfection the heart sought: sin was misplaced love, love guided by the restless, needy heart instead of God.

Emerson taught a different lesson. Strictly speaking, he offered his listeners heresy. The heart was perfect, if only we would listen to it, not to custom or tradition or the demands of others. "If a man is at heart just, then in so far is he God," Emerson declared, and by listening to his heart, "a man is made the Providence to himself." A just heart, moreover, was not a heart of laws or principles but one in tune with its own love. The heart's spontaneous voice was all the God men could know: "That which shows God in me, fortifies me. That which shows God out of me, makes me a wart and a wen. . . . Only by coming again to themselves, or to God in themselves, can [people] grow forevermore." The only sin that Emerson acknowledged was failure to listen to the heart: deafness or indifference to one's own true voice was the source of all sin. Because churches, creeds, and divinity schools housed custom and ritual, they came between a man and his divine heart. Redemption required leaving them behind. Emerson declared before a class of freshly trained ministers

In the soul . . . let the redemption be sought. Wherever a man comes, there comes revolution. *The old is for slaves.* When a man comes, all books are legible,

all things transparent, all religions are forms. He is religious. Man is the wonderworker.

There would still be Christianity, Emerson wrote, but it must be returned to what he called its truth: "a faith like Christ's in the infinitude of man." If only we could be true to ourselves, we would be divine to one another, and truth, beauty, and desire would be one. Conformity, laziness, and cowardice stood in the way of this humanist trinity. What we had to overcome to achieve it was "our soul-destroying slavery to habit."

Happiness as Truth, and Other Heresies

OLIVER WENDELL HOLMES SR., father of the great jurist and a major figure in his own right, called Emerson the author of "our intellectual Declaration of Independence" from Europe and custom. Emerson, for his part, seemed to regard the Declaration much as he did churches and stories of the life of Jesus: as enervating vessels for a spirit that each person had to encounter directly or not at all. He wrote scornfully, "[N]othing is more disgusting than the crowing about liberty by slaves, as most men are, and the flippant mistaking for freedom of some paper preamble like a 'Declaration of Independence,' or the statute right to vote, by those who have never dared to think or to act." Emerson praised resistance to all earthly dogma, all fixed conclusions, for these were impediments to insight and experience: principles could become deadly if allowed to suffocate living feeling.

Emerson, the descendant of generations of ministers, intensified the sovereignty of personal conscience as Douglass expanded the demand for honor and standing among others. Emerson voiced a radical and secular version of what Burke had ascribed to New Englanders, the dissidents' "refinement on the principle of resistance." What John Adams called the "staring timidity" of feudalism and Catholicism, Emerson found in the conventional religion and social conformity of the recently independent United States. Critics had warned that an "unalienable" right to liberty, if taken seriously, would dissolve all the laws that kept men from one another's throats. The Americans, then, could not mean the fine phrases they used because, taken seriously, they would mean anarchy. Here, though, was an American who seemed to mean just that, who said that conscience was the only law, not a conscience of guilt or reproach, but one lit up with love and delight.

The phrase in the Declaration of Independence closest to Emerson's spirit is also the most slippery and open-ended—and, as it happens, the one that has stuck most prominently in the American mind. It is the last in the triad of unalienable rights: life, liberty, and *the pursuit of happiness*. That word, as used in the Declaration, is a miniature of several centuries of changing ideas about the human situation. *Happiness* is an Anglo-Saxon word closely related to *happenstance, perhaps,* and *happen,* as in "I just happened to be here today." Its roots lie in fortune, serendipity, and random chance. A happy man was a lucky man, one whom fortune smiled on, a man with good breaks. Happiness as good fortune, however, was not something one pursued. One might propitiate the Fates, crossing one's fingers and

knocking on wood. But *pursuit* would have been wrong. The old sense of happiness bespoke human helplessness in a world governed by powers beyond our control—not least, the power of social and political superiors.

In the seventeenth and, especially, the eighteenth centuries, *happiness* took on a different meaning: well-being, even flourishing, which people could aim at and achieve. This was the happiness that moral philosopher Francis Hutcheson, an early luminary of the Scottish Enlightenment, had in mind when he identified the purpose of society as producing "the greatest happiness of the greatest number." The difference becomes clear if you imagine the absurdity of proposing "random good luck for everyone" as a social program. The new idea of happiness asserted a new image of human beings as active creators of the world they inhabited. The idea of pursuing happiness now made sense.

"The pursuit of happiness" also suggested a specific understanding of what the unalienable right of liberty might mean. The happiness that Emerson praised is an experience in the body and mind, a sense of satisfaction, well-being, and capability. We know what makes us happy only by the circular measure of our own happiness. Every discovery establishes, and changes, the nature of the happiness we are seeking. Guaranteeing the pursuit of happiness thus means protecting an ongoing, open-ended exploration of oneself and one's own experience. This search has no pre-set shape, and there is no saying just where it will end up. In this respect, it is very much an Emersonian idea. Indeed, unlike some severe intellectuals, Emerson almost always used *happiness* as a term of high praise, a sign of the heart's personal encounter with truth.

Such a version of happiness, though, becomes so intensely individual that Hutcheson's formula, the "greatest happiness of the greatest number," can no longer rest on it. A happiness that belongs to irreducibly individual experience cannot be added up alongside all other irreducibly individual experience. As Emerson wrote on this point, "[A]ll loves and friendships are momentary. Do you love me? means, Do you see the same truth? If you do, we are happy with the same happiness: but presently one of us passes into the perception of new truth; we are divorced, and no tension in nature can hold us to each other." Emerson's insistence on the truths of the individual heart could seem to dissolve all human bonds except those based on spiritual overlap, with no mercy to ties of family, country, or previous love. The self that Emerson prophesied might be sovereign and majestic in its own experience, but it could also seem vagrant and wayward in relation to the lives of others.

Emerson, then, could stand as evidence either that American freedom was even greater than its founders could understand or that it was self-immolating. On the side of greatness, Emerson's motto "Trust thyself" crystallizes the insistence on personal authenticity that is near the heart of today's ideal of freedom. Accept no compromise with a world that schemes to make you untrue to yourself, to trick you into a false word, a lying smile, work undertaken without passion, reading and writing without inspiration, or companionship without love. Tyranny is whatever draws you away from your true self and occludes the clarity of your judgments and the immediacy of your experience, whether it is called monarchy, democracy, abolitionism, marriage, or your job. Emerson's phrases from the Divinity School

Address echo today in millions of children's defiance of their parents, in spouses' decisions to divorce, and in choices to come out of the closet: "I must be myself. I cannot break myself any longer for you, or you. If you can love me for what I am, we shall be the happier." Emerson saw the promise of democracy in his vision of "a nation of men" all following this creed, which would be the world's first free country by his new measure of freedom. He also saw that ideal as the standard that would judge American democracy: if Americans failed to be true to themselves, the country would be just a richer, faster-paced, and grubbier successor to all earlier spiritual tyrannies.

We Americans today are Emersonians when we seek fulfillment in work and love, when we ask ourselves what we really feel, when we find our way through a conversation by the intuition that some words feel true and others would sell us out if we spoke them. Our therapeutic culture aims less at the manageable depression that Freud made the goal for his fin de siècle Viennese patients and more at an Emersonian clarity about who we are and what it will take to make us more fully ourselves—a clarity that can bring Emersonian rapture when we catch a note of it. Constitutional law took an Emersonian turn—not its first—in 2003 when the Supreme Court ruled that laws banning sodomy "demean the existence" of citizens whose intimacy was a way of working out the "meaning of their lives and the mystery of the universe"—problems, the Court implied, not for doctrine or custom but for unbound personal exploration. Even many American evangelicals are Emersonians in their emphasis on feeling, sincerity, and the guiding power of a pure heart. As much as any idea can be, this is not a set of propositions

but a way of meeting one's own life, understanding eagerness and delight not as symptoms or sins but as signs pointing toward a personal truth.

Declarations of Independence

DOUGLASS AND EMERSON amplified the same spirit that infuriated Samuel Johnson and left Edmund Burke divided: insistence on one's own rights, integrity, and conscience against all received authority. Douglass's declaration made real a nightmare of the founding generation: slave revolt, a "domestic insurrection" on their own principles of liberty. Emerson fulfilled the prophecy of the Americans' critics: he asserted the boundless prerogative of a conscience that withheld its consent from whatever custom offended it. Both men's acts redefined the principles of the American founding, giving its promise of freedom larger scope and richer meaning. They showed that the first rebellion reached further than those who made it imagined.

Each of these declarations turns a privilege into a right, an indulgence from a superior into an inherent power of human beings. In defiance, a slave's dignity ceases being the master's plaything and becomes the boundary where the master's abuse must stop. As Douglass wrote to his former owner on the tenth anniversary of his escape, "In leaving you, I took nothing but what belonged to me." For Emerson, an American's conscience was not the product of moral instruction by neighbors and churches but the inner compass that judged these, and this alone imparted its authority. Each declaration says, in effect, "Freedom—in politics, in conscience, in my own body—was never yours to give me.

It was always mine, and it still is. My freedom is not the gift of your power, but the standard I will use to judge your power."

Each declaration carries the potential to destroy the order it challenges, and perhaps even to shake the basis of all order. The original Declaration asserted a people's power to resist and replace their government, which is what brought the charge of anarchism against the colonists. Douglass condemned a class of property and the economic order that rested on it. What he called freedom, the law and the Constitution regarded as theft. Emerson set his conscience against all contrary custom and teaching. Warned that his heart's voice might be sinful, not virtuous, he replied, "If I am the devil's child, I will live then from the devil. No law can be sacred to me but that of my nature." Each declaration in its own way threatened "an axe to the root of all government."

Each declaration also contains something generous and constructive, the beginning of a new kind of order. The act of rebellion begins in self-certainty. The American colonists had no doubt that the king had violated their rights; Douglass and Emerson were sure that they had to resist or die an inner death. As Douglass observed at Rochester, "There is not a man beneath the canopy of heaven, that does not know that slavery is wrong *for him*." But—just as Douglass meant to show—identifying with the part of oneself that resists oppression implies identifying with that part of every person. It is possible, of course, to keep the impulse selfish and the principle solipsistic but integrity and the very impulse of rebellion press the other way. It would have been unthinkable for Douglass, having reached his truth as he did, to join some free blacks in holding slaves of his own.

His rebellion also implied supporting equality for women: he was one of a handful of men to sign a Declaration of Sentiments extending the original Declaration's demands to American women, and the motto of the *North Star* began "Right is of no sex." Emerson, for all his antinomianism, did not aim at solitude. He hoped to clear the way for new versions of friendship and love, based not on obligation but on the heart's desire. Both men found in the American history of rebellion, with all its parochialism, hypocrisy, and selfishness, an impulse toward broadening and deepening personal freedom into a new form of community, which was theirs to claim and extend.

CHAPTER 2

The Search for Civic Dignity

ABRAHAM LINCOLN's reflections on the meaning of the Civil War rightly belong to the American canon. His call in the Gettysburg Address for "a new birth of freedom" and in his second inaugural to "bind up the . . . wounds" of the war express the two ideals that animated him through this time: justice and reconciliation. Another speech is scarcely remembered, but it, too, might deserve a place. Thirteen days after his second inaugural and less than a month before his assassination, Lincoln addressed the 140th Indiana Regiment in Washington, D.C. It was a brief talk, probably impromptu, and, unlike the other two, funny. The transcript reports eruptions of laughter and applause among the soldiers.

The 140th was made up mostly of farmers, like many volunteer regiments. Its soldiers had fought their way through Tennessee and North Carolina, ending in garrison duty in Washington. Lincoln spoke not just plainly, as he usually did in his late addresses, but casually, seemingly aware of addressing listeners who could once have been his neighbors. He described a desperate Confederate effort to enlist slaves as soldiers. Seizing on the irony of ordering

men to fight for their own enslavement, he remarked, "I have in my lifetime heard many arguments why the negroes ought to be slaves; but if they fight for those who would keep them in slavery it will be a better argument than any I have yet heard." The Indianans laughed and applauded. Lincoln continued, "He who would fight for that ought to be a slave." More applause. Lincoln was condemning slavery, but he was also playing on the prejudice of whites who might have enjoyed suspecting that blacks were just stupid and subservient enough to take orders from Confederate commanders. This was, after all, the same president who had denied favoring social equality between the races and noted that, even if he believed otherwise, national attitudes would forbid integration.

Having found a vein, he seemed to continue in it: "While I have often said that all men ought to be free, yet I would allow those colored persons to be slaves who want to be." Then Lincoln veered in a new and unexpected direction—"and next to them those white persons who argue in favor of making other people slaves." Applause. "I am in favor of giving an opportunity to such white men to try it on for themselves." The soldiers cheered.

Lincoln's rhetorical brilliance was connected with a temperamental inability to make things easy for his audiences. When he was in his mature voice, he spoke simply but unsettlingly. His second inaugural address, like every other presidential inaugural in history, invoked God; unlike any other, it refused to assert that divinity was on the nation's side. In his speech to the 140th, rather than simply praise his listeners and play a little on their racial attitudes, he

addressed the question that the war's end presented, the same that had divided Frederick Douglass from Justice Roger Brooke Taney: Who now was an American? A white man? No. A freeman? But all were now free, or about to be. What, then, did it mean to be American? Perhaps it would help to ask who was not an American. A slave had always been, in some way, the opposite of an American. That opposition was the key to the sensation of freedom that powered the colonists' revolt. Taney had insisted on this in his racist interpretation of the Constitution. Douglass, too, had relied on it when he denied that the Fourth of July belonged to slaves, calling it "your celebration."

Lincoln proposed that the only American who deserved to be a slave was one who believed that others deserved it. That was a dark but funny ironist's way of saying that to be American meant believing that no one deserved slavery and that this principle would henceforward be the American premise. It was not, however, so much a solution as the statement of a problem. How, after all the blood, should we look at one another? What could be the dignity of membership in a community not founded on anyone's exclusion or degradation? How would Americans achieve honor without rank?

Presidents, Citizens, and the Common Good

WOODROW WILSON turned to the same question in his first inaugural address, in 1913, offering a vision of common life for twentieth-century America. He offered "to interpret the occasion" of his inauguration and argued that the Dem-

ocratic victory was important not for the sake of the party but because "the Nation . . . now seeks to use the Democratic Party . . . to interpret a change in its own plans and point of view." This imagery added something new and essential to the president's role. Earlier presidents had cast themselves foremost as bearers of constitutional principle, not wholly unlike the justices of the Supreme Court. Wilson's new description was more romantic and visionary. The president was to propose a coherent aim and attitude for the diverse forces that had swept him to power. He was now a kind of democratic oracle, tasked with giving voice to the people's collective power to redefine their political life. Wilson said the election had brought "a new insight into our own life . . . a vision . . . of our life as a whole," and called the challenge of the time "whether we be able to understand our time and the need of our people, whether we be indeed their spokesmen and interpreters."

In some respects, Wilson was offering a new role for the presidency. He would soon break the tradition, established by Thomas Jefferson, of presenting the State of the Union report to Congress in writing rather than delivering it in person. Speaking in person was especially important because Wilson was the first post–Civil War president to transcend the nineteenth-century system of political parties: although he won office as a Democrat, he established himself as an independent voice, directly addressing the American people. With this change, Wilson set in motion the central dynamic of twentieth-century American politics: the unique role of the president as spokesperson and emblematic personality of the American nation. Later, radio

carried Franklin Roosevelt's voice into kitchens and living rooms, and television became inextricable from John F. Kennedy's appeal, but Wilson first achieved the change in presidential role that others would perfect.

In other ways, however, Wilson only updated a perennial role of presidential language, which Lincoln, too, had caught in midstream: connecting the national community with the meaning and purpose of citizens' lives. Certain questions are permanent in a modern political order. How, if at all, does citizenship contribute to personal dignity and meaning? How tightly does the country bind all Americans to a common destiny? Is American life today closer to the mythic community of purpose sometimes evoked in accounts of the founding generation, and later in Lincoln's vision of freedom at the end of the Civil War, or to a nation of strangers bound by happenstance and mutual convenience? In what ways do all Americans count equally just for showing up, and in what ways are some more equal than others?

As Burke said of abstract liberty, abstract answers to these questions are secondary. Their foundation in political life is a "sensible object," a vision of the dignity and purpose of American life, and of the part that citizenship plays in making these real. Because it works on the level of identity, such a vision of politics goes beyond the very important and useful things that government may provide, such as schools, hospitals, and highways. It also goes beyond so-called public goods that only government can secure, such as national defense and environmental protection. An idea of common good is not about what you get but about who you are, the

part of your identity that comes from being American. (It may imply that being American means getting certain things, but it does not begin from that question.)

An idea of the common good, then, addresses basic needs that are harder to measure than physical and financial security but just as real. One is dignity, the feeling that you matter and command the respect of others, not just because of what you do or own, but because of who you are. Another is recognition, the sensation that you are not a stranger in your world but, instead, it is made to house people like you, and you are made for it. Connectedness, being tied to others rather than isolated, and purpose, contact with a larger meaning that helps to orient your life, fill out this set of needs. The sum of these needs is having a place to stand in the world and a sense of the worth and importance of your life. Hardly anyone satisfies those needs mostly through citizenship, and our individualistic idea of freedom makes the demands of national community light enough that no one should have to. Nonetheless, what it means to be American is part of how most of us make sense of our lives. Perhaps more important, political decisions shape the world in which we satisfy these needs or find them thwarted, and those decisions, in turn, both draw on and shape visions of citizenship and the nation.

American visions of common good express a struggle to join the sensation of personal freedom to a compelling image of citizenship and national community. These visions have grown and changed with the rise of a complex national and international economy, the massive growth of government, and the eclipse of traditional civic life by consumer culture. Here, too, Wilson's first inaugural marked a turning

point. His was the first presidential vision of citizenship to begin from an industrial society and a national economy. He turned from old images of Americans as self-reliant pioneers and entrepreneurs to a new acknowledgment that personal fate depended on vast and impersonal forces, which could willy-nilly crush or elevate a vulnerable individual. His was a vision of Americans with vulnerable bodies as well as masterful wills, thrown into a world they had not chosen and could neither control nor entirely understand, for whom the Industrial Revolution, despite all the new powers and wealth it brought, had re-created some of the dependence of slavery. Wilson's was also a vision that included some of the Americans for whom the old ideal of mastery had always been false. Tellingly, his was the first inaugural address to include women and children, as well as grown men, in its portrait of Americans. This picture of the nation formed the basis of a new role for government as the one power strong enough to master vast social and economic forces and create a country in which vulnerable individuals could achieve meaningful freedom. Defining an idea of civic dignity and common good for this changed world remained a major task of presidential language for nearly seventy years. In some ways, it remains the challenge of today's public language.

The Tepid Consensus

IN OTHER WAYS, we live in the wreckage of Wilson's project. Recent presidential language shows ideas of civic dignity and common good in quiet crisis. Rather than explain how belonging to the nation might add to dignity

and freedom, the last three presidents have mostly given up this aim. For twenty years, since the election of George H. W. Bush in 1988, the main themes of American political language have not been political at all. Instead, they have concentrated on personal virtue, the qualities that uphold families, workplaces, and civic organizations. Although this kind of presidential talk has deep historical roots, it is new in important ways. Its central ideas—character, responsibility, and service—have never before figured so prominently or in such intensely nonpolitical ways as they do now.

The major landmarks in this consensus, the two inaugural addresses apiece of Bill Clinton and George W. Bush, took place in decades of intense political animosity. Partisans on both sides learned to disdain the other party's president as a moral or intellectual degenerate and suspect his strong supporters of being not fully American—or, maybe, the wrong kind of American. While there is nothing to the often-heard conceit that the country has recently been uniquely divided, dislike and resentment have been fierce. But imagine you were to read both presidents' addresses as a visitor from another century, unfamiliar with local partisan cues such as Republicans' propensity to praise charter schools and Democrats' silence born of their debt to teachers' unions. You would notice a difference of degree in religious language: God figures in the critical moments of Clinton's speeches but appears throughout Bush's. Otherwise, you would probably get the impression of a culture of profound moral consensus, where the same terms and ideas anchor both parties' rhetoric. You might also suspect that

you had come across a political culture whose members have no clear idea of the purpose of their political life.

Responsibility is a keystone word for both Clinton and Bush. Clinton in his first inaugural defined "what America does best: offer more opportunity to all and demand more responsibility from all." It was time, he said, "to break the bad habit of expecting something for nothing, from our government or from each other," and time to "all take more responsibility, not only for ourselves and our families but for our communities and our country." Four years later, he announced that "we need a new sense of responsibility for a new century" and, again, that "every one of us, in our own way, must assume personal responsibility, not only for ourselves and our families, but for our neighbors and our nation." George W. Bush dedicated his 2000 nomination address to the theme of responsibility, urging a "responsibility era," and in his first inaugural he called America "at its best . . . a place where personal responsibility is valued and expected." He celebrated responsibility as "a call to conscience" that, although "it requires sacrifice," brings us into "the fullness of life not only in options but in commitments."

Service, too, is central in both presidents' language. In his first inaugural, Clinton "challenge[d] a new generation of young Americans to a season of service," called "serving" the key to the "simple but powerful truth [that] we need each other," and declared, "From this joyful mountaintop of celebration, we hear a call to service in the valley." In 2001, explaining that "[w]hat you do is as important as anything government does," Bush urged citizens "to serve your

nation, beginning with your neighbor" and "build communities of service and a nation of character."

Character is another defining word in this lexicon. In an alliterative catalog of personal virtues, Bush in 2001 called for "a new commitment to live out our nation's promise through civility, courage, compassion and character." Four years later, he explained

> In America's ideal of freedom, the public interest depends on private character—on integrity, and tolerance toward others, and the rule of conscience in our own lives. Self-government relies, in the end, on the governing of the self. That edifice of character is built in families, supported by communities with standards, and sustained in our national life by the truths of Sinai, the Sermon on the Mount, the words of the Koran, and the varied faiths of our people.

Clinton did not rely in the same way on the word *character,* but he did declare in 1997, "The greatest progress we have made, and the greatest progress we have yet to make, is in the human heart. In the end, all the world's wealth and a thousand armies are no match for the strength and decency of the human spirit."

This constellation of virtues is essentially about people's ineradicable ties to others. Interdependence is the key moral insight for both presidents and unites their language across partisan differences. While Clinton announced the "simple but powerful truth [that] we need each other [a]nd we must care for one another," Bush explained "the exercise of rights is ennobled by service" because "liberty for all does not mean

independence from one another." In keeping with that emphasis, this political language also leans heavily on *community* and *communities,* not as mere descriptions but as moral terms for groups of people who recognize their responsibility of service to one another. Character, similarly, is not a description of good, bad, or merely quirky personality but a moral word for the qualities of responsibility and service that make community possible.

Of course these virtues matter. Failures of character, responsibility, and service can be terrible: abandoned children, broken promises, places neglected or despoiled. Without social virtue, moreover, government could not be both free and effective: it takes good faith—a willingness not to cheat on taxes, steal when the chance arises, litter and pollute profligately, and so forth—to keep up good order without constant incursion on private life. But these truths do not form a vision of political community. They are a thin substitute for it, a confection of undeniable facts about human beings in general that says little about the dignity and responsibility of American citizenship in particular.

This political language is something new. To be sure, George Washington held that a country's political institutions depend ultimately on the virtue of its people, but for roughly the first two centuries of American independence, political language concentrated on specifically political qualities. *Character* was a description of personality or outlook, not a moral term, and *virtue,* its obvious cognate, tended to mean such political virtues as love of liberty and respect for rule of law. *Responsibility* and *service* overwhelmingly referred to the duties of public office. The language of sacrifice and dedication, famously associated with John F.

Kennedy's inaugural call to "ask what you can do for your country," was reserved for wartime and the geopolitical struggle of the Cold War, which was how both Kennedy and Dwight Eisenhower used it. (Kennedy's famous sentence was a bridge in a series of exhortations to advance the cause of American freedom around the world.) Even Lincoln's Gettysburg Address is a call not for sacrifice—the melancholy and humane president was out of appetite for that, if he ever had any—but for political hope in sacrifice's aftermath. *Community* was a neutral noun rather than a moral concept; it designated communities of interest, political jurisdictions, and the international community of civilized nations.

Private virtue began to occupy the center of political language only with Richard Nixon. Nixon's were the first inaugural addresses to use *responsibility* in its private sense. He argued in 1969 that national greatness rested above all on "those small, splendid efforts that make headlines in the neighborhood newspaper instead of the national journal." Pressing the theme further in 1973, he urged the country to turn away from "attempting to gather all power and responsibility in Washington. Instead, he insisted, "A person can be expected to act responsibly only if he has responsibility. . . . Let us locate responsibility in more places. Let us measure what we will do for others by what they will do for themselves. . . . Let us remember that America was built not by government, but by people—not by welfare, but by work—not by shirking responsibility, but by seeking responsibility." These passages form a kind of bridge between the old, political register of virtue and the new, private register.

The way Nixon introduced the theme is a second key to understanding today's political language. Private virtue, particularly "responsibility," was the counterpoint to Washington and "government." Responsibility filled the void that opened up when the ambitions of government receded. It was a major theme of both Nixon's inaugurals, especially his second, that Americans had asked too much of government and not enough of one another and themselves. Characteristically, Nixon managed to sound small spirited as he self-consciously echoed Kennedy: "[L]et each of us ask—not just what will government do for me, but what can I do for myself?" Nonetheless, he pioneered a formula that pervades today's political speech. Bill Clinton's language of service and responsibility was a way of working out the idea, shared with Nixon, that, while government was not the source of all problems, "government is not the solution. We, the American people, we are the solution." These virtues answered the need for "work to do, work that government alone cannot do" and, again, formed a counterpoint to "the bad habit of expecting something for nothing, from our government or from each other." Indeed, Clinton's insistence on the limits of government was louder than George W. Bush's, perhaps because he was pressing against the stereotype of the big-government liberal, while Bush did not labor under that shadow. In Bush's speeches, it was not necessary to contrast private virtue with statist overreach, because dreams of ambitious domestic government were so clearly finished as anchors for political language. The divorce of civic identity from government, which Nixon set in motion, is nearly complete in Bush's speeches. (Bush's language is, of course,

self-consciously that of wartime. This is the topic of the next chapter.)

In connecting public life to personal meaning and purpose, recent presidential language relies almost entirely on a vision of private and social virtues. In this vision, personal connection works outward through affection and interdependence, from family to church, friendship, and other concrete forms of moral community. Government, in this image, is the thing that went away and cleared the space now filled by private virtue. The only political quality in this speech is that the speaker occupies the country's most powerful and visible political office. The president addresses people as moral and social beings, but not as citizens, unless *citizen* means simply a person who is aware of interdependence and takes it seriously.

When intense partisan hostility coexists with rhetorical agreement about the moral vision of politics, that may show that political language is exhausted. This is the more so when political speech portrays political acts and values as inferior to personal ones. Americans have recently felt that the best and highest goods in life come through family, friendship, spiritual development, and the rest of personal experience. We have tended not to believe that something is ennobled because it is touched by state power or a partisan movement, preferring our values concrete, present in our own experience and in people that we can see and touch and name. For twenty years, political language has answered to this attitude and tutored us in it.

This apolitical political language is unusual in history. Its key terms are new, at least in the ways they are now used, and its distance from distinctly political questions is singu-

lar. How did it come to define so much of our political imagination? The answer involves the whole story of American political language. It begins in early efforts to define a vision of the nation and the dignity of citizens. It continues in the major theme of the twentieth century: the attempt to create an image of civic dignity that could flourish in the complex economy and expanded government of the twentieth century. As we shall see, Ronald Reagan achieved one of his greatest imaginative triumphs by repudiating that effort. We have thus been living in the remnants of a collapsed rhetorical tradition. Our intensely personal language of political community, composed in the absence of political vision, is what the collapse left us.

Freedom and Dignity in Nineteenth-Century America

IN HIS FIRST INAUGURAL, Thomas Jefferson described Americans as "possessing a chosen country, with room enough for our descendants to the thousandth and thousandth generation." By *chosen* he meant not that the country was divinely ordained but that Americans had chosen their country by coming to North America and creating a nation through revolution and constitutional politics. They had conquered, occupied, and shaped a continent of plenty, where westward expansion would create prosperous and self-governing communities deep into the future. There would be no need for the hierarchy and dependence of feudal orders, where men, crowded together in old countries, rested their wealth and freedom on the abjection of others. Nor would Americans suffer the chaos and predation of cities, those crucibles of dependence and exploitation. The

chosen country was ample, and every American could have a life worth living there.

In the country Jefferson envisioned, the role of government was modest and clearly defined. "[A] wise and frugal government," he explained, "shall restrain men from injuring one another, shall leave them otherwise free to regulate their own pursuits of industry and improvement, and shall not take from the mouth of labor the bread it has earned. This is the sum of good government." Jefferson portrayed a government of what some would later call negative liberty, securing citizens from violence and theft and otherwise leaving them free to order their own lives. His embrace of negative liberty, though, arose from a vision of the positive powers of individuals engaged in "industry and improvement" to "regulate their own pursuits" without impeding one another's freedom and to make a good living by their labor. This version of negative liberty begins not in abstract principles but in a picture of the lives of Americans on a rich continent.

Jefferson's "essential principles" of American constitutionalism had the same spirit: "Equal and exact justice to all men," regular elections and majority rule, "economy in the public expense, that labor may be lightly burdened . . . encouragement of agriculture, and of commerce as its handmaid; the diffusion of information and arraignment of all abuses at the bar of the public reason; freedom of religion; freedom of the press, and freedom of person under the protection of the habeas corpus, and trial by juries impartially selected." These principles, Jefferson held, "guided our steps through an age of revolution and reformation" and "should be the creed of our political faith, the text of civic instruc-

tion, the touchstone by which to try the services of those we trust." These were to be the principles of legitimate American government. Deviation from them would be a sign of overreaching power. They were principles for a nation of the upright and strong, people able to take advantage of economic opportunity and apply reason, judgment, and energy to give their lives the shapes they wanted. The dignity of such Americans lay in their powers of free action and self-mastery. Threats to their freedom came mainly from government itself: censorship of opinion, excessive taxation, improper arrest and prosecution, or failure to administer "equal and exact justice."

Being this kind of American was the main source of personal dignity in the political community—a community that honored each (white, male, property-holding) citizen as master of his own life, standing foursquare with all others. This was an important part of what Jefferson and others meant when they called the United States *republican*. A second meaning of "republican," and another source of citizen dignity, was found in the idea that each American had an equal part in forming the sovereignty of the United States, the body of political power. The idea that power flowed from the whole political community to the government, which held it in "trust," was central to American political language in the nineteenth century. American rhetoricians contrasted this republican image of sovereignty with the monarchical vision of political power as descending from the king. So Franklin Pierce held that any American citizen could "stand unabashed even in the presence of princes, with a proud consciousness that he is himself one of a nation of sovereigns." Defending the principle of universal

male suffrage even for uneducated former slaves, James Garfield put the contrast more starkly: "If in other lands it is high treason to compass the death of the king, it shall be counted no less a crime here to strangle our sovereign power and stifle its voice." In this image, the least able and most scorned citizen had the same sovereign dignity as European royalty. In other respects—including political practice—the racist and recently slaveholding United States would enforce hierarchy among its people, but in the republican vision of sovereignty, each citizen contributed to the shape of the nation.

These ideas—particularly the image of self-mastery—governed nineteenth-century American political language. They had profound affinities with the social vision that became the unofficial ideology of the northern states before the Civil War and, in the war's aftermath, formed the centerpiece of American identity. This was the idea of free labor: that American freedom rested on the power to choose and pursue a career, acquire property, and trade one's time and talent for whatever pay they could command. This ideal of self-mastery was linked to a vision of social mobility, in which nearly everyone—following Jefferson's picture of life in a plentiful and chosen country—could end up as a prosperous property holder. Emerson sketched an archetypal free-labor biography in his essay "Self-Reliance," where he praised the "sturdy lad from New Hampshire or Vermont, who in turn tries all the professions, who teams it, farms it, peddles, keeps a school, preaches, edits a newspaper, goes to Congress, buys a township, and so forth, in successive years." It is impossible to miss either the ideal of self-mastery in this sketch, one of the most concrete pas-

sages in a long paean to "self-trust," or the expectation of plenty: a township waiting for a purchaser.

This ideal carried a demanding, sometimes merciless counterpart: those who fail must deserve it. The large-hearted Abraham Lincoln, in the course of defending free labor as a principle of equal dignity for democratic citizens, paused to assert, "If any continue through life in the condition of the hired laborer [rather than become a proprietor], it is not the fault of the system, but because of either a dependent nature which prefers it, or improvidence, folly, or singular misfortune." American dignity implied overwhelming responsibility, even culpability: if you could not pull off success, then failure was all yours.

The Failure of Free Labor and the Progressive Search for Dignity

THERE WAS ALWAYS a big element of myth in the world-view of free labor. But there was also plentiful opportunity in a continent opened for settlement in a time when land was the source of most wealth. That continent, however, changed in the nineteenth century. The Industrial Revolution moved production from farms and workshops, which laborers could hope to acquire for themselves, to factories, which they could not. The national economy overwhelmed local markets and produced semimonopolist trusts, which regulated their industries in their own favor. In face of these new facts, free-labor thought came to seem more complacent than hopeful and dignifying. The most notorious expression of this decrepit period is the Supreme Court's

opinion in *Lochner v. New York*, striking down a labor law
that set maximum weekly hours for bakers because such
regulation violated workers' freedom to contract for whatever terms they liked. If followed consistently, that principle
would have forbidden workers and other less wealthy
groups from using politics to change the balance of economic power. Indeed at the end of the nineteenth century,
Grover Cleveland denounced such political efforts as
"paternalism . . . the bane of republican institutions." Paternalism, he insisted, "perverts the patriotic sentiments of our
countrymen and tempts them to pitiful calculation of . . .
sordid gains. It undermines the self-reliance of our people
and substitutes in its place dependence upon governmental
favoritism. It . . . stupefies every ennobling trait of American
citizenship. . . . While the people should patriotically and
cheerfully support their Government its functions do not
include the support of the people."

When a president could denounce minimum-wage and
maximum-hours laws as threats to American dignity, equat-
ing a sometimes brutal industrial economy with Jefferson's
open frontier, free labor thought was close to exhaustion.
Whatever the experience of earlier generations had actually
been, workers, farmers, and small businessmen began to feel
that they were not masters of their own destinies but play-
things of complex systems that they could only partly
understand, let alone control. These changing realities inter-
acted with changing ideas to challenge the individualism of
free labor. A generation of elites studied economics and politics at German universities and returned with images of a
nation as an organic whole, like a living body, in which the
national spirit or character must be deeply entwined with

political and economic institutions. They tended to deplore the political economy of free labor as illusory atomism, a false image of society as an assembly of "sovereigns" rather than the complex organism they believed it really was.

Teddy Roosevelt and Woodrow Wilson were the first presidents to reject free-labor language. Deeply influenced by the Progressive movement, they believed that government must be strong enough to control private economic power in the interest of the vulnerable. In a critical respect, their vision of the nation was nearly opposite the image of self-mastery that had animated free labor. Instead, they portrayed Americans as vulnerable to vast economic and social forces that only government could discipline. The failure that Lincoln attributed to "dependent character" or "singular misfortune" was now the ordinary possibility that haunted everyone. What Cleveland had denounced as debasing "paternalism," Wilson made the moral justification of government. With ideas such as Cleveland's in his sights, Wilson in 1913 lamented that the country had not "studied and perfected the means by which government may be put at the service of humanity, in safeguarding the health of the Nation, the health of its men and its women and its children, as well as their rights in the struggle for existence." Wilson replaced the negative liberty of free labor with an almost parental duty for the state to provide succor to its needy and fragile people. He continued, "There can be no equality of opportunity, the first essential of justice in the body politic, if men and women and children be not shielded in their lives, their very vitality, from the consequences of great industrial and social processes which they cannot alter, control, or singly cope with."

This was new language in two ways. As mentioned earlier, it was the first appearance of women and children in an inaugural address. That change expanded the circle of citizens whom the president addressed beyond adult men to include the whole social body. Wilson's address was also the first portrayal of Americans in the terms the Progressives had pioneered: as limited in their powers of self-mastery and small before large "industrial and social processes" that could overpower them without the state's protection. Wilson replaced an image of the citizen as a man who mastered his own fate with a picture of human beings of all sexes and ages who were often mastered by the impersonal Fates of a complex economy. Such imagery persisted through much of the twentieth century. In 1937, Franklin Roosevelt proposed this purpose for government: "to solve for the individual the ever-rising problems of a complex civilization," problems that "without the aid of government had left us baffled and bewildered," the victims of "blind economic forces and blindly selfish men." Almost thirty years later, Lyndon Johnson cautioned that the American ideal, "a place where each man could be proud of himself . . . rejoicing in his work, important in the life of his neighbors and his nation," had "become more difficult in a world where change and growth seem to tower beyond the control and even the judgment of men." The world was too much with us, and perhaps too much for us.

The change brought a problem. How could the new description of the vulnerable individual watched over by a powerful state sustain a vision of personal dignity? Having set aside the mythic imagery of free labor, what did Progressives offer in its place?

Franklin Roosevelt and Civilian Honor

ADDRESSING SAN FRANCISCO'S Commonwealth Club in 1932, Franklin Roosevelt offered a version of personal dignity that did not repudiate the old free-labor idea but instead adapted it to the new era. Rather than present the expansive Progressive state as the antithesis of self-reliant individualism, Roosevelt described his government as the only power that could secure those old values in new times. He began by identifying two perennial American rights, the first free conscience and judgment, the second protection of property. Free conscience, he claimed, was unchanged since the time of Jefferson, whom Roosevelt invoked as his model. Property rights, however, had changed in the industrial era. The point of property rights, Roosevelt said, was to enjoy personal security: assurance against starvation, sickness, and old age, and a place to stand in the world. In the industrial twentieth century, that security was not as simple as it had (allegedly) been on the frontier. Roosevelt called "the highly centralized economic system . . . the despot of the twentieth century, on whom great masses of individuals relied for their safety and their livelihood, and whose irresponsibility and greed (if it were not controlled) would reduce them to starvation and penury." Once, political tyranny, feudal privilege, and enslavement had denied men security. Firm property rights had helped to protect them from these abuses. Now a complex economy—paradoxically, an achievement built out of firm property rights, especially those of the owners of capital—fostered insecurity. The solution was to create new sources of economic security and opportunity. According to Roosevelt, this was not an anti-individualist

position: it was only a way of doing for industrial-era self-reliance what simpler economic arrangements had achieved in an agrarian age. Americans needed "a more permanently safe order of things . . . not to hamper individualism, but to protect it."

Of course, Roosevelt's image of modern, state-supported self-reliance as a simple extension of timeless American values was unabashed mythmaking. Little about these values was timeless. Emerson and other Romantics had transformed the meaning of free conscience, making it a far more personal, intimate idea than even the freethinking Jefferson would have envisaged. Douglass, Lincoln, and the triumph of free labor had made self-mastery a universal ideal (for men, anyway), but it had begun as a doctrine for masters, rooted in domination over others. In telling his story of American rights, Roosevelt set out to do what Emerson and Douglass had done, if with somewhat less personal heroism: change the meaning of the American legacy to take in a new image of freedom.

Lyndon Johnson later deepened Roosevelt's idea by finding heroic Emersonian individualism in ordinary lives. Describing his "Great Society," he evoked a world of ceaseless self-discovery and self-creation, declaring in 1965, "I do not believe that the Great Society is the ordered, changeless, and sterile battalion of the ants. It is the excitement of becoming—always becoming, trying, probing, falling, resting, and trying again—but always trying and always gaining." Johnson was echoing FDR, who had described the founding spirit of the United States as the power to begin the world again in one's own life. Roosevelt had called this urge the engine of democracy throughout history. Johnson

developed this idea by defining the Great Society as a humanist paradise, "where leisure is a welcome chance to rebuild and reflect, not a feared cause of boredom and restlessness . . . where the city of man serves not only the needs of the body and the demands of commerce, but the desire for beauty and the hunger for community." He imagined a country without poverty or racial injustice but also one "where the meaning of our lives matches the marvelous products of our labor." He linked the goals of security and comfort to an Emersonian enterprise: developing new versions, extensions, and variations of oneself, not as passive enjoyment but as active exploration and creation.

Language Lost

THESE VERSIONS of political language were attempts to locate personal dignity within national community and to define the role of government in a complex economy. Roosevelt, Johnson, and others tried to avoid the shadow that haunted Wilson's first inaugural and the whole Progressive view of society: the image of women and men as flotsam on the seas of economic change, passive objects of the state's solicitude, lacking the mastery that had always been the heart of American dignity.

It was naturally tempting to reject this awkward and experimental language in favor of familiar ideas: that men and women were innately the masters of their own lives, government power was usually a threat to mastery, and there was no need for a new way to put together personal dignity with citizenship. As we saw earlier, these ideas reentered the center of political language with Richard Nixon's presi-

dency. Nixon was in many respects part of the midcentury consensus that modern life required a powerful government, a consensus that united Democrats such as Harry Truman and Republicans such as Dwight Eisenhower. Nixon, however, had to address attacks on government from the New Right of Barry Goldwater and the anti-integration populism of George C. Wallace. He was also a man with a finely developed sense of resentment, able to register the ways that others felt hemmed in and disrespected—as he did himself, even as president—and begin translating those into political language. This blend of political strategy and personal temperament set him up to open several rhetorical paths. Nixon first brought to presidential language the theme that the most important values are private and personal—in contrast to government, not enabled by it as Johnson proposed. Nixon set out the idea that government should be a slightly shamed moral underling of private life. Turning around Kennedy's famous exhortation, asking instead what people could do for themselves, he captured the feeling that government was taking too much from honest citizens, giving too many rewards to the undeserving, and preening too proudly the whole time.

Nixon's language was stammering and inconsistent, shifting from midcentury pieties about the necessity of government to resentment-laden slashes at paternalism. Ronald Reagan brought force and clarity to these themes, reasserting the nineteenth-century idea of civic dignity and rejecting outright the Progressive vision of government and society. Reagan also reacted to Jimmy Carter's failed attempt to give the country a new idea of itself. Carter followed the new conservatives of the 1960s in arguing that

government had overreached important limits, and he set in motion some practical moves away from regulation that Reagan would accelerate. To the Democratic Party's staunch liberals, he looked like a candidate of the right. His belief that government had limits, however, was of a piece with his traditional Southern Christianity, quick to see sin, pride, and folly in any self-assured act. He offered an image of a humbled country. In an exemplary passage in 1977, he said,

> We have learned that "more" is not necessarily "better," that even our great nation has its recognized limits, and that we can neither answer all questions nor solve all problems. We cannot afford to do everything, nor can we afford to lack boldness as we meet the future. So, together, in a spirit of individual sacrifice for the common good, we must simply do our best.

While "boldness" was in the paragraph, it was swaddled in negation upon negation—"nor can we afford to lack." Carter's emphasis was on what the country could not be, could not afford, could not permit itself. To "simply do our best" is a more limited, less self-assured thing than to do our best. Amid newfound limits, "individual sacrifice" had a grim cast without much uplift. When Carter said, "We have already found a high degree of personal liberty, and we are now struggling to enhance equality of opportunity," the "already" hinted at enough, if not too much, and "found," so much weaker than "achieved," suggested limited feeling for the personal liberty that was so important to the

American experience of dignity. "[I]f we despise our own government," he said, "we have no future"; the phrase might have left a listener unsure whether we did have a future, after all.

The born-again Carter offered limits and constraint as cornerstones of American identity. Puritan ministers and their descendants would have recognized the call to self-abasement as a form of moral instruction for creatures whose wish to do and be all things was a symptom of sinful pride. In the great tradition of the political sermon, stretching back to the early colonies of New England, such humbling reunited the covenantal community with its moral purposes and its members with one another. Carter, however, addressed a people deeply shaped by ideas of self-mastery and authenticity, without the religious consensus that supported the old-school sermon. He was left with mandatory uplift, which was weighted down fatally by the ballast of his pessimistic and reproachful words. He spoke from a tradition that had grown alien to the public language and sentiments of the United States.

In his first inaugural, Reagan rejected both Carter's chastened tone and the larger twentieth-century idea that a modern vision of freedom required a strong government. Referring to recession and rising deficits (which would grow much greater under his administration), he declared, "In this present crisis, government is not the solution to our problem." He went on to a direct assault on Progressive premises: "From time to time, we have been tempted to believe that society has become too complex to be managed by self-rule, that government by an elite group is superior to government for, by, and of the people." Presidents from

Wilson to Carter had mostly accepted that complex, impersonal systems outstripped individual will and understanding. This was nonsense, Reagan answered: common sense and free choice could grasp and master the social world as well as ever. People might feel overwhelmed by powers greater than they, but Reagan could explain that experience: "[O]ur present troubles parallel and are proportionate to the intervention and intrusion in our lives that result from unnecessary and excessive growth of government." What held people back, cast them aside, and failed to show due respect for their values and hopes was government itself, which Reagan would tame. Reclaiming lost mastery only required getting government out of the way. This was a brilliant recasting of the presidential role that Wilson and Franklin Roosevelt had pioneered: Reagan remained the master interpreter of American experience, but he would turn his office against the expanded government that they pioneered.

This picture cleared space for Reagan to reassert old images of individual freedom and dignity without the twentieth-century burden of complexity. He fiercely repudiated Carter and all the prophets of diminution before him. "It is time for us to realize," he said, "that we are too great a nation to limit ourselves to small dreams." Instead, "We have every right to dream heroic dreams." Reagan volunteered to be the vessel of a newly expansive imagination: "Your dreams, your hopes, your goals are going to be the dreams, the hopes, and the goals of this administration, so help me God." An administration with dreams first among its attributes! This was something new—but also not so new. Franklin Roosevelt had governed with Emersonian

buoyancy, a merry confidence in the nation's powers and future. Lyndon Johnson had evoked the spirit of individual exploration and self-invention, made possible by the generous provision and social engineering of the Great Society. Reagan gave voice to the same vital faith that the world exists to make our wishes real. He left out only the idea that this condition is a complex and partly political achievement in an always-changing world. Instead, he called that magical condition an American birthright. Reagan's first inaugural address was a rhetorical Iwo Jima, reclaiming American innocence by force.

By 1985 the reclamation was complete. Reagan portrayed the twentieth century as marked by capitulation to government, which went hand in hand with failing self-confidence and will. The end of that decline came in 1980, when "we knew it was time to renew our faith, to strive with all our strength toward the ultimate in individual freedom consistent with an orderly society." That meant—contrary to Carter and seventy years of political language before him—that "there are no limits to growth and human progress when men and women are free to follow their dreams." Citizenship required "our willingness to believe in ourselves and to believe in our capacity to perform great deeds . . . why shouldn't we believe that? We are Americans." Self-trust was our duty and our privilege.

In the twenty years since Reagan finished his second term, our politics has lived mainly in the landscape he created. It has been nearly impossible to speak of a special role for government, let alone link it to personal dignity and freedom. Since Carter, describing limits or loss of mastery has been thought to be political poison. Bill Clinton

attempted some of Roosevelt's political optimism in his first inaugural, calling on the country to embrace change and adapt to the new challenges of globalization—an implicitly political task. After his party's crushing defeat in 1994, he returned, chastened, to the images of personal and social virtue that he shared with George W. Bush. This language is a kind of proto-politics, a recognition that Reagan's endlessly hopeful individuals exist in communities and families—which Reagan himself glimpsed with praise of "compassion" in both inaugurals. The vision of interdependence that it conjures up, however, has no space for the more complex dependence that ties personal fates to institutions and the sweeping trends of economic life—the original rationale of twentieth-century government. As a matter of politics, our political language has been a socialized, rhetorically humane version of nineteenth-century individualism. The president, as interpreter in chief, has reminded us of the virtues we are charged to maintain.

CHAPTER 3

War and Its Equivalents

ONE OF THE BEST PIECES ever in *The Onion*, the satirical newspaper whose articles make up a parallel history of the last two decades, appeared just after September 11, 2001. It opened, "Feeling helpless in the wake of the horrible September 11 terrorist attacks that killed thousands, Christine Pearson baked a cake and decorated it like an American flag Monday." True to form, the article is lightly ironic as it traces the fictional Topeka legal secretary's rummage through her kitchen cabinets in a frenzy of distress and media saturation. It concludes, though, with a middle-American version of the "Yes" at the end of James Joyce's *Ulysses* as Pearson presents the confection to her neighbors:

"I baked a cake," said Pearson, shrugging her shoulders and forcing a smile as she unveiled the dessert in the Overstreet household later that evening. "I made it into a flag."

Pearson and the Overstreets stared at the cake in silence for nearly a minute, until Cassie hugged Pearson.

"It's beautiful," Cassie said. "The cake is beautiful."

good for a country that is much more diverse and, in some ways, equal than any previous America. The New Deal, the greatest American political experiment in social solidarity, addressed a national community with white-supremacist struts. Roosevelt held his indispensable congressional majority only through concessions to Southern Democrats who refused to have their system of racial caste dismantled. He went as far as declining to support an anti-lynching law, a shameful capitulation to the ugliest and most lawless form of American violence. The part of the Great Society that we remember—the War on Poverty—had real failings, but it was also broken on racial resentment, precisely because Lyndon Johnson would not limit its reach along the racial lines that Roosevelt accepted. Decades of growing tolerance and openness have made the country a much better one but have also made us more nearly a country of strangers. The equality of tolerance is not that far from indifference, and very far from the equality of opportunity that LBJ envisioned. As political scientist Robert Putnam has recently argued, there is no reason to deny in principle that diversity and solidarity can coexist; that said, we have not found a convincing register for their coexistence in American politics.

Finally, a language of common good would have to contend with the enrichment of private life. The search for a fuller life is under way everywhere but in government: it is the personal utopianism of yoga and Pilates studios, mega-churches and living rooms, pharmaceutical labs and psychotherapy clinics, and the editorial offices of *Dwell* and *Saveur*—the hundreds of thousands of places where billions of dollars and hours drive the unending search for meaning

and satisfaction. Americans have always been amateur specialists in self-transformation, but the practice has never been more elaborate, mainstream, or sorted into lifestyle-compatible market segments. If there was a hint of unique adventure and transformative possibility in the politics of past generations, it is harder to find now, partly by contrast with the multifarious growth of possibility elsewhere in life.

At least some of a language that worked might extend Roosevelt's and Johnson's images of citizens whose free personal activity is enabled by shared institutions. Such language might begin with the paradox of American individualism—a new version of what Progressive critics of free labor described a century ago. On one hand, we experience ourselves as vessels of infinite possibility, and we have more tools and techniques to make that possibility real than anyone else in history. We feel correspondingly entitled to make good on at least a generous portion of what we might become, and disappointed and wronged if we find we cannot. On the other hand, we are not much less buffeted by economic and institutional fate than earlier Americans. Tens of millions lack the basic security of health insurance. Globalization, the decline of private-sector unions, and new corporate models all make unemployment an ordinary interruption for the fortunate and a long-term threat for the unlucky. It is fashionable to praise the flexibility and self-revision that these changes necessitate, and there is some basis for the praise; but "reinventing" yourself is much more fun when you choose the occasion than when circumstances pick you out for reinvention. The Progressive criticism of laissez-faire began in the clash between the ideal of self-mastery and the reality that people were vulnerable to

impersonal forces whose dictates could feel as arbitrary as the Greek Fates and that, like those iconic powers, made a mockery of human will. The world has changed since 1905: we are much richer, and real deprivation is less likely. Nonetheless, the psychic whiplash that strikes when our vast sense of possibility meets unyielding constraint is as acute as ever. A competent, innovative government might pick up this problem—which it is fair to describe as the politics of the American dream—where Johnson set it down when the Great Society yielded to bureaucratic overreach, racial anger, and a war the country was coming to hate, which the president did not know how to end. There is more on this possibility in later chapters on the economy of freedom.

War and Its Equivalents

MAYBE, THOUGH, there needs to be more. In an 1895 Harvard commencement address, Oliver Wendell Holmes Jr., the Civil War veteran and future Supreme Court justice, attacked the Progressive concern with personal security and comfort as spiritually insufficient. Holmes and some of his contemporaries might have predicted the developments described in the previous chapter: the failure of Progressive politics to sustain an idea of common good and the retreat of public values into personal virtue. For them, the lives that Progressives tried to make possible for all citizens could not sustain the idea of citizenship itself. Citizenship, as a status and source of dignity, relied on an idea of civic honor. Honor was a quality of soldiers, not homemakers, and there was no way to save it in a world of safe private lives. "War is out of

fashion," Holmes complained to the listening Harvard graduates, and he derided the "society for which many philanthropists, labor reformers, and men of fashion unite in longing . . . one in which they may be comfortable and may shine without much trouble or any danger." Progressives wanted less pain, less suffering, less failure, and, at the end of history, a world "cut up into five-acre lots, and having no man upon it who [is] not well fed and well housed." But such a world, Holmes complained, would be intolerable, because it would contain no honor, that is, no earned dignity. All previous ideas of honor, he insisted, had been based on the virtues of war: the willingness to die for something greater than oneself. If Progressives wanted civic dignity, they were trying to have it both ways, to "steal the good will without the responsibilities of the place."

Holmes did not argue that a country needed soldiers to protect its home fires and permit its citizens their innocent, decadent pleasures. His was not a practical argument but a spiritual one. He argued that a man needed to be a soldier to be a man. A citizen needed to be a soldier to have honor. And being a soldier was as personal a spiritual posture as being an Emersonian individual, except that, for Emerson's resolute openness and self-trust, Holmes substituted a self-sacrificing dedication to struggle as such, which approached impassioned nihilism. He said,

> I do not know what is true. I do not know the meaning of the universe. But in the midst of doubt, in the collapse of creeds, there is one thing I do not doubt, that no man who lives in the same world with most of us can doubt, and that is that the faith is true and

adorable which leads a soldier to throw away his life in obedience to a blindly accepted duty, in a cause which he little understands, in a cause in a plan of campaign of which he has little notion, under tactics of which he does not see the use.

It was a Romantic idea, far from the practical concerns of the founding generation. Jefferson had described a continent of homesteads as an empire of liberty, full of clear-headed and self-reliant citizens. Holmes answered that a nation of prosperous house lots was a kind of spiritual prison. He portrayed human life as shadowed by ignorance and confusion but pierced and illuminated by pure commitment, regardless of its object, with self-sacrifice as its defining emblem. The idea that materialistic, democratic modernity had eroded heroism, and sacrifice could restore it, would later become a Fascist theme. Holmes's call for blind collectivism, however, was thoroughly and paradoxically individualist at its core. The point of unreflecting duty in battle was to experience one's own "heroism." A man had to do this to confront his own soul, "to know that one's final judge and only rival is oneself."

Holmes had seen nightmarish battles. Teddy Roosevelt, who had seen only the quick and victorious kind, was so impressed by Holmes's address that he selected the Massachusetts judge for the Supreme Court. (Holmes was a major jurist and scholar, so it was not an eccentric choice; but the Harvard address helped to persuade the young president that he had found his justice.) In an 1899 speech in Chicago, Roosevelt sounded like Holmes as he poured scorn on "the men who fear the strenuous life, who fear the only kind of

national life which is really worth leading." He celebrated
the search for new challenges, the vitality of "men with
empire in their brains," and denounced "the timid man, the
lazy man, the man who distrusts his country, the over civilized man, who has lost the great fighting, masterful virtues."
In one way, Roosevelt's address was less militarist than
Holmes's, for although he praised the moral greatness of
war, he did not embrace blind sacrifice, and he imagined the
fighting spirit of great souls expressed in writing, politics,
commerce, any field where ability was pressed to its limit.

Unlike Holmes, however, Roosevelt had in mind an
actual and ongoing military campaign: the reconstruction of
the Philippines, recently taken from Spain, where United
States forces were locked in bloody combat with guerrillas.
The "empires" he praised were literal, and he offered them
as a national purpose greater than mere wealth and comfort.
He proposed as a model British imperial rule in Egypt and
India, which, he said, had educated imperial officials in
public-spiritedness while preparing the colonized peoples
for self-government. War, conquest, and self-overcoming in
all forms were his exemplars of greatness. The industrial
magnates who had built the country's factories and railroads
might be great souls, but neither their clerks nor their workers found much honor in Roosevelt's picture. Those who
were concerned "only with the wants of our bodies for the
day" would consign America to "the part of China, and be
content to rot by inches in ignoble ease within our borders,
taking no interest in what goes on beyond them, sunk in a
scrambling commercialism; heedless of the higher life, the
life of aspiration, of toil and risk." Like Holmes, he implied
that the modern world provided a spiritually intolerable life

nation that was both true to itself and good would ennoble citizens, or so this idea ran.

Developing this theme, Franklin Roosevelt declared in 1941,

> A nation, like a person, has a body [that] must be fed and clothed and housed, invigorated and rested . . . a mind that must be kept informed and able, that must know itself, that understands the hopes and the needs of its neighbors. . . . And a nation, like a person, has something deeper, something more permanent, something larger than the sum of all its parts . . . which matters most for its future—which calls forth the most sacred guarding of its present.

Roosevelt called the deep and authentic character of the country its "spirit," the greatest of the three, and warned that if it ever "were killed, even though the Nation's body and mind, constricted in an alien world, lived on, the America we know would have perished."

Another approach was a language of mobilization, in which politics and reform became James's "moral equivalent of war." In this image, collective action, with clear purpose and dramatic effect, was far more charismatic than the scattered acts of individuals. Wilson's language of national vision and insight had portrayed the nation as a single mind and spirit. The language of mobilization drew the country as a single body composed of millions of parts, each contributing to the power of the whole. This vision proposed about politics what James had said about combat (though

this was not his own view): "It is the essential form of the State, and the only function in which peoples can employ all their powers at once and convergently."

Interestingly, such images did not appear in presidential language during or after the Civil War. Lincoln's spirit was profoundly nonmartial: in major speeches he portrayed war as tragedy as much as heroism and ascribed the North's victory to God's inscrutable will as much as to the efforts of Union soldiers. It was only after the country's second experience of mass-mobilization warfare, in World War I, that presidents began to use major addresses to envision Americans in peacetime as an army on the march. Warren Harding, well after the armistice but seeming to savor his vision of another war, first spoke of combat's power to "unify our collective and individual strength and consecrate all America [,] body and soul, to national defense . . . all in the sublime sacrifice for country."

Franklin Roosevelt picked up this strand of language in his 1933 inaugural, well before real war returned to American life. Here Roosevelt came near to his cousin Teddy and to William James, Progressives who tried to infuse reformist politics with the heroism of mass combat. This was also where Roosevelt fell furthest from the other, resolutely civilian version of Progressive common good, which he had expressed in his Commonwealth Club speech promising to protect American individualism by way of a strong state. In the worst period of the Great Depression, Roosevelt announced,

[I]f we are to go forward, we must move as a trained and loyal army, willing to sacrifice for the good of a

common discipline, because without such discipline no progress is made, no leadership becomes effective. We are, I know, ready and willing to submit our lives and property to such discipline, because it makes possible a leadership which aims at a larger good. This I propose to offer, pledging that the larger purposes will bind upon us all as a sacred obligation with a duty hitherto evoked only in time of armed strife. With this pledge taken, I assume unhesitatingly the leadership of this great army of our people dedicated to a disciplined attack upon our common problems.

Roosevelt promised his listeners the "warm courage of the national unity[,] clear consciousness of seeking old and precious moral values," and "clean satisfaction that comes from the stern performance of duty by old and young alike." Lucid, vigorous action by the people as a whole was what Roosevelt called "the future of essential democracy." It required a leader to provide voice and coherence. Thus the American people proved their democratic vitality when they "asked for discipline and direction under leadership" and "made me the present instrument of their wishes."

This language was an attempt to achieve for Progressive politics what William James had seen as the great gift of being a soldier at war: pride in oneself that arises from pride in a larger movement or action. As James put it, describing service to nation and humanity as substitutes for war, "We should be *owned*, as soldiers are by the army, and our pride would rise accordingly." James meant that, like instruments of a higher will, people should take purpose and dignity from fulfilling the aims of the nation or humanity. Other

sources of pride would then shrink in importance. Like military officers, they could be poor without shame. Like doctors, they would find their energy and skills shaped by service to the needs of others. In this way, the blind and bloody devotion that Holmes praised could become a more generous and clear-eyed sentiment. As James put it, "Why should men not some day feel that it is worth a blood-tax to belong to a collectivity superior in *any* respect? Why should they not blush with indignant shame if the community that owns them is vile in any way whatsoever?" Such sentiment could grow from older and more violent ideas: "On the ruins of the old morals of military honor, a stable system of morals of civic honor builds itself up. What the whole community comes to believe in grasps the individual as in a vise."

Ironically, James's image of the individual "in a vise" of community opinions was a perfect if inadvertent metaphor for what the defiant, emancipating strain of American freedom had always stood against: subjection to the mind and will of another. So too was his choice of being "owned" as a way of describing a soldier's source of pride. A human being who is owned, after all, is a slave. Even in Holmes's praise of the unreasoning, self-forgetful experience of war, there was a strange but essential core of individualism that made his sentiment seem a shadowed and bloodstained cousin to Emerson's. Not so for James, who seemed to imagine individual pride and devotion as functions of the attitudes of the majority. He even called for "skillful propagandism" to inculcate the right kind of patriotism.

Perhaps these unattractive associations doomed the Progressive image of national community as a form of mobilization. It may be that the American register of dignity was

too deeply individualist to support a wish for the vise grip of ownership. A different weakness afflicted the other Progressive idea of greatness, that of a collective American soul. In their praise of national "vision" and "spirit," Wilson and Roosevelt offered images of national community that, while powerful in their way, were abstract from the life of anyone other than the president—and perhaps even from his. The language was, finally, mystical, envisioning a communion between the soul of the citizen and that of the nation: But where was the nation's soul to be found? What was the prayer that brought it into the heart of everyday life? What concrete reminders were there of the higher life of the whole? The image of organic wholeness was caught between two bad alternatives. On one hand, it could threaten to swallow up all-important American individuality in Roosevelt's presidential "discipline." On the other, it could become an impossible exhortation to unite with a remote abstraction.

History as Heroism

HOLMES, whose praise of war showed at once the bloodiest mind and the clearest vision among the militarists, observed in his Harvard address that the glory of war tended to exist only in hindsight:

> War, when you are at it, is horrible and dull. It is only when time has passed that you see that its message was divine. I hope it may be long before we are called again to sit at that master's feet. But some teacher of the kind we all need. In this snug, over-safe corner of

the world we need it, that we may realize that our comfortable routine is no eternal necessity of things, but merely a little space of calm in the midst of the tempestuous untamed streaming of the world, and in order that we may be ready for danger.

Part of the gift of war, if it was a gift, was acute awareness of repose as a moment saved from a surrounding storm, justice as an exception carved from tyranny, and all such good things as products of human struggle. That awareness adjusted one's sense of human powers, making them seem paradoxically both smaller and larger than they might appear in a complacent mood. They were smaller and less permanent than "the tempestuous untamed streaming" of a world not made for human convenience or ideals. Human will was also, however, larger than fate or inheritance because it was the only power that could bend Holmes's "untamed streaming" toward comfort or justice. In this way, what Holmes called for was fearless knowledge of history as a thing made by often violent and desperate struggle, and always, in the end, temporary in achievement.

It is not only war that can give history this quality. Maybe our moral equivalent of war could be an attitude toward history itself, the history of our most basic principles, our sensations of freedom and community, and our place in that history. It is possible to think of a constitutional tradition in this way: as a set of achievements wrenched from injustice and chaos, which, when we remember it, makes our sense of the present more vivid and purposeful. Consider three attitudes toward American history, of which only one comes close to capturing the tragic,

clarifying, and paradoxically empowering perspective that Holmes described.

One attitude glides over the failures of American history, its betrayals of freedom and equality, its deep connection with slavery and genocide. From this point of view, the essence of American freedom was an accomplished fact from the beginning. The problems along the way were failures in application, due to inconsistency or intermittent selfishness. Getting over those was a matter of setting right in detail what was always right at the core. This attitude toward American experience was central to the language of the New Right in the middle of the twentieth century. Barry Goldwater, denouncing the ambitions of the New Deal and Lyndon Johnson's reforms, assured listeners in July of 1964, "[W]e Americans understand freedom. We have earned it: we have lived for it, and we have died for it. This nation and its people are freedom's models in a searching world. We can be freedom's missionaries in a doubting world." He did not say that, along with these—true—historical achievements, Americans had gained insight into, let alone changed the meaning of freedom. *That* we already knew, from the time when "the Good Lord raised this mighty Republican Republic to be a home for the brave and to flourish as the land of the free." Freedom could be defended and preserved; it could not, however, reveal itself in new qualities and forms through history's struggles. American freedom needed defenders and missionaries, not doubting but hopeful explorers. These were the same themes that Ronald Reagan would bring to his first inaugural address, fewer than twenty years later. He was already part of Goldwater's restorationist movement in 1964, assailing doubters with the assurance

that "the martyrs of history were not fools." Martyrs die to confirm eternal truths.

The second attitude is the opposite of the first. It is an attitude of repudiation, holding that America has been not right but wrong all along. Addressing the sweeping language of the Declaration of Independence in 1844, William Lloyd Garrison announced, "[O]ur fathers were intent on securing liberty to themselves . . . and though *in words* they recognized occasionally the brotherhood of the human race, *in practice* they continually denied it." It was time to throw out the convenient lie that freedom and equality formed the heart of American constitutional tradition. In the name of honesty and principle, Garrison called on abolitionists to reject the Constitution, withdraw from a government corrupted by slavery, and hasten the conflict that would end that system and establish a new order. This attitude had adherents in the Progressive Era, who saw the American emphasis on personal rights and limited government as one part philosophical mistake, one part the self-serving strategy of wealthy elites in the founding generation who schemed to preserve their property and privilege against a more robust democracy. In this view, as for some of the abolitionists, the way forward for Americans began with discarding the flawed legacy of hypocritical ancestors. Today this attitude appears in the tendency of some on the left to define American life by its worst aspects, insisting that progress has occurred despite, not through, the country's announced values and official milestones.

The third attitude toward history found a voice in Lyndon Johnson's 1965 address to Congress on the Voting

Rights Act. Johnson proposed that the failures of American history should instruct and temper Americans' national identity. Johnson identified the moment as "a turning-point in man's unending search for freedom," a search that Americans were part of but had not completed. The United States was "the first nation in the history of the world to be founded with a purpose," making itself a vessel of that search, but the same ideal of freedom that anchored national purpose was also the measure of national failures. More than a century after the Emancipation Proclamation, "the Negro . . . is not fully free tonight" and "emancipation is a proclamation and not a fact." That situation presented the country with a question to "bare the secret heart of America," the question of what it meant to belong—for blacks and whites—to a nation whose members often feared and hated one another. As a question of self-definition, it meant the country could "fail as a people and as a nation . . . gain[ing] the whole world, and los[ing its] own soul." This was the language, too, of Martin Luther King Jr., who had called the broadest phrases of the Declaration of Independence and the Constitution "a promissory note" for a later generation to make good when it would "rise up and live out the true meaning of its creed." The principles were a challenge to the living, one lodged at the center of what it meant to be American.

Johnson proposed that Americans can become a better version of themselves only by repudiating something they have been. Setting ourselves free from a cramped vision of the country is the first step in entering a larger one. Identifying American life with fixed and perfect freedom is never enough. Instead, Americans should see the country as

moved by an impulse to freedom that runs from the past and opens into the future. The meaning of American freedom is what we make of it, the dignity and mastery Americans are able to command together. We understand these principles partly because we have lived with, and sometimes struggled to overcome, their opposites. This approach takes the country's failings as real and basic but, instead of demanding guilt or diminution, treats failure as a starting point for appreciating what it would mean for the country to be greater. This is true to national history. It is also true to the experience of any reflective person, who must know that life—for an individual as for a country—is a braid of aspiration, disappointment, and change that combines loss and progress, and that success is not a perfect resting point but a direction.

The tradition of Johnson and King acknowledges that the meaning of American freedom, and so the meanings of citizenship and patriotism, changes as its limits expand. A country that extends civic dignity to those who once formed a slave caste has changed the dignity of being American. Gone is the pride of racial supremacy, of belonging to a master caste and lording it over others with the humiliations that the powerful can exact. What takes its place is a new version of dignity drawn from a history of both freedom and abjection. This is a familiar, now even commonplace, idea of what it means to be American. It is also a triumph of moral and political imagination, which required citizens to set themselves loose from an old idea of national identity and find their way into another. That kind of self-transforming consummation is the special power of this way of imagining, and speaking in public about, the country.

This attitude approaches what William James said Progressives would need to find if they were to achieve civic dignity in a complex world: the moral equivalent of war. James was mistaken when he supposed that the moral equivalent of war would have to be an activity that resembled war, such as mass mobilization for national service. The same confusion sometimes affected Franklin Roosevelt's way of describing the New Deal, aligning it with a militarized image of the country. Those were not viable images of American life, and if they had been, they would not have been good. The historical attitude that Johnson and King expressed, however, was a "moral equivalent" of war in a different way. It showed how human goods, especially dignity, peace, and justice, are not natural gifts but achievements won from their opposites in a history of struggle.

This attitude also made American identity a source of duty: not strict rules but a moral orientation toward an ideal of equal freedom. The version of mobilization this attitude offered was the movement of struggle across generations, an inheritance of effort pressing forward and failure falling back, and successive efforts to adapt a broad ideal to each new time.

This attitude toward American history enables its members to reject and remake the world in which they are born, not in simple repudiation but in completion of a promise not yet kept. This attitude also makes possible a particular form of patriotism, which I would call constitutional patriotism. This is more than a rational appreciation of the benefits that orderly government power provides to citizens, but it is also something other than blind devotion to what is one's own. It is an emotional identification with the country

that sweeps in how it came to be as it is and what it might become. A constitutional patriot's loyalty is not restricted to what exists. It is also loyalty to possibility. It may be that a patriot, like a lover or friend, often sees the country in the best light possible. This habit can obscure vision, politically as much as personally, if it means willfully overlooking problems. It can also train attention toward the possibility of change and show that change is sometimes not self-surrender but movement toward a completeness that, by its nature, a country never reaches.

The country has recently seen too much war for too little purpose. Most of us nonetheless feel our first loyalty to the peaceful goals that Teddy Roosevelt and Holmes called sad and dishonorable: family life, personal development, comfort, pleasure, and security. And so we should. The American experience in Iraq has confirmed the obvious: we do not believe it is a high human good to lose one's life, for purposes one does not understand, in a senseless strategy. Nonetheless, there is something to the idea that modern citizenship requires its own version of heroism. We might still hope to find that in our own brutal and hopeful history and the principles we take from it, which we can ever and again aim to make good this time.

Is Freedom Empty?
Citizenship, Sodomy,
and the Meaning of Life

ONE EARLY CHALLENGE to the American idea of freedom was that it would be fatal to social and political community—the prophecy that Samuel Johnson captured in his gleeful set piece of the starving frontiersman and his impudent cur. The images of national community that fill the previous two chapters are efforts to answer that charge. Another dire forecast was the one that Emerson's Divinity School Address seemed to confirm—that inalienable rights of life and liberty, in the end, gave absolute power to the wayward judgment of the individual American. The Americans, Johnson's "kings of ME," were zealots of conscience, and this made their doctrine a charter of anarchy. The only freedom that would satisfy them would amount to chaos.

We do not need to reach back to Johnson for this anxiety. In 2004, James Dobson, founder of the Christian-right group Focus on the Family, called Supreme Court justice Anthony Kennedy "the most dangerous man in America." Kennedy was an odd choice for that dubious

honor. A lifelong Republican and Roman Catholic, he has a reputation for intellectual modesty and concern with others' opinions. As a Supreme Court justice, he is a member of the one branch of government that controls no money, police force, or army. The courts cannot bribe, starve, or bludgeon others into obeying them. Their authority depends on willing consent to their judgment.

So where was the danger? In 2003, Kennedy wrote the Court's opinion in *Lawrence v. Texas*, ruling that states could not forbid homosexual relations between consenting adults. The decision reversed the Court's ruling seventeen years earlier in *Bowers v. Hardwick*, which had allowed states to ban sodomy. Setting out his reasoning under the due process clause of the Fourteenth Amendment to the Constitution, Kennedy wrote an uncommonly winged piece of judicial prose:

> These matters, involving the most intimate and personal choices a person may make in a lifetime, choices central to personal dignity and autonomy, are central to the liberty protected by the Fourteenth Amendment. At the heart of liberty is the right to define one's own concept of existence, of meaning, of the universe, and of the mystery of human life.

That passage incited Dobson to reignite an old and persistent problem: Is freedom meaningless? When we have taken away the last constraint, will we know what to do with ourselves? Or will we be left purposeless, indifferent? Will freedom turn out to be, after all, another word for nothing left to lose, the vertigo of an American road trip collapsed in

exhaustion? Worse, would people with no constraints turn into predatory animals, the strong using the weak for pleasure or convenience? That would mean that complete freedom would return to something like its opposite, the naked exploitation of slavery. Could it be that the boundaries that growing freedom has rejected are all that ever kept us human?

The Case Against Freedom

CRITICS CHARGE THAT FREEDOM is an empty idea, that it is powerful for the destructive work of breaking chains but ends by crushing the gentler constraints that give life shape and meaning, while bringing no shape of its own. Whether for an individual trying to make sense of his own life or a judge interpreting the Constitution, taking freedom as a guide can only produce confusion. This idea unites religious conservatives such as James Dobson with more moderate and politically complicated ministers such as Rick Warren, a much less fire-and-brimstone evangelical; so-called communitarians of the left; and other critics of the narcissism and frivolity of American life. Dobson argues that same-sex marriage would erode the relationship in which two people forsake all others and commit themselves to bringing up the next generation. It would turn all intimate relations into transient fun seeking: "Imagine an environment where nothing is stable and where people think primarily about themselves and their own self-preservation," Dobson writes, calling up the world of Thomas Hobbes lucidly enough to pass an undergraduate philosophy exam. Although gay activists seek " 'freedom'

from the shackles of moral law and traditional institutions," their freedom is chaos and violence, one of the confused self-indulgences by which "we can wound ourselves and devastate those around us." In contrast, "true freedom and genuine fulfillment can be found only when we live in harmony with our design," the divine order that Dobson believes includes the traditional American family.

For a less-right-wing version of the idea that becoming "free" inspires people to debase themselves and one another, consider Warren's Christian self-help tract, *The Purpose-Driven Life.* The book is all about what Justice Kennedy calls the meaning of the universe and the mystery of human life. Warren's starting point is that without God there is no reason to do anything but seek pleasure. "If your time on earth were all there is to your life," he writes, "I would suggest you start living it up immediately. You could forget being good and ethical, and you wouldn't have to worry about any consequences of your actions. You could indulge yourself in total self-centeredness because your actions would have no long-term repercussions." In this view, a human being without external law is just a pleasure machine, indifferent to others' needs and suffering.

This idea is not restricted to conservatives. Maybe its most lucid spokesman is Michael Sandel, a Harvard professor and political liberal, although he has often argued that "liberal" political philosophers place too much weight on choice and individual rights. Describing what he sees as the moral danger of genetic engineering, Sandel argues that life loses its purpose precisely when all choices are open. If our mastery over our lives ever became so complete that we could redesign life itself, that power would leave us with

"nothing to affirm or behold outside our own will." Human choice, Sandel implies, is an empty and rudderless thing without outside purpose to guide it. He argues that purpose comes from a love of what is given to us, what we have no power to choose or decline, a quality he calls "giftedness." The given includes our genetic traits and those of our family and friends—what we think of as talent and character. It may also include traditions, such as the meaning of a sport that genetic enhancement would change, or that of family, marriage, or romantic love. Without the givenness of our culture, as well as that of our personal makeup, we would be adrift. If we press freedom past the outer bonds of the given, so goes the argument, we will win only chaos. When Justice Kennedy hinted at a constitutional law of radical personal autonomy, he became the focal point of a fear: that freedom will set loose self-indulgent and predatory impulses that tradition has kept under control. In this view, the free man is lonely, hungry, and destructive—roughly Dobson's portrait of the homosexual man who, if traditional marriage falls, will become the model of all American men.

A Countertradition

THESE ANXIETIES express a whole interpretation of American experience, a countertradition in a country otherwise enamored of freedom. At the extreme was Stephen Elliott of Georgia, the only bishop ever to preside over the Protestant Episcopal Church in the Confederate States of America. Elliott preached to his state's clergy in 1862 that to preserve social order, the South must reject the Declaration of Independence. By embracing radical principles of liberty,

American revolutionaries had put the Republic on an untenable course. "Carried away by our opposition to monarchy and an established Church," he declared of the revolutionary generation, "we declared war against all authority and against all form. The reason of man was exalted to an impious degree, and in the face not only of experience, but of the revealed word of God, all men were declared to be created equal, and man was pronounced capable of self-government." For Elliott and many theologians, jurists, and journalists across the South, this was a philosophical error masquerading as a principle of government. According to him,

> Man is not capable of self-government because he is a fallen creature, and interest, passion, ambition, lust, sway him far more than reason or honor. As for equality among men, whether by creation or birth, or in any other way, it is a miserable ignis fatuus [will-o'-the-wisp]. . . . Upon principles as false and as foolish as these was our late Government founded.

This strand of thought was not restricted to Southern defenders of slavery. In the North, versions appeared in the speeches and writings of such major figures as Timothy Dwight, revolutionary and later president of Yale, and Lyman Beecher, the father of abolitionist novelist Harriet Beecher Stowe and abolitionist celebrity minister Henry Ward Beecher. The elder Beecher warned that if the new American freedom meant being "loose from wholesome restraint," it would "begin the work of self-destruction . . . a malignant exercise, which has no parallel in the annals of

time, and . . . attended with miseries, such as the sun has never looked upon." He envisioned the rising democracy as a regime of moral decline, in which licentious citizens and indulgent rulers entered into a tacit conspiracy to tolerate crimes such as drunkenness, slovenly discipline in child rearing, and failure to keep the Sabbath. A country founded in ancestral virtue was consuming its moral capital and had lost the discipline necessary to renew it. Beecher warned,

> We are becoming another people. Our habits have held us, long after those moral causes which formed them had in a great degree ceased to operate. Those habits, at length, are giving way. So many hands, have so long been employed to pull away foundations, and so few to repair the breaches, that the building totters. So much enterprise has been displayed, in removing obstructions from the current of human depravity, and so little to restore them, that the stream at length is beginning to run. It may be stopped now, but soon it will become deep, and broad, and rapid, and irresistible.

Dwight sounded the same notes in 1801, warning that "man, unrestrained by law and religion, is a mere beast of prey." For him as for other conservatives, the Revolution was a dubious period, marred by "visionary ideas of patriotism," "wild moments of enthusiasm," and the presence of agents from philosophically decadent France.

Beecher predicted that if Americans squandered their inheritance of good moral habits, they would never recover their "demolished institutions," the unique creation of Puri-

tan settlers and constitutional architects. He called on
Americans to re-create a moral consensus by mobilizing a
moral militia, called out to defend "our altars and our fire-
sides," and restore values eroded by licentiousness and neglect. As Beecher put it, this was to be a war for "the standard
which our fathers reared; and our motto is, 'the inheritance
which they bequeathed us, no man shall take from us.'"
This was traditionalism for a country unsure whether it had
traditions to maintain.

The Countertradition and the Constitution

LAWRENCE V. TEXAS was not the first time Kennedy set
out his praise of liberty in a momentous opinion. In 1992, in
Planned Parenthood of Pennsylvania v. Casey, he authored a
joint opinion with two other justices, David Souter and
Sandra Day O'Connor, upholding the right to abortion that
the Court first announced in *Roe v. Wade*. Evoking the personal and often painful decision whether to bear a child,
Kennedy set down the same words that I earlier quoted
from *Lawrence*. He ended that discussion by writing, "The
destiny of the woman must be shaped to a large extent on
her own conception of her spiritual imperatives and her
place in society." Those "spiritual imperatives" centered on
"one's own concept of existence . . . and the mystery of
human life." Respect for them pressed the hand of the state
away from regulating women's choices about abortion.
Eleven years later in *Lawrence*, the same respect for citizens'
"own conception of . . . spiritual imperatives" forbade the
state to regulate the intimate lives of adults. The Supreme

Court's old rule, permitting government regulation of sexuality and finding, in the words of the *Bowers* opinion, no "fundamental right to homosexual sodomy," had become unacceptable. In Kennedy's words, its persistence as constitutional law "demean[ed] the existence of homosexual persons," and the state had no right "to demean their existence or control their destiny by making their private sexual behavior a crime."

Justice Antonin Scalia dissented from the 1992 abortion ruling in *Casey*, predicting—accurately—that constitutional protection of "intimate" and "deeply personal" decisions would open the way for a right to same-sex intimacy. He warned darkly that once the Court had started down Kennedy's path, it would find no way to distinguish between the choice to have an abortion and the choice of a lover. The one was just as intimate, just as deeply personal, as the other. When his forecast came true in *Lawrence*, Scalia made a radical declaration: a Court that was seriously committed to protecting personal actions based on "the concept of existence" and "the mystery of human life" would have to override any law expressing moral judgment, because such judgment always intrudes on self-exploration and self-expression. Although Scalia did not put it this way, laws expressing moral judgment present a form of Sandel's "given" to individuals, embodying some of the traditions in which they choose and act. Such laws also provide a "given" to judges, a way of orienting their reasoning along lines of custom and authority. Without such restrictions, a judge wielding a wide-open concept of personal freedom would be akin to Sandel's Promethean genetic engineer, with nothing

to affirm outside his own will. Thus Scalia derided the soaring sentences of Kennedy's opinion as "the passage that ate the rule of law."

Scalia did not argue, however, that *Lawrence* would in fact lead the Court to invalidate all laws based on moral judgments—say, laws against bestiality and drug use. His point was that "the mystery of human life" is a broad and imprecise phrase, sure to mean very different things to different people. If the "liberty" protected in the due process clause includes the freedom to act on one's own conception of life's meaning, then a great vagueness lies near the heart of constitutional law. As nature rushes to fill a vacuum, politics quickly fills out such potent vagueness with exact accounts of the liberty the Constitution secures. Scalia saw *Lawrence* as setting judges free to impose their own ideas of personal liberty on the country, taking advantage of loose phrases to write into the Constitution whatever political platform they liked. In *Lawrence,* he glowered, that platform was "the so-called homosexual agenda," an activist program to erase moral disapproval of homosexuality. Tomorrow it might be something completely different.

In the same vein, dissenting from the Court's partial preservation of abortion rights in *Casey,* Scalia compared the joint opinion which Kennedy joined to that of the willful Chief Justice Taney in that moral disaster of American law, *Dred Scott v. Sandford.* When Taney wrote that black Americans could not become citizens because the framers had enshrined a political culture based on white supremacy, a dissenter from that judgment accused him of doing just what Scalia believed Kennedy was doing: reading his own vision of American society into the Constitution to force it

on the country. When judges can do that, the dissenting justice warned, "we no longer have a Constitution; we are under the power of individual men, who for the time being have the power to declare what the Constitution is, according to their own views of what it ought to mean." Scalia similarly set himself against an imagined tyranny of judges. While Scalia's main concern was constitutional interpretation and Dobson's was the culture of marriage, both argued that the idea of freedom can go too far, becoming a destructive principle that tears down necessary inheritances and leaves nothing to steer by but will, whim, or appetite— backed up, in the end, by power. One person's arbitrary power over another was what American freedom started out by rejecting, whether in the literal slavery of personal relations or the figurative slavery of political tyranny. Pressing against such bonds, rebels and reformers experienced what Michael Sandel calls "something appealing, even intoxicating, about a vision of freedom unfettered by the given." Now their critics warn that the vision of freedom that they produced is the long way around to a rebirth of tyranny.

If this were true, it would be a devastating judgment on a way of life. It would make the United States a country founded on a philosophical error, as Samuel Johnson and many other English observers believed. It would suggest that the road ahead will bring either new guiding principles or cultural disaster—which some, such as Dobson, believe is already on us. The line of criticism that Scalia and Dobson share is also the most venerable argument against the principles that became American freedom. Conservatives denounced the radicalism of the American Revolution as a formula for anarchy and tyranny, dressed as demands for

freedom. Later conservatives, politically heterodox communitarians, and other critics have repeated the argument ever
since.

The Sensations of Order

LET US PAY THIS VIEW the respect Burke showed the
American colonists. Instead of treating it as a philosophical
sparring partner, let us look at what Burke would have called
its sensible object, the vision in which order is the most precious and endangered quality in human life. Two images
interact here. One portrays the solitary individual as a sad
and deprived creature. In this view, we have no great inner
truth, only what we have learned and gleaned from the
inheritance around us. Our inner cathedrals are miniatures
of the great edifices we inhabit together, and if we tear those
down we should not expect to build something new in their
place. No one is born human, let alone noble, heroic, or dignified: we learn to be those ways, and to regard others similarly, by the customs of our time and place. If there is an
inalienable right, it is the right to what makes us human: the
principles of our law, the habits of our social life, the inspiration and consolation of our religion and our society's forms
of friendship and love. The justice we should seek is not
against society but part of our membership in society, which
will fail if we turn the demand for justice against society
itself. Burke expressed this idea in his attack on the French
Revolution, contrasting the "rights of man," which the revolutionaries advanced, with "the real rights of men . . . to the
acquisitions of their parents, to the nourishment and

improvement of their offspring, to instruction in life, and to consolation in death."

This appreciation of custom as a source of dignity and comfort can incline a person toward a conservative temperament: a preference for what he knows over the untried; for facts over promises and promises over mysteries; and a love of continuity and an intuition that change always brings loss. One way to understand this temperament is as an abiding attachment to the finitude of human life, its brevity and smallness and vulnerability, which greatly amplifies the value of any fine, lasting, or protective thing.

The love of order also has a darker side. This is a sense that order is fragile, the edifices of everyday life cannot take much shaking, and something dangerous seethes beneath the familiar surfaces that one loves. Douglass said he found the hunger for freedom in human nature itself, and he staked that against the authority of slave master Covey. Burke spoke for a whole tradition that answered: human nature is not discovered but formed by custom. Strip away custom—particularly the customs of authority, the rules and hierarchies of your time and place—and you will find nothing lovely or heroic, only chaotic appetites for pleasure and power and a violent passion to dominate others. In this vision, to be a man, just a man, was not the achievement Douglass described but a terrible nakedness verging on formlessness. When Emerson wrote in "Self-Reliance" that if his unchained heart showed him to be the devil's child, then that was who he would be, he echoed back his enemies' fear as a promise.

In both of its aspects, the love of order is rooted in the

sense that human beings are defined as much by our limitations as by our powers. Perhaps it is the perennial counterpoint to the impulses of American freedom because it highlights truths that the quest for mastery and authenticity can easily overlook, and qualities that the drive to freedom can harm: We are vulnerable, needy, finite, and often unable to be good. We need one another, and we hurt one another. Without order that is older and larger than we are, we can become less dignified, sadder, and more dangerous. Much of the power and grace of what we do comes not from ourselves alone but from custom and inheritance. From this perspective, declarations of independence easily overestimate the powers of living human beings and weaken us just where they set out to make us stronger.

Demands for freedom are their own kind of tradition, in place at the time of the American Revolution and open to radical expansions by figures such as Douglass and Emerson. But what if the demand for freedom tends to undermine all forms, constraints, and qualifications, destroying the bases of common life and, finally, of individual freedom itself? That challenge deserves a direct answer.

A Little Context

SUCH BROAD WAYS of putting a problem can make it a shadow-puppet of the imagination. It is helpful, instead, to stay with specifics. What made Kennedy's opinion in *Lawrence* possible, and what does that tell us about the relationship between freedom and order? Several strands of constitutional politics and history came together there. First is the very idea of the Constitution as a charter of individual

liberty defining national citizenship by the rights that citizens hold. Although this may seem obvious today, it formed no part of the design of the Constitution of 1787. Even the Bill of Rights, the original ten rights-protecting amendments to the Constitution, provided protection only against the federal government, not guarantees of individual rights as such. Under that constitutional scheme, the sodomy ban at issue in *Lawrence* would have been immune to challenge because it was a Texas state statute, not a federal law. The idea that the Constitution defined personal rights of national citizenship triumphed in the aftermath of the Civil War, when the Reconstruction Congress pushed through the Thirteenth, Fourteenth, and Fifteenth Amendments to the Constitution. The Fourteenth Amendment extended American citizenship to everyone born in the United States and forbade state governments to intrude on the rights of national citizenship, a change that courts gradually came to interpret as applying nearly all of the Bill of Rights to states as well as the federal government.

The second strand that contributed to Justice Kennedy's opinion was a distinctive idea of the content of national citizenship: freedom to engage in a personal search for the meaning of life. It was, in a sense, a claim for the rights pronounced in Emerson's Divinity School Address. This, too, was something new. Until the New Deal, the touchstone personal right of national citizenship was freedom of contract, the right to buy and sell one's own labor without "constraints" such as minimum-wage and maximum-hours laws. (That vision of freedom, like the idea of national citizenship itself, traced some of its origin to the rejection of racial caste. Slavery was the antithesis of free contract because the slave,

being property, had no choice in entering his relationship with his master and no freedom to leave it.) Otherwise, with the exception of some protection of political speech and such "fundamental rights" as the freedom to educate one's children outside the public schools, courts gave little content to the idea of a constitution of personal liberty. The line of cases including *Roe v. Wade, Casey,* and now *Lawrence* lent the idea of constitutional liberty a new dimension. Justice Kennedy's version, in particular, gave full voice to the idea of freedom as emancipation and authenticity. His "concept of . . . the universe, and of the mystery of human life" echoed, probably without intending it, Emerson's challenge to his fellow Americans to achieve "an original relation to the universe." What was exhortation and wish for Emerson became constitutional doctrine at the turn of the twenty-first century. What Emerson set as an aim for the individual personality, Kennedy offered as a key to the purpose of American political community and the limits of government power.

The third change that Justice Kennedy's opinion took in was in some ways the most important, although it was unspoken—except by Scalia, who got near it in his disdainful dissent. The majority, Scalia pointed out, was vague about what had changed in constitutional law between *Bowers* and *Lawrence.* What exactly was the right the earlier Court had failed to recognize, which the present one was enforcing? What were its metes and bounds? The *Bowers* Court had found no "fundamental right to homosexual sodomy" in American constitutional law, and Kennedy did not claim to have discovered such a right. Was the right, then, to be completely unhindered in all quests for mean-

ing and identity, whether undertaken through sex, drugs, or, for that matter, working for less than the minimum wage? As a matter of principled reasoning, it was not hard to charge that Kennedy's opinion changed either nothing or everything.

Here is one version of what changed between 1986 and 2003. Kennedy wrote that when the *Bowers* Court described the question before it as whether the Constitution enshrined a right of homosexual sodomy, it "disclose[d] the Court's own failure to appreciate the extent of the liberty at stake." The earlier Court's interpretation of the issue "demean[ed] the claim the individual put forward, just as it would demean a married couple were it to be said marriage is simply about the right to have sexual intercourse." What was clear in 2003, Kennedy wrote, was that regarding a sexual relationship as an isolated act was (at least sometimes) a mistake. Intimacy could also be "an element of a personal bond that is more enduring." It was forging such bonds with other people, not simply pursuing pleasure as the impulse arose, that put same-sex intimacy in the constitutionally protected category of activity in which people work out the meaning of their lives.

Kennedy's opinion, then, did not turn only on a fine point of principle. In fact, it may not have turned on such a point at all. The crux of the case was the Court's vision of the human acts brought before it, not so much the law as the facts that the law had to assess. In 1986, a majority of the Court could see these acts as the "buggery" that many states had long banned, an action just as much subject to prohibition as, say, injecting heroin or stealing a loaf of bread. In 2003, a majority understood the same acts as parts of

meaning-making relationships in which people explored their identities and gave shape to their lives—akin to marriage, a domain of protected liberty. The difference between the cases lay not so much in what the justices thought as in what they saw: not, that is, so much in their elaboration of constitutional principle as in their views of the world.

But this is a false contrast. Any body of principle arises from Burke's "sensible objects," images of the social world it is meant to govern. For instance, Justice Kennedy's seeing same-sex intimacy as being like marriage also expressed an idea of what marriage is for: intimacy, fulfillment, and lasting personal bonds, but not (necessarily) reproduction or forging financial and social ties between extended families. In many times, places, and systems of thought, those latter purposes would have seemed obviously paramount. In a traditional view, the emphasis on reproduction would make the analogy to same-sex intimacy a stretch. The idea that marriage weaves together large family networks would make most modern marriage seem a vagrant, idle thing. Our idea of marriage puts chosen intimacy at the center of authentic and emancipated lives. That made Justice Kennedy's expansion of intimate freedom in *Lawrence* plausible.

The constitutional expansion of Lawrence also drew force from another change that took place between 1986 and 2003. Largely outside courts and legislatures, lesbians and gay men let the country know that they existed and wanted respect and recognition. The most visible face of this change was the explosion in sympathetic gay characters on television and in movies, particularly after the mid-1990s. Less visible but probably more important were tens of millions of

personal conversations in which gay people who would once have kept their secret for a lifetime came out to parents, friends, and colleagues. The cumulative effect was to force the American moral imagination open a little wider than it had been, drawing gay lives into the broadened circle of national life. Notoriously, when *Bowers* was decided, Justice Lewis Powell, who cast the deciding vote, reflected aloud that he had never even met a gay person—this, in a cruel irony, to a closeted gay clerk. Thanks to many acts of personal courage, Justice Powell's deluded complacency became anachronistic in just seventeen years.

The people who changed the social world that the Supreme Court justices—and everyone else—confronted were, then, engaged in a kind of constitutional interpretation, an interpretation of the meaning of *liberty*. When critical passages of a constitution rest on such broad terms, and doubly when that constitution is received as a charter of individual and even Romantic freedom, such popular interpretation becomes unavoidable. What it means for people to uncover or build the meaning of their lives is not the sort of fact that will stand still. People who insisted that others take them as they were, often at the cost of considerable discomfort on both sides, were announcing what it meant for them to be free, and in doing so they changed both the meaning of their sexual acts and the meaning of American freedom. The problem of interpreting changing social practices presents itself uninvited, and no doubt it both prompted and shaped Kennedy's opinion.

Freedom's Gifts

THE HISTORY behind Kennedy's opinion shows that, far from being empty or merely destructive, freedom has its own version of "giftedness," philosopher Michael Sandel's word for qualities we can neither choose nor refuse, which are simply part of what makes us ourselves. In this respect, even the most disruptive and radical act expresses not arbitrary choice and naked power but a web of belief and experience that, like Sandel's giftedness, must be taken partly on faith. This reality shows itself in several ways.

First, the demand for personal freedom is an American tradition in its own right. Our most radical repudiations are expressions of an inheritance. Even Douglass's resistance to Edward Covey asserted dignity built from a cultural inheritance that included the natural-rights doctrine of the Declaration of Independence, revolutionary slave masters' sensitivity about freedom and honor, and the Christian doctrines of redemption and conscience. Douglass's personal milestones were also, at Rochester, a stage in the nation's constitutional tradition and, on the Maryland plantation, a choice to make American sensations of personal dignity his own. The Declaration of Independence itself was an act of constitutional interpretation within the British tradition of struggle between the people and their rulers, as were the doctrines of liberty that Samuel Johnson called a charter of anarchy. Emerson's denunciation of tradition, too, belonged to a tradition, the New Englanders' iron defense of conscience that Burke had described decades earlier and that Emerson's Congregationalist ancestors had developed in the

sermons that formed the model for the nineteenth-century heretic's addresses.

That people learn to be human from the traditions they inherit need not be a conservative truth. Tradition can make us rebels, innovators, people determined to find new ways for order and emancipation to coexist. Some of the power of American freedom lies in its being a tradition of this kind. It is alive in experience as much as in texts or principles, in the many attempts of young women and men to achieve what the punctilious Hillary Rodham called, in an address at her graduation from Wellesley College, "more immediate, penetrating, and ecstatic modes of living." It is the dawning realization in rebellious young adults that their parents might have attempted such a thing, and might someday understand their children's attempts with sympathy born of their own experience. It is the attitude of parents who reverse the lesson of the Prodigal Son, loving their rebellious children fully, not because they return to the original customs of the fold, but because in rebellion they become themselves.

Second, the experience of personal truthfulness and falsity that drives expanding freedom is itself a fact, a refutation of the idea that free choice leaves nothing to affirm outside the arbitrary will. When Emerson wrote that "imitation is suicide," he did not believe he was using hyperbole. Romanticism, American and otherwise, developed the Protestant belief in an inherent conscience, a living truth that, having felt it, one has to choose either to live by or to mutilate and suppress. Romanticism succeeded, making Emerson and Walt Whitman the often unacknowledged

authors of American experience, because so many ordinary people found the Romantics' words true in their lives. Sodomy bans "demeaned" gay people not because they prohibited a self-indulgent excess but because the way the plaintiffs experienced intimacy was a part of them. It might be intensely personal, but there was nothing arbitrary about it.

Even the most personal act of rebellion not only repudiates order but also seeks a different order. It is a demand not to be left alone but to live among other free people. The attack on freedom usually involves the charge that others will be mere instruments for the whim and pleasure of the unbound self, but portraying personal freedom as moral solipsism betrays a misunderstanding. Douglass and Emerson aimed at a life to live that is one's own, in a world not determined to crush it. Their demands posed a threat to present order, but they were essentially motivated by the wish for a different kind of livable world. This is also a love of order, but an order that does not yet exist, which requires faith that it is possible even though those who demand it cannot know that yet. Emerson praised forms of friendship and love that began in genuine mutual recognition, demanding not concealment and self-mutilation but openness and honesty. This personal impulse found a voice as an ideal of political community in Walt Whitman, Emerson's self-appointed and rebellious disciple, for whom the whole purpose of democracy was to integrate radical respect for individuality with profound attachment to the nation. Only a country that could respect all its citizens was capable of this integration. Today what we mean by friendship is what Emerson meant, and one important ideal of national com-

munity is substantially Whitman's. That is why Justice Kennedy's image of American constitutional community as one that does not demean the personal imperatives of its members captures a vision of citizenship and patriotism. The American experience of freedom is deeply connected with the needs for dignity, respect, and recognition. These are not only personal conditions but interpersonal ones, ways of being among other people. Integrating individual freedom into national community is not simply a way to bring it under control: it is a way to make its most basic motives real.

The fracture in attitudes toward the unbound self is not really between fundamentalist allies of James Dobson, on the one hand, and Emersonian fundamentalists, on the other. By and large the only people who take such pure views of American life are those who, like Dobson, make their livings by peddling divisive opinions. Evangelicals experience the tug of authenticity, and purported Emersonians find their personal truths in quiet and conventional lives. The relation between authenticity and convention is not so much a culture war as a balance within each life. For most people, taking Dobson's line seriously would extinguish a whole body of vital experience, while at the same time, vitality arises from commitment and belief, not just whim. We live in a middle ground between the shaping nurturance of custom and the charge and urgency of self-discovery and self-expression. These two, very different, versions of giftedness turn out to be complementary in practice.

The Constitution, too, has this double character. Seen one way, it is simply a set of procedures, rules, and principles

laid out by some Americans and interpreted by others, including some who are alive today. As something we made, and continue to make by reinterpreting it, it is by definition also something we could ignore or destroy. And yet in order to be a constitution, to be authoritative today and to connect the present to past and future, it must also be more than that. Once we have created it, and even as we remake it, we experience it as something that stands apart from us, exists before our judgments of it, and, mysteriously, can make us more ourselves by constraining us—even though we made it in the first place. This, of course, is a quality it can have only if we approach it in a certain attitude. It is, like the American tradition of freedom itself, a way that we work to reconcile our capacity for disruption and emancipation with our interdependence and need for order. Citizens who live with the Constitution, in a country that works out many of its basic political values through that document, will unavoidably aim to make the Constitution their own as the plaintiffs in *Lawrence* did. If the American ideal of freedom is meaningless, then we live on mistaken premises, in our politics and constitutional law, and also in our intimate lives and everywhere between those poles of public and private. But the fact that these are our lives is the nearest thing we have to a refutation of the claim that our freedom is meaningless.

CHAPTER 5

American Utopias

TO THEIR CRITICS, American revolutionaries were utopians. Intoxicated by political ideals—Samuel Johnson's "delirious dream of republican fanaticism"—they ignored the limits of reality and sought an impossible world. The Methodist leader John Wesley tried to instruct the colonists in 1775:

> Would the being independent of England make you more free? Far, very far from it. It would hardly be possible for you to steer clear, between anarchy and tyranny. But suppose, after numberless dangers and mischiefs, you should settle into one or more republics: would a republican government give you more liberty, either religious or civil? By no means. No governments under heaven are so despotic as the republican: no subjects are governed in so arbitrary a manner, as those of a commonwealth.

The Americans' vision of a free society struck Wesley as self-immolating. Like many of the best minds of his time, he would have quashed the project before it began, saving

the world the human cost of what he expected to be a disastrous experiment. It took a gamble on an untested idea—fanaticism, snorted Johnson—to prove the naysayers wrong.

The twentieth century was bled and scarred by political utopias. Delirious dreams and unchecked brutality were the cocktail of tyranny in the Soviet Union, Germany, China, Cambodia, and elsewhere. The horrors of the century led many Anglo-American thinkers, liberal and conservative alike, to fresh disdain for radical experiment. Isaiah Berlin, a powerfully skeptical liberal, defined utopianism as ideological certainty backed by power, the source of "failed revolutions . . . the oceans of blood which have led not to the Kingdom of Love but to further blood, more misery."

The American relation to utopian dreams is fraught with irony. On one hand, the home of the world's first utopian success soon acquired a trademark indifference to political ideas. With mostly trivial exceptions, Americans shrugged off the ideological currents of hope and terror that shook the last century. Louis Hartz, in his classic 1956 study, *The Liberal Tradition in America*, accused his countrymen of believing in the naturalness, inevitability, and perfection of their ideas, blissfully ignorant that earlier generations had struggled to invent and establish them. He wrote with impatience and some disdain of a country with no political philosophy, "only . . . the American Way of Life, a nationalist articulation of [John] Locke which usually does not know that Locke himself is involved." On the other hand, American politics is no great redoubt of what Isaiah Berlin praised as utopianism's opposite, "the sense of reality," the power to appreciate the many-textured parts of human life and integrate them into one skein of experience and

judgment. To the contrary, American politics produces intermittent and terrible utopian exercises, mostly exported. The Iraq adventure is just the kind of utopia that Berlin attacked: undertaken with blind self-confidence, powered by ideas that seemed obvious and irresistible to believers, and proved equal parts futile and destructive in practice. Sadly, this effort to create a republic abroad would have vindicated Wesley's grim forecast, which the Americans refuted so soundly in their own country.

American politics at home can be as oblivious to reality as our foreign adventures. Consider this finding, from a poll conducted in 2001, during the debate on repeal of the federal estate tax: 20 percent of respondents identified themselves as members of the country's wealthiest 1 percent, while another 19 percent admitted they had not yet reached that charmed circle but predicted they soon would. That amounts to nearly two-fifths of Americans believing themselves in or near the highest altitudes of wealth. It isn't hard to see what that tilted vision means for tax politics. It also shows the persistence of the free-labor vision of an American life: the young man works hard and, after some years of just rewards, can buy himself a township. The mathematical impossibility is no match for the power of the image. This is a subtle kind of utopianism. Instead of "delirious dreams" of an ideal society, it ascribes dreamlike qualities to familiar institutions, envisioning the American economy as a loaves-and-fishes enterprise in which one percent quickly becomes thirty-nine, and to be ordinary is to be extraordinary. In another way, it assigns utopian power not to any social program but to one's own life, a place where dreams defy statistics to become real. This charismatic unreality is

the image of American life that Ronald Reagan placed at the center of politics, in which personal dreams and an endlessly responsive economy together create an alchemy of wish fulfillment.

These ironies and confusions are symptoms of deeper difficulties. While the Americans' critics were wrong to denounce the nascent national project as doomed, skeptical friends such as Edmund Burke were right in seeing it as profoundly vexed. No one then could know what it would mean to found a tradition on rebellion and repudiation, a social order on the rights and consent of each member. These difficulties became clearer, but did not grow simpler, in centuries of debate over civic dignity and national community. They emerged in efforts to reconcile opposed aspects of the American self. Each person is a vessel of infinite possibility and limitless demands for dignity and recognition; each one also depends profoundly on institutions and circumstances, which enable some to realize their potential and smother that of others. We sometimes cannot be the people we believe we must, and when we can, the achievement is not altogether our own. In the same way, each heart is a compass of personal truth, source of its own lessons whose authority must be final, on penalty of self-betrayal; but each person is also part of a community and tradition, and his wishes and imagination are creatures of those common worlds. Our precious, irreducible uniqueness is our most ordinary and derivative quality. These cross-pressures, created by conflicting parts of American experience, drive our ambivalent utopianism.

Three American traditions have emerged to bridge the gap between the utopian demand for a world as capacious as

our dreams and the persistent reality of limits. One is the idea of common sense, the doctrine that ordinary, untrained judgment can solve any moral or practical problem. A radical doctrine on its face, this conceit in fact throws us back on unspoken and shared attitudes, which tame our response, coaxing it along to familiar and reassuring conclusions. Another is personal utopianism, the conviction that, although American institutions may be forever fixed, our private lives are open to infinite change. Although common sense has a conservative tack and personal utopianism is beloved of the cultural left, both are aspects of a single tendency: splitting the radicalism and conservatism of the American inheritance, with the result that neither achieves its full power. The third tradition represents the best attempt to take seriously the complex relationship between personal freedom and the context of culture and institutions. This is the tradition of vision and experiment, which acknowledges both the utopian impulse and the reality of constraint and tries to change the world by increments to make constraint less fatal.

American Common Sense

AMERICANS' FOREMOST SECULAR CREED is the belief that common sense, the heart's impulse and the mind's untrained judgment, solves all problems and removes all mysteries. This appealingly democratic idea has the price of honoring our habits and prejudices as self-evident truths, enabling us to hold together our radicalism and our conservatism without fully confronting either.

Treating what he called "the philosophical approach of

the Americans," Alexis de Tocqueville described the following procedure. Confronted with a new question, the typical
American would not reach for the precepts of tradition or
the values of his family or his class. Instead, whether the
problem was scientific, theological, or political, the American would make his own observations, apply his judgment,
and come up with a conclusion he could call his own. This
attitude involved quiet but supreme self-confidence: obscure
and complex problems must yield to the same common-
sense approach as patching a roof or designing a sod house.
Indeed, Tocqueville thought the American genius for practical action underwrote faith in intellectual common sense:
"Seeing that they are successful in resolving unaided all the
little difficulties they encounter in everyday affairs, they are
easily led to the conclusion that everything in the world can
be explained and that nothing passes beyond the limits of
intelligence"—specifically, the unaided intelligence of the
commonsensical ordinary American.

American common sense trusts gut instinct but over-
looks that the gut is a conventional organ. Put aside received
ideas, ignore the nattering of elites, and sit still with your
conscience, your intelligence, and your God; then follow the
answer you find, whatever the results. That is the method of
prophets, those turners-over of traditional order. It was
Emerson's formula, and Douglass's. Often, though, American answers turn out to be familiar and nondisruptive,
truths the self-reliant American has heard somewhere
before. Neighbors' and parents' ideas return to us with the
dignity of self-evidence. And, ironically, it becomes difficult
to imagine that others could think differently, when so
many free minds have reached the same conclusions.

Tocqueville spotted this paradox. He thought personal experience too narrow, knowledge too limited, and life too short to build a view of the world from the ground up. Most of what people believe, they must take on trust from others. There was no embarrassment in this: it was just the nature of knowledge. The curious thing was that Americans imagined—sincerely—that they did not rely on received wisdom but formed independent judgments as they went along. The result was that they resisted explicit forms of authority—priests, leaders, traditions—and ended up relying instead on the subtle, ambient pressure of popular opinion. Seeking their own judgments, they again and again reached the same conclusions as their countrymen. The obviousness of the conclusions seemed to be proof of the power of common sense. In fact, it was just as much proof of the power of public opinion to give some thoughts the clear ring of the obvious, others the clink of the unbelievable or absurd.

This sort of self-certainty seemed to underlie George W. Bush's confidence in the success of the Iraq invasion, which he ascribed not to the foreign-policy expertise of men like his father but to "a higher father." The president's vision was both strategic and theological. Strategically, in his second inaugural address he professed the discovery that "America's vital interests and our deepest beliefs are now one" because only promoting freedom could keep us safe. Theologically, Bush declared in his 2005 State of the Union address, "I believe God has planted in every heart the desire to live in freedom." The ideas united in a single harmony: the order of each freedom-loving heart upheld that of a free society, which in turn would create a peaceful world.

No doubt other sources helped to make Bush's vision for

Iraq believable: the seemingly spontaneous fall of Communist dictatorships in Central Europe; the wave of imperfect but real democracy that followed; and American military success in the first Gulf War and during humanitarian interventions in Bosnia and Kosovo. Just as important, however, was the president's faith that Iraqis would create a peaceful and democratic world if they were just set free from tyranny—almost regardless of what the American occupiers did in the meantime. This is the faith in common sense, the belief that the ordinary heart contains a blueprint for moral and social life, which is sufficient if we listen to it. It is a humane and hopeful idea, and there is truth in it. As a formula for using political power, it is also dangerously close to willful naïveté. It suggests that one's own heart is transparent, and those of others the same, and that if one's own intentions are pure, one can do no harm. In such a vision, power serves the harmonious pattern that President Bush evoked to defend the Iraq invasion: a good heart, a free society, and a peaceful world. This kind of innocence frees power from knowledge and responsibility. It is political utopianism of the kind Isaiah Berlin decried, but shorn of all obvious radicalism.

One reason so much of the world doubts American good faith in the Iraq invasion is that the naïveté appears willful, like a perverse caricature of a theory of politics. It seems the geostrategic equivalent of Bush's notorious report that he had looked into the eyes of Russia's then president, Vladimir Putin, and found a trustworthy soul in the autocrat and former KGB officer. In this respect the American political worldview sincerely tends toward self-caricature.

Every error of common sense was on display in the inva-

sion and occupation of Iraq. Confident in their humane motives, the president and his more idealistic advisers scarcely considered the inhumane effects their acts might have: the heart, astonishingly, seemed to be enough. Trusting that what seemed clear to them must be equally clear to others, the war's supporters imagined themselves in a concert of freedom-promoting motives with Iraqis, an illusion that took months of growing chaos to unravel. Above all, the architects of the occupation were indifferent to the basic institutions of order, allowing the tasks of government to slip through their fingers. They waited for freedom to arise while squandering its preconditions.

Common Sense: An American History

THE ORIGINS OF American common sense are roughly equal parts political and religious. To appreciate the religious dimension, consider this 1812 sermon at the opening of the Presbyterian church of Port Republic, Virginia. The speaker was George Bourne, no political conservative but an abolitionist who would eventually leave the South and become a contributor to the *Liberator*, the abolitionist newspaper that Frederick Douglass called "my meat and my drink" during his early years of freedom. Discussing the nature of salvation, Bourne stressed the need for "self-loathing and abasement, [and] contempt of the world." There could be no reconciliation between men and God "until we know 'we are wretched, and miserable, and poor, and blind, and naked.' " He followed that biblical quote by asserting in his own voice, "[T]he Judge is not our friend and a resident in our souls."

Contrast Bourne with the wildly influential evangelical preacher Rick Warren, whose *Purpose-Driven Life* has sold tens of millions of copies around the world. "God," Warren writes, "wants to be your best friend." He goes on to assure readers that God can "handle . . . frank, intense honesty from you." The point of being direct with God, even to the point of insulting him, is that God wants individuality, not in Bourne's sense but in ours: "What may appear as *audacity* God views as *authenticity*. God listens to the passionate words of his friends; he is bored with pious, predictable clichés."

Warren's doctrine starts from the problem of all free individuals: what to do with your life. People struggle with meaninglessness, lack of purpose, the feeling that they drift through existence. That feeling, in turn, arises from the unspoken belief that life is meant to have a purpose, that without a clear path something we are supposed to feel is missing. Warren's answer is that each person already has a purpose, a way she is meant to live and things she is supposed to do. That purpose is part of a divine plan, inscribed in the heart at the moment of creation. You discover your part in that plan by looking within, to your heart, which Warren defines as "the bundle of desires, hopes, interests, ambitions, dreams, and affections you have." He continues, "Your heart reveals the *real* you—what you truly are. . . . We instinctively care about some things and not about others. These are clues to where you should be serving." In other words, God *is* "a resident in our souls," exactly what George Bourne claimed he was not and could not be. To find God, you look within. In this picture, knowledge of the divine plan begins and ends in the self, and its achievement is a

celebration of the self and the world, once a person learns to identify those as God's plan. For George Bourne, God was the scourge of the wretched self as well as its eventual salvation. Almost none of that remains in Warren's theology.

The passage from Bourne to Warren marks an American transformation. The country was founded amid religious ideas that included an emphasis on human depravity, the idea that the Presbyterian abolitionist Bourne expressed when he called human beings wretched, poor, miserable, and naked. This strain of pessimism about human nature prompted the New Haven minister Lyman Beecher to reflect approvingly in 1812, "Our fathers were not fools. . . . Their fundamental maxim was, that man is desperately wicked, and cannot be qualified for good membership in society without the influence of moral restraint."

Beecher exaggerated: religious pessimism was not especially the attitude of America's founding politicians. Most were in some measure republicans, members of a political tradition that stressed the human aptitude for self-rule. Alexander Hamilton opened the first paper in *The Federalist*, the now-canonical defense of the proposed United States Constitution, by suggesting that independent America was exploring, on behalf of all humanity, "the important question, whether societies of men are really capable or not of establishing good government from reflection and choice, or whether they are forever destined to depend for their political constitutions on accident and force." Hamilton sided with reflection and choice, and so did his fellow revolutionaries and constitutional framers.

Religious thinkers had long regarded republicanism as too humanistic and this-worldly. Indeed, Enlightenment

optimists such as Thomas Jefferson, institution builders such as Hamilton, and choleric and dour characters such as John Adams had in common that their worldviews were formed more by political than by religious ideas. Like any generalization, this one has its exceptions. John Jay and John Witherspoon, in particular, were evangelicals in a way we might recognize today. They, and others such as Patrick Henry and Samuel Adams, supported hereditary church establishments as bulwarks of social order. The most prominent founders, however, tended to be either Deists, who denied the divinity of Jesus and believed in a lawmaker God who took no active part in human affairs, or so reticent about their personal religious beliefs as to make the issue moot. In this respect, the Revolution's political leaders were representative of their society as well as its elite: Americans in 1776 and 1787 were much less "churched" than those of the next generation.

The first decades of independence brought dramatic change to American life. Two developments especially contributed to the rise of common sense. The first was an alliance among republicanism, patriotism, and Christianity. It made political liberty, American nationalism, and religious belief parts of a single creed. The second was a new version of Christianity emphasizing innate potential for goodness in the human heart, a set of moral and religious instincts that provided trustworthy guides to judgment and action. The first change repudiated John Wesley's political pessimism and set up George W. Bush's confidence that democratic freedom was enough to change the world itself. The second rejected the view of human depravity that George Bourne and Timothy Dwight expressed, replacing it with a new trust in moral intuition.

Christian Patriotism

THE RAPPROCHEMENT BETWEEN Christianity and American political culture had several sources. One was the political and social ferment that the Revolution set in motion. American independence arrived in a frontier society. Scant authority checked the passions and ambitions of the new country's young population. Americans sprinted after open land, financial schemes, and personal pleasure. If accounts from the time are accurate, drunkenness, fornication, public swearing, and indifference to Sabbath customs all grew more visible—unsurprising on any frontier. The changes stirred suspicion that religious conservatives had been right all along: depraved humanity could not keep itself in order. As a young man, Timothy Dwight had supported the Revolution. As president of Yale, he declared of independent America,

> Never were men so entirely lovers of their own selves,
> covetous, boasters, proud, blasphemers, disobedient
> to parents, unthankful, unholy; without natural
> affection, truce breakers, false accusers, incontinent,
> fierce, despisers of those that are good; traitors,
> heady, high minded, lovers of pleasures more than
> lovers of God.

The source of all this moral chaos was the false liberty of men with appetites unchecked by social discipline. These were "infidels" who believed in the rational freedom of the Enlightenment. Dwight urged his listeners to shun them:

Their neighborhood is contagious; their friendship is a blast [a plague, not a good time]; their communion is death. Will you imbibe their principles? Will you copy their practices? Will you teach your children, that death is an eternal sleep? That the end sanctifies the means? That moral obligation is a dream? Religion a farce? And your Savior the spurious offspring of pollution [born naturally rather than miraculously]? . . . Will you make marriage the mockery of a register's office? Will you become the rulers of Sodom, and the people of Gomorrah? . . . Will you enthrone a Goddess of Reason before the table of Christ? Will you burn your Bibles? Will you crucify anew your Redeemer? Will you deny your God?

In North Carolina, far from bluestocking New Haven, Samuel McCorkle sounded all the same notes in 1798. McCorkle was a Presbyterian minister, a Princeton graduate, and a principal founder of the University of North Carolina. Like Dwight and Beecher, he saw the secular political philosophy of Enlightenment as a threat to moral and social order. He argued that Americans confronted a choice between two versions of freedom connected with two versions of religion. The first, French Deism, was the religion of rationalists and a stalking horse for a radical Enlightenment "conspiracy against all the religions and governments of Europe." The aims of this conspiracy were to restore "sensual pleasures" to an honored place in life and to establish as natural rights political equality and "freedom from all government or control but reason." McCorkle's "French" conspiracy contained the premises of today's freedom:

democracy, political equality, and personal liberty. For him and other conservatives these principles were dark doorways to ungoverned appetites, social chaos, and eventual tyranny. The anarchic principles had crossed the Atlantic from mad France to the newly independent United States. McCorkle reported that the three or four years leading up to his sermon had seen more Sabbath breaking, riots, murder, suicide, adultery, fornication, rape, robbery, perjury, forgery, bribery, speculation, bankruptcy, and imprisonment than all his earlier life. These disasters gave fresh force to the old wisdom: only reverence for a supernatural God could constrain human depravity and maintain social order. McCorkle concluded that Deism had undermined itself by showing that moral principles were impotent unless believed to be divine.

Members of the revolutionary generation sounded similar same notes as they watched their republic fall into what seemed a chaos of greed and pleasure seeking. Benjamin Rush, one of the most hopeful leaders of the Revolution, declared the United States in 1812 "a bebanked, a bewhiskied, and a bedollared nation," an experiment that "will certainly fail" and "has already disappointed the expectations of its most sanguine and ardent friends." He judged that "nothing but the gospel of Jesus Christ will effect the mighty work of making nations happy."

John Adams, always more skeptical than Rush, nonetheless in the 1770s had linked American rebellion to the progress of the human mind and the spirit of liberty against political oppression and mental darkness. In 1813, in a lament typical of his late life, he asked, "Where is now, the progress of the Human Mind? . . . When? Where? And

How? is the present Chaos to be arranged into order?" Jefferson and Hamilton, too, described themselves as aliens in the new and tumultuous America that they, patron saints of democracy and commerce respectively, had done so much to create.

Religious revivalists—who in the view of rationalists like Jefferson and Adams were part of the problem—offered themselves as the solution. Every minister who warned against the country's decline into sensualism, drunkenness, Sabbath breaking, and rationalism also called for a return to godly order. They did not envision that order as the old church-and-crown hierarchy of England but as the proper republican government of a United States disciplined by respect for law and reverence toward God. Lyman Beecher's 1812 New Haven sermon, for all its pessimism about licentious democracy, was titled "A Reformation of Morals Practicable and Indispensable," and Beecher argued that the rising evangelical wave was "turning back the captivity of our land." He envisioned not just a moral revival but a civic one: as mentioned earlier, he urged virtuous believers to keep democracy upright by serving as "a sort of disciplined moral militia" acting for traditional values and the public good. Unlike in many earlier jeremiads, religion did not stand just to repudiate a sinful age or forecast divine punishment: it came as a social force to heal and complete the new American freedom.

Religious revivalists' views found allies in the political class. As the religious historian Mark Noll puts it, the last decade of the eighteenth century brought broad consensus around the idea that "religion should and could contribute

to the morality that was necessary to the virtuous citizens, without which a republic could not survive."

The canonical statement of this idea came in George Washington's 1796 Farewell Address: "Of all the dispositions and habits which lead to political prosperity, Religion and morality are indispensable supports. In vain would that man claim the tribute of Patriotism, who should labor to subvert these great Pillars of human happiness, these firmest props of the duties of Men and citizens." This idea, which became conventional across American politics, is exactly the argument of the revivalists: liberty without religion tends to disintegration, but liberty rooted in religion forms the most virtuous political order.

This combination of beliefs avoided two poles of a conflict that wracked Europe for more than another century. One pole was radical, or secular, Enlightenment, which envisioned both politics and morality as independent of religion—the French Deism that Samuel McCorkle attacked in North Carolina. That view had been a contender for the spirit of the American Revolution: it was the outlook of Thomas Paine, author of the revolutionary pamphlet *Common Sense,* and it would have fit the rationalism and Deism of many founders. The other pole was anti-Enlightenment reaction: the doctrine that social order depended on traditional hierarchy and the age of revolution was a great crime that could be remedied only by restoring the old ranks and forms. American revivalists adopted some of this diagnosis—it gave them their vocabulary of licentiousness, anarchy, and moral decline—but not its authoritarian and theocratic prescription. Instead, they created a

kind of evangelical Enlightenment, embracing increased freedom and equality but insisting that those changes would be desirable and sustainable only if thoroughly imbued with religion. Progress was real, not a self-destructive delusion, but it would undermine itself without the support of religion.

Several features of American experience helped make this synthesis work. One was the long-standing form of the New England political sermon. Delivered on election days and on the dates of public fasts (which were fairly frequent), the political sermon was a genre distinct from the ordinary Sunday address. Where Sabbath sermons concentrated on individual salvation, political sermons addressed the community's divine covenant, warning that sinful behavior could drive God to abandon the colonists. These sermons urged listeners to return to God so that the community could uphold proper order and deserve divine blessings. They thus established a vocabulary, and a habit of mind, that linked religious revival to the preservation of social life. Punishment always lurked in these sermons, but the promise of restoration and continuity was just as important. The sermons cast religion, just government, and personal virtue as achieving those ends together. This formula was thus available in the early Republic as a way to understand and address two concrete problems: for those worried about the chaotic tendencies of the new American freedom, how to stabilize freedom without surrendering it; and for religious leaders seeking their place in the new order, a model of freedom that cast them as indispensable collaborators.

It also helped that organized religion and republican political sentiment had been congenial to each other in the

American colonies before and during the Revolution. New Englanders such as John Adams and the Boston minister Henry Mayhew identified colonial resistance with Protestant nationalism. In their interpretation of the Revolution, English settlement of the American colonies carried on the traditions of both the Protestant Reformation and Parliamentary republican struggles against royal power in the English Civil War of the seventeenth century. Parliamentary forces were adamant in their defense of traditional rights, often radical in their ideal of self-government, marked by the prominence of dissenting Protestants in their ranks, and vituperative and paranoid in their horror of Catholicism. American resistance to the king after 1776 often seemed a resurgence of that spirit. What in England had been a factional position in a bloody war became in North America a candidate—at least a regional candidate—for a new national identity.

Another reason the synthesis worked was that American conservatives and moderates struggled to distinguish *their* Revolution from that of France, which collapsed into domestic terror and open war just years after the American states adopted the Constitution. Paine and many Jeffersonians were early supporters of the French revolutionaries, but as tales spread of mob violence and the guillotine, and Paine himself was imprisoned during the Terror, France became a pariah cause. This was potentially awkward, because each revolution pronounced the inalienable rights of men, asserted popular sovereignty against a monarch, and produced its own experiments with "anarchy." One way to put distance between the two was to emphasize the radical Enlightenment rationalism of the French. Robes-

pierre, the personification of the Terror, tried in 1793 and 1794 to inaugurate a Deist Cult of the Supreme Being as a new civic religion. His yet more radical opponents countered with a Cult of Reason, to be embodied in a statue of the goddess of rationality. Timothy Dwight invoked the image of this goddess "at the table of Christ" in his 1801 parade of licentious horribles. Finer-grained distinctions between the French and American experiences gave way to the formula that zealous trust in reason made the French revolutionaries bloody-minded radicals, while religious faith kept the American rebels temperate and fundamentally orderly.

Thus several strands of motive, thought, and rhetoric came together in an American attitude to religion and politics. The marriage of the two was firm by the early decades of the nineteenth century. As Tocqueville described it in the 1830s, "I do not know if all Americans have faith in their religion . . . but I am sure that they believe it necessary to the maintenance of republican institutions. This opinion does not belong only to one class of citizens or to one party, but to the entire nation; one finds it in all ranks." Writing in 1833, Supreme Court justice Joseph Story, in his *Commentaries on the Constitution*, embodied the attitude that Tocqueville sketched: "Indeed, in a republic, there would seem to be a peculiar propriety in viewing the Christian religion, as the great basis, on which it must rest for its support and permanence, if it be . . . the religion of liberty." A partnership had been formed that covered the distance from John Wesley's eighteenth-century abhorrence of republics to his fellow Methodist George W. Bush's twenty-first century embrace of freedom as God's gift to humanity and the

United States as freedom's special vessel. Every element of Bush's formula was already present in the nineteenth century's distinctly American synthesis, the evangelical Enlightenment. That development stamped familiar institutions with divine approval, a blessing that was indispensable to the self-assurance of American common sense.

Common Sense and Moral Knowledge

ANOTHER SIGNAL CHANGE at the root of the doctrine of common sense was a new idea of how people make moral judgments. The traditional view of human depravity, that God was no resident of the human heart, made individual judgment a thin and hazardous reed. But in the eighteenth century, a contrary idea was developing in Scotland, particularly in the work of the Irish-born philosopher and theologian Francis Hutcheson. Hutcheson argued for an inherent "moral sense" that disclosed the rightness and wrongness of actions as naturally as perception conveyed the properties of the physical world. Hutcheson's thought had much in common with that of economist and moral philosopher Adam Smith, who described innate "passions" and moral judgment as keeping social life orderly with no need for salvation to heal a mutilated human nature. Theories of social passions and the moral sense were influential in the mid–eighteenth century at Princeton, where James Madison and John Witherspoon studied, and at Glasgow and Edinburgh, where Pennsylvanian and American founder James Wilson was educated. Hutcheson was a major influence on George Wythe, Thomas Jefferson's mentor and "second father," and his ideas almost certainly influenced Jefferson's confidence

in the unaided human judgment that might find con-
tentious "truths to be self-evident."

In America, "moral sense" ran together with the broader
idea of "common sense"—*common* with the double meaning
of being universal and of being ordinary, plain, and simple.
The heart of the idea was that everyday people, without special training, could solve practical, moral, and theological
problems. The same Timothy Dwight who warned Yale
against licentious freedoms declared in 1793 that "Common-
sense" qualified a "plain man" to know "as perfectly as Aris-
totle, or Sir Isaac Newton . . . whether Christ lived,
preached, wrought miracles, suffered, died, appeared alive
after death, and ascended to Heaven. The testimony of the
senses, under the direction of Common-sense, is the deciding, and the only testimony, by which the existence of these
facts must be determined."

The long-ago events that Christian creeds affirmed were
as evident to the senses as, say, how to fix a gap in a fence.
This radical proposition did not stay within the university
walls of New Haven. Lorenzo Dow, a fiery-eyed itinerant
preacher of the early nineteenth century, caught the spirit of
the time when he identified Martin Luther's rejection of
Catholic Church government as a reassertion of "common
sense [that] had become . . . blinded by the ignorance of
darkness."

Dow went on to praise the American colonists as
defenders of "common sense" and "the liberty to think, and
judge, and act for themselves." He expressed confidence that
common sense and proper social reform would go together:
"A few plain Rules, properly enforced, will prove of more
consequence than tyrannical barbarity, or despotic cruelty.

This is self-evident to those who reflect on the various modes of family government." Common sense honed on everyday experience was enough to solve the most complex problems of social life.

Few went quite as far as Dow, who accompanied his doctrine of democracy and natural rights with a long-haired, prophetic appearance. (His was, however, an age that produced plenty of American prophets and sects, Joseph Smith and Mormonism being the most prominent and lasting.) But one has only to see the common thread between his thought and that of the conservative Timothy Dwight to appreciate how widespread the faith in common sense became in those decades. There were, of course, serious disputes about how far to take the doctrine: Dwight, a member of an older generation and of the ministerial elite, objected to the untrained interpretations of amateur preachers, noting with bitter irony that the same citizens who would not hire an unqualified builder would put their souls in the hands of an autodidact prophet. Nonetheless, by embracing the doctrine of common sense and the evangelical movements that carried it, even conservatives such as Dwight reinforced the very process they futilely tried to slow or redirect.

Two polestars of the rising evangelical culture gave the idea of common sense especially vivid expression. One was biblical literalism, the belief that the Bible is the transcribed word of God and true in every particular. The radicalism of this idea lies in the belief that lurks behind it: any literate reader can reach the meaning of God's word by sitting down with the plain text. Literalism in practice is less about where the words come from than about who can understand them,

and how. For literalists, interpretation requires no training or even special intelligence. *Literal* meant plain and accessible. As historian Nathan Hatch concludes, this change "empowered ordinary people by taking their deepest spiritual impulses at face value rather than subjecting them to the scrutiny of orthodox doctrine and the frowns of respectable clergymen."

Evangelical ministers also appealed to emotion and intuition in their calls for conversion and revival. This was not exactly new, of course: Saul was overcome on the road to Damascus, and Saint Augustine's conversion, famously recorded in his *Confessions,* was an ecstatic, mystical experience. Jonathan Edwards and other leaders of the Great Awakening of the 1730s and 1740s made more emotional appeals than their predecessors. But in the early decades of independence, a religious establishment that mistrusted emotional "enthusiasm" gave way to a passionate embrace of feeling as the key to spiritual truth. Dwight, a bridging figure in this change as in much else, defended emotional revivalism against the charge of enthusiasm, arguing that a matter as important as salvation *should* bring intense feeling: "seasons of deep despondence, and successive transport," misery and ecstasy. In defending American liberty against the infidels' disbelief and sensuality, he found he much preferred religious enthusiasm to "a cold, contemptuous indifference toward every moral and religious subject."

With such praise of feeling, the heart was on its way to becoming the American moral compass. Religious revivals became notorious for their physical displays of ecstasy. An aging Jefferson complained that worshippers "pour forth the effusions of their love to Jesus, in terms as amatory and car-

nal, as their modesty would permit them to use to a mere earthly lover." To a more charitable observer, these "effusions" were the outward signs of an inward transformation: being "born again" or "born in the spirit" was the touchstone of almost all evangelical revival. Rebirth turned the heart, renewed it, and made it whole. God the Judge did not reside in the heart, the Calvinist George Bourne had insisted; but for the new evangelicals, Methodists, Baptists, and others, truth entered the heart and announced its presence there.

The role that religion assumed in the developing American experience of freedom was complex, even paradoxical. On one hand, religious conviction and community—Dwight's "moral militia"—were tasked to preserve virtue and order by limiting the excesses of "licentious" freedom. On the other, faith increasingly depended on the passionate feelings whose unchecked power had long frightened the conservative enemies of both political radicalism and religious "enthusiasm." Those impulses, once so suspect, were now the handmaidens of moral renewal. Religious feeling was the passionate path to chastity, the ecstatic helper of continence, the intoxicating gateway to orderliness and sobriety. The world of Puritan settlers and Deist and republican revolutionaries was giving way to the virtuous enthusiasms that would eventually produce George W. Bush and Rick Warren.

Religious feeling could play this part only bolstered by belief in something like Hutcheson's moral sense. There must be no danger of confusion between the passions of sin and those of religious rebirth. Biblical literalism held that God's word was clear and coherent, open to any lay reader. The same idea now came to apply to the human heart, at

least when the heart was open to God. Otherwise, religious feeling would have been no safe guide to life or salvation. Otherwise the charismatic leaders who filled revival tents might be quacks and demagogues. If that proved true, then the new evangelical movements might become the anarchic mob that enemies of democracy had always feared. Hence, common sense had to be as conventional in substance as it was self-assured in attitude.

Personal Utopianism

UTOPIAN NEEDS TO BE more than an insult. Taking the word in a neutral sense, the first lines of the Declaration of Independence are utopian, envisioning a world of unprecedented political freedom and equality. Frederick Douglass's insistence on equal dignity and Emerson's on the sovereignty of conscience are utopian also. In this neutral sense, utopianism has two aspects: a judgment that what now exists in the world, however familiar and lawful, is intolerable; and a choice to assert the demands of feeling and conscience, however unlikely their success. What is intolerable in the world and what is irresistible in our innermost and most persistent demands (Emerson called it the "soul['s] ... enormous claim") are two sides of the same experience: the discovery of a need that has no answer in the present world. The discovery may come in some moment of ordinary experience: a joy in being alive that one cannot explain, a fleeting intimacy with another person whom one is otherwise forbidden to know or touch (think of interracial love in the age of miscegenation bans), a taste of what it would be like to work from delight. Or the wish may begin in the language

and images of the common culture, in a biblical prophecy of justice and plenty, or in haunting words: "that all men are created equal." The utopian impulse makes that wish a demand, a project to reshape the world by answering a human need that will otherwise have to be put away and forgotten—until it appears again.

Ironically, we successors to American utopianism now inhabit only a personal version of that spirit, which makes us revolutionary in our private lives and mores but complacent about our institutions. This is foremost a utopianism of the individual life. It does not pay less honor to the impulses at the core of utopianism, but it does them less good, and makes them less credible, than would a version looking to both the heart and the world in which it must live.

To appreciate this peculiar development, consider an unrecognized forerunner of American ideas: Charles Fourier, the embittered French salesman and clerk who spent his evenings at the start of the nineteenth century filling notebooks with vivid rants against commercial civilization and plans for idyllic communities of spontaneous work and free love. Inhabitants of Fourier's "phalanxes" would be assigned tasks and lovers based on their place in Fourier's map of the 810 personality types. "Courts of Love," meeting at night, would assign amorous duties to ensure that every member of the community received a "sexual minimum" of erotic satisfaction. Fourier once predicted that, when his principles governed the world, life would be so sweet that the seas would turn to lemonade.

Fourier's comical excess captures how Americans tend to think of political utopianism, if we do at all: as a cocktail of hyperbureaucratic imagination, unrealistic ideas about

human nature, and, at root, the alienation and grudges of people who probably can't put their pants on straight, let alone find a sexual partner in the usual way. Rather than lemonade oceans, Fourier's legacy was small bands of alienated intellectuals grubbing in the dirt, falling into sexual jealousy, and soon coming apart. Such doomed experiments became an indelible image in popular culture. Monty Python had exemplary fun with futile utopianism in *The Holy Grail*, in which King Arthur encounters Dennis the anarcho-syndicalist, whose comrades reject the king's authority, run their community by a complex system of rotating power, and otherwise spend their time digging in the unpromising muck of the British countryside.

But something strange happened while we were laughing, ruefully or sadistically, at idealists who wound up squabbling over lovers and potatoes. The utopian Fourier won by losing.

Fourier's basic idea was that human desire, which he called passion, did not have to be at war with social order. Peace and prosperity didn't require people to accept chastity or to do the often spirit-crushing labor that tradition or the market dealt them. Traditional thought regarded human life as tragic: society held together only if people refrained from expressing their passions, despite the pain of the suppression. Without the discipline of repression, most imagined, chaos would consume social order. The only way to secure a life together was for most people to die thousands of small deaths, putting away their wishes to be great, do joyous work, and love intensely all their lives. Priests and moralists condemned these disruptive passions as sin and taught ordinary people to die their small deaths quietly while calling

that a virtuous life. Bitter, frustrated, half-crazy Fourier answered that this mass sacrifice of the human spirit was no more necessary than any other superstitious offering. There was no contradiction between passion and prosperity. People would produce more if they could do work that answered their deepest desires. They should have a variety of tasks through the day, including breaks for play. In this way they could satisfy "the butterfly passion," the wish to move among activities and keep the whole personality alert and involved. Acknowledging the taste for competition, Fourier proposed dividing workplaces into teams that would seek to outdo one another while ties among their members grew stronger. By reorganizing work to respond to what naturally moved people in their lives, he proposed to get more out of people while making them happier and more fulfilled.

Take out the phalanxes and the 810-part personality chart, and how far is this from today's ordinary dreams? Rick Warren calls "[y]our emotional heartbeat" the key to selecting the right work and writes that dissatisfaction comes from failure to know ourselves. Warren sets this idea in an evangelical worldview, but it is the core of the broader American ideal of vocation: do what you love, what makes you happy and feels right; follow your bliss. Not everyone believes in this ideal, of course, and of those who believe in it, not all get to live it; but it is our ideal nonetheless. We have nearly discarded the old idea, which Fourier attacked, of work as a person's assigned place in a hierarchical social order, and while many still regard their jobs as what Fourier believed most work was—a barter of daylight hours for evenings and weekends—most would exchange that experi-

ence for purpose and fulfillment if they could. That is why people have bought tens of millions of copies of Warren's *Purpose-Driven Life*, along with so many other guides to meaning in work and life. Fourier's utopianism is our everyday ambition.

None of this is to say that Fourier's thought has directly influenced American life. The point is that his ideas, once the epitome of unrealistic radicalism, now share much with common sense. That change suggests how deeply common sense can change, and how strong the utopian element is in our version of it. Fourier's phalanxes, for their part, have become the workplaces of the American elite. The corporate campuses of Silicon Valley were celebrated in the 1990s for mixing work and play, with volleyball courts outside and foosball tables amid the cubicles, and for letting gifted and productive workers set their own schedules and, sometimes, their own projects. They did not always make good on that image, but the appeal of the image bespeaks how the ideal of work has changed. Fourier's cooperatively competitive teams dot the workplaces of entertainment, technology, and consulting, to name a few. Those industries, in turn, have incubated a new generation of truly voluntary work: collaborative making and sharing, linked by digital technology. The best-known product of this movement is Wikipedia, the sprawling online encyclopedia created by volunteer enthusiasts around the world. Less famous collaborative projects, from maps of the surface of Mars (assembled by dispersed volunteers from snippets of massive digital photo files) to online photomontages, are everywhere. We share the ideal of doing work from passion and in the spirit of play.

If Fourier's prescriptions for passionate work have often seemed fatuous and doomed even as they were winning, his sexual ideas were much more scandalous. They were so unconventional in his lifetime that he concealed most of them, filling personal notebooks with elaborate plans for freeing bodily passion but providing only hints in his published works. Fourier believed that shutting down sexual desire bent the whole personality out of shape, making it difficult to form bonds of any kind, especially the ideal love that combined erotic satisfaction with deep affection. He raged against the strictures that denied young people sexual love until they married and denied it to the aged and luckless because they were deemed undesirable. He promised that in the phalanxes, old and young alike would enjoy "amorous illusions and distractions." In Fourier's thought, no social order that called itself humane could deny "the mutiny of love," the insistence on erotic satisfaction and passionate attachment. "When love has gone," he wrote, "man can only vegetate." In a sentence Rick Warren might have written—and has amply paraphrased—he declared, "God shares this conviction; he thinks that man is an incomplete being without love."

Where do Fourier's fantasies stand today? If we once again excise the Gallic bureaucratic imagination, setting aside the Courts of Love, we look remarkably like Fourier's children. The mutiny of love is complete, and the mutineers now steer the ship. Not everyone has gone along: some evangelicals and others maintain a traditional view of sexual virtue, and from time to time an iconoclast calls for a revival of chastity. But today the traditionalists, not the libertines, are iconoclasts. In high school, college, and beyond, sexual

exploration is a human right, a natural activity that nearly everyone joins. A subtle, shifting set of distinctions has emerged to parallel the ones Fourier imagined: hookups, friends with benefits, lovers, and, when passionate attachment arrives, boyfriends and girlfriends, wives and husbands. Here in the aftermath of the mutiny of love, people marry later, but they do marry, and those who marry late are the most likely to stay married. And for those who, for whatever reason, are happier on their own, that too is now more a choice, less a shame.

In other words, we hardheaded, commonsensical Americans have created our own phalanx. Our version of Fourier's utopian vision has come about by distinctly American means. Where he proposed a bureaucracy of experts governed by a nearly mathematical code, we have achieved something like a free market in sex. Where he envisioned a social right to a minimum of sexual satisfaction, akin to European protections for income, housing, and employment, we have arrived at an American-style right to private sexual choice and otherwise left people to do as well as they can. Our institutional imagination has produced match.com and speed dating, not by-laws for phalanxes. In place of Fourier's Court of Love, which was to dispense erotic satisfaction by principles of justice and equity, we have erected a Bazaar of Love. Our spirit, though, is utopian. Or, rather, it was utopian. Today, in the quarters that have taken it up, it is common sense. Because it is common sense, it is invisible as radicalism, as mutiny, as utopianism.

Utopianism as Conservatism

BOTH COMMON SENSE and personal utopianism reinforce the sense that, while our judgment is omnipotent and
our personal lives deeply free, our institutions are unchang-
ing. Personal utopianism nearly requires believing in our
institutions' perfection. Trusting that one can remake one's
own life depends on confidence that the world will rise up
to meet the heart's desire. That amounts to confidence that
existing political and economic institutions produce just the
right degree of freedom—the freedom one needs to be oneself. One telling symptom of this belief is that mathematical
anomaly, the nearly 40 percent of Americans who believe
they are or will soon be among the country's wealthiest
1 percent. This version of utopianism envisions almost infinite plasticity for personal life and nearly perfect rigidity for
the institutions that so profoundly shape individual lives. It
portrays institutions as if they were natural facts, personal
life as the product of wide-open choice, when in fact institutions arise from collective choices and personal life takes
wings or chains from its institutional setting. In this respect,
personal utopianism is a recipe for persistent frustration.
With scant programmatic impulse or social vision, it aims
not to reform the world to meet human wishes but to find
the key in which those wishes reach their preordained harmony with the world.

In its favor, our utopianism discourages the sense of personal futility that Fourier himself embodied and that has
dogged other frustrated dreamers. The personal utopian does
not know what he cannot do. This self-confidence has made
private life and personality into ongoing experiments in liv-

ing. A nation of personal utopians will push some of the central experiments of modern freedom to their limits. It will test every allegedly unavoidable limit on mobility, self-invention, and forms of community. Everything close enough to touch, personal utopians will remake just to see whether they can live with it remade. And they will find out firsthand just how much of life can take its shape from the free activity of unconfined individuals, not in theory but in practice.

That achievement, however, comes along with forgetfulness about politics and institutions. Modern explorations of freedom began in the gamble that the world could accommodate, even answer, more from us than we knew. Our personal utopianism has moved the center of this gamble from politics to individual life and from theory to experience. There it has all the power of what is lived rather than merely imagined or argued. It also has all the limitations of acts that are only individual. Where our most personal wishes would require a changed world to make them real, we approach that prospect haltingly, if at all. American utopianism found its power by escaping from politics, and it finds its limits in the same escape. Neglecting concrete constraints and the changes that would be necessary to make our wishes real, we may frustrate dreams that would otherwise be achievable. We would pursue our personal utopian projects more effectively if we stopped imagining that our wishes have the power to make themselves true.

Vision and Experiment

THE RESTLESSNESS OF AMERICAN FREEDOM has produced a practical tradition of experiment and innovation,

made up of millions of small declarations of independence from hierarchy, constraint, and fear. Every successful advance in freedom has been an experiment in reordering some part of life to make real a greater range of human possibility. These have generally not been sweeping, ideological reforms, the "visionary politics" that antiutopians disdain. Instead, the experiments have mostly been incremental, advancing where they succeed, and succeeding where they make enlarged lives possible.

Experiment is the best light in which to understand many American achievements. Political democracy is an experiment in organizing government power, the greatest coercive power in modern life, on the principle that everyone must have a fair part in directing it. Imperfect as its results are, this is a root-and-branch rejection of the idea that societies must choose among fixed tradition, bare authority, and anarchy. It is also a rejection of the idea that political communities must be divided between those who have a share in sovereign power—whites in antebellum America, men before universal suffrage, property holders throughout much of history in England and America—and those who obey law but do not shape it: blacks, women, landless laborers, migrant workers, and, where the institution existed, slaves. As a refutation of those ideas, democracy is a successful experiment, and there is no reason to regard it as complete.

The market economy, too, is an experiment. It entrusts to personal choice decisions about sharing and using the world's riches. Whatever failures and injuries markets bring, the principle that billions of individual choices can order the world's work and play is as radical in its way as political

democracy. It replaces a system in which fathers, husbands, and masters stood at the peak of a pyramid, commanding those who depended on them much as they used their tools and their lands—and, in turn, took commands from other men who outranked them. The early American ideal simply removed those higher-ups from the picture, so that each free man stood on his apex beneath only the sky, foursquare with other such men, and dominant over his servants, household members, and slaves. Moving from that vision of equality among masters to one in which all were masters of themselves turned the world inside out, and continues to do so today.

The freeing of intimacy, too, was a radical experiment in ordering life. The power of the father was the model of all traditional authority. It rested on a picture of the family as a system of command, obedience, and discipline of sexual appetite. From the beginning, critics saw rising freedom and equality as threatening to make all appetites equal and unbounded. So they denounced political democracy, the market, and each change in the family and sexual mores as a formula for license and anarchy. They still do. Yet the modern world has not abolished marriage but changed its ideal to a relationship of intimacy, affection, and desire—with the remarkable result that what two men or two women seek in demanding the right to marry is substantially what one man and one woman hope to achieve. Sex has run far from custom and hierarchy to become a way of forming, remaking, and breaking ties to others and elaborating one's understanding of oneself.

Freedom is thus an engagement with open questions. In economic life, how much free choice of work, how much

self-expression, how much control over our daily labor, are compatible with expanding wealth? How much security—the freedom of knowing your job will remain yours, or that you will have care when you are sick—is compatible with innovation, which gives us new powers every decade? In politics, how much democracy is compatible with order and the rule of law? How strong can individual rights be without undermining security against criminals, or, these days, terrorists? The unhappy conundrum of our time, that neither security nor liberty is worth having without the other, brings home that both are elements of freedom, enabling us to lead the lives we wish to lead, even as each presses against, and sometimes overwhelms, the other. In intimate life, how much freedom of the heart can coexist with the perennial tasks of families and communities to give succor to our vulnerability and neediness and to raise the next generation? We approach these questions as traditionalists and experimenters, incremental reformers of our own order.

To say that Americans have no political philosophy, as some have claimed, is to miss the daring and incisive inquiry—call it philosophical if you like—that Douglass, Emerson, and countless others conducted into the human meaning of American freedom. They did not work mainly with political doctrine, but they made the doctrines of their time, spoken and unspoken, answer to their intimate and unbreakable demands. Their premise was that we cannot know the meaning of "life, liberty, and the pursuit of happiness" *for us* unless we try them in forms that fit our lives, that answer what Emerson called the soul's enormous claim. These principles should make life's power and possibility manifest, not replace them with dead abstractions.

A full remembrance of American traditions of freedom would recognize how often our experiments have shocked observers and surprised even those who undertook them: the revolutionaries proved "anarchy" could be tolerable, Douglass showed that slave revolt could be a path to constitutional interpretation, and Emerson insisted that self-knowledge was worth the risk of turning out to be the devil's child. Our conventional wisdom today is a legacy from dead radicals who risked the impossible. The impossible became ordinary only because they succeeded. Fixing the meaning of our freedom, imagining that some earlier declaration of independence was the last one ever, would be false to our actual tradition, a tradition not of fixity but of radical experiment. Without that spirit, we would inhabit a dead tradition, a dogma.

One way to understand the last several centuries is as a story of freedom's expansion in an order that invites further experiments in freedom. That expansion is not something that has befallen us, nor been bequeathed by technology or historical chance or divine plan, but something we have achieved. We have achieved it because of who we are—freedom-seeking people. We may not have evolved or been created to seek freedom, but it is what we have learned to do. We have remade the world in the image of our freedom and remade ourselves by inhabiting it. We live in the midst of both those projects.

The greatest difficulty in this tradition has been to integrate the emancipating demands—the insistence on our own innermost truths that makes us utopians—with the recognition of our frailty and interdependence. This recognition is absolutely necessary for any utopian impulse to

translate to shaping a real and habitable place, and its lack has often made utopian efforts seem morally blind and humanly obtuse. We are infinite in possibility and importance, and in trying to create communities of free people we acknowledge the infinite in one another. We are also terribly finite and small, able to spend lifetimes in confusion or die instantly and senselessly. Like gods, we can remake our world through imagination and action. Yet all our visions are arid and our wishes hollow without one another's sympathy and care, without the patience for our weakness that is just as important as recognition of our strength. As history's hostages and its dependent children, we are one another's prisoners, caretakers, and rescuers.

The most hopeful response to this condition is a vision to guide our experiments, a way of seeing one another that recognizes that our power is inseparable from our dependence, our greatness from our need. It is because we are free that we can change our lives, institutions, and rules to answer our own demands; yet it is because we are limited and vulnerable that we need institutions, rules, and, above all, one another to make our freedom real, and we must make each change with care and respect for what it disrupts. Such a vision can contribute to integrating highly personal experiences of freedom and order into a picture of institutions: citizenship, the government, the economy. Our idea of freedom is a deceptively difficult one. It requires both restraint and engagement from government, regulation and laissez-faire in economic life, and a picture of citizenship that acknowledges both autonomy and interdependence. The most difficult integration contains all of these and goes beyond them. To be realists about ourselves, we must also be

utopians, because that is the truth of our condition and aspiration. To be successful utopians, we must also be realists, because what we wish becomes true when we find ways to change the world as well as ourselves and enter a new world together.

CHAPTER 6

The Economics of 1776, and Today

THIS IS AN AGE of economics. The market often seems as basic as physics and as sweeping and decisive as war. Finance and start-ups show their charisma by attracting the most able and ambitious young people. They produce celebrities—who has not heard of Bill Gates or George Soros?—and political leaders, recently New York's financier-mayor. Managing money, or the corporations that make it, has become the hallmark of talent, ambition, and that all-important American quality, realism. The surest sign of competence and adulthood is to have made money; staying poor brings both under suspicion. Investment decisions provide metaphors for all choice. Who under thirty-five does not instinctively weigh upsides, downsides, options, and, as often as not, opportunity costs? Whoso would be a man, wrote Emerson, must be a nonconformist: nowadays, he must also be an investor.

The market is both a spectator's game and a participant sport. The boom of the late 1990s moved financial markets from specialized news to the same general-interest category as sports scores. Investment—in a home, for retirement, for

simple gain—is ordinary and much discussed among people who, two generations ago, would have kept it between themselves and their accountants, or not thought much about it at all. This goes as much for the young, bohemian, and fashionable as for the older and more staid. In fact, it may be the greatest gain for the lords of the market that since Tom Wolfe called them "masters of the universe," they have taken back the cachet they once yielded to edgier types. Those who make the money are now widely suspected of having better parties, better clothes, and more fun than others—and, maybe more to the point, more initiative and creativity in their work.

In some ways, none of this is new. As we have seen, some of the more idealistic American founders complained at the start of the nineteenth century that the country they created had been overrun by money-grubbers. Alexis de Tocqueville noted that Americans in the 1830s sought wealth relentlessly because money had replaced all other sources of esteem. Writing after the Civil War, Walt Whitman attacked an amoral "realism" that valued profit and nothing else—and that attack came before the high period of the Gilded Age, at the close of the nineteenth century, when robber barons ruled economy and politics alike. Progressive twentieth-century presidents from Woodrow Wilson to Franklin Roosevelt asserted that the country had lost its way, pursuing money over fairness and equal opportunity. What they attacked was clear. Exactly what they proposed to restore was not. The United States was founded on speculation, quick profit, and sometimes breathtaking mobility, which always came with crassness and exploitation. Being poor has

seldom been a good plan anywhere, but Americans show a singular lack of interest in any mark of status or worth besides wealth. The other forms of esteem we provide, mostly fame and politics, are fungible: there are no poor celebrities or penniless former presidents. There is no American idea of honorable poverty to match the ascetic or scholarly ideals of many cultures.

So there is nothing strange in the economy's power over American life and imagination. What is strange is that at various moments most of us hold two almost completely opposite visions of "the economy." One might think of these as two folk economies. One is the image of the market as a realm of creativity, excitement, and mastery, far more vivid and efficacious than fractious, bloviating politics or ethereal scholarship. This is not just a heroic picture of elite entrepreneurs and hedge-fund managers but an idea of economic life that many Americans expect to join. In this folk economy, as mentioned earlier, nearly 40 percent of people say they are in, or will soon join, the nation's wealthiest 1 percent, and two-thirds say that wealth comes from talent and effort, not luck. (That is twice the rate of Europeans who say so.) Nor is the heroic folk economy only a matter of making money. American consumption, too, is more and more about self-transformation. While some critics lament the death of political "soulcraft," industries of the soul proliferate, from self-help and psychotherapy to burgeoning legal drugs that change mood and even personality. Gyms, personal trainers, and videos offer a growing menu of ways to sculpt the body. Food and design have become new democratic art forms, bringing novelty—and status anxiety—to

areas recently reserved to elites and aesthetes. Whether you are earning or consuming, this folk economy sells change and mastery above all.

Yet the other American folk economy is the antithesis of mastery. This is the image of "market forces" as relentless powers pressing history along a course that human choice cannot change. Does any executive want, as a personal matter, to organize the takeover that throws middle-aged workers into pensionless unemployment, press the bargain that strips employees of health insurance, or organize outsourcing to polluting Chinese factories? The shareholders who own publicly traded companies, too, would think twice before making these decisions, if they were deciding as citizens, neighbors, or family members, rather than as abstract profit makers. The professionals who staff the deals sometimes openly regret the human cost of their work. But they will keep doing it as long as it is legal. More important, they will have no choice unless they change jobs—and then someone else in the same job will soon face the same nonchoice. Anyone who tries to make different decisions will rapidly meet a series of punishments known collectively as market discipline. For executives, these include falling stock prices if quarterly earnings come in lower than expected or the company has not adopted the most aggressive profit-making strategy, and flight by customers if prices are higher than competitors' because, say, they reflect health benefits or American wages. For financiers, the threat is low returns on investment funds, compared with competitors who will happily buy established companies to slash payrolls and sell off assets, or otherwise make a quick, high-margin return. The point is not that corporate execu-

tives and financiers are evil but that taking on those roles means accepting rules that recognize one goal: maximum profit within (usually) the limits of law. Masters of the universe keep their positions by accepting universal laws that are as unyielding as Isaac Newton's formulas: as with gravity, you do not ignore such rules for long or with good results.

What is true of the most powerful players in the economy goes many times over for everyone else. The undulations of a fast-moving global market have made household income fluctuate more dramatically in recent years than in earlier decades. A market-driven health insurance system has pressed the number of uninsured Americans up almost annually since the 1980s. Even for those who do well, there is an aspect of the lottery in the whole system. Who knew in 1970 that American heavy industry would disappear, sending union workers with high school educations into retail and service work at fractions of the pay they had expected when they took their first jobs? Who could say in 1990 that private-sector lawyers' salaries would rocket skyward, while nonspecialist doctors and architects would fall behind in professional earnings? Was there any way to know that a computer science degree would soon be extraordinarily lucrative, while training in other technical and demanding fields would produce unemployed research scientists? What wisdom or virtue was involved in buying real estate just before the great boom at the start of the millennium, or stock eight years earlier? It is universal habit, and American habit in particular, to take credit for one's own successes—and, often, the blame for disappointments; but from a clear-eyed perspective, the market lands the kinds of heavy,

unaccountable blows that used to be attributed to the Fates, and its rewards can be just as mysterious. At the heart of our imagined mastery, what we most hope for or fear can turn out to be what we least control.

There is a way of seeing disruption and insecurity as necessary and good. The market rewards those who make or do what others will pay them for, and it shows no mercy to those who do otherwise. The rewards are even larger for innovators who find new ways to fulfill desires. In search of these rewards, people set out to do what they believe others want: build cars or computers, write songs, resculpt the crooked noses of the wealthy, or grow organic vegetables as comely as their chemical-drenched cousins. This striving to bring the greatest happiness to the greatest number of others produces a perennial churn, which the economist Joseph Schumpeter famously called creative destruction. New technologies obliterate old industries. New pleasures eclipse old habits. The capable flee declining industries to enter rising ones. In turn, industries bolt from expensive or otherwise inefficient regions and countries and find places where they can do their work more cheaply. The result is more of what people want—satisfied desires, summed up in such economic abstractions as rising productivity and growing national income.

Security is the enemy of creative destruction. Every middle-aged worker entitled to keep his job in a declining industry, every outmoded company shored up by protection from imports or foreign investment, represents a drag on innovation and efficient deployment of capital and labor. That, in turn, means a cost in satisfied desires. The rules of the market turn the world economy into a global desire-

satisfaction machine. Anyone who tries to hold on to a piece of security in violation of these rules puts her own satisfaction over a larger portion of others'. This is the moral logic of rigid market rules. The straightforward irony of the market, made famous by Adam Smith's image of an invisible hand aligning personal and public interests, is that it directs individual selfishness to the generous result of growing overall satisfaction. A more subtle irony is this: in the moral logic of the market, we are supposed to be selfish within the rules but altruistic about the rules, accepting the personal insecurity or loss that comes with the logic of overall benefit.

This vision of economic life as expressing inflexible but ultimately benign rules has several sources. In twentieth-century public life, however, it has served a special role as the solution to a political problem. Maximum overall prosperity is a version of the common good, a candidate to be the goal of policy and object of civic loyalty. It is especially congenial to the diversity of national life. Whatever you want, from a high-performance car to wilderness hiking, from Shakespeare productions to televangelism broadcasts, producing the means to get yourself more is simpler than persuading others to value it, too. Harold Ickes, a prominent New Dealer, made this point when he argued that consumer welfare should be paramount over partisan disputes. "It is as consumers," Ickes insisted, "that we all have a common interest." Following Ickes's logic, politicians in the last century treated economic questions as what John F. Kennedy called "technical problems . . . administrative problems," not political decisions. The point was to apply the laws of economics correctly.

Although all of this can seem obvious today, it is a drastic departure from tradition to think of economic life as a set of mainly technical problems. Historically, economic thought is deeply entwined with ideas about what freedom means and what would be necessary to achieve it in social life. That history is not an anachronism today: economic life remains essentially tied to themes of freedom. Indeed, the first folk economy, linking economic life to freedom and mastery, is the persistent voice of a long-standing ideal, that the economy exists to make us freer. The second folk economy, the one that understands economics as a set of implacable, superhuman forces, is so powerful today partly because we tend to forget that economies serve human purposes, freedom above all.

Economies of Freedom

SEVENTEEN SEVENTY-SIX, best remembered in the United States for producing the Declaration of Independence, was also the year that Adam Smith's *Wealth of Nations* appeared in print. Smith's book is often described as a declaration of independence for economics, because his target was mercantilism, an approach to economic policy that entwined government with industry. Mercantilist policies picked out favored sectors, protected them with tariffs, granted monopolies to the politically connected, and aimed to build up trade surpluses and the coffers of the state. Smith answered all of this with the revolutionary contention that unregulated, self-interested individual choices would produce the most wealth overall—the proposal captured in the image of the invisible hand.

Yet Smith's vision of economics was as much moral and political as technical. He was equal parts political economist, jurist, psychologist, and moral philosopher, as well as a student of rhetoric and persuasion. Smith believed in "natural liberty," including freedom to choose a trade, move freely in search of business or work, and enter or leave economic relationships by choice. On its face, this falls close to a simple libertarian formula, but Smith had something more complicated in mind. He cared most about the relationships that an economic system created among people, which shaped how they regarded themselves and others. His touchstone values in judging relationships were reciprocity, which he honored and worked to promote, and domination, which he abhorred. He saw market society as embodying the greatest degree of reciprocity possible in his time and showed this by contrasting it with slavery and feudal relations. In those more hierarchical orders, Smith argued, some people depended fundamentally on the will of others for their security and freedom of action. The powerful learned to give commands and their dependents learned to take them. The result was a zero-sum system in which the dignity of the powerful depended on the subjection of their dependents. Those who gave orders commanded respect, while those who took them commanded none.

In the system of "natural liberty" that Smith recommended, no one had a simple power of command: if you wanted someone's time and energy, you had to persuade him to give them to you. That meant addressing his interests, affections, and attachments—in sum, whatever motivated him. It meant, that is, addressing another person, someone with goals and values like, or unlike, your own. Smith

believed that the need to bargain trained the powerful away from domination and toward more subtle ways of seeing and engaging others. He also believed that bargaining taught the humble to exercise judgment and self-respect. Natural liberty created a little zone of free choice, the power to say no, and the corresponding need for others to persuade you to say yes. In that zone, people learned what it was to make choices, what they wanted to pursue, and what they would not accept unless it was a matter of life or death. They learned to think of themselves as people with values and aims, entitled to pursue those. Historian Emma Rothschild has summed up Smith's goals by saying that he hoped economic reform would make human minds less frightened and the world less frightening.

Smith imagined that a market society might honor, not the man who wielded power over the largest number of dependents, but the one who could persuade others to join their efforts freely to his. Smith thought such a person would display competence, self-command, and the ability to engage others sympathetically while keeping his own integrity. In such a world, ordinary interaction could enhance the dignity of all rather than building up some at the cost of pressing down others.

Bringing about that world was a political program: Smith and his admirers were reformers. Natural liberty was not a natural fact, but an ideal that would become real only if law created and enforced it. That reform required a massive transfer of property rights: eliminating all the ways that people owned one another's energy and talents, from indentured servitude to outright slavery, and making individuals the owners of their own bodies and time. Such laws literally

created the market economy. They also contributed to an ideal of free personality and a version of dignity. Smith's treatment of freedom and dignity aligned him with the goals of the American founding, in which political freedom meant much the same thing that economic freedom was for Smith: the opposite of slavery—depending abjectly on no one, having a place of one's own to stand, and asserting the judgment of an independent mind.

The legacy of Adam Smith's 1776 has mattered nearly as much to American life as that of the founders' 1776. The irony in both cases has been a tendency to hold on to the ideal of freedom while forgetting its complicated relationship to institutions and politics. The most treacherously seductive American habit of thought is thinking of political freedom as a set of permanent rights and economic freedom as a system of rigid and relentless rules, then falling into puzzled disaffection when these principles fail to perfect personal freedom. But this is not the only American tradition: at times, political vision and economic experiment have made good on ideals of freedom and dignity. Those times form the model for the practical pursuit of American freedom.

Free Labor: The Opposite of Slavery?

BOTH THE POLITICAL AND ECONOMIC VISIONS of 1776 defined freedom as the opposite of slavery. This meant not depending on the will of another for personal liberty or well-being. It meant having a place to stand in the world, beneath no one, from which to freely exercise will and judgment. Being a free man was a status that gave dignity and

self-respect, not a mere convenience but the keystone of identity. This vision implied a social order in which people's relations to one another would be, somehow, the opposite of slavery. Abraham Lincoln expressed this when he wrote in 1858, "As I would not be a slave, so I would not be a master. This expresses my idea of democracy. Whatever differs from this, to the extent of the difference, is no democracy."

Lincoln's ideal was a long way from the reality of American life between 1776 and the Civil War. American law recognized again and again that slaves were legal chimeras, "persons" and "men," but also "property," "chattels," and "things." As human beings they were "created equal," but they were also the opposite: property subject to an owner's will. The ideal of American freedom relied on the image of slavery, the thing that it was not, just as, in practice, the freedom of the free was entwined with the subjection of the slave.

Americans split angrily over the meaning of this paradox. For some, it was in the nature of things, not a contradiction but a fact of life that should trouble no one. For others, it was an inescapable tragedy, a contradiction Americans would live with because they had no way to solve it. For still others, whose numbers grew before the Civil War, slavery was a challenge to be met, a searing reminder that American freedom was an unfinished project. In 1827, Judge William Brockenbrough of Virginia, a friend of James and Dolly Madison and frequent social host to Chief Justice John Marshall of the Supreme Court, took the complacent view. Brockenbrough argued that there was "no incompatibility" between the personal liberty and security of a slave and a master's rights of ownership. The relationship was a

basically harmonious one, like that of parent and child or master and apprentice, and all it required was for the master to show "due moderation" in his demands and discipline. Brockenbrough's approach, which he set out in a criminal case against a master who had "cruelly beaten" a slave, was humanitarian in its sanguine way. Brockenbrough saw no need, and no defense, for cruelty. But at the same time, he would have excised the radical promise of the Declaration from American life. Freedom in his vision really was the freedom of masters, the highest point in a pyramid of rights and privileges. Rights were relative to where one stood along that pyramid, not universal or inalienable. Just as life took place in a world of adults and children, so it also took place in a world of masters and apprentices, and masters and slaves. Economic life had hierarchy, not freedom, as its touchstone.

Another Southern judge, Thomas Ruffin of North Carolina, expressed a more tragic view in 1829, the year he joined his state's supreme court. The case, *State v. Mann*, was another criminal action, this one against a master who shot and wounded a woman slave as she fled from punishment for "some small offence." Like Brockenbrough, Ruffin was an elite Southerner, in his case a graduate of Princeton. Unlike the Virginian judge, he portrayed slavery as a bitter anomaly in American law. He rejected the idea that owning another human being had anything in common with raising a child or training an apprentice. Enslavement erased the defining powers of the freeman, leaving the slave "doomed . . . to live without knowledge, and without the capacity to make any thing his own, and to toil that another may reap the fruits." There was no way the law could honor

the humanity of a person in such a position: having defined him as a thing, it had to treat him as a thing. "For a slave," Ruffin wrote, "obedience is the consequence only of uncontrolled authority over the body," and so "the power of the master must be absolute, to render the submission of the slave perfect." Slavery really was the opposite of freedom, the living embodiment of all that the Declaration rejected. Nonetheless, it was enshrined in American life and law, and no clear-eyed view of the country could deny it.

Ruffin's opinion suggested a man who had come to reluctant terms with slavery, at least in his public role as a judge. Nonetheless, his stark language gave him an ironic charisma among abolitionists. Like him, they despised as a cozy lie the complacent approach, which covered slavery in the gauze of family ties and moral reciprocity. Shared contempt suggested a kindred spirit. Harriet Beecher Stowe thought the opinion displayed a great soul wrestling with a terrible reality. For her and other abolitionists, slavery betrayed the American promise of universal freedom and also set a standard for reformers: to end human bondage and find a way to make the opening lines of the Declaration real.

Ruffin was plainly torn, but his abolitionist admirers may have underestimated his allegiance to the realities of his time and place. Alongside his diagnosis of slavery as a tyrannical relationship, he expressed hope that public opinion and legislation would make it more humane, though he believed that judges must not try to make those reforms themselves. For all his ambivalence, his description of slavery as a tragic aberration captured in vivid language what many believed, including some who were far from being abolitionists. Defenders of slavery often referred with regret

to the institution's "necessity." That idea had various mean-ings. It could mean that free workers would refuse to accept the jobs that slaves did, especially plantation labor. It could mean that, in a world of scarcity and hard choices, owner-ship was the most humane relation between rich and poor, however morally regrettable it might seem. In the United States, *necessity* frequently referred to an idea that Ruffin had discussed with his father in letters home from col-lege: once Americans had created an enslaved class, they had no way to emancipate it without risking a race war. Growing racism in the nineteenth century added force to this idea, as it became ever less imaginable that whites could share the continent with former slaves and their descendants.

Americans who denied that slavery was either necessary or legitimate therefore had to answer the claim that enslave-ment was "necessary" by developing a political economy of freedom, a theory of economic life that lived up to the stan-dards of the Declaration. It was partly under the pressure of this need that the American idea of free labor developed in the early and middle decades of the nineteenth century. (There were, however, many crosscurrents. Free labor had origins in Adam Smith's thought and took its early Ameri-can form, in the era of Andrew Jackson, as a vision of democratic, yeoman dignity for white citizens, in opposition to hierarchy, paternalism, and monopolies.) In its early-nineteenth-century versions, the idea that economic life should take shape from the free agreements of legally equal individuals, and nothing else, had been called on to recon-cile the reality of popular government with the ideal of indi-vidual autonomy. This was its role in Thomas Jefferson's

inaugural formula that government should ensure the rights
of citizens and go no further, and in the thought of Jackson-
era Democrats such as New York newspaper editor William
Leggett, who argued in 1834 that government had the power
to protect individual liberty and property but not "to tamper
with individual industry a single hair's breadth beyond." In
this role, as a theory of state power that promised to leave
personal freedom undisturbed, free labor governed the relations of nonslaves in a nation where many were enslaved: it
was a doctrine for free citizens but not a principle of universal freedom.

In the aftermath of the Civil War, with slavery abolished
by the Thirteenth Amendment (prohibiting "involuntary
servitude" except as punishment for crime), free labor
became the leading candidate for a role the country badly
needed to fill, a political economy of universal freedom. The
challenge was to define a political and economic order that
gave life to the ideals of dignity and self-mastery. Free labor
was supposed to solve two basic questions about the meaning of a free society. One was political: What power could
government exercise over free people? The other question
was the problem of political economy: How could free individuals coordinate their lives of production, consumption,
and exchange in a way that honored one another's freedom
and did not bow to the cruel "necessity" that thinkers such as
Justice Ruffin accepted? Addressing these questions, the
engineers of Reconstruction called free labor "the noblest
principle on earth" and the "foundation of civilization"
because it promised to reconcile "free choice and social
order."

Particularly in the postemancipation South, free labor

was often more myth than reality, as white landowners pushed black laborers into long-term contracts surrendering the all-important right to quit. A more fundamental problem was whether free labor could ever be an adequate principle for a free economy, even if it were put into unstinting effect. As both Abraham Lincoln and Ralph Waldo Emerson stressed in their descriptions of American dignity, free labor was not just a set of legal and economic rules but also a narrative for a life. One might be a wage laborer for a time, but those who worked hard and avoided what Lincoln called "singular misfortune" should end up as property owners, taking orders from no one. Historian Eric Foner has emphasized that keeping western lands open to small proprietors rather than slave plantations was one reason that free labor was tied closely to "free soil," the political vision of a yeoman frontier without slaves. This ideal was never as straightforward as its advocates made out, but it became particularly vexed at the end of the nineteenth century. The industrial economy that grew up in the United States took its power from large concentrations of capital, an entirely new scale of machines and factories. In the past, farmworkers and apprentices had been a few steps—not easy steps, to be sure, but often possible ones—from becoming craftsmen and farmers. A wage laborer could work a dozen lifetimes in one of the new factories and never imagine operating his own. The division between those who owned the factories and those who worked in them now seemed nearly as stark and permanent as the old division between plantation owners and their slaves.

The scale of the industrial economy lent urgency to another difficulty in free labor: Were contracts between

workers and their employers really the agreements of free and equal individuals? That was the principle that supposedly enabled free labor to reconcile freedom and social order. What, however, was the equality between a factory owner and any of the hundreds of employees and potential employees who bargained with him? What was the freedom of a worker with no property, who sold his time for a living and had to take the going rate for his skills or stop feeding his family? As a formal matter, the capitalist's freedom to fire and the worker's freedom to quit were two sides of the same right, held equally by both parties. Many doubted, however, that letting that principle resolve the issue would make dignity and mastery real in economic life. Even the justices of the conservative Supreme Court expressed doubt that free-labor principles alone could justly govern the relations of miners and mine owners, women laborers and factory owners, or even full-grown men in ordinary trades and the capitalists who drove hard bargains while holding the threat of firing over their heads.

Versions of Freedom in the Industrial Age

THESE DIFFICULTIES INSPIRED several responses. One was to keep the commitment to laissez-faire principles and simply accept inequality of power and opportunity. This approach rested on belief that making one's own economic choices was the core of freedom. Frequently it also drew on something alien to the antebellum pioneers of free labor: biological ideas, associated with Charles Darwin and the English laissez-faire theorist Herbert Spencer, which portrayed social life as a "struggle for existence," with mar-

ket capitalism its highest form. This image sharpened the idea of freedom to a fine point: freedom to compete, to struggle for survival, was the basic and perennial human interest.

The Darwinist version of a free economy also differed from earlier visions in its contempt for politics, which the new laissez-faire thinkers tended to see as a conspiracy of the weak to hobble and rob the strong. Where Lincoln had defined democracy as life without slaves or masters, William Graham Sumner, a Yale professor and leading social Darwinist, dismissed democracy as "a word to conjure with." Sumner insisted that freedom came not from political choices but from the material progress that competition produced, and he denied that "the men of 1787" who wrote and adopted the Constitution had done much to form American life. Democracy, he insisted, could mean only one of two things. Taken in the best sense, it meant individual freedom to compete, the laissez-faire that Americans already enjoyed, with some of the kinks removed. Given any other sense—an ambition to "democratize" the industrial economy, for instance—it was "only a rule of division for robbers who have to divide plunder or monks who have to divide gifts." Democracy was an unproductive form of the struggle for survival, sure to "waste capital and bring us all to poverty" and "set loose greed and envy as ruling social passions."

The Darwinist image of social life was both more individualist and more collectivist than earlier American thinking. Its individualism was straightforward: to be human was to struggle for personal survival, with wide-open market competition the proper legal frame for the struggle. Sumner

called social protection against hardship "go[ing] back to slavery." On the collectivist side, Darwinists did not see nations as the Lockean founders had, as associations of naturally free and distinct individuals. Instead, following Old World social thought, they portrayed society as a kind of superorganism, built out of the competitive cooperation of millions of individuals, who played the role of cells in the body. While competition appeared to individuals as a quest for life over death, a long step back revealed that every battle for survival added its part to the wealth, complexity, and scale of the whole. Men and women might try desperately "to avoid being converted into food," as sociologist Franklin Giddings serenely but evocatively described Darwin's formula, but in that frenzy they inadvertently created history and society, a festival of the strong atop a necropolis of the weak and unlucky. In this picture, free judgment, which had mattered so much to the antislavery view of freedom, was left to elites who could survey the sweep of history and social order. (Even their judgment, moreover, consisted mainly of apprehending and approving the Darwinist facts.) For most people, there were only "herd habits" and "folkways," which Giddings called "a tyranny ... that perfects the group in cohesion and in unity of purpose." It was a use of *tyranny* that John Adams and Thomas Jefferson would have recognized as accurate. Giddings, however, meant it not as denunciation but as lightly ironic praise. For him and many like him, a clear-eyed view of the industrial age meant accepting the tyranny of Darwinist principles as a version of freedom.

The laissez-faire camp had no monopoly on Darwinist metaphors or organic images of society. As earlier chapters

set out, Woodrow Wilson and William James imagined individuals taking dignity from the greatness of the social order, which Wilson in particular portrayed as a common mind, finding its voice in a presidential oracle. Franklin Roosevelt, too, described a nation as having a body, a mind, and a soul, each requiring its own form of sustenance—an idea that would have been strange even as metaphor to the founding generation but intuitive to the laissez-faire Darwinists whose policies Roosevelt repudiated. Indeed, the whole Progressive concern to preserve individual mastery and honor in a complex and regulated society was not only an effort to save the antislavery and free-labor visions of dignity. It was also a program for a Darwinist age, an answer to the charge that social protection weakened the super-organism and left people unfit for life's struggle. Wilson described social protection as meant to ensure weaker citizens' "rights in the struggle for existence," and proregulatory justices of the Supreme Court used the same phrase to explain why laws protecting workers were necessary to bring them up to the starting line of competitive social life. Many political camps shared the biological image of human beings as small and interdependent parts of a vast system, which ran by rules indifferent to individuals.

In this spirit, a second approach to the industrial age seized on the collectivist strand of the new social thought and dismissed traditional individualism as the vestige of a long-gone pioneer society. At its most extreme, this approach could lead to sympathy for totalitarian experiments. Stuart Chase, a Progressive economist sometimes credited with coining the term *New Deal* for Roosevelt's program, returned from a junket to the Soviet Union dis-

missing laissez-faire as a doctrine for the age of covered wagons and asked in 1932, "Why should Russians have all the fun remaking a world?" Also on that excursion was Columbia economist Rexford Tugwell, an important New Deal figure who would later argue that "in a pioneer society liberties are allowed the individual which cannot be allowed when civilization is further advanced." Tugwell defended "repressive action by the group" as the means for curbing pioneer liberties in a higher state of civilization.

Despite disastrous remarks like these, most Progressives did not think freedom obsolete in the industrial economy, nor were they prepared to hand over Americans to totalitarian experiments. Nonetheless, many did suspect that the old image of individual freedom, with its emphasis on independence and mastery, offered living Americans only false promises. They rejected that idea of freedom partly because it seemed so much the hobbyhorse of their enemies, the laissez-faire apologists who treated competitive individualism as an immutable law of nature. They rejected individualism also partly because it stood athwart the vision of society as an organic system of systems they shared with many conservatives. Thinking of a cell as if it were an individual is a category mistake: a cell works as a function of its place in a body. Many believed that, in a complex society, personal fate depended so much on impersonal systems that imagining people as masters of their own lives was fatally unrealistic.

This attitude did not define a political camp, at least in the United States. Instead, it described a tendency in thinking, a disregard for individual choice and democratic action in favor of expert management. Even Franklin Roosevelt,

in the same Commonwealth Club address in which he called for a renewal of individualism and self-reliance, announced that initiative and energy alone could not sustain a complex economy: "[T]he day of enlightened administration has come." Roosevelt was very far from imagining individual freedom or democracy as being outmoded. In fact, adapting them to modern conditions was the closest thing to a unifying theme in his often helter-skelter political thinking. But in setting out the "new terms of our old social contract," Roosevelt and other Progressives sometimes seemed to doubt whether the old touchstones of independence and mastery could survive in any form.

On both sides of the Atlantic, the Progressive ideal of freedom began by repudiating what many derided as the "negative" liberty of laissez-faire. As Woodrow Wilson put it in *The New Freedom*, "[T]o let the individual alone is to leave him helpless as against the obstacles with which he has to contend." Instead, they tacked toward various versions of "positive freedom." In its broad sense, that term referred to what individuals actually had the power to do in economic life as against what they were merely not prohibited from doing. Free choice in employment contracts did not make a worker more free if he could choose only among terrible offers. The right of a worker to quit a job with no other good prospect was not, contrary to free-labor thinking, the same as the power of an employer to fire a worker with a dozen job seekers lined up to replace him. The law's protection of property had a very different meaning for the owner of a factory or an estate than for an indigent laborer: it gave the first man enormous power, while its effect on the second was to make him subject to that power—an employee in the

factory, a trespasser on the estate. Taken in this way, positive freedom implied that government should arrange economic life not to protect the often meaningless freedom of free labor but instead to spread meaningful opportunities broadly among citizens. Thus Roosevelt proposed at the Commonwealth Club that property rights, once the guarantors of negative freedom, should now be reshaped to ensure the economic security of the old and young, the sick and the unlucky. That is, traditional ownership should become instead the right to subsistence, which the welfare state would provide. The old idea of property as a carapace, a hard shell set against the world, had made sense in an era when the task of politics was to break people out of dependent relationships, slavery above all. Now, Progressives imagined, property would mean something closer to a socially guaranteed power to live without deprivation.

The same period also brought another new version of economic freedom: the freedom of the consumer. John M. Clark, a New Deal economist deeply concerned with the political regulation of business, saw the twentieth-century version of individualism as "soften[ing] the ideal of maximum self-assertion to maximum self-realization." The ideal of self-realization meant that what counted as individual freedom was to be able to lead the life you thought best and felt was authentically yours. That meant—in keeping with the broad idea of positive freedom—having the wealth and security to pursue your personal ideal. Just as important, it relocated the center of negative freedom, the core of personal rights that government must not violate. The economic rights of property and contract, the cornerstones of laissez-faire, began to give way to rights of conscience,

speech, and personal association. These rights were essential to discovering and expressing authentic personal aims. With this emphasis in place, the rights of free labor looked less like basic guarantees of personal freedom and more like tools to achieve personal ends, tools that government could and should adjust to make them more effective.

This version of personal freedom was in the spirit of Emerson's marriage of Romanticism to American individualism. It helped to power the culture of Romantic consumerism, the world of products, services, and brands that promise to help users discover and achieve truer versions of themselves. In older images of American economic life, it was as a producer—a farmer, a craftsman, or an entrepreneur—that a man showed his substance. The idea of consumption as a path to authenticity was something new.

Markets and Freedoms Now

THESE ALTERNATIVES still pretty much describe American attitudes to economic life. When we inhabit the folk economy of permanent and implacable rules, we are reluctant Darwinists locked in the struggle for existence. When we inhabit the folk economy of heroic mastery, of dashing entrepreneurship and finance, we give updated expression to the free-labor ideal. As consumers more than as producers, but also in some creative careers, we follow the Romantic individualism that aims at "maximum self-realization." In general, however, it is fair to say that we are not entirely satisfied with our solutions. Our infinite—or at least generous—sense of personal possibility still clashes with the

unyielding constraints of the market. Our folk economies still describe different worlds.

There are other difficulties, too. As sophisticated economists emphasize, the abstract set of rules that we call the market has some basic defects as a way of integrating diverse values. There are three enormous reasons for this. First is that *market* is a thoroughly incomplete way of describing any economy. The term broadly means that many valuable resources are privately owned and traded by willing agreement. It is silent as to extremely basic questions. Who owns what? How equal or unequal is the distribution of ownership? What is owned at all? Can people own one another? Are music, images, stories, and ideas private property, or are they open for anyone to use? Moreover, what, exactly, can owners do? Can you, for instance, fill in wetlands on your property or sell your body for sexual pleasure or your personal services for two dollars an hour? Until you have answered these questions, you know very little about what it means to live in any particular "market society."

Second, markets don't actually maximize the sum of human satisfactions, even when they work perfectly. They maximize the sum of satisfaction to those who have the spending power to get what they want. In a world with profoundly unequal distribution of wealth, markets will guarantee lots of attention to the desires of the wealthy, such as entertainment, fitness, and cosmetic surgery, and very little to those of the poor, such as mosquito netting and anti-malaria vaccines. In an economy in which formulas for medical drugs are private property, this will mean that even when treatments exist for the diseases of the poor, the poor will often be unable to afford them. This is so despite

the fact that antiretroviral treatment for an indigent HIV-positive Ugandan will make a much more profound difference in her life than Botox treatment for a Palo Alto professional (and thus, although it seems trivial to add, presumably provide greater satisfaction).

Third, markets take account only of satisfactions and harms that people can find a way to price. The elegant logic of the market does not touch externalities, the good or bad effects of people's actions that they are neither charged nor rewarded for. Pollution is a classic example: as long as polluting is free, economically rational actors will spew junk into air and water, even though this takes a toll on everyone's well-being. Climate change threatens to become, fairly literally, the externality that ate the world. The last two hundred years of economic growth have been not just a preference-satisfaction machine but an externality machine, churning out greenhouse gases that cost polluters nothing and disperse through the atmosphere to affect the whole globe.

These observations are sometimes presented as criticisms of markets, but it is more helpful to take them as cues for the political decisions that shape any market economy. In shaping their markets, societies are free to choose the themes of the economics of 1776: reciprocity, dignity, and freedom. This requires taking responsibility for the political decisions that stand behind markets and give them their shape. It also means getting past the most pessimistic folk economy, the one that envisions a system of implacable and inevitable rules, and trying to make good on the optimistic one, the vision of economic life as a system of freedom. When Americans do this, they pick up the ambition that

Franklin Roosevelt described in his Commonwealth Club address: giving new life to old ideas of freedom in deeply changed circumstances. They also reconnect with the tradition of freedom-promoting economic reform that Adam Smith set in motion, which deeply respects the market but demands that it serve human values. Economics is not just a science but a tradition, not just a system of rules but a mode of action.

CHAPTER 7

The Value of Freedom

ADAM SMITH'S preoccupation with the economics of freedom makes as much sense today as it did in his time. The motives that powered his thought count everywhere today: in politics and personal life, as we have already seen, and also—maybe less expectedly—in economics itself. A discipline famously described as "the dismal science" and often denounced for a flat and mechanical picture of human beings has potential to become, again, a source of insight into Smith's themes: the value of freedom and dignity in social life.

Dignity and Reciprocity in Economics Today

ONE OF THE AXIOMS of today's mainstream economics is that "preferences are exogenous," or given, which simply means that people want what they want regardless of the contexts in which they pursue it. This premise has analytic benefits for economists: it enables them to model individual behavior as the pursuit of consistent goals through ever-changing obstacle courses. It is also the target of some of the more vituperative criticism of economic thought, having

elicited the charge that economists envision people as acting on blind desires rather than deliberating about values. It need not have that meaning, of course: it is an analytic tool, not a claim about how people really are. Even as an analytic premise, however, it tends to blind economic thought to one of the ideas that most engaged Adam Smith: that when the context changes, people may pursue different goals than they otherwise would have.

Recent experiments on how people make choices have brought economists to a renewed interest in just this issue—often in terms that Smith would recognize. Researchers find that Smith's touchstones, dignity and reciprocity, reinforce each other and together shape choices. Some institutional designs promote dignity and reciprocity, while others undermine them. These findings underscore the value of recovering Smith's orientation and again thinking of economic institutions as generators of reciprocity and dignity.

Modern economics is sometimes defined as the study of how people choose under constraint. *Constraint* means all the inconvenient but unavoidable facts of life: limited time, money, and supplies of the things we want, as well as the rules that govern our competition and cooperation with others. Economics starts by assuming that people always make choices that will get them more of what they want than the alternatives. As a matter of fact, it turns out that most people's choices depart from this model in predictable ways. For instance, they value what they already have more than what they only stand a chance of acquiring. They value the first small increase over what they have more than further increases, so that although more may be better, the first dose of more has a headier effect than the twelfth dose

of the same size. Behavioral economists, who concentrate on the ways people actually make choices, have worked up these anomalies into an approach to decision making, which they call prospect theory.

Some of the most interesting experiments in choice add still more to the standard model. They provide good reasons to expand its focus to revive the questions Adam Smith asked. In these experiments, people regularly give up selfish material advantage for social and emotional reasons, mainly to uphold their own dignity and to share in reciprocity with others. Although it is true that, strictly speaking, they are choosing to get more of something, the "something" is dignity and reciprocity, which often seem to be at war with the quest for greater wealth. The mind of the person choosing is not a machine for maximizing overall gain, but an impassioned argument over what kind of value is worth pursuing.

Other experiments contradict the premise that preferences are exogenous, that is, that what people want is fixed before they start choosing. In fact, the contexts in which people make choices shape the values they pursue. Depending how their dealings with one another are set up, people will pursue more reciprocity and dignity or more financial gain. These different values will be either more at odds or more complementary, also depending on the context. This is exactly what Adam Smith believed: that status and respect were as important in economic life as material interests, and that a good economy made these motives mutually reinforcing by enabling people to pursue self-interest and dignity all at once.

One of these telling experiments is the ultimatum game, a rapid transaction between two strangers in a laboratory. The experiment features a pot of money, which the experi-

menters provide. One player offers a split of the money between herself and the other player. The second then accepts or rejects the offer. If she accepts, the players share the money accordingly. If she rejects the offer, the game is over and the experimenters keep the money—in other words, the transaction blows up and the players go home with no deal. If both players were rationally self-interested in keeping with economists' models, and out for monetary gain, the first player would always offer the smallest possible amount, aiming to get as much as possible for himself, and the second player would always accept because some gain is better than none.

The results are very different from that forecast. The first player's average offer is usually between 40 and 45 percent of the pot, and the most common offer tends to be an even split. When the offer falls below 20 percent of the pot, the second player rejects it about half the time. These results hold even when the stakes are as large as $400 in wealthy countries and, in some developing countries, a month's income. Critics have suggested that players must imagine they are building up reputations for generosity that will benefit them down the line, but the results persist even when players clearly understand that the game is a onetime event between strangers.

Clearly, people are doing something other than maximizing their cash take. Experimenters designed some variations on the basic game to try to get at that nonmonetary X factor. One result suggested that players are reacting to perceptions of respect or disrespect. Experimenters told players that some of the offers they were considering were generated automatically by computers, while others came from human players, whom the participants briefly met

before the games began. In fact, these were lies: the experimenters rigged the game, ensuring that each player faced the same spread of high offers, such as even splits, and low ones, such as 90/10 and 80/20 divisions. As usual, players accepted almost all the high offers and rejected many of the low ones. The telling result was that rejection rates were at least twenty points higher when players believed that low offers came from other human beings rather than from computers. The motive for rejecting a low offer, then, has to do with another person's willfully withholding a larger share. The rejection is a way of striking back at the disrespect implicit in a low offer, a motive that makes sense toward another person, but not toward an algorithm.

Another experiment, tellingly called a trust game, also highlights how decisions respond to respect and disrespect. In this game, players take turns deciding between two options: take the money (an amount set by the rules) and run, which ends the game, or let the game go forward, which gives the other player the chance to cash out and quit. The longer the game goes, the larger the potential rewards get for each player; but continuing the game also creates more opportunities for each player to quit and short the other. The interesting finding from the trust game is that, when one player shows trust by letting the game go forward, the other becomes much less likely to defect and cash out, compared with other situations that are identical except for the earlier act of trust.

Personal interaction made the difference in both games. Players in the ultimatum game who believed they were being shorted by other human beings reacted by sinking the whole ship, pot of money and all. Players in the trust game

who had been trusted reciprocated, to their potential financial disadvantage, twice as often as those who had not.

To say that personal interaction was key, however, gets only half the story. The other half is that the rules of the game made the difference. Some versions of the trust game provided no chance for an initial trusting move, which meant there was always less reciprocity down the road. Rules that created chances for reciprocity produced a (small, transient) world in which a majority of players would give up a benefit to themselves to reward someone else for trusting them, producing greater overall wealth in the process. Versions that made no room for displays of trust produced less generous choices.

Understanding Dignity and Reciprocity

THESE RESULTS SUGGEST that what people value is not fixed. Instead, values in the trust game emerge from a three-way interaction among the person choosing, the other player, and the rules that structure their interaction. What is still obscure in this picture, though, is the nature of the non-monetary X factor, the motive that gets engaged by certain personal interactions, such as trust, reciprocity, or feeling slighted or shortchanged. One way of getting at this motive, or cluster of motives, is by observing the brains of people making choices. Neuroscientists find that areas of the brain are associated with particular experiences, such as thirst, pain, or receiving a reward, or with activities, such as social interaction or rule-governed calculation and control. By watching which areas become active as people make a

choice, they can learn something about the motives of that choice.

Researchers observing the brains of players in the rigged ultimatum game, the one in which some offers supposedly came from computers and others from human players, found that while players decided whether to accept a low, potentially insulting offer, two brain areas were engaged. One, the dorsolateral prefrontal cortex, is associated with what we might think of as adult cognitive work: applying abstract principles to a particular case, overcoming immediate gratification to achieve a longer-term goal, and generally being the chief financial officer of the self. You might think of it as the accountant brain. The other, the anterior insula, is associated with negative emotional states such as anger and disgust and sensations of hunger and thirst. You might think of it as the hurt brain. When players accepted low offers, the accountant brain was more active than the hurt brain. When they rejected such offers as insulting, the hurt brain was more active. There seemed to be two kinds of motives at work, one abstractly self-interested, the other emotional and connected with basic experiences of need and deprivation. The first pushed toward taking whatever money was on the table, the second toward striking back against the sting of a perceived insult. Because of the way the game was set up, the two motives were at odds, engaged in a neural contest of strength.

The brains of players engaged in successful trust games, some lasting for many rounds, also show distinctive patterns. When players settle into reciprocating strategies, their brain activity is associated with receiving rewards and other

pleasurable feedback—in short, reinforcement by other people. As in the ultimatum game, this activity is greater with two human players than when one person plays a trust game with a computer. Social-reinforcement brain activity is also higher in players who seek reciprocating strategies than in those who do not, and it falls sharply when the other player defects. In an intriguing twist, players with lower levels of this activity not only tend not to reciprocate: they also show as much (or as little) social-reinforcement brain activity when playing with a computer as when playing with a human being, suggesting blunted interpersonal experience generally.

This discussion has ventured pretty far into the laboratories of behavioral economists and neuroscientists. Let's return to the economics of 1776 and Adam Smith's idea that a market economy could advance dignity and freedom by directing bargaining toward reciprocity rather than domination. The role of reciprocity in these experiments is strikingly close to what Smith envisioned. Consider the decisions that both the ultimatum game and the trust game present. When the first player in the ultimatum game makes a generous offer, she does something much like what the first mover in a trust game does by letting the game go to a second round: offer the other player a chance to benefit them both by reciprocating. In the trust game, the second player decides whether to give up a gain for himself to benefit the first player, who has already trusted him. In the ultimatum game, the second player decides whether to give up a benefit to punish the other player for making a low offer. Although superficially opposite, these responses are two sides of the same coin. What the trusting player in the trust

game does, and what the stingy first player in the ultimatum game does not, are the same: offer reciprocity.

Offering reciprocity means approaching another person in particular ways: regarding the other as having judgment, interests, goals, and emotions; addressing her as a possible collaborator rather than an object of coercion or manipulation; and, maybe most important, making oneself vulnerable to her rejection or defection. A trusting move in a trust game takes into account the other's interests by enabling her to gain more than she would if the game ended immediately. It treats her as a potential collaborator by making the result of the game, the division of rewards, depend on her choice. It makes the trusting player vulnerable to the second player's power to defect. A low offer in an ultimatum game does the opposite: it is an attempt at domination. It ignores the second player's interest in sharing the windfall pot of money (which, after all, neither player did anything to deserve), as well as her sensitivity to the slight of a low offer. A low offer also treats the second player as if she had no alternative but to accept any offer, even an insulting one, an attitude akin to approaching her as an object of manipulation rather than a collaborator. While the rules of the ultimatum game prevent the first player from insulating himself against rejection, a low offer is an attempt to override that vulnerability by reminding the second player that she is in a rational-choice corner and gains nothing by rejecting an offer. It is because people do not like being put in corners that this strategy increases the likelihood of rejection.

Reciprocity is a basic category of human experience, and its opposite is not self-interest, as some of the experiments might seem to suggest, but domination. Its association with

rewards and other pleasurable feedback suggests that it is an elementally satisfying way of being among others. Failures of reciprocity—attempts at domination—are equally basic and aligned with essential feelings of deprivation (hunger and thirst), threats to bodily integrity (pain), and the emotions that enable us to defend ourselves against these (anger). The needs that reciprocity satisfies are as basic emotionally as food and wholeness are physically. They are the needs for respect and recognition, the bases of dignity and self-regard. These, recall, are also the values at the heart of the American sensation of freedom. Reciprocity is an essential part of how we make that freedom real in social life.

Although reciprocity and monetary self-interest pull against each other in the trust and ultimatum games, they can also be mutually reinforcing. In the slave and feudal societies that Adam Smith denounced, the two motives were opposed because both material gain and respect came from domination, and offering reciprocity would have been unsatisfying for the powerful, hazardous for the weak. Some social practices, however, integrate reciprocity and self-interest. Studies of citizen psychology suggest that customs such as voting and paying taxes, which benefit everyone but tempt nearly anyone to defect from them, work only because of the perception of reciprocity. People willingly uphold the practices as long as they believe most others do the same. When this is true, participating is a mark of belonging and having status in society, rather than evidence of being a sucker. A good market economy should integrate reciprocity and self-interest, producing both wealth and dignity and distributing them broadly.

Contemporary economics, then, gives ample reason to take seriously the themes of the economics of 1776: reciprocity, dignity, and freedom. Those themes also tie economics to the politics of 1776, with its core idea of freedom as rooted in the dignity and mastery of individuals. Recovering this connection more fully would mean appreciating that the economy is, like politics, both something we confront as a fact and something we shape by shared choices. We don't always have to accept insecurity and harm as products of inevitable rules. We don't have to imagine that our economy is, just by its nature, all it can be. Instead, we can engage our economy politically, as a system of rules that aims to reconcile security with innovation, wealth with reciprocity, and all of these with a vision of freedom. Rightly understood, an economy is an integrating institution that human beings use to put our values together.

Freedom as Wealth

WHAT MIGHT THIS MEAN concretely? Just as politics must come in to fill out economists' incomplete definition of a market, so economics can help political thinking to be as precise as possible. Amartya Sen, who received the 1998 Nobel Prize in economics, argues that his field needs a rich idea of freedom to do its best work. Many of Sen's major contributions are in welfare economics, which evaluates institutions and social arrangements by the level of well-being they create. The first question to ask about that project, of course, is what counts as well-being and how to measure it. From the late eighteenth century until early in the twentieth, most English-speaking welfare economists

worked with versions of classical utilitarianism. This meant estimating people's well-being more or less directly, like taking a read of body temperature or a count of white blood cells, and adding that well-being up or averaging it. There are serious theoretical problems with that approach: there is in fact no way to measure well-being (or happiness, which was often what utilitarians aimed at) like body temperature, for it is a subjective state that may vary from person to person for all kinds of reasons, from differences in their bodies to differences in their values. As a practical matter, traditional welfare economics was less vexed. It mostly guided policy decisions, and economists just assumed that basic material needs came before aesthetic satisfaction or sheer pleasure. Faced with a choice between a public-health project that would free some number of Londoners from cholera and building an opera house that would seat the same number of people in the course of a year, they would have had no difficulty judging that fighting cholera added more to well-being.

This approach came under heavy theoretical attack in the early twentieth century. A new generation of economists (taking inspiration from earlier skeptics) argued that because well-being was subjective, attempts to measure it were unscientific and spurious. They also appealed to personal freedom: given that people could and did pursue diverse values, was it not disrespectful at best, authoritarian at worst, to sweep that diversity aside and say that well-being is whatever welfare economists think most important? Isn't the only freedom-respecting measure of well-being whether you get what you want? That is, shouldn't the measure of well-being be satisfaction of preferences? And since there

was no way to compare the happiness or well-being that one person got from his satisfied preferences with someone else's happiness from her satisfied preferences, the only cogent question welfare economists could ask was whether any particular person would prefer one social arrangement to another. This greatly straitened approach led welfare economists to adopt the mildly famous Pareto principle (named for a nineteenth-century Italian economist): a state of affairs is better than another if at least one person would prefer it and no one would prefer the other. Many economists, notably Sen, have pointed out that whether a state of affairs passes this test reveals almost nothing that anyone would want to know about it. Recognizing this, those making practical applications of welfare economics often ask instead what arrangement would produce the most wealth, which has the advantage of being concrete and measurable. Others do more or less what the old-style utilitarian economists did, conducting a "cost-benefit analysis" that tries to assign monetary value to experiences as diverse as illness, death, and the pleasure one might take in a beautiful landscape.

Sen argues that all these so-called scientific approaches to welfare economics distort the reality of human choice. He insists that to be useful, welfare economics must address what it is that people value about their social arrangements, even though that means trying to get hold of diverse, conflicting values, many of them difficult or impossible to measure directly. It must also take seriously that economics is an inquiry about choice, individual and collective, and that choice is an exercise of freedom, a statement about who one is, or who we are, that contributes to creating the world

in which all future choices will take place. If economics is a science, then, it is a science of freedom, specifically of the relationship between freedom and constraint.

Sen argues that what we value about an economy is its power to promote and secure freedom. The right question to ask about any economic arrangement is how well it does this. That question is not at all simple, because freedom, as we keep seeing, is a value with several faces. It includes the negative freedom from interference with decisions—now greatly expanded into choices about childbearing and intimacy. It includes the Progressive redefinition of freedom as what some called positive liberty: not just choosing unhindered, but choosing among many attractive alternatives, rather than in a Hobson's choice. This is the sense in which the factory owner is freer than the laborer in a company town, even though both enjoy the same laissez-faire rights. Freedom also includes a third element, glimpsed in both the old antislavery emphasis on free judgment and the newer ideal of authenticity. This is the psychological capacity to make good on potential freedom, to recognize, act on, and change one's own projects and values. This capacity arises from a sense of oneself as having equal standing with other free human beings. In this respect, it is closely tied to the early American obsession with unfettered conscience and judgment, the ideal that Emerson worked into a doctrine of the free mind. These three aspects of freedom may come into conflict in any economy: the whole history of antislavery, free labor, and the effort to reclaim and expand personal freedom in the industrial economy has been driven by their conflict. These same dimensions of freedom must also be

complementary, for without any one of them, the other two would be meaningless. Indeed, a common purpose holds them together and reveals their respective limits. That goal is a country where dignity, mastery, and authenticity are possible in every life and social bonds arise from reciprocity, in which people recognize and respect these qualities in one another.

CHAPTER 8

Fragments of a Free Economy

"ACONSTITUTION," wrote Oliver Wendell Holmes Jr. in 1905, "is not intended to embody a particular economic theory." Holmes was dissenting from his Supreme Court colleagues' ruling, in *Lochner v. New York*, that the New York legislature had violated a constitutional right of contract when it passed a law limiting bakers to working no more than sixty hours per week. Holmes's dissent became canonical among critics of the Gilded Age courts' desultory laissez-faire jurisprudence. Although Holmes himself did not share the Progressive faith in political reform, his *Lochner* opinion fit the Progressive idea that no economic system was natural or fixed, and that politics and expert administration should bring economic life in line with national ideals. After 1937, when the Supreme Court gave in to the New Deal and dropped most constitutional limits on economic regulation, Holmes's words made him seem a prophet in the wilderness, pronouncing constitutional truth thirty years before it finally became law.

More than a century after he announced it, Holmes's view remains constitutional law. His dictum about constitutions and economic life, however, obscures an important

truth. Any idea of freedom in a national community implies a picture of economic life, whether libertarian, Progressive, or otherwise. Imagining the economy as a technical field concerned only with gross national product and marginal gains in productivity is false to tradition and experience. Our economic life remains one of the places where we give meaning to the opposites of slavery, the ideals of dignity, mastery, and free judgment. Taking this fact seriously today has two meanings, one that will seem conservative, the other radical or at least reformist. On the conservative side, we should recognize our existing market economy as a powerful system of freedom. By basing economic life on willing agreements among workers, employers, owners, and financiers, it secures free choice. The importance of choice is the hard crystal of truth in all libertarianism, which reaches back to the repudiation of slavery and political tyranny. For example, there is no parity between being assigned a career that suits you fairly well and choosing one for yourself. Freedom is not just where you end up but also how you get there.

At the same time, where you end up also matters, and that depends on the great themes of Progressive freedom: what choices you face, what resources you have, and therefore what you are able, and so truly free, to choose. Our market economy addresses this aspect of freedom, too, by increasing wealth. This formula has its limits, which I sketched earlier, but growing wealth has greatly expanded human powers. In medicine that extends and improves life, instant global communication, and safe and fast transport, to take just a few cases among thousands, we are different creatures from our ancestors, able to act in ways that they could only imagine as magic.

That is the conservative side of the story. On the reformist side, this description of the market as promoting freedom is a starting point, not a resting place. To envision the market as a system of freedom is usually a right-wing attitude, a favorite of antigovernment conservatives who invoke the memory of Adam Smith against the minimum wage and national health care. But a free economy, like American freedom in general, is as much a challenge as a fact. Taking up the challenge requires asking what it means for our economy to serve human purposes, finding ways to pursue all dimensions of freedom further than we have before now. Two examples of such reforms will give a sense of what this means.

More Responsibility with Less Cruelty

THE FIRST EXAMPLE starts from this uncomfortable fact: people's economic fates depend as much on sweeping technological and other changes as on their own skills and energy. Recall the American factory worker in 1970 and the computer scientist in 1985, headed in opposite directions for reasons they could not control and, often, could not have foreseen. The forces that elevated one and disinherited the other are also the drivers of creative destruction, with its gifts of innovation and growing wealth. By setting up our economy to embrace creative destruction, we decide, though we seldom admit it, to make economic sacrifices of those who become obsolete, like furniture thrown overboard from a wagon traveling west. A changing world greatly diminishes their real choices and power to act.

Moreover, anticipating such disruption can push per-

sonal choices toward excessive caution. For instance, some who might have trained as researchers in a high-risk, high-reward field of science, such as genetic engineering or nanotechnology, end up in civil engineering or law school because the downside risk of specialized training is too great, and while there are second acts in American economic life, they are uncertain and often a long time in coming. The cost of these self-protective choices is partly in a loss to innovation, which happens when able people take risks. There is also a cost to free judgment and authenticity in these cautious choices: people with a sense of vocation give it up for something safer that also feels less compelling.

The sense that all of this is arbitrary, possibly inefficient, and costly to the human spirit has motivated Romantic programs to enable people to choose their work without regard to the market—from each according to his inclination. The problem with an economy of bliss followers is that many sources of bliss produce nothing of value to anyone else. Guaranteeing everyone a substantial income whatever work they chose to do would produce a world with more bad poetry, boring independent films, and hours spent watching reality television. Economists call this phenomenon moral hazard: if you protect people against the consequences of unproductive behavior, they will be more likely to behave unproductively. After a generation, such a policy would have exacted a severe cost in wealth and innovation.

But is there a way to have more of both—more real choices now without so much sacrifice of the future? Yale economist Robert Shiller has proposed an approach that might work, by protecting people against the downside risk of daring choices without encouraging wasteful careers and

idle noncareers. The idea is that, when someone began training in a field, she could acquire a unique form of income insurance. Instead of guaranteeing her a personal level of income, it would promise that, if the field she entered—such as nanotechnology or intellectual-property law—performed worse than expected, she would receive an income subsidy, regardless of her own situation. By contrast, if her field did better than expected, meaning someone with her training should have ample chances to make a good living, she would receive no income support, even if she had bad luck or bailed to become an independent filmmaker. How fields were "expected" to do would be a function of market pricing, just like more familiar kinds of insurance. (Because many young trainees have little money, it might be appropriate to finance insurance along the lines of a student loan.) This would amount to setting up voluntary risk sharing across sectors of the economy, making it possible to share the benefits of creative destruction while limiting its costs. Because the policies would be market driven rather than simply redistributive, and because individuals could not game the system by opting out of productive careers, this scheme would also be compatible with market efficiency. From the point of view of individual choice, it would be a way to create both more security and more freedom to choose a career, and to stop sacrificing the futures of the unlucky to overall economic dynamism. This reform suggests that at least some of the tragic relationship between the two folk economies is not inevitable but open to change. Aversion to this kind of risk-sharing reform is usually rooted in the fantasy of the first folk economy, that what we get is what we choose and deserve, so sharing—upside or

downside—is a rule for robbers or monks. The special elegance of a well-designed insurance program is that it can help us to believe this ideal somewhat less, while at the same time bringing reality closer to it. We may believe it less because risk sharing is an acknowledgment that much of what befalls us is nothing we choose or deserve. The truth may still come nearer to the ideal because insurance buffers us against some of what we cannot control, leaving the course of our lives more reliant on the choices we can in fact make.

The American conviction that individuals author their own lives, limited only by energy and initiative, is a halfway splendid idea. The splendid half is the idea of responsibility: that people are able to make and follow out their own choices. Recall Frederick Douglass's conclusion from his time in slavery: that human nature is incapable of respecting a powerless man, though it may pity him. The belief that others have the power to shape their lives is also the premise that they can command our respect; in one's own life, the same belief is a premise of self-respect. But this idea has a cruel corollary: your failure is your own. Moreover, failure is crushing, because it defines you as a person deserving pity, not respect. The belief that people get what they deserve manages to be both optimistic and merciless, respectful and cruel.

The paradox shows the human value of a social contract that fosters the greatest possible amount of achievement, on the one hand, and, on the other, protects people as far as possible from extremes of misfortune such as illness, deprivation, and economic failure. It is not just that those policies are fair or just according to some abstract standard, or that

they fit one party's political preference. It is that they may be the only way for Americans to preserve our ideals of responsibility and respect for others without falling into contempt for those who fail. The best way to make good on these ideals is to minimize failure and create the maximum opportunity for success. That is the way to approach the best version of values that are defining and profoundly admirable, but intensely tricky nonetheless.

A Little More Freedom

THAT EXAMPLE is about reconciling wealth and innovation with personal choice and opportunity, integrating aspects of freedom that are often at odds. The next is about how economic life interacts with politics, enriching or limiting exploration of what freedom means. The starting point is the last two decades of expansion in digital technology. In 1990, the work of creators—books, movies, songs—was always fixed in physical form, a hardcover or pocket edition, a film reel, vinyl, or a CD. Culture, the sum of all of those creations and whatever spirit is greater than the sum, was on the one hand a galaxy of words, notes, images, and ideas but, on the other, a library, an arsenal of imprinted paper and plastic. Each of those physical objects took time and effort to make and was difficult or impossible to revise once it existed. (Thomas Jefferson edited the New Testament with a razor, taking out the supernatural events and preserving what he deemed the sound ethical teaching; reworking a vinyl version of the Beatles' *White Album* with even the finest cutting tool would not produce a coherent alternative version.) They were no easier to share than cars or chairs:

you could borrow my copy of *Middlemarch*, but we couldn't read it at the same time.

Digital technology turned these works into nearly pure information: albums, images, and, increasingly, books and movies are now electronic files, with no physical form except their appearance on a screen or in headphones. That change means a few big things. Files are very easy to share. When one person has a song and an Internet connection, in principle everyone with the same technology could be listening to that song a day later—everyone in the world, each with an electronic "copy" on her computer. Digital files are also easy to create and edit. Even recording a song or filming a simple movie used to require something like the workshop of a master craftsman, expensive tools that took technical expertise to use. Sharing a creation meant moving from the craftsman level to the factory scale. Books (always the easiest to create), albums, and films passed through vast, capital-intensive institutions before they reached the public, because it took a literal factory to produce a first run of a novel or a record. That gave these industries enormous influence over what went into stores, what was featured on display stands, and even what was reviewed. All this meant that sheer technological requirements drove an industrial model of popular culture.

That doesn't mean that the result was the cultural equivalent of canned soup. The last sixty years have been, in many ways, a wonderful time to be a reader, listener, and viewer. What's new today is the power to make and share your own creations without ever passing through the factory. Anyone who has downloaded independent musicians' songs (or just a friend's) or watched amateur videos on YouTube knows

how easy this is to do. While much of it is silly (though lots of silliness comes through the factory, too), some amateur work is superb.

These changes are a catalyst for creativity in more subtle ways, too. Most creation does not involve just making something the world has never seen (such as, alas, a home video of your cat) but recasting parts of what others have done into a new whole. That's notorious in songwriting and literature: everyone knows about Shakespeare's plagiarism and the way songwriters from Bob Dylan to Gillian Welch have reworked old lines and motifs, and earlier reworkings of these, creating unmistakable personal styles that are also unmistakably drawn from a long history. From the playful to the profound, all culture works this way. Frederick Douglass and other radicals reached back to the words of the Declaration of Independence to give old principles new meaning. Now, for the first time ever, anyone with some fairly affordable and simple equipment can rework or remix the songs and images that others made.

In a culture that revolves around images and sound as much as words, this kind of remixing is near the heart of political commentary. In the run-up to the Iraq War, nothing better expressed what many skeptics thought of the new transatlantic "special relationship" than a widely watched satirical clip of George W. Bush and Tony Blair as mutually enamored young lovers lip-synching "Endless Love" (with the prime minister singing the female part). One of the sharper comments on foreign-policy developments between 2001 and 2004 was Jon Stewart's use of video collage to stage an acrimonious debate between George W. Bush, the isolationist of the 2000 presidential campaign,

and George W. Bush, the Wilsonian idealist of four years later. The difficulty is that such commentary—like DJ Dangermouse's reworking of the *White Album* and Jay-Z's *Black Album* into the hybrid *Grey Album*—uses material that someone else made and legally owns. (More typically, it is material that someone else made and that a corporation owns.) That means the owners can stop the remixers and impose heavy fines to discourage others from picking up where they left off. They can do so because they don't like the message the remixer is sounding or just because they don't want anyone, no matter how benign, messing with their stuff and encouraging others to do the same.

This is not the place for a primer on the law of intellectual property, which governs who owns cultural goods and what owners can prevent others from doing with their property. The basic point is that new kinds of creativity and commentary are running headlong into property rights designed for industrial-era culture, and much of the potential that technology has created could remain empty possibility. There are fairly simple ways to rebalance intellectual property, but lawmakers, under heavy lobbying from the culture industry, have ignored them. (The most effective reform so far is a voluntary one, in which creators give up some of their ownership rights, authorizing others to draw on what they have done and announcing to all that *this* song or book is available for further creative use.) Lawrence Lessig, a law professor at Stanford, calls the choice that the law is now making one between "free culture" and "permission culture." These are not just differently tweaked legal regimes, but different ways of living in a culture. A free culture is one in which whatever comes in through your eyes

and ears is something you might recast a little, remark upon, mash together with another thing, or borrow from in making your own magnum opus. A permission culture is one in which every composition of words, images, and sounds belongs to somebody, and if you don't ask before doing your own thing with it, you will be nailed for the intellectual-property version of trespassing on another person's land.

Consider again the confidence that Douglass had to have to make the Declaration of Independence and the Constitution his own. He had to believe—or act as if he believed—that the world he lived in was for him, as much as it was for the slave owners who had drafted and signed the Declaration. He had to act as if the life he inherited was not the only one he—or the country—could have, and that the language around him was a living instrument to change that life. That is also the attitude of a hoped-for free culture—that of a democratic personality that might adjust the world at any moment in some small or large way. An economy of creativity can help to train people in that attitude by making culture into raw material for everybody's joint creation of the next moment, or it can foster the opposite spirit by presenting a world of fixed creations, each carrying a serious penalty for anyone who tries to remake it according to his imagination.

Whether free culture would have the democratic virtues I have sketched is not something we can know before we try. These kinds of thoughts about economic life as a system of personal freedom and cultural democracy must begin as exercises of imagination. They describe a pair of possible worlds, one more closed and the other more open, one freer and the other less free. The freer world is the one better able

to integrate the diverse dimensions of freedom: free choice; the power to act effectively and choose from among many alternatives; and the psychological capacity for free judgment, imagination, and healthy self-regard. Having imagined a more free world, we then have to ask which political and legal decisions could move us closer to it. The answers to that question cannot have mathematical precision. Instead, they are more or less hopeful glimpses of what we might all become if we chose different rules: bolder, more capable people in a more emboldening world.

These fairly modest examples anchor this chapter because they are less obvious than some others. Larger ones are also in some ways more straightforward. An efficient system of universal health insurance would express a sense of fairness and belonging, enable people to make freer decisions (not least because they would not depend on their current employers for health care and so could change jobs when that otherwise made sense), and make American business more competitive (by removing the burden on large employers that insure their workers in a hugely expensive system). That would be a centerpiece of any program to do in the twenty-first century what Franklin Roosevelt proposed to do for the twentieth: make a changed economy serve the American vision of a nation of free individuals whose dignity begins in their freedom. Another centerpiece would be integrating environmental protection and workers' rights into trade agreements, seeking to rest the international economy on fairness and responsibility just as the national economy of the late nineteenth century rested on mobility and freedom of contract. Dawning recognition of global climate change highlights how urgent this change is,

and may help to make it politically possible. These aims are obviously desirable if there are ways to pursue them effectively. The serious question is whether there are technical reasons, ranging from the limits of information to the ways political decisions are made, that the goals are impossible or come at an intolerably high cost. Those questions are partly for experts and partly for experiment. When a country is open to some experiment with its institutions, experts need to be skilled not just in the details of existing institutions, but in connecting those with the use of political imagination.

This way of thinking about economic life may seem unduly idealist, taken with abstract ideas of freedom remote from the practicalities of production and exchange. That response is understandable, but it is exactly backward. Our economic inheritance is a thoroughly idealistic one, shaped by ideas of how free people can organize their practical lives together on the basis of their freedom. The most hardheaded premises of economic life are the residue of earlier political programs that set out new ways to make people free. The fixed points of our reasoning should be not implacable market rules but the several distinct strands of freedom, sometimes conflicting and sometimes supporting one another, which the economy exists to serve. The market is a superior tool for this purpose, and like any tool it has forms and constraints that a competent user must respect. The first thing he has to know, though, is what he is trying to accomplish. American economic life has always been a pursuit of freedom, and it is still that today. We must pose our economic questions in that light to know what we are asking.

*   *   *

Recall the charge against American freedom from critics in the pessimistic countertradition: that it is self-immolating, a purely negative force that breaks down barriers until social life, bereft of sustaining forms, collapses into chaos. If one wanted to give that idea new life today, the best starting place would not be sexuality, secularism, or hedonism: it would be climate change. Here, more than anywhere else, it is clear that the logic of a free society threatens that society with self-destruction. Understanding how this works is not so complicated. Appreciating how to overcome it requires using the lessons of all the strands of this book: the history of economics, the repeated transformations of American political community, and the ever-changing idea of freedom itself.

To begin with the problem: the central principle of the market economy is that most of the time individuals pursuing their self-interest will spontaneously produce benefits for all, and that this process should give economies their shapes. Although it is familiar today, this idea is as radical as any advance in freedom. It is among our foremost ways of putting into effect that prophetic Enlightenment slogan "the pursuit of happiness"—ordering our lives of production and exchange not by the word of a sovereign nor by a religious vision of the cosmos, but by millions of personal needs and desires, the innumerable notes of an unlikely harmony.

As noted, however, the market's license for personal selfishness includes ignoring those effects of our actions that neither harm nor benefit us personally, and instead fall on others—what economists call *externalities*. Such thoroughgoing self-concern is part of the reason critics damned the

market as a system for sociopaths; but externalities turn out to be open to political repair. Laws controlling pollution, setting minimum wages, guaranteeing health benefits, and otherwise limiting our ability to take advantage of others— all these set ground rules for basic responsibility. Today, though, climate change threatens to become the externality that ate the world, a spiraling harm built into the logic of our economy, which neither individual nor political decisions are well positioned to correct.

Competent introductions to the science of climate change are easy to find these days, and new details develop monthly. The briefest refresher: human emissions of heat-trapping gases are changing the composition of the earth's atmosphere in a way that is all but certain to drive up global temperatures. These changes involve complex and poorly understood systems, full of feedback effects and tipping points, so that even the most sophisticated forecasts are guesswork. Leading predictions of the consequences include rising sea levels, disastrous floods, huge storms, ever more intense droughts, and changing global weather patterns that could turn today's croplands into deserts. The effects on humans could include expanding tropical diseases, famines, huge flows of ecological refugees, and wars over diminishing arable land and disappearing water. Even if some regions—such as the Russian and Canadian tundra—were to benefit for a time, the disasters in densely populated areas would strain both political order and natural resources. All of this is the part we understand, relatively speaking. Beyond that, the enormous complexity of the global climate makes responsible forecasting all but impossible, but we know that the planet has gone through climate shocks be-

fore, in which temperatures have spiked or plummeted, devastating ecosystems and species. It would be irresponsible not to consider the possibility that we are contributing to such a shock now.

The aspect of climate change that is rooted in personal decisions is not hard to see. The greenhouse gases that fossil fuels emit when burned are a nearly perfect externality, dispersing through the entire global atmosphere, while the person burning the fuel enjoys cheap and fast travel, instant communication, heat and cooling (the ironically named climate control), and the other technologies that have done so much to make the world the playground of our desires. Anyone who stops burning fossil fuels would give up all the benefits herself for an imperceptible help to others. The unhappy choice for individuals is between being part of the problem and being, well, a sucker. The same logic holds for countries. Even 300 million Americans' making very substantial cuts in emissions would not change basic global trends. (In 2007, China passed the United States as the world's largest source of greenhouse gases.) Moreover, these idealistic Americans would absorb the full sacrifice of wealth and freedom that comes with giving up the dominant modern technology, while dispersing the modest climate benefit across the world. If personal carbon reductions are, practically speaking, a futile form of sainthood, national reductions are a minimally effective version of foreign aid. This is the key to the political problem of climate change: the collective decisions that control externalities happen at a scale that does not begin to match the problem. A country, like an individual, would have to be close to altruistic to give up fossil fuels in a meaningful way, and even then it could

not hope to make a great difference by its own actions. Adding a dollop of insult, it would also have to be altruistic toward the future: although democracies make political decisions on a scale of two to seven years, climate change works itself out over many decades, so that the largest effects of today's decisions fall on a generation that is still unborn. Neither kind of altruism, by and large, describes how countries behave, nor does *saintly* describe many individuals.

Take a step back to recall the story that this book tells, and consider how it might come to a very unhappy ending. Imagine the history our disappointed descendants might write. For centuries, the moral teachings of a civilization held self-interest and self-trust to be the sins of frail and deluded humanity. These traditional teachings denied that societies could discern distinct and viable principles of order and design their own institutions accordingly. They denounced such efforts as doomed hubris. Then, in an unprecedented experiment, some people rejected the old wisdom. They took the heart's desire and the body's appetite as compass points and rededicated human ingenuity to serving them. They created new forms of order to house these inverted values. For a time, the experiment succeeded, changing life so dramatically that the utopian visions of one century became the pedestrian common sense of the next.

Then, suddenly and drastically, the experiment failed. Self-interest and self-trust proved to be formulas for devastating the world. Democratic polities, the other moral center of the great experiment, could not stop runaway self-destruction and turned out to abet it instead. Faced with

overwhelming evidence that they were on an unsustainable course, the freedom-loving peoples of the twenty-first century wrung their hands, congratulated themselves on their hybrid cars and locally grown food, and changed little, because it never made sense for anyone or any country to do so. Today the wiser descendants of that age, survivors in a changed and inhospitable world, teach their children the ideas of their ancestors' critics, the pessimists who saw through their blithe hubris. They recognize the twenty-first century as the apex of an experiment whose logic set it up to fail from the start.

It is not so hard to imagine the future vantage from which our present would seem a disastrous mistake. So what are the resources—technological, to be sure, but also political and cultural—that we have to avert it? The leading response to climate change is a suite of proposals to retool economic life, balancing global emissions of greenhouse gases with natural and industrial uptake of them, thus stabilizing the atmospheric chemistry. This is the ideal captured in the phrase *carbon-neutral*. (Carbon is the most important of the six major greenhouse gases, and it is often used as a stand-in for them all.) There is a habit, inherited from a puritanical strain of environmentalism, of understanding this change as quashing self-indulgence and returning humanity to a severe kind of virtue. That way of seeing our situation is of a piece with the grim backward-looking story set out just above. It is a mistake, and a counterproductive one. The more we understand our freedom as mere self-indulgence, the less likely it seems that we will be able to change direction and avert possible disaster. That is, the shallower our picture of our own tradition, the more likely it

becomes that our descendants will see it as a tragic and wasteful error.

But there is another way of understanding the tradition of American freedom, in both the sweeping spirit of the pursuit of happiness and the particulars of economic and political life. From this perspective, the point of American freedom has been to discern and create the best kinds of limits, and to experience them as the consummation of personal freedom and basis of its social practice, rather than its opposite. To appreciate this, consider how our ecologically hell-bent economy arose. The principles of the American economy do not embody any nihilistic or merely selfish vision of human beings, even if that is how economic life sometimes seems to play out.

Take the libertarian core of American economic life, the principle that each person's main concern should be to look out for her own interests. As we have seen, this is a powerful driver of the spiral of externalities behind climate change. In fact, the premise that self-concern should be one's main motive creates the definition of an *externality*, that which is outside oneself. As we have also seen, however, the roots of this principle lie not in mutual indifference, but in a series of attempts to imagine and create a community of equals. This was what Adam Smith aimed at when he portrayed markets as ways of putting persuasion and reciprocity, rather than command and hierarchy, at the center of everyday life. It was the reason that Abraham Lincoln's democratic creed—that there should be no slaves and no masters—seemed to him to imply the doctrine of free labor.

Our familiar libertarianism began as a principle for a new kind of common life. It also began, ironically enough, in a request for sacrifice. Smith and Lincoln asked masters, lords, all those at the top of the zero-sum hierarchy of honor and power, to give up a share of their command to make possible a society of equals. Sometimes the change was willing, and sometimes law or war had to break the privileges of the old order to inaugurate the new. Either way, masters surrendered a whole repertoire of power, honor, and identity to clear the way for new, still uncertain ways for people to live together. For those persuaded to undertake the change willingly, the hope was that the surrender would open better kinds of power, honor, and identity, in which no one would have to be abject.

Take another anchor of modern economic life, regulation and intervention by government, which aims at ensuring wealth and security for the nation. Here, too, our system looks unlikely to address climate change because selfishness looms too large among its principles: a government that addresses climate change will impose burdens on its own people out of proportion to the benefits, which they will share with the rest of the world and future generations. At least since the start of the twentieth century, there has been near-agreement that one of the major purposes of government is to improve the material lives of its people. Some on the right, such as Oliver Wendell Holmes in his "Soldier's Faith" address, have called the goal of material well-being callow and demeaning, while others on the left, such as Michael Sandel, have linked it to the collapse of strong public values. Seen as these critics see it, regulation aimed at national prosperity does appear to be a principle of collective

selfishness as strong as the axiom of individual self-interest, a decisive argument against curbing our own greenhouse gas emissions to help other peoples or future generations.

Consider, however, that such welfare-state regulation has another, very different aspect. It entered national political identity through the addresses of Woodrow Wilson and Franklin Roosevelt, who defended the new role for government not by invoking simple self-interest but by giving voice to a new moral image of the American polity. Wilson presented far more inclusive images of citizenship than earlier presidents had. His portrait of the country included women, children, and factory workers—citizens whose defining characteristic was their vulnerability. They were the Americans for whom libertarian principles were more a hollow promise than a guarantee of dignity and respect. When Wilson argued that government must step in to protect these Americans with laws ensuring minimum wages, maximum hours, and safe workplaces, he was partly licensing a bureaucratic state, but partly insisting that Americans' vision was large enough to encompass both autonomy and vulnerability. This idea, like Lincoln's, required sacrifice: surrendering the myth of self-reliance and making room in the national idea for people other than successful adult men. Its compensating promise was an image of the country that could reconcile compassion with respect, doing more honor to both than would be possible with either alone. This image is not a license for simple selfishness on the national scale, any more than the individualism of the market, rightly understood, is a license for simple personal selfishness.

This history is a reminder that the freedom our economic life embodies has never been an attempt to discard all

barriers to self-interest and selfish satisfaction. Instead, it has been an effort to replace needless and demeaning constraints—the traditional slur that desire is sinful, the belief that order can come only from hierarchy—with limits that prove both more enduring and more dignifying. Both these sweeping changes in economic life were deeply tied to evolving ideas of personal freedom and national community. Each change also expressed the belief in our power to transform ourselves. American freedom has always involved the ability to discern a better—more realistic and dignifying—set of limits and reimagine ourselves within their confines. Our economic life has always been in part an institutional embodiment of the ways we have come to understand our freedom.

Could there be a similar idea of a carbon-neutral economy, an economy consistent with global ecological stewardship? The limits such an economy would begin by recognizing are akin to those of earlier eras: for free labor, the autonomy and dignity of others, and for the regulatory state, vulnerability and interdependence. Like those, the ecological limits of a fossil-fuel economy express basic facts about the conditions in which we live and act. The principle of emitting only the greenhouse gases the earth's systems can process would be foundational for the economy of a country that adopted it, directly or indirectly affecting every choice in investment, production, and consumption. (Today's economy reflects the opposite principle: our car-based transport systems, sprawling communities, large houses, and intercoastal and intercontinental families are all features of a system in which energy is priced as if it were environmentally costless.) Are these limits we could embrace as enriching our freedom?

There are important differences between these prospective new limits and earlier ones. Earlier transformations addressed human beings, not the natural world: those changes were thoroughly about what it meant to recognize one another as free people. The deep and defining limits on personal action that they adopted—no enslavement and a social obligation to care for the weak and vulnerable—expressed ideas about what a community of free individuals would look like. Earlier sets of limits fell entirely within the arena of human freedom, while climate change presents a boundary from outside. Moreover, there may seem to be something mistaken in identifying as part of freedom something that is so palpably a constraint. What part of ourselves would we answer or perfect by giving up, perhaps until technology changed and perhaps forever, some of our convenience, mobility, and choice? Is that not the bad old constraint that economic and political progress has rolled back for centuries? If so, calling the limits a form of freedom would be a misuse of language.

If so, it would be best to admit it. It is also possible, however, that we can devise a response to climate change that is not just a surrender of some of our present convenience, but also a development in our ideas of freedom and dignity. One strain of the American tradition this book traces is the ambition to acknowledge and take account of what seems true, in oneself or in the larger world, even when society appears to be in a conspiracy to deny it. This is the ideal of the free mind and sovereign conscience, with its early American voice in John Adams, its landmarks in Emerson's and Douglass's refusals to deny what they felt to be true in themselves, and its present battlefields, from intimacy and

identity to free culture and permission culture. This ideal has made a contribution to both environmentalism and the politics of dissent generally through the work of Henry David Thoreau, the prophet of attentiveness and delineation, who devoted his writing to sorting confusion from clarity, ephemerae from what would last, unwelcome and burdensome borrowings from what was one's own, and the optional shackles of false necessity from the necessary limits of reality. He took as the theme of his work that living in truth—the phrase of a later generation of constructive rebels—was the highest form of freedom and taproot of an unbreakable dignity.

That ideal of truthfulness has been a dissenting chord in politics, the special province of the civilly disobedient and other idealists who follow Thoreau in preferring integrity to effectiveness. It has, in other words, been an aspect of freedom at odds with the compromises and incidental injuries of everyday life. The idea of a carbon-neutral economy promises to move the ideal to the center of ordinary practice. It presents a promise Thoreau might have welcomed: a complete acknowledgment and accounting of the effects of our actions, and, in that respect, an economy that does not require its participants to look away from what they do. This is the aspect of American freedom we now have the greatest need to integrate with the rest. It is the best stay against the strain of national temper that runs to sheer fantasy (such as Ronald Reagan's promise to restore a nineteenth-century ideal in twentieth-century conditions) or hysteria (such as the climate of fear and quiescence that quashed important public questions about the invasion of Iraq). Moreover, it is likely to be our best resource in acknowledging ecological

limits as a part of our freedom, rather than a contradiction of it. If we can learn to see the challenge of climate change in that way, we are more likely to succeed in answering it and to preserve the best parts of our tradition while doing so. While it remains true that American action alone cannot avert a global ecological crisis, American leadership and participation may well make the difference in creating a worldwide response.

None of this means that a stern puritanical economy is the best or the most likely response to climate change. We should expect, and seek, revolutions in energy sources, transport design, housing, and communication to preserve and enhance as much as possible of what we value in today's prosperity. The main point of a carbon-neutral economy would be to value and encourage the innovation that would bring those changes sooner rather than later, because waiting for an ecologically blind economy to drive us to a new approach means waiting for disaster. The minor—but critical—point of a carbon-neutral economy would be acceptance of those sacrifices of convenience and comfort that we cannot avoid as we remake our economy and the world it shapes. Both changes would begin in a public language of civic dignity for an ecological age and a vision, both moral and practical, of an economy that could integrate environmental limits into the other values it embodies. The greatest encouragement we have in starting that process is that it is more like than unlike other great changes we have managed, and that the same tradition of freedom that drove those changes has resources for this one, if only we remember it rightly.

Afterword

THIS BOOK is an exploration of the American sensation of freedom, the quality John Adams named, Edmund Burke diagnosed, and each of the book's characters and episodes elaborated and reshaped. It is part history, part political theory, and part an incomplete topography of a field of ideas that we each must find our own way of inhabiting. American freedom has emerged through a series of momentous discoveries: that limits previously thought inescapable were, after all, unnecessary and forms of order believed impossible could become ordinary. One of the first such discoveries was in revolutionary Massachusetts, where political order emerged without inherited authority—as a worried Burke put it, anarchy proved tolerable. The end of slavery, the rise of democracy, the freeing of intimacy, each repeated the unsettling discovery. We are most true to the American tradition of freedom when we take chances with our institutions and ideas and try to become the parents of a future world that many in the present think impossible. At its best, this tradition is a concert of unbreakable individual demands for dignity and a vision of the country as a community of equal dignity. A tradition of repudiation and

innovation, it imparts a way of understanding the most radical breaks with the past as true to an inheritance. Its spirit is no simple fulfillment of some original promise contained in the country's founding, although many have expressed it that way. Instead, it is a practice of answering to new discoveries about who we individually are and what a country, taken whole, might be, which draws on the past for help in steering by glimpses of the possible future.

Our changes are always incomplete efforts to integrate values that are often at odds, and which bring bad with good, confusion as well as clarity. The American sensation of freedom has come nearest to confusion when it has seemed simple and final. It is complex because it includes several values—the defiant spirit of declarations of independence, mastery and authenticity, civic dignity, the wish for heroism, and the love of order and recognition of vulnerability and interdependence—which different people inevitably understand in different ways. Moreover, there will always be sincere disagreement over how to put it into practice. Acknowledging its complexity is, in fact, one of the first responsibilities it imposes.

Writing about American politics, Emerson once distinguished between "the party of memory"—the conservatives—and "the party of hope," the reformers. That contrast looks very different in American life today. In the traditions that Emerson, Douglass, and others helped to create, memory is a source of hope and its indispensable helper. The lesson of our history is that the demand for greater freedom is real and right: it expresses the elemental needs for a place to stand, a sense of dignity, and a life among other free people. The demand for freedom is the engine of our history, not

the enemy of order but the beginning of each new form of order. Joining in American memory means remembering this, drawing on the past to make sense of the new possibility of the present.

Our history is also a reminder that freedom and order stand in a difficult and sometimes tragic relationship. We make good on our capacity for freedom only by upholding common institutions that sometimes constrain us and frustrate our sense of limitless potential. We honor one another when we can see, at once, infinite possibility and deep vulnerability and need. We take in the full dignity of our constitutional community only by accepting the country's failures as much as its promise and understanding that, as citizens, we work to redeem some of both. We fully appreciate freedom when we understand that it arises both from radical acts of defiance and self-assertion and the slow, imperfect work of integration with inherited values and a sometimes obdurate world. If we pretend that any of this is simple, we fall into the bad American habit of self-trust without self-knowledge, optimism unanchored in experience, which ironically leaves us disappointed and cynical. If we take it whole, we have a beginning. The shape of American hope is an endless chain of these beginnings.

Thank You

BRUCE ACKERMAN, Lindsay Andrews, Jessica Areen, Ben and Karen Barker, David Barron, Kate Bartlett, Ryan Bates, James Boyle, Corey Brettschneider, Daniela Cammack, Michael Calabrese, Brady Case, Josh Cohen, Reid Cramer, Erin Daly, Christopher Elmendorf, Owen Fiss, Philip Frickey, Robert Gordon, Ashbel Green, David Grewal, Melissa Healy, Megan Hinkle, Jennifer Jenkins, Larry Kramer, Anthony Kronman, Sidney Kwiran, Roland Lamb, Larry Lessig, Michael Lind, Charles Ludington, David Maxted, Pratap Mehta, Andrew Miller, Martha Minow, Nicholas Parillo, Philip Pettit, Robert Post, Jeff Powell, Hannah Purdy, Walter and Deirdre Purdy, Aziz Rana, Lauren Redniss, Robert Reich, Chris Schroeder, Neil Siegel, Reva Siegel, Sara Sherbill, Joseph William Singer, Zephyr Teachout, Dennis Thompson, Michael Tomasky, Erin Trenda, Lisa Tust, Sheilah Villalobos, Jennifer Wimsatt, and Kim Witherspoon.

Students in my seminars at Duke Law School and Harvard Law School and participants in the Harvard University Ethics seminar and several presentations at the New America Foundation.

Duke Law School, Harvard Law School, the Harvard University Ethics Center, Yale Law School, Boalt Hall Law School at the Univeristy of California at Berkeley, Colorado Law School, the Center for American Progress, and the New America Foundation.

Notes

Introduction: The Sensations of Freedom

3 "zealots of anarchy": Samuel Johnson, *Taxation No Tyranny: An Answer to the Resolutions of the American Congress*, 2.

"these lords of themselves": Ibid., 36.

4 in awe: See Conor Cruise O'Brien, *The Great Melody: A Thematic Biography of Edmund Burke*, 101–2.

4 "whether the white people": Edmund Burke, letter to Miss Mary Palmer, Jan. 19, 1786, in *On Empire, Liberty, and Reform: Speeches and Letters*, ed. David Bromwich.

4 "I do not know": Edmund Burke, *Speech on Conciliation with America*, Mar. 22, 1775, 45.

5 "life, liberty, and property": Johnson, *Taxation No Tyranny*, 35.

5 "making slaves": Ibid., 65.

5 "wild, indefinite, and obscure": Ibid., 55.

5 Both men also hated: On Johnson, see David Brion Davis, *The Problem of Slavery in the Age of Revolution, 1770–1823*, 398 ("Samuel Johnson, who . . . reportedly toasted at Oxford 'to the next insurrection of the negroes in the West Indies,' took up the black man's cause with a seriousness that distressed Boswell"). On Burke, see ibid., 358 (Burke an "outspoken opponent . . . of Negro slavery"), 405 (referring to "the antislavery eloquence of a . . . Burke"). See also O'Brien, *Great Melody*, 91 ("Burke hated slavery").

5 "Why is it": Johnson, *Taxation No Tyranny*, 89.

6 "put the axe": John Lind, *An Answer to the Declaration of the American Congress*, 122.

6 he gleefully imagined: Johnson, *Taxation No Tyranny*, 11–12.

6 "disbursed impiety": See O'Brien, *Great Melody*, 93.

7 "Sir, I am": James Boswell, *The Life of Samuel Johnson, L.L.D.*, 116.

7 "All government is": Johnson, *Taxation No Tyranny*, 23.

7 "the rights of man": Edmund Burke, *Reflections on the Revolution in France*, 58–59.

7 "unsuspecting confidence is": Burke, "Letter to the Sheriffs of Bristol on the Affairs of America," in *On Empire*, 174.

7 "The Spirit of America": See O'Brien, *Great Melody*, 155.

8 "the delirious dream": Johnson, *Taxation No Tyranny*, 35.
the infatuated and the corrupt: Ibid., 70 ("men who, by whatever corruptions or whatever infatuation, have undertaken to defend the Americans").

8 "Abstract liberty": Burke, *Speech on Conciliation*, 26.

8 "the sensations": John Adams, *Dissertation on the Canon and the Feudal Law* (1765), in *The Political Writings of John Adams*.

9 "those who are": Burke, *Speech on Conciliation*, 30.

9 "the haughtiness of": Ibid., 30–31.

9 "have sprung up": Ibid.

9 "a refinement on": Ibid., 29.

10 "communion of the spirit": Burke, *Speech on Conciliation*.

10 "minds to a state": Adams, *Dissertation*.

10 "infernal confederacy": Ibid.

10 "civil and political slavery": Adams, *Dissertation*.

10 "zealots of anarchy": Johnson, *Taxation No Tyranny*, 2.

10 called "civil slavery": Adams, *Dissertation*.

11 As the Americans saw: Besides the material cited in this book, this account of the constitutional culture of early America draws on John Philip Reid, *The Ancient Constitution and the Origins of Anglo-American Liberty*; Larry Kramer, *The People Themselves: Popular Constitutionalism and Judicial Review*, 9–34; Gordon S. Wood, *The Creation of the American Republic*, 3–90; Bernard Bailyn, *The Ideological Origins of the American Revolution*, 55–143; John Philip Reid, *The Concept of Liberty in the Age of the American Revolution* (Chicago: Chicago University Press, 1988).

11 It draws insistently: For instance, the complaint about quartering soldiers appears in the Declaration of Independence, the English Bill of Rights of 1689, and the Petition of Right of 1628. The complaint against taxation without the consent of representatives also appears in all three documents. So do objections to interference

with the meeting and activity of Parliament and with the traditional procedures of rule of law.

12 "wild and obscure": Johnson, *Taxation No Tyranny*, 55.

13 For Burke, this ambition: Although this idea is amply expressed throughout Burke's work, the best exposition is Bromwich, ed., introduction to *Burke on Empire*, 1–38.

13 "confident that the first": Burke, *Speech on Conciliation*, 26.

14 "A new, strange, and unexpected": Ibid., 37

15 "wild, obscure, and indefinite": Johnson, *Taxation No Tyranny*, 55.

18 "All men are born": Massachusetts Constitution of 1780, art. 1.

19 "spirit" that Burke warned: O'Brien, *Great Melody*, 155.

22 "dissidence of dissent": Burke, *Speech on Conciliation*.

1: Declarations of Independence

24 "He has excited": Declaration of Independence.

25 "arbitrary . . . absolute rule": Ibid.

26 when he merged: See John Stauffer, "Frederick Douglass," in Frederick Douglass, *My Bondage and My Freedom*, ed. Stauffer.

26 "[M]y husband": See James Oakes, *The Radical and the Republican*, 245.

26 Eleven years earlier: Douglass recounted his own life in three biographies. In this work I draw mainly on *My Bondage and My Freedom* and *The Life of Frederick Douglass, an American Slave*. These were written closer to the events discussed in this book than "Life and Times of Frederick Douglass," in *Frederick Douglass: Autobiographies*, which appeared in 1881 while the earlier two both predated the Civil War.

26 "What have I": Frederick Douglass, "What to the Slave Is the Fourth of July?" in *The American Intellectual Tradition*, vol. 1, *1630–1865*, ed. David A. Hollinger and Charles Capper, 448.

26 "This Fourth of July": Ibid., 449.

26 "for revolting barbarity": Ibid., 451.

27 "your celebration": Ibid.

27 "scorching irony": Ibid.

27 "I am ashamed": William Lloyd Garrison, "Address to the Colonization Society (July 4, 1829), "in *A House Divided: The Antebellum Slavery Debates in the United States, 1776–1865*, ed. Mason I. Lowance Jr., 340.

27   "a covenant with death": William Lloyd Garrison, "Address to the
     Friends of Freedom and Emancipation in the United States," in
     Hollinger and Capper, *1630–1865,* 438.

27   "the ring-bolt": Douglass, "What to the Slave," 446.

28   "are all saving principles": Ibid.

28   "interpreted as it ought": Ibid., 458.

28   "importation of persons": U.S. Constitution, art. 1, sec. 9, cl. 1.

28   "person held to service": U.S. Constitution, art. 4, sec. 2, cl. 3.

28   "three fifths": U.S. Constitution, art. 1, sec. 2, cl. 3.

28   "I hold": Douglass, "What to the Slave," 458.

29   "With them": Ibid., 447.

30   "regarded as beings": *Dred Scott v. Sandford,* 60 U.S. 393, 407 (1856).

30   Showing a keen eye: Ibid., 408–10.

31   "[T]he men who framed": Ibid., 410.

31   Taney wrote: Ibid., 405:

>   It is not the province of the court to decide upon the jus-
>   tice or injustice, the policy or impolicy, of these laws. The
>   decision of that question belonged to the political or law-
>   making power; to those who formed the sovereignty and
>   framed the Constitution. The duty of the court is, to inter-
>   pret the instrument they have framed, with the best lights
>   we can obtain on the subject, and to administer it as we find
>   it, according to its true intent and meaning when it was
>   adopted.

31   In a memoir: The events mentioned here are recounted in Dou-
     glass, *My Bondage and My Freedom,* 114–41.

32   "the turning point of my life": Ibid., 140.

32   "and our sacred honor": Declaration of Independence.

33   "The grass grows": "An Address," in *The Essential Writings of Ralph
     Waldo Emerson,* ed. Brooks Atkinson, 63.

33   "then is the end": Emerson, "An Address," 64.

33   Saint Paul: Romans 7:15.

34   Saint Augustine: The best account of this interpretation of experi-
     ence is in book 3 of Augustine's *Confessions.*

34   "If a man is": Emerson, "An Address," 64.

34   "a man is made": Ibid., 65.

34   "That which shows": Ibid., 69.

34   "In the soul": Ibid., 75.

35   "a faith like": Emerson, "An Address," 75.

35   "our soul-destroying slavery": Ibid., 76.

35   "our intellectual Declaration": Quoted in *Library of Literary Criticism of English and American Authors,* vol. 7, *1875–1890,* ed. Charles Wells Moulton, 377.

35   "[N]othing is more": Ralph Waldo Emerson, "Fate," in *The Conduct of Life,* 1–51, 23.

36   Emerson voiced a radical: For Burke and Adams; the reference is to the discussion in the introduction.

36   Critics had warned: The reference is to the discussion in the introduction of Samuel Johnson and other critics of American independence.

36   *the pursuit of happiness:* The discussion of happiness in this paragraph and those that follow borrows from that of Garry Wills in *Inventing America: Jefferson's Declaration of Independence.*

37   "the greatest happiness": On Hutcheson's use of the phrase, and its variations, see William Robert Scott, *Francis Hutcheson: His Life, Teaching, and Position in the History of Philosophy,* 275.

38   "[A]ll loves and friendships": Ralph Waldo Emerson, "Swedenborg; or, The Mystic," in *Representative Men* (Boston: Houghton Mifflin, 1903), 91–146, 128.

38   "Trust thyself": Emerson, "Self-Reliance," in *Essential Writings,* 133.

39   "I must be myself": Ibid., 145.

39   "a nation of men": Emerson, "The American Scholar," in *Essential Writings,* 59.

39   manageable depression: On Freud's view of therapy and its aims, see Peter Gay, *Freud: A Life for Our Time,* 244–305.

39   "demean the existence": *Lawrence v. Texas,* 539 U.S. 558, 578 (2003), Justice Kennedy.

40   "domestic insurrection": The reference is to the language of the Declaration of Independence, cited in the introduction, pages 24–25.

40   "In leaving you": Douglass, "Letter to His Old Master," in *My Bondage and My Freedom,* 259.

41   "If I am": Emerson, "Self-Reliance," 135.

41   "an axe to the root": The reference is to the discussion in the introduction, pages 6, 13.

41   "There is not": Douglass, "What to the Slave," 450.

42   "Right is of": See Deborah E. McDowell, introduction to Doug-
      lass, *Narrative of the Life of Frederick Douglass, an American
      Slave*, xxv.

2: The Search for Civic Dignity

43   "a new birth": Abraham Lincoln, Gettysburg Address (Nov. 19,
      1863).

43   "bind up": Abraham Lincoln, second inaugural address (Mar. 4,
      1865).

44   "I have in my lifetime": Abraham Lincoln, speech to the 140th
      Indiana Regiment (Mar. 17, 1865).

45   "your celebration": The reference is to Douglass's Independence
      Day 1852 address at Rochester, New York, discussed in chapter 1,
      page 25.

45   "to interpret": Woodrow Wilson, first inaugural address (Mar. 4,
      1913).

46   "a new insight": Ibid.

46   In some respects: For a valuable introduction to the history of pres-
      idential speech and Wilson's pivotal role in it, see Jeffrey K. Tulis,
      The Rhetorical Presidency.

47   "sensible object": The reference is to Burke's remark on the charac-
      ter of abstract ideas, discussed in the introduction pages 8–9.

48   Another is recognition: For some valuable discussions of the idea of
      recognition, see Axel Honneth, *The Struggle for Recognition: The
      Moral Grammar of Social Conflicts*, 131–40, 145–79; Charles Taylor,
      "The Politics of Recognition," in *Philosophical Arguments*.

50   While there is nothing: See Morris P. Fiorina, *Culture War? The
      Myth of a Polarized America*, 2d ed.; Alan Wolfe, *One Nation After
      All*.

51   "what America does": William J. Clinton, first inaugural address
      (Jan. 20, 1993).

51   "we need a new sense": William J. Clinton, second inaugural
      address (Jan. 20, 1997).

51   "responsibility era": George W. Bush, nomination acceptance
      speech at Republican National Convention (July 31, 2000).

51   "at its best": George W. Bush, first inaugural address (Jan. 20,
      2001).

51   "challenge[d] a new": Clinton, first inaugural address.

51   "simple but powerful": Clinton, first inaugural address.

51   "[w]hat you do": Bush, first inaugural address.

52   "a new commitment": Ibid.

52   "In America's ideal": George W. Bush, second inaugural address
      (Jan. 20, 2005).

52   "The greatest progress": Clinton, second inaugural address.

52   "the exercise of": Bush, second inaugural address.

53   George Washington held: See George Washington, first inaugural
      address (Apr. 30, 1789), "the foundation of our national policy will
      be laid in the pure and immutable principles of private morality."

53   *Character* was a description: See Thomas Jefferson, second inaugu-
      ral address (Mar. 4, 1805), referring to the "reflecting characters of
      the citizens at large" in considering public affairs and the "zeal and
      wisdom of the characters" whom they elect; James Monroe, inau-
      gural address (Mar. 4, 1817), "We must support our rights or lose
      our character"; Andrew Jackson, second inaugural address (Mar. 4,
      1833), asserting that successful foreign policy "has elevated our
      character among the nations of the earth"; William Henry Harri-
      son, inaugural address (Mar. 4, 1841), referring to a love of power as
      anathema to the "character of a devoted republican patriot";
      Rutherford B. Hayes, inaugural address (Mar. 5, 1877), describing
      civil-service reform as ensuring that an occupant of certain posi-
      tions should keep his job "as long as his personal character remains
      untarnished"; Grover Cleveland, inaugural address (Mar. 4, 1893),
      warning against policy that "saps the strength and sturdiness of our
      national character"; Lyndon Johnson, inaugural address (Jan. 20,
      1965), "Our destiny in the midst of change will depend on the
      unchanged character of our people, and on their faith."

53   and *virtue:* John Adams, inaugural address (Mar. 4, 1797), referring,
      in a discussion of republican political culture, to the "general dis-
      semination of knowledge and virtue" as the test of such a govern-
      ment; James Monroe, inaugural address (Mar. 4, 1817), proposing to
      maintain the near perfection of American government by "preserv-
      ing the virtue and enlightening the minds" of citizens; William
      Henry Harrison, inaugural address (Mar. 4, 1841), referring to love
      of country and of liberty as "public virtue"; Benjamin Harrison,
      inaugural address (Mar. 4, 1889), referring to "virtues of courage
      and patriotism." The first hint of a contemporary sense of the word
      comes in the middle term of Dwight Eisenhower's "virtues most

cherished by free people—love of truth, pride in work, devotion to country," which he held out as bases of civic dignity. Dwight D. Eisenhower, first inaugural address (Jan. 20, 1953). The word does not appear in inaugural addresses thereafter.

53 *Responsibility* and *service:* See Washington, first inaugural address, referring to "service to my country" as military and political service; James Madison, first inaugural address (Mar. 4, 1809), referring to "the honor and the responsibility allotted to me"; John Quincy Adams, inaugural address (Mar. 4, 1825), referring to "my public service" as his ensuing presidential term; James Knox Polk, inaugural address (Mar. 4, 1845), insisting that the president, in executing his office, "shrinks from no proper responsibility"; Grover Cleveland, first inaugural address (Mar. 4, 1885), referring to his "solemn sense of responsibility" upon assuming the presidency; Warren G. Harding, inaugural address (Mar. 4, 1921), using "universal service" to refer literally to draft enlistment; John F. Kennedy, inaugural address (Jan. 20, 1961), identifying the "call to service" with American soldiers buried abroad). It is worth noting that *service* does get an early use in something close to its contemporary sense, although with a more civic inflection than is typical now. See Wilson, second inaugural (Mar. 4, 1917), referring to "an America united in feeling, in purpose and in its vision of duty, of opportunity and of service."

54 "those small, splendid": Richard Nixon, first inaugural address (Jan. 20, 1969).

54 "attempting to gather": Richard Nixon, second inaugural address (Jan. 20, 1973).

55 "[L]et each of us": Nixon, second inaugural address.

55 "government is not": Clinton, second inaugural address.

55 "work to do": Clinton, first inaugural address.

55 "the bad habit": Ibid.

57 "possessing a chosen": Thomas Jefferson, first inaugural address (Mar. 4, 1801). For one discussion of Jefferson's vision, see Drew R. McCoy, *The Elusive Republic: Political Economy in Jeffersonian America.*

58 "[A] wise and": Jefferson, first inaugural address.

58 "industry and improvement": Ibid.

58 "essential principles": Ibid.

58 "guided our steps": Ibid.

59 meaning of *republican:* On the significance of this idea, see Philip

Pettit, *Republicanism: A Theory of Freedom and Government*, 1–128;
Gregory S. Alexander, *Commodity and Propriety: Competing Visions
of Property in American Legal Thought, 1776–1970*, 1–77; Michael J.
Sandel, *Democracy's Discontent: America in Search of a Public Philosophy*; McCoy, *Elusive Republic*.

59　held it in "trust": See James Madison, first inaugural address (Mar.
4, 1809), referring to his "awful sense of the trust to be assumed");
James Madison, second inaugural address (Mar. 4, 1813), invoking
"the momentous period at which the trust has been renewed";
James Monroe, first inaugural address (Mar. 4, 1817), referring to
the need for a president to hold "a just estimate of the importance
of the trust and of the nature and extent of its duties"; ibid., referring to American government officials as "the faithful and able
depositaries of their trust [that of the American people]"; Andrew
Jackson, second inaugural address (Mar. 4, 1833), referring to the
office as a "sacred trust" that he "receive[d] from the people."

59　"stand unabashed even": Franklin Pierce, inaugural address (Mar. 4,
1853).

59　"If in other lands": James Garfield, inaugural address (Mar. 4, 1881).

60　idea of free labor: The canonical introduction to the work is Eric
Foner, *Free Soil, Free Labor, Free Men: The Ideology of the Republican
Party Before the Civil War*. For a further examination of the ideological stakes of the ideas of self-ownership and freedom of contract, see Charles W. McCurdy, "The 'Liberty of Contract' Regime
in American Law," in *The State and Freedom of Contract*, ed. Harry
N. Scheiber (Stanford, CA: Stanford University Press, 1998),
161–97. For a sketch of historiographic developments about the origins and legacy of free labor, see Manuel Cachan, "Justice Stephen
Field and 'Free Soil, Free Labor Constitutionalism': Reconsidering
Revisionism," *Law and History Review* 20 (2002): 541, and Stephen
A. Siegel, "The Revision Thickens," *Law and History Review* 20
(2002): 631.

60　"sturdy lad from": Emerson, "Self-Reliance," 147.

61　"If any continue": Abraham Lincoln, address to the Wisconsin
State Agricultural Society (Sept. 30, 1859).

61　a big element: See Robert J. Steinfeld, *Coercion, Contract, and Free
Labor in the Nineteenth Century*, 3–38.

61　The Industrial Revolution: On the growth of the industrial economy and the challenges it presented to received ideas of economic

freedom and legal order, some starting points are John Fabian Witt, *The Accidental Republic: Crippled Workingmen, Destitute Widows, and the Remaking of American Law;* Morton Keller, *Regulating a New Economy: Public Policy and Economic Change in America, 1900–1933;* Keller, *Regulating a New Society;* Daniel T. Rodgers, *Atlantic Crossings: Social Politics in a Progressive Age.*

62 "paternalism . . . the bane": Grover Cleveland, second inaugural address (Mar. 4, 1893).

62 Whatever the experience: Witt, *Accidental Republic;* Keller, *Regulating a New Economy;* Keller, *Regulating a New Society;* Rodgers, *Atlantic Crossings.*

62 A generation of elites: See Rodgers, *Atlantic Crossings,* 33–111.

63 "dependent character": Lincoln, address to Wisconsin State Agricultural Society.

63 as debasing "paternalism": Cleveland, second inaugural address.

63 "studied and perfected": Wilson, first inaugural address.

64 "industrial and social": Wilson, first inaugural address.

64 "to solve for": Franklin D. Roosevelt, second inaugural address (Jan. 20, 1937).

64 "a place where": Lyndon B. Johnson, inaugural address (Jan. 20, 1965).

65 "the highly centralized": Franklin D. Roosevelt, address to the Commonwealth Club of San Francisco (Sept. 23, 1932).

66 "a more permanently safe": Ibid.

66 "I do not": Lyndon B. Johnson, Great Society speech (May 22, 1964).

67 "where leisure is": Ibid.

67 "where the meaning" Ibid.

68 Richard Nixon's presidency: See John Mickelthwait and Adrian Wooldridge, *The Right Nation: Conservative Power in America,* 68–71.

69 "We have learned": Jimmy Carter, first inaugural address (Jan. 20, 1977).

69 "We have already": Ibid.

70 "[I]f we despise": Ibid.

70 In the great tradition: On the tradition of the political sermon, see Harry N. Stout, *The New England Soul: Preaching and Religious Culture in Colonial New England,* 13–29.

70 "In this present": Ronald Reagan, first inaugural address (Jan. 20, 1981).

71 "Our present troubles": Ibid.
71 "It is time": Ibid.
72 "we knew it": Ronald Reagan, second inaugural address (Jan. 21, 1985).

3: War and Its Equivalents

74 "Feeling helpless": "Not Knowing What Else to Do, Woman Bakes American-Flag Cake," *The Onion*, Sept. 26, 2001 (available at http://www.theonion.com/content/node/28148).

76 "mystic chords of memory": Abraham Lincoln, first inaugural address (Mar. 4, 1861).

77 political scientist Robert Putnam: See Robert D. Putnam, "E Pluribus Unum: Diversity and Community in the Twenty-First Century: The 2006 Johann Skytte Prize Lecture," *Scandinavian Political Studies* 137, no. 30.2 (2007).

78 are not much: For an introduction to the changing shape and distribution of economic risk in the United States, see Jacob S. Hacker, *The Great Risk Shift*.

79 "War is out": Oliver Wendell Holmes, "The Soldier's Faith" (commencement address, Cambridge, MA) (May 30, 1895).

80 "I do not know": Ibid.
81 "heroism": Ibid.
81 "the men who": Theodore Roosevelt, "The Strenuous Life" (Chicago, Apr. 10, 1899).

82 "only with the wants": Roosevelt, "Strenuous Life."

83 "healthy-minded person"; "No collectivity is"; "[I]t has to be": William James, "The Moral Equivalent of War" Lecture, (San Francisco, 1906).

83 "moral equivalent": James, "Moral Equivalent of War."

85 "A nation": Franklin D. Roosevelt, third inaugural address (Jan. 20, 1941).

86 "It is the essential": James, "Moral Equivalent of War."

86 Lincoln's spirit: Especially telling here are the Gettysburg Address and the second inaugural address.

86 "unify our collective": Warren G. Harding, inaugural address (Mar. 4, 1921).

86 "[I]f we are": Franklin D. Roosevelt, first inaugural address (Mar. 4, 1933).

87   "We should be *owned*": James, "Moral Equivalent of War."

88   "Why should men not": Ibid.

88   "skillful propagandism": Ibid.

89   "War, when you are": Holmes, "Soldier's Faith."

91   "[W]e Americans understand": Barry Goldwater, "Extremism in Defense of Liberty Is No Vice" (San Francisco, July 16, 1964).

92   "the martyrs of history": Ronald Reagan, "A Time for Choosing" (nationwide television address, Oct. 27, 1964).

92   "[O]ur fathers were": William Lloyd Garrison, "Address to the Friends of Freedom and Emancipation in the United States," Charles Capper, *1630–1865*, 444.

92   This attitude had adherents: The preeminent scholarly expression of this view of American history is Charles A. Beard, *An Economic Interpretation of the Constitution.*

93   "a turning-point": Lyndon B. Johnson, speech before Congress on Voting Rights Act (Mar. 15, 1965).

93   "a promissory note": Martin Luther King, "I Have a Dream" (Washington, DC, Aug. 28, 1963).

4: Is Freedom Empty? Citizenship, Sodomy, and the Meaning of Life

97   "kings of ME": The reference is to the discussion of Johnson's criticism of the Americans' rhetoric of freedom, in the introduction, page 3.

97   "the most dangerous man": James Dobson, *Marriage Under Fire: Why We Must Win This Battle*, 40.

98   "These matters": *Lawrence v. Texas*, 539 U.S. 574 (2003).

99   "Imagine an environment": Dobson, *Marriage Under Fire*, 55.

99   " 'freedom' from the shackles": Ibid., 18.

100 "If your time": Rick Warren, *The Purpose-Driven Life: What on Earth Am I Here For?*, 38.

101 "nothing to affirm": Michael Sandel, "The Case Against Perfection," *Atlantic Monthly* (Apr. 2004).

101 "giftedness": Ibid.

102 "Carried away": Stephen Elliott, *New Wine Not to Be Put into Old Bottles*, 10. Originally a sermon preached at Savannah, GA, Feb. 28, 1862).

102 "Man is not": Ibid., 10-11.

102 "loose from wholesome restraint": Henry Ward Beecher, *A Refor-*

mation of Morals Practicable and Indispensable, 29. Originally a sermon delivered at New Haven, Connecticut, Oct. 27, 1812.

103   "We are becoming": Ibid., 27.

103   "man, unrestrained": Timothy Dwight, *A Discourse on Some Events of the Last Century,* 33. Originally a lecture delivered at New Haven, CT, Jan. 7, 1801.

103   "demolished institutions": Beecher, *A Reformation,* 28.

104   "our altars": Ibid., 32.

104   "The destiny": *Planned Parenthood of Pennsylvania v. Casey,* 505 U.S. 833, 852 (1992), Justices Kennedy, Souter, O'Connor.

105   "fundamental right": *Bowers v. Hardwick,* 478 U.S. 186, 190 (1986), Justice White.

105   "demean[ed] the existence": *Lawrence,* 539 U.S. 575.

105   "intimate" and "deeply personal": These words refer to Justice Kennedy's language in *Lawrence v. Texas,* discussed earlier, and not to any introduced by Justice Scalia.

105   "the concept of existence": Ibid.

105   Sandel's "given": The term refers to the same concept that Michael Sandel argues for as necessary to moral reasoning, as discussed earlier in this chapter.

106   "the passage": *Lawrence,* 539 U.S. 588. Justice Scalia dissenting.

106   "the so-called": *Lawrence,* 539 U.S. 601. Justice Scalia dissenting.

107   "we no longer": *Casey,* 505 U.S. 984. Justice Scalia dissenting and quoting *Dred Scott v. Sandford,* 19 How., 393, 621 (1856), Justice Curtis dissenting.

107   "something appealing": Sandel, "Case Against Perfection."

108   "the real rights": Burke, *Reflections on the Revolution,* 58–59.

109   a conservative temperament: The image of conservative temperament set out in this paragraph takes some of its shape from that of Michael Oakeshott, "On Being Conservative," in *Rationalism in Politics and Other Essays.*

112   "an original relation": Ralph Waldo Emerson, "Nature," in *Essential Writings,* 3.

113   "disclose[d] the Court's": *Lawrence,* 567.

115   Justice Lewis Powell: See John C. Jeffries Jr., *Justice Lewis F. Powell, Jr.* (New York: Fordham University Press, 2001), 528.

117   "more immediate, penetrating": See William H. Chafe, *Private Lives, Public Consequences: Personality and Politics in Modern America* (Cambridge, MA: Harvard University Press, 2005), 342.

117 "imitation is suicide": Emerson, "Self-Reliance," in *Essential Writings*, 133.

119 The Constitution, too: The image of a constitution in this passage expresses a debt to Robert Cover, "Nomos and Narrative," *Harvard Law Review*, no. 97 (1983): 4–68.

5: American Utopias

121 "delirious dream": This language, from Johnson's attack on American conceptions of freedom, is quoted in the introduction, pages 5, 8, and 16.

121 "Would the being independent": John Wesley, "A Calm Address to Our American Colonies," in *The Works of the Rev. John Wesley, A.M.*, vol. 6, ed. John Emory, 298.

122 "failed revolutions": Isaiah Berlin, *The Sense of Reality: Studies in Ideas and Their History*, ed. Henry Hardy, 32.

122 "only . . . the American": Louis Hartz, *The Liberal Tradition in America*, 11.

122 "the sense of reality": "The Sense of Reality," in *Sense of Reality*, 1–39.

123 Consider this finding: For the statistic on Americans' impressions of where they stand in the national distribution of wealth, see David Brooks, "The Triumph of Hope over Self-Interest," *New York Times*, Jan. 12, 2003.

125 "the philosophical approach": See Alexis de Tocqueville, *Democracy in America*, ed. J. P. Mayer, trans. George Lawrence, 429–33.

126 "Seeing that they": Ibid., 430.

127 "a higher father": See William Hamilton, "Bush Began to Plan War Three Months After 9/11," *Washington Post*, Apr. 17, 2004.

127 "America's vital interests": George W. Bush, second inaugural address (January 20, 2005).

127 "I believe God": Bush, State of the Union Address, 2005.

127 No doubt other: These explanations are ably sketched in Francis Fukuyama, *America at the Crossroads: Democracy, Power, and the Neoconservative Legacy*.

128 Bush's notorious report: See Robert H. Donaldson and Joseph L. Nogee, *The Foreign Policy of Russia: Changing Systems, Enduring Interests*, 358.

129 "my meat and my drink": Frederick Douglass, *Narrative of the Life of Frederick Douglass*, 100.

129 "self-loathing and abasement": George Bourne, *The Majesty and Condescension of God*, 35. Originally a sermon delivered at Port Republic, VA, Dec. 25, 1812.

130 "God," Warren writes: Warren, *Purpose-Driven Life*, 85.

130 "handle . . . frank, intense": Ibid., 94.

130 "What may appear": Ibid.

130 "the bundle of desires": Warren, *Purpose-Driven Life*, 237.

130 "Your heart reveals": Ibid., 238.

130 "a resident in our souls": These words are Bourne's and not, so far as I know, Warren's.

131 "Our fathers were": Lyman Beecher, *A Reformation of Morals Practicable and Indispensable*, 16.

131 "the important question": Alexander Hamilton, *The Federalist*, no. 1 (Oct. 27, 1827).

131 Religious thinkers had: The characterizations of founding-era religious attitudes in these passages draws on Mark A. Noll, *America's God: From Jonathan Edwards to Abraham Lincoln*, 53–226. The entire discussion of the development of commonsense attitudes in the passages that follow reflects a great debt to Noll's work, and indeed he uses "common sense" to describe a distinctive American synthesis of religious, political, and epistemic attitudes.

133 "Never were men": Timothy Dwight, *A Discourse on Some Events of the Last Century*, 38. For a sketch of the mood of these complaints, see Gordon S. Wood, *Radicalism of the American Revolution*, 325–28.

133 "infidels": Dwight, "Discourse," 21–22.

134 "Their neighborhood is": Ibid., 45.

134 French Deism: Samuel E. McCorkle, *The Work of God for the French Republic and Then Her Reformation or Ruin*, 21. Originally a fast-day sermon delivered in Salisbury, NC.

134 "conspiracy against all": Ibid., 12.

134 "sensual pleasures": Ibid.

134 "freedom from all": Ibid., 12–13.

135 McCorkle concluded: Ibid., 28.

135 "a bebanked, a bewhiskied": Wood, *Radicalism*, 366.

135 "Where is now": Wood, *Radicalism*, 366–67.

136 Jefferson and Hamilton, too: Ibid., 367–68.

136 "turning back": Beecher, "Reformation of Morals," 28.

136 "a sort of": Ibid., 18. Much of the sermon is an argument for the coercive force of public opinion and moral suasion on sinners.

136 "religion should and could": Noll, *America's God*, 203.

137 "Of all the dispositions": George Washington, Farewell Address (Sept. 17, 1796).

138 One was the long-standing: The account of election sermons here owes a lot to Harry N. Stout, *The New England Soul: Preaching and Religious Culture in Colonial New England*, 13–31, 70–77.

139 such as John Adams: The source for Adams's Protestant nationalism is his "Dissertation on the Canon and Feudal Law," in *The Political Writings of John Adams*, ed. George A. Peek.

139 Boston minister Henry Mayhew: Jonathan Mayhew, "A Discourse Concerning Unlimited Submission and Non-Resistance to the Higher Powers" (Boston, 1750), http://www.lawandliberty.org/mayhew.htm.

139 Another reason the synthesis: On the effort to distinguish the United States from France, see Noll, *America's God*, 87-88. This theme also emerges in Sean Wilentz's discussion of the fate of Democrat-Republican radicalism in the early Republic; see Wilentz, *The Rise of American Democracy: Jefferson to Lincoln*, 40–140. As has been clear, this was a major theme of revivalist sermons throughout this period.

140 "I do not know": Tocqueville, *Democracy in America*, 293.

141 Theories of social passions: For a good introduction to the influence of these ideas in colonial and early republican America, with particular attention to Hutcheson and Jefferson, see Garry Wills, *Inventing America: Jefferson's Declaration of Independence*. Also helpful here is Noll, *America's God*, 92–113.

142 "Common-sense" qualified: Noll, *America's God*, 10.

143 "common sense [that] had": Lorenzo Dow, *Analects, or Reflections upon Natural, Moral, and Political Society* (original copyright illegible), 44.

143 "common sense" and: Ibid., 47.

143 "A few plain": Ibid., 59.

144 "empowered ordinary people": Nathan O. Hatch, *The Democratization of American Christianity*, 10.

144 "seasons of deep": Dwight, "Discourse," 18.

145   "a cold, contemptuous": Ibid., 19.

145   "pour forth": Thomas Jefferson, letter to Dr. Thomas Cooper, Nov.
      2, 1822, in *Jefferson: Writings*, ed. Merrill D. Peterson (New York:
      Library of America, 1984), 1464.

147   "soul['s] . . . enormous claim": Emerson, "The Over-Soul," in
      Essential Writings, 236.

147   Inhabitants of Fourier's "phalanxes": See Charles Fourier, *The
      Utopian Vision of Charles Fourier*, ed. Jonathan Beecher and Richard
      Bienvenu, 387–95.

147   "sexual minimum": Ibid., 336.

149   "the butterfly passion": Ibid., 48.

149   "[y]our emotional heartbeat": Warren, *Purpose-Driven Life*, 238.

150   collaborative making and sharing: On these forms of "dispersed
      creativity," see Yochai Benkler, *The Wealth of Networks*, 59–90.

151   "amorous illusions": Fourier, *Utopian Vision*, 333.

151   "the mutiny of love": Ibid., 340.

151   "When love has": Ibid., 332.

153   nearly 40 percent: See David Brooks, "The Triumph of Hope over
      Self-Interest," *New York Times* (Jan. 12, 2003).

6: The Economics of 1776, and Today

162   "masters of the universe": The famous phrase comes from Tom
      Wolfe, *The Bonfire of the Vanities*.

162   Some of the more idealistic: See Gordon S. Wood, *The Radicalism
      of the American Revolution*, 364–69.

162   Alexis de Tocqueville noted: See Alexis de Tocqueville, *Democracy
      in America*, ed. J. P. Mayer, trans. George Lawrence, 50, "I know of
      no other country where love of money has such a grip on men's
      hearts"; 627, "The first thing that strikes one in the United States is
      the innumerable crowd of those striving to escape from their origi-
      nal social condition; and the second is the rarity, in a land where all
      are actively ambitious, of any lofty ambition."

162   Walt Whitman attacked: See David Bromwich, "Lincoln and
      Whitman as Representative Americans," in *Democratic Vistas:
      Reflections on the Life of American Democracy*, ed. Jedediah Purdy, 40.
      Whitman expresses the idea powerfully in *Democratic Vistas*—
      "Never was there, perhaps, more hollowness at heart than at

present"—in *The Portable Walt Whitman,* ed. Mark van Doren, 325–28.

162 Progressive twentieth-century presidents: See the discussion of Wilson and Franklin D. Roosevelt on these themes in chapters 2 and 3, pages 63–66 and 84–86.

163 two-thirds say: See Andrew Kohut and Bruce Stokes, *Two Americas, One American* (Washington, DC: Pew Research Center, June 6, 2006). For a book-length treatment of these themes, look at Jennifer L. Hochschild, *Facing Up to the American Dream: Race, Class, and the Soul of America.*

163 "soulcraft": Michael J. Sandel, *Democracy's Discontent: America in Search of a Public Philosophy,* 319. Sandel discusses this issue at length on pages 1–24 and 317–28.

165 Who could say in 1990: This discussion draws on Robert Shiller, *The New Financial Order,* 107–13.

166 economist Joseph Schumpeter: See Joseph A. Schumpeter, *Capitalism, Socialism and Democracy,* 81–87.

167 Adam Smith's image: For a discussion of the precedents and context of this image, see Emma Rothschild, *Economic Sentiments: Adam Smith, Condorcet, and the Enlightenment,* 116–56.

167 Harold Ickes: See Sandel, *Democracy's Discontent,* 267, quoting Ickes.

167 John F. Kennedy: See Sandel, *Democracy's Discontent,* 265–66, quoting Kennedy.

168 Historically, economic thought: Although the discussion that follows relies heavily on the work of Adam Smith, there is a large and rich body of work on this theme. Some starting points are Rothschild, *Economic Sentiments,* especially 7–86; Sandel, *Democracy's Discontent,* especially 123–249; Barbara Fried, *The Progressive Assault on Laissez Faire: Robert Hale and the First Law and Economics Movement,* 29–70; Gregory S. Alexander, *Commodity and Propriety: Competing Visions of Property in American Legal Thought, 1776–1970;* Istvan Hont, *Jealousy of Trade: International Competition and the Nation-State in Historical Perspective;* and for a more critical assessment of the development of economic ideology and social relations in the United States, Morton J. Horwitz, *The Transformation of American Law, 1780–1860.*

168 target was mercantilism: See Adam Smith, *An Inquiry into the*

Nature and Causes of the Wealth of Nations, vol. 1, ed. R. H. Campbell and A. S. Skinner, 135–59.

169   "natural liberty": Smith, *Wealth of Nations*, vol. 2, 687.

169   degree of reciprocity: On Smith's vision of reciprocity and social relations, see Rothschild, *Economic Sentiments*, 7–15.

169   Smith recommended: For Smith's idea of free choice, persuasion, and reciprocity, see Adam Smith, *Lectures on Jurisprudence*, ed. R. L. Meek et al., 352:

> The offering of a shilling, which to us appears to have so plain and simple a meaning, is in reality offering an argument *to persuade one to do so and so as it is in his interest.* Men always endeavour to persuade others to be of their opinion even when the matter is of no consequence to them. . . . And in this manner, every one is practising oratory on others thro the whole of his life.—You are uneasy whenever one differs from you, and you endeavour to persuade [him] to be of your mind. . . . In this manner [people] acquire a certain dexterity and adress [*sic*] in managing their affairs, or in other words in managing of men. . . . That is bartering, by which they adress [*sic*] themselves to the self interest of the person and seldom fail immediately to gain their end. The brutes have no notion of this.

I have made this argument with more systematic reference to Smith's writings in two articles: Jedediah Purdy, "A Freedom-Promoting Approach to Property: A Renewed Tradition for New Debates," *University of Chicago Law Review* 72 (2005): 1237; and Jedediah Purdy, "People as Resources: Recruitment and Reciprocity in the Freedom-Promoting Approach to Property," 56 *Duke Law Journal* 1047 (2007).

170   Historian Emma Rothschild: Ibid., 14.

170   Smith imagined that: See Adam Smith, *The Theory of Moral Sentiments*, 77.

172   "As I would not": See Bromwich, "Lincoln and Whitman," 38.

172   American law recognized: For "person," and "property," see *United States v. Amy*, 24 F. Cas. 792, 810 (C.C.D. Va. 1859) U.S. Supreme Court chief justice Roger Brooke Taney, riding circuit: "We must

not lose sight of the twofold character which belongs to the slave. He is a person, and also property." For "men" and "chattels," see *State v. Jones,* 1 Miss. 83, 85 (1820): "In some respects, slaves may be considered as chattels, but in others, they are regarded as men."

172 "things": *Jarman v. Patterson,* 23 Ky. 644, 644 (1828), "In other respects, slaves are regarded by our law . . . not as persons, but as things."

172 "created equal": The language quoted refers to the Declaration of Independence.

172 Brockenbrough argued that: Brockenbrough's language in *Commonwealth v. Turner,* 26 Va. 678, Justice Brockenbrough dissenting.

173 he portrayed slavery: Ruffin's language in *State v. Mann,* 13 N.C. 263 (1829). For discussions of this much-studied case, see Mark V. Tushnet, *Slave Law in the American South: State v. Mann in History and Literature;* Robert M. Cover, *Justice Accused: Antislavery and the Judicial Process* (New Haven, CT: Yale University Press, 1974), 77–78; Eugene Genovese, *Roll, Jordan, Roll: The World the Slaves Made,* 35.

174 Harriet Beecher Stowe: See Cover, *Justice Accused,* 78.

175 referred . . . to the institution's "necessity": For a survey of arguments in favor of slavery's necessity to orderly society, either intrinsically or as it had developed in the United States, see Elizabeth Fox-Genovese and Eugene D. Genovese, *The Mind of the Master Class: History and Faith in the Southern Slaveholders' Worldview,* 11–68, 201–48.

175 Ruffin had discussed: For Ruffin's correspondence with his father, see Tushnet, *Slave Law,* 91–92.

175 idea of free labor: For a survey of material related to free labor, see the note on page 243 to chapter 2, page 60, "idea of free labor."

176 Jefferson's inaugural formula: The reference is to Jefferson's first inaugural address, discussed on pages 57–59.

176 "to tamper": William Leggett, "True Functions of Government," in *The American Intellectual Tradition* (*Evening Post,* Nov. 21, 1834), 239.

176 engineers of Reconstruction: See Eric Foner, *Reconstruction: America's Unfinished Revolution, 1863–1877,* 155, 164, quoting Northerners committed to free labor as a principle for rebuilding a postslavery South.

177 more myth than reality: For a very illuminating discussion of this

point, see Foner, *Reconstruction,* 155–68, and Robert J. Steinfeld, *Coercion, Contract, and Free Labor in the Nineteenth Century,* 3–38.

177 Abraham Lincoln and Ralph Waldo Emerson: The reference is to the discussion in chapter 2, pages 60–61.

177 Foner has emphasized: See Foner, *Free Soil,* 27–29.

177 industrial economy that grew: On the growth of the industrial economy and the challenges it presented to received ideas of economic freedom and legal order, some starting points are John Fabian Witt, *The Accidental Republic: Crippled Workingmen, Destitute Widows, and the Remaking of American Law;* Morton Keller, *Regulating a New Economy: Public Policy and Economic Change in America, 1900–1933;* Keller, *Regulating a New Society;* Daniel T. Rodgers, *Atlantic Crossings: Social Politics in a Progressive Age.*

178 Even the justices: See *Holden v. Hardy,* 169 U.S. 366, 397 (1898), "[T]he proprietors of [mines and smelters] and their [employees] do not stand upon an equality"; *Lochner v. New York,* 198 U.S. 45 (1905), featuring a debate between the majority and the dissent over whether the same condition holds between bakers and their employers; *Muller v. Oregon,* 208 U.S. 412 (1908), holding that women employees are relatively vulnerable and so constitutionally eligible for special legislative protection.

179 "struggle for existence": For a sketch of the varieties, origins, and effects of social Darwinism in American thought, see Rick Tilman, introduction to *Darwin's Impact: Social Evolution in America, 1880–1920,* ed. Frank X. Ryan. The phrase and variants on it became commonplace. The Supreme Court observed in *Muller v. Oregon,* for instance, that women faced a "disadvantage in the struggle for subsistence," 208 U.S. 412, 420. Sociologist Franklin H. Giddings noted at the time that the two phrases tended, even in Darwin's use, to have identical meanings. See Giddings, "The Struggle for Human Existence" (1922), in *Darwin's Impact,* 43.

179 "a word to conjure": William Graham Sumner, "The Absurd Effort to Make the World Over" (1894), in *Darwin's Impact,* 16.

179 "the men of 1787": William Graham Sumner, "What Emancipates" (1890), in *Darwin's Impact,* 23.

179 ambition to "democratize": For meanings of *democratize,* see Sumner, "Absurd Effort," 19.

180 "to avoid being converted": Giddings, "Struggle for Human Existence," 43.

180   "herd habits" and "folkways": Ibid., 46.

180   As earlier chapters mention: The reference is to the discussions in
       chapters 2 and 3, pages 45–47 and 83–85.

181   Franklin Roosevelt, too: Roosevelt, third inaugural address (Jan.
       20, 1941).

181   "rights in the struggle": Woodrow Wilson, first inaugural address
       (Mar. 4, 1913). The Darwinian image of the struggle for existence
       was central in Wilson's account of the purposes of Progressive gov-
       ernance. The full passage is

> Nor have we studied and perfected the means by which gov-
> ernment may be put at the service of humanity, in safeguard-
> ing the health of the Nation, the health of its men and its
> women and its children, as well as their rights in *the struggle
> for existence.* This is no sentimental duty. The firm basis of
> government is justice, not pity. These are matters of justice.
> There can be no equality or opportunity, the first essential of
> justice in the body politic, if men and women and children
> be not shielded in their lives, their very vitality, from the
> consequences of great industrial and social processes which
> they can not alter, control, or singly cope with.

181   the Supreme Court used: The reference is to the passage from
       Muller v. Oregon discussed in the note on page 255 to chapter 6,
       page 179, "struggle for existence."

181   Stuart Chase, a Progressive: See Otis L. Graham, *Toward a
       Planned Society: From Roosevelt to Nixon,* 14.

182   economist Rexford Tugwell: See Fried, *Progressive Assault,* 38–39.

182   Nonetheless, many did suspect: Good discussions of the am-
       bivalence of Progressives appear in Fried, *Progressive Assault,*
       particularly 29–70; Leon Fink, *Progressive Intellectuals and the
       Dilemmas of Democratic Commitment;* and Edward A. Purcell, *The
       Crisis of Democratic Theory: Scientific Naturalism and the Problem of
       Value.*

182   Even Franklin Roosevelt: Franklin Roosevelt, address to the Com-
       monwealth Club of San Francisco (Sept. 23, 1932). A fine introduc-
       tion to the larger intellectual and cultural themes in which
       Progressive commitments were formed, and their variance from the

mainstream of nineteenth-century models, is Rodgers, *Atlantic Crossings*.

183 "[T]o let the individual": See Fried, *Progressive Assault*, 41.

184 "soften[ing] the ideal": Ibid., 42.

186 First is that *market:* A valuable discussion of the incompleteness of "market" appears in Amartya Sen, "The Moral Standing of the Market," in *Ethics and Economics*, ed. Ellen Frankel Paul et al., 1–19.

7: The Value of Freedom

189 "the dismal science": The derogatory designation comes from Thomas Carlyle's "Occasional on the Negro Question" (1849). See Mancur Olson and Satu Kahkonen, introduction to *A Not-So Dismal Science: A Broader View of Economies and Societies*, 7.

189 "preferences are exogenous": For a critical and illuminating discussion of this premise, see Amartya Sen, "Rationality and Social Choice," in *Rationality and Freedom*, 285–89.

190 Modern economics is: The source of this definition is Lionel Robbins, *An Essay on the Nature and Significance of Economic Science*, 2d ed. (London: Macmillan, 1945), 16, "Economics is the science which studies human behaviour as a relationship between ends and scarce means which have alternative uses."

191 prospect theory: For one quick introduction to this material, see Diane Coyle, *The Soulful Science: What Economists Really Do and Why It Matters*, 131–32, 142–44.

191 the ultimatum game: These accounts of the ultimatum game come from Joseph Heinrech et al., " 'Economic Man' in Cross-Cultural Perspective: Behavioral Experiments in 15 Small-Scale Societies," 28 *Behavior and Brain Science* 795 (2005); Terence Chorvat and Kevin McCabe, "The Brain and the Law," 359 *Philosophical Transcripts of the Royal Society of London* 1727 (2004); Alan G. Sanfey et al., "The Neural Basis of Economic Decision-Making in the Ultimatum Game," 300 *Science* 1755 (2003); Ernst Fehr and Urs Fischbacher, "The Nature of Human Altruism," 425 *Nature* 785 (2003).

193 called a trust game: These accounts of the trust game come from Jonathan D. Cohen, "The Vulcanization of the Human Brain: A Neural Perspective on Interactions Between Cognition and Emo-

tion," *Journal of Economic Perspectives* 19, no. 4 (2005): 3–24; Vernon L. Smith, "Constructivist and Ecological Rationality in Economics," *American Economic Review* 93 (2003): 465; James K. Rilling et al., "A Neural Basis for Social Cooperation," *Neuron* 35, no. 2, (2002): 395–405; Kevin McCabe et al., "A Functional Imaging Study of Cooperation in Two-Person Reciprocal Exchange," *Proceedings of the National Academies of Science* 98, no. 20 (Sept. 25, 2001): 11832–35.

194 Neuroscientists find that: See Rilling, "A Neural Basis"; McCabe, "Functional Imaging Study."

197 Offering reciprocity means: For a valuable synthetic study of reciprocity, see Dan M. Kahan, "The Logic of Reciprocity: Trust, Collective Action, and Law," in *Moral Sentiments and Material Interests: On the Foundations of Cooperation in Economic Life,* ed. Herbert Gintis et al.

199 Amartya Sen, who received: See Amartya Sen, "Rationality and Freedom," in Sen, *Rationality and Freedom,* 3–65.

199 From the late eighteenth century: For a valuable sketch of this aspect of economic history, see Robert Cooter and Peter Rappoport, "Were the Ordinalists Wrong about Welfare Economics?" *Journal of Economic Literature* 22 (1982): 507, 520–24.

200 heavy theoretical attack: The exemplary and probably decisive attack is Robbins, *Nature and Significance of Economic Science,* 1–21, 104–58.

201 Many economists: For a balanced but critical assessment of the Pareto criterion, see Sen, "The Possibility of Social Choice," in *Rationality and Freedom,* 92–94.

201 Others do more or less: For explanations, defenses, and prominent applications of cost-benefit analysis to contemporary problems, see Cass R. Sunstein, *Worst-Case Scenarios,* 176–274.

201 Sen argues that: For discussions of these issues, see Sen, "Rationality and Freedom," "Possibility of Social Choice," and "Processes, Liberty and Rights," in *Rationality and Freedom,* 623–58.

202 power to promote freedom: Ibid., particularly "Processes, Liberty, and Rights." For a more accessible statement of the argument that the aims of economic life should be identified with freedom, see Amartya Sen, *Development as Freedom,* 13–53.

8: Fragments of a Free Economy

204 "A constitution": *Lochner v. New York,* 198 U.S. 45 (1905), Justice Holmes dissenting.

204 Holmes himself did not: Holmes's devastating assessment of reform's effect on this human spirit is apparent in his lecture, "The Soldier's Faith," delivered at Harvard on May 30, 1895.

204 After 1937: The touchstone case repudiating laissez-faire jurisprudence is *West Coast Hotel v. Parrish,* 300 U.S. 379 (1937). For a discussion of Franklin Roosevelt's triumph over a recalcitrant Supreme Court, see Lawrence M. Friedman, *American Law in the Twentieth Century,* 151–83.

205 On the conservative side: For discussions of the core libertarian commitment from a libertarian perspective, take a look at Richard Epstein, *Simple Rules for a Complex World,* and Charles Murray, *What It Means to Be a Libertarian.*

205 The importance of choice: For a highly respectful look at this issue from a nonlibertarian, see Amartya Sen, "Markets and Freedoms," in *Rationality and Freedom,* 501–31.

205 themes of Progressive freedom: There is a terrific discussion contrasting laissez-faire and "positive" ideas of freedom in Barbara Fried, *The Progressive Assault on Laissez-Faire: Robert Hale and First Law and Economics Movement,* 29–70. For two examples of the attempt to work the idea in its early-twentieth-century American crucible, see Herbert Croly, *The Promise of American Life,* and Woodrow Wilson, *The New Freedom..*

206 drivers of creative destruction: This sketch of some of the costs to individual choice of creative destruction draws heavily on the discussion of Robert Shiller, *The New Financial Order,* 1–68, a valuable primer on picturing risk as the center of economic life.

207 motivated Romantic programs: For Charles Fourier's proposals to overcome these limitations, see *The Utopian Vision of Charles Fourier: Selected Texts on Work, Love, and Passionate Attraction,* ed. Jonathan Beecher and Richard Bienvenu, 271–328.

207 Yale economist Robert Shiller: Shiller, *New Financial Order,* 107–21.

209 robbers or monks: The allusion is to Sumner, "Absurd Effort," 19, calling economic democracy "a rule of division for robbers who have to divide plunder or monks who have to divide gifts."

209 The American conviction: This paragraph's discussion refers to research mentioned earlier finding that two-thirds of Americans believe people's lives and fortunes are determined by choices, not forces beyond their control, and that only about half as many Germans (and fewer than 50 percent of Britons) believe this. Andrew Kohut and Bruce Stokes, *Two Americas, One American.* For a book-length treatment of these themes, look at Jennifer L. Hochschild, *Facing Up to the American Dream: Race, Class, and the Soul of America.*

209 Frederick Douglass's conclusion: Frederick Douglass, *My Bondage and My Freedom,* 140, "Human nature is so constituted that, that it cannot *honor* a helpless man, though it can *pity* him; and even this it cannot do long, if the signs of power do not arise."

209 contract that fosters: The idea sketched here is very close to that at the center of Shiller, *New Financial Order,* especially pages 1–20. It also, of course, has much in common with the tradition of efforts in distributive justice to minimize the influence of morally arbitrary factors on the outcomes of people's lives. See John Rawls, *A Theory of Justice,* 11–16, 65–89; Ronald Dworkin, *Is Democracy Possible Here?,* 17–21, 116–160.

210 The next is about: The technological developments and allied cultural events sketched here are set out in rich detail in James Boyle, *The Public Domain: An Environmentalism for the Common of the Mind;* Yochai Benkler, *The Wealth of Networks: How Social Production Transforms Markets and Freedom;* Lawrence Lessig, *Free Culture: How Big Media Uses Technology and the Law to Lock Down Culture and Control Creativity.*

210 Thomas Jefferson edited: Jefferson refers to this procedure in a letter to John Adams dated Oct. 12, 1813. See *Jefferson: Writings,* ed. Merrill D. Peterson, 1300–1304.

213 This is not the place: Those seeking a primer on intellectual property's doctrines, purposes, and politics can do no better than Boyle, *Public Domain.*

213 The most effective reform: This refers to Creative Commons, an organization that facilitates such partial donations to the public domain. For a sketch of its operations, see Lessig, *Free Culture,* 282–86.

213 Lawrence Lessig, a law professor: Lessig, *Free Culture,* xiii–xvi,

172–73. For a more extensive treatment of freedom in the digital and cultural realms, see Benkler, *Wealth of Networks*, 133–300.

214   better able to integrate: The image of economic decision making as aiming at integrating the widest possible set of values is close to the analysis of Benkler, *Wealth of Networks*, 133–382, and, at a higher level of abstraction, Sen, *Development as Freedom*, 282–99.

215   what Franklin Roosevelt proposed: The reference is to Roosevelt's Commonwealth Club address, discussed on pages 183–84.

Bibliographic Essay

WHAT ARE the meanings of freedom, the touchstone value of American life, and do they add up to a good, or even coherent, idea? How can a political community express respect for the dignity of every member? What, if anything, would it mean for an economy to do the same?

Political theorists and moral philosophers have made heroic efforts to answer these questions in the abstract. More practical-minded people often set them aside as unanswerable. This book steers a middle path between the huge ambition of the first approach and the quietism of the second. The questions are not really optional, and their answers come concretely, in the history and politics, literature and spiritual searching, in which people explore them. This book is a treatment of American engagement with the questions.

Introduction

THE INTRODUCTION tries to frame the whole discussion in this spirit. People act in ways that are deeply shaped by ideas, but the ideas are not abstract propositions: they are intuitions, perceptions, unspoken beliefs about how the world works and what matters most. As a theoretical matter, I owe this formulation to the work of philosopher Charles Taylor. In his three collections of

philosophical papers, *Human Agency and Language, Philosophy and the Human Sciences,* and *Philosophical Arguments,* Taylor has rigorously set out the idea that people live by their interpretations of the world, the geographies of their shared headspace. His two vast works of cultural and intellectual history, *Sources of the Self* and *A Secular Age,* have framed my sense of how the Western worldview has developed over recent centuries, how we have literally become different creatures as our vocabularies and registers of experience have deepened and changed. Also influential on this view of value and judgment was Martha Nussbaum's *Fragility of Goodness.*

This idea is not uniquely philosophical. Taylor shares it with historians of early America who put ideas about power and legitimacy at the center of their analyses: Gordon S. Wood in *The Creation of the American Republic* and *The Radicalism of the American Revolution,* Bernard Bailyn in *The Ideological Origins of the American Revolution,* and John Philip Reid in *The Ancient Constitution and the Origins of Anglo-American Liberty* and *The Concept of Liberty in the Age of the American Revolution.* These shaped my sense of what is salient in writing about the early American experience: what liberty meant, how it registered in experience, how it created theories of legitimacy and resistance.

I spent time with primary texts such as John Adams's *Dissertation on the Canon and Feudal Law* and *Novanglus,* Jefferson's writings, and Henry Mayhew's sermon linking the American cause to the Parliamentary side in the English Civil War, as well as documents from the Civil War itself. (No one can read the Petition of Right of 1628, which sounded an opening salvo nearly two decades before open conflict, nor the Bill of Rights of 1688, which brought the reopened struggle to a final conclusion, without recognizing that these are parts of a constitutional tradition to which the American founders also belonged.) I was drawn to the English debate over the American rebellion because those observers, rather like me, were trying to understand something both far away

and familiar, which struck them by turns as inspiring and lunatic. A measure of both sympathy and detached understanding helped them to lay out the stakes of the Americans' insurgent theories. British apologists such as the hilarious and indignant John Lind, whose *Answer to the Declaration of the American Congress* Lord North commissioned, and the rather deeper-cutting Samuel Johnson, greatly illuminated the picture, showing how sensible, humane figures could regard the American cause as either criminal or insane. While the Americans had stalwart defenders such as Richard Price, who identified them as avatars of English liberty, it was the complicated and ambivalent Edmund Burke who became my touchstone.

Burke is an astonishing figure. I have thought so since reading his speeches on India, years ago, but it was late in this project that his view of the Americans came to figure centrally in mine. He admired the colonists and saw clearly the radicalism and traditionalism that intertwined in their rebellion and the uncertain prospect of combining these into a new kind of tradition. When he declared that freedom always has a "sensible object," he put in words exactly what I had been trying to say about the American colonists' worldview. To understand how he thought about politics—as an attempt to get inside the moral and emotional experience of others—it is invaluable to read his speeches, including the full text of "On Conciliation with America," his opening of impeachment proceedings against Indian governor-general Warren Hastings, his speech on Charles James Fox's reform bill for East Indian governance, and his other great American speech, "On American Taxation." His *Reflections on the Revolution in France* is sometimes brilliant, of course, but it is also sometimes unhinged—not just because Burke was old and wounded by disappointment but also because he was at his steadiest when he had an audience before him and a problem in his hands. Although obsessed with abstraction, which both seduced and repelled him—his attacks on

abstraction are themselves great works of abstract political prose—he found his genius in the face of political decisions. On Burke, I have benefited from Conor Cruise O'Brien's vast, vigorous, and highly partisan "thematic biography," *The Great Melody*, but even more from the sensitive work of a teacher and friend, David Bromwich. Bromwich's introduction to his edited collection, *Burke on Empire, Liberty, and Reform*, is a wonderfully acute description of Burke's temperament and view of the world.

I learned a lot about ideas of freedom from some major theoretical and historical treatments of the issue, especially Orlando Patterson's *Freedom;* Edmund Morgan's *American Slavery, American Freedom;* Philip Pettit's *Republicanism;* Barbara Fried's *Assault on Laissez-Faire;* and Isaiah Berlin's classic essay "Two Concepts of Liberty." Taken with the widespread effort to understand freedom by reference to its opposite or negative, I also began reading in the history of slavery, especially David Brion Davis's classics, *The Problem of Slavery in Western Thought* and *The Problem of Slavery in the Age of Revolution*, plus his recent collection of articles and essays, *Inhuman Bondage*. In the end, all purely theoretical questions about freedom's nature were resolved into this book's attention to the competing strands of American tradition and the "sensible objects" that populate their images of freedom.

Chapter 1

FREDERICK DOUGLASS is another arresting figure best approached through his own words. Like Burke, he provided many. In this book, I rely mostly on the two autobiographies that he wrote before the Civil War, the *Narrative of the Life of Frederick Douglass* and *My Bondage and My Freedom*. It was particularly illuminating to get acquainted with the varieties of antislavery politics and constitutional interpretation that were active before the Civil War, and so to see the distinctiveness and courage of the

path Douglass set himself. Central texts for this are Lysander Spooner's *The Unconstitutionality of Slavery;* William Goodell's *Slavery and Anti-Slavery;* and the thought of Gerrit Smith, which comes closest to Douglass's own final position: that the Constitution is an antislavery document but is not self-executing, instead requiring a democratic people to assert the power to interpret it in an antislavery spirit. Smith was the subject of several early biographies, and one can learn a lot about his ideas from Ralph Volney Harlow, *Gerrit Smith: Philanthropist and Reformer* (1939). A good relatively recent and scholarly essay on Smith's connection to Douglass's thinking is John R. McKivigan, "The Frederick Douglass-Gerrit Smith Friendship and Political Abolitionism in the 1850s," in *Frederick Douglass: New Literary and Historical Essays*, ed. Eric Sundquist.

In reading Emerson, I have relied almost completely on his own essays and speeches, mostly but not only those cited in the text. I read Emerson's thought through Charles Taylor's account of the rise of Romanticism in *Sources of the Self* and *A Secular Age:* as an objection to the utilitarian account of progress and formalistic idea of negative liberty that the Romantics saw (with significant justification) as characterizing the Enlightenment of the eighteenth and early nineteenth centuries and as essentially shaping early American self-understanding. Such critics would have appreciated F. C. Montague's characterization of the utilitarian reformers in his introduction to an eighteenth-century edition of Jeremy Bentham's *Fragment upon Government,* in which he refers to that school's "immense hopefulness for the future joined with extravagant contempt for the past; its generous humanity alloyed with a somewhat sordid conception of human nature; its venturous scientific spirit suffused with the most arrogant dogmatism; its grotesque pedantry blended with the shrewdest common sense." As emerges in my discussion, there also seem to me to be real continuities between Emerson's insistence on the integrity of

judgment and conscience and the ideal of the free mind that figures in polemics such as John Adams's *Dissertation on the Canon and Feudal Law* and in Burke's characterization of the Americans. The tradition began and continued in insistence on oneself, one's own experience, judgment, and feeling; what changed in Emerson was the content of those, which became intimate, personal, alive with feeling—in a word, Romantic.

Chapters 2 and 3

THESE BEGAN AS EXERCISES in doing just what the text implies: reading every presidential inaugural address, from Washington through the second Bush, along with some other major addresses by presidents and their contemporaries. My aim was to find a constant thread to trace the development of a national political vocabulary and, in that vocabulary, images of citizenship and national community. I was looking, in other words, for a "sensible object" of American citizenship, with an eye to seeing both its change and its continuity. The themes of these chapters are the ones I found in that reading. I was led to William James, Oliver Wendell Holmes's "Soldier's Faith," and Teddy Roosevelt's "Strenuous Life," for instance, by the impression that Progressive presidents struggled to find a register of civic dignity after the era of free labor. What I did not expect to find—perhaps naïvely—was how much of the Romantic spirit of Emerson appeared in the militarism of the late nineteenth and early twentieth centuries.

The discussion of constitutional tradition toward the end of chapter 3 is very much of a piece with that of the tradition of repudiation in chapter 1 and the arguments at the conclusion of chapter 4. In developing this idea, I have been strongly influenced by Robert Cover's classic essay on law and constitutionalism, "Nomos and Narrative"; the account of constitutionalism as a tradition in the work of my friend and colleague H. Jefferson Powell,

notably in *A Community Built on Words;* and nearly all the work of Reva Siegel and Robert Post, a pair of constitutional theorists and historians with whom I taught at Harvard Law School in 2006 and who understand a constitution as a point of unity that lends felt coherence to conflict, both across the political community and across time. In back of all of these are more theoretical efforts to understand the nature of traditions and political communities: John Rawls's *Political Liberalism,* with its argument for a strong shared vocabulary of principle, an "overlapping consensus"; Alasdair MacIntyre's work on the nature of traditions in moral reasoning, developed in *After Virtue, Whose Justice? Which Rationality?* and *Three Rival Traditions in Moral Inquiry;* and William Connolly's argument for the necessity and appropriateness of conflict in moral reasoning, *Identity\Difference.* In taking up a constitutional and political tradition rather than a philosophical problem, I am expressing two judgments. The first is that the issue matters most when it is made concrete in a particular tradition. The second is that concrete traditions, in which people work out themes of continuity and change in response to actual problems, often do a better job of defining and mediating among conflicting values and alternative visions than abstract consideration can do.

Chapter 4

THE QUESTION about whether modern ideas of freedom undermine themselves also began as a theoretical one. The idea that they do goes back to attacks on natural-rights theory as old as Robert Filmer's "Patriarcha" (to which John Locke was responding in developing his own natural-rights theory) and Joseph de Maistre's attacks on the French Revolution, notably his *Considerations on France* and *Against Rousseau.* This tradition ran strong as late as the mid–nineteenth century in the United States, when George Fitzhugh marshaled it against the liberal view of free soci-

ety in two defenses of slavery, *Cannibals All!* and *Sociology for the South*. Contemporary versions of the same argument have come in Leo Strauss's *Natural Right and History*, MacIntyre's *After Virtue*, and the closing chapter of Taylor's *Sources of the Self* (although Taylor was cautious about the idea and has moved further from it in later writings).

This is just the idea that James Dobson develops in his attacks on *Lawrence v. Texas*, gay rights, and same-sex marriage in *Marriage Under Fire*. It is also the view that former federal appeals court judge and Supreme Court nominee Robert Bork expresses in *Slouching Towards Gomorrah* and *A Country I Do Not Recognize*. Leon Kass, former head of George W. Bush's Council on Bioethics, has made similar arguments in a variety of places, including the edited volume *Life, Liberty, and the Defense of Dignity*. As I argue in the chapter, it has an analogue in the theories of interpretation that Justice Scalia has advanced in his dissents from due process cases, and the analogue is fairly significant because, in both contexts, what is under interpretation is the meaning of liberty. It strikes me as worth recognizing that this is not only an idea of the political right. On the contrary, it finds strong voice in the politically liberal communitarianism of Michael Sandel in both *Justice and the Limits of Liberalism* and *Democracy's Discontent*, as well as in his recent *Case Against Perfection*. Legal scholars such as Gregory S. Alexander, in his account of theoretical alternatives in *Commodity and Propriety*, make similar arguments.

My decision to focus on the problem in a concrete legal case and a specific social issue is helpful, I think, in taking it outside theoretical alternatives and into the experience of those whose lives constitute the "problem." The answer, as far as there is one, does not arise from theoretical truths about freedom, social order, or moral reasoning but from experiments in the meaning of freedom, the demands it can make on order, and the forms order can take.

Chapter 5

I HAD BEEN thinking for some time about the commonsense presuppositions of American life and the character of the utopian impulse. I came to the first in thinking about the political language and temperament of George W. Bush, whose confidence in his own judgment—sometimes imagining divine backing, sometimes not—powerfully arrested my attention. The backdrop was, no doubt, Tocqueville's argument about why Americans so confidently rely on common sense. Some political science and sociology work on American intuitions about the world was also important, notably Jennifer Hochschild's *Facing Up to the American Dream* and other works and Robert Bellah's (with collaborators) *Habits of the Heart*.

· In thinking about the utopian impulse, I began from sharply critical assessments by Isaiah Berlin and Mark Lilla, two liberals (in the broad sense of the term) who understand utopianism as a misplaced and destructive effort to load politics with aspirations it cannot carry, such as love, the desire for completeness, or the wish for perfection. (I am thinking particularly of most of the essays in Berlin's *Sense of Reality* and of Lilla's *Reckless Mind: Intellectuals in Politics*). Although these influenced me, studying the American tradition and some of its antecedents in the moderate Enlightenment persuaded me that such pessimism could not be the whole story. Agitators for values we now regard as obvious, such as political equality and labor markets without slavery, were attacked as utopians by the "countertradition" critics whose work I consider in chapter 4. Our ordinary political attitudes, the same ones that today's antiutopians hold, were themselves touchstones for utopian projects. This led me to believe that the utopian demand for a world that can accommodate more of our nature than the present is a permanent and valid part of progress. This image of

utopianism has something in common with the one Roberto Unger advances in *Passion* and *False Necessity*, although Unger's embrace of a disruptive spirit is farther reaching and more consistent than mine.

Chapters 6–8

THESE CHAPTERS are very much of a piece. For more than a decade I have been asking an unoriginal question: What relationship does a market economy have to democratic community? Having said a fair amount about democratic community up to this point, it seemed essential to turn back to the economic part of the question. I had also been thinking about this question somewhat independently in teaching a first-year law course on property, a topic that sets out the legal basis of market relations.

There are stylized alternatives in this debate, and they are completely unhelpful. There is still a conservative tendency, as in Richard Pipes's *Property and Freedom*, to identify personal and political freedom pretty comprehensively with markets. There is also a leftover antimarket animus on the left, a tendency to see the political equality of democracy and the economic differentiation of markets as indicating that the two systems are basically opposed. I see parts of this in work I admire, such as Sandel's *Democracy's Discontent* and republican histories such as Drew R. McCoy's *Elusive Republic*.

My way out began in reading Adam Smith, not just *The Wealth of Nations* but also *The Theory of Moral Sentiments* and *Lectures on Jurisprudence*. I found in Smith a visionary reformer, concerned with every aspect of social life, who put markets at the center of what was, in ways, a radical vision. I found myself tracing parts of this influence into early American thought, in conservatives such as James Kent in his *Commentaries on American Law*, but also democratic radicals such as the Jacksonian William Leggett. At

the same time, I began reading on the origins and commitments of Smith's Scottish Enlightenment, especially Emma Rothschild's *Economic Sentiments,* Istvan Hont's *Jealousy of Trade,* and the earlier collection edited by Hont and Michael Ignatieff, *Wealth and Virtue.*

In contemporary work, I found inspiring an approach to economics that has much in common with Smith's: that of Amartya Sen, who won the Nobel Prize for economics in 1998. I have learned immensely from Sen's work in *Inequality Reexamined; Resources, Values, and Development; The Quality of Life* (an edited volume with Martha Nussbaum); and the invaluable collection *Rationality and Freedom.* I have also benefited, both in reading and in teaching Sen's work, from his more accessible summary of his thought, *Development as Freedom.*

Despite his productive involvement in important issues of development and equality, Sen is primarily a theorist. In thinking about how to approach today's economic decisions in a spirit both realistic and utopian, I looked to people involved in areas where technology is changing fast enough that basic questions about how to order rights and interests are open and alive. I found these especially in intellectual property, where my friend and colleague James Boyle (*The Public Domain*), Yochai Benkler (*The Wealth of Networks*), and Lawrence Lessig (*Free Culture, Code,* and *The Future of Ideas*) have shed a lot of light on just the kinds of questions I argue we should pose; and in finance, where Robert Shiller (*The New Financial Order*) showed me an immense amount about how complex financial structures can be either profreedom or antifreedom.

Bibliography

Adams, John. *The Political Writings of John Adams.* Ed. George A. Peek. New York: Hackett, 2003.

Alexander, Gregory S. *Commodity and Propriety: Competing Visions of Property in American Legal Thought, 1776–1970.* Chicago: University of Chicago Press, 1997.

Armitage, David. *The Declaration of Independence.* (Cambridge, MA: Harvard University Press, 2007).

Bailyn, Bernard. *The Ideological Origins of the American Revolution.* Cambridge, MA: Harvard University Press, 1992.

Beard, Charles A. *An Economic Interpretation of the Constitution.* Edison, NJ: Transaction Publishers, 1998.

Beecher, Lyman. *A Reformation of Morals Practicable and Indispensable.* New Haven, CT: Eli Hudson, 1813.

Benkler, Yochai. *The Wealth of Networks: How Social Production Transforms Markets and Freedom.* New Haven, CT: Yale University Press, 2006.

Berlin, Isaiah. *The Sense of Reality: Studies in Ideas and Their History.* Ed. Henry Hardy. New York: Farrar, Straus & Giroux, 1996.

Boswell, James. *The Life of Samuel Johnson, L.L.D.* Edinburgh: William P. Nimmo, 1873.

Bourne, George. *The Majesty and Condescension of God.* Staunton, VA: Isaac Collett, 1813.

Boyle, James. *The Public Domain: An Environmentalism for the Commons of the Mind.* New Haven, CT: Yale University Press, 2009.

Bromwich, David. *Democratic Vistas: Reflections on the Life of American Democracy.* Ed. Jedediah Purdy. New Haven, CT: Yale University Press, 2004.

Brooks, David. "The Triumph of Hope over Self-Interest." *New York Times,* Jan. 12, 2003.

Burke, Edmund. *On Empire, Liberty, and Reform: Speeches and Letters.* Ed. David Bromwich. New Haven, CT: Yale University Press, 2000.

———. *Reflections on the Revolution in France.* Oxford: Oxford University Press, 1999.

———. *Speech on Conciliation with America.* New York: Harper & Bros., 1945.

Cachan, Manuel. "Justice Stephen Field and 'Free Soil, Free Labor Constitutionalism': Reconsidering Revisionism." *Law and History Review* 20 (2002): 541.

Chafe, William H. *Private Lives, Public Consequences: Personality and Politics in Modern America.* Cambridge, MA: Harvard University Press, 2005.

Casey v. Planned Parenthood of Pennsylvania. 505 US 833 (1992).

Chorvat, Terence, and Kevin McCabe. "The Brain and the Law." *Philosophical Transcripts of the Royal Society of London* 359 (2004): 1727.

Cohen, Jonathan D. "The Vulcanization of the Human Brain: A Neural Perspective on Interactions Between Cognition and Emotion." *Journal of Economic Perspectives* 19, no. 4 (2005).

Commonwealth v. Turner. 26 Va. 678 (1827).

Cooter, Robert, and Peter Rappoport. "Were the Ordinalists Wrong About Welfare Economics?" *Journal of Economic Literature* 22 (1982): 507, 520–24.

Cover, Robert. "Nomos and Narrative." *Harvard Law Review* 97 (1983): 4.

Cover, Robert M. *Justice Accused: Antislavery and the Judicial Process.* New Haven, CT: Yale University Press, 1974.

Coyle, Diane. *The Soulful Science: What Economists Really Do and Why It Matters.* Princeton, NJ: Princeton University Press, 2007.

Croly, Herbert. *The Promise of American Life.* New York: Macmillan, 1911.

Davis, David Brion. *The Problem of Slavery in the Age of Revolution, 1770–1823.* Oxford: Oxford University Press, 1999.

Dobson, James. *Marriage Under Fire: Why We Must Win this Battle.* Sisters, OR: Multnomah Publishers, 2004.

Donaldson, Robert H., and Joseph L. Nogee. *The Foreign Policy of Russia: Changing Systems, Enduring Interests.* New York: M. E. Sharpe, 2005.

Douglass, Frederick. "Life and Times of Frederick Douglass." In *Frederick Douglass: Autobiographies.* New York: Library of America, 1994.

———. *My Bondage and My Freedom.* New York: Modern Library, 2003.

————. *The Life of Frederick Douglass, an American Slave.* Oxford: Oxford University Press, 1999.

Dred Scott v. Sandford. 60 US 393, 407 (1856).

Dwight, Timothy. *A Discourse on Some Events of the Last Century.* New Haven, CT: Ezra Read, 1801.

Dworkin, Ronald. *Is Democracy Possible Here?* Princeton, NJ: Princeton University Press, 2006.

Elliott, Stephen. *New Wine Not to Be Put into Old Bottles.* Savannah, GA: Steam Power Press of John M. Cooper, 1862.

Emerson, Ralph Waldo. *The Conduct of Life.* Boston: Houghton Mifflin, 1904.

————. *The Essential Writings of Ralph Waldo Emerson.* Ed. Brooks Atkinson. New York: Modern Library, 2000.

————. *Representative Men.* Boston: Houghton Mifflin, 1903.

Epstein, Richard. *Simple Rules for a Complex World.* Cambridge, MA: Harvard University Press, 1995.

Fehr, Ernst, and Urs Fischbacher. "The Nature of Human Altruism." *Nature* 425 (2003): 785.

Fink, Leon. *Progressive Intellectuals and the Dilemmas of Democratic Commitment.* Cambridge, MA: Harvard University Press, 1997.

Fiorina, Morris P. *Culture War? The Myth of a Polarized America.* 2d ed. New York: Pearson Longman, 2006.

Foner, Eric. *Free Soil, Free Labor, Free Men: The Ideology of the Republican Party Before the Civil War.* Oxford: Oxford University Press, 1970.

————. *Reconstruction: America's Unfinished Revolution, 1863–1877.* New York: Perennial, 1988.

Fourier, Charles. *The Utopian Vision of Charles Fourier: Selected Texts on Work, Love, and Passionate Attraction.* Ed. Jonathan Beecher and Richard Bienvenu. Boston: Beacon Press, 1971.

Fox-Genovese, Elizabeth, and Eugene D. Genovese. *The Mind of the Master Class: History and Faith in the Southern Slaveholders' Worldview.* Cambridge: Cambridge University Press, 2005.

Fried, Barbara. *The Progressive Assault on Laissez-Faire: Robert Hale and the First Law and Economics Movement.* Cambridge, MA: Harvard University Press, 2001.

Friedman, Lawrence M. *American Law in the Twentieth Century.* New Haven, CT: Yale University Press, 2002.

Fukuyama, Francis. *America at the Crossroads: Democracy, Power, and the Neoconservative Legacy.* New Haven, CT: Yale University Press, 2006.

Garrison, William Lloyd. "Address to the Colonization Society." In *A House Divided: The Antebellum Slavery Debates in the United States, 1776–1865,* ed. Mason I. Lowance Jr. Princeton, NJ: Princeton University Press, 2003.

————. "Address to the Friends of Freedom and Emancipation in the United States." In *The American Intellectual Tradition.* Vol. 1, *1630–1865,* ed. David A. Hollinger and Charles Capper. Oxford: Oxford University Press, 1977.

Gay, Peter. *Freud: A Life for Our Time.* New York: Norton, 2006.

Genovese, Eugene. *Roll, Jordan, Roll: The World the Slaves Made.* New York: Vintage, 1974.

Goldwater, Barry. "Extremism in Defense of Liberty Is No Vice." In *Twentieth-Century Speeches,* ed. Brian MacArthur. 348–51. New York: Penguin, 2000.

Goodell, William. *Slavery and Anti-Slavery.* New York: William Harned, 1852.

Graham, Otis L. *Toward a Planned Society: From Roosevelt to Nixon.* Oxford: Oxford University Press: 1976.

Hacker, Jacob S. *The Great Risk Shift.* Oxford: Oxford University Press, 2006.

Hamilton, Alexander. *The Federalist.* No. 1. Oct. 27, 1827.

Hamilton, William. "Bush Began to Plan War Three Months After 9/11." *Washington Post,* April 17, 2004.

Hartz, Louis. *The Liberal Tradition in America.* New York: Harvest, 1991.

Hatch, Nathan O. *The Democratization of American Christianity.* New Haven, CT: Yale University Press, 1991.

Heinrech, Joseph, et al. " 'Economic Man' in Cross-Cultural Perspective: Behavioral Experiments in 15 Small-Scale Societies." *Behavior and Brain Science* 28 (2005): 795.

Hochschild, Jennifer L. *Facing Up to the American Dream: Race, Class, and the Soul of America.* Princeton, NJ: Princeton University Press, 1995.

Holden v. Hardy. 169 U.S. (1898).

Hollinger, David A., and Charles Capper, eds. *The American Intellectual Tradition.* Vol. 1, *1630–1865.* Oxford: Oxford University Press, 1997.

Holmes, Oliver Wendell, Sr. *Library of Literary Criticism of English and American Authors.* Vol. 7, *1875–90.* Ed. Charles Wells Moulton. New York: Henry Malkan, 1910.

Holmes, Oliver Wendell, Jr. "The Soldier's Faith." Commencement address. Cambridge, MA. May 30, 1895.

Honneth, Axel. *The Struggle for Recognition: The Moral Grammar of Social Conflicts*. Cambridge, MA: MIT Press, 1996.

Hont, Istvan. *Jealousy of Trade: International Competition and the Nation-State in Historical Perspective*. Cambridge, MA: Harvard University Press, 2005.

Horwitz, Morton J. *The Transformation of American Law, 1780–1860*. Cambridge, MA: Harvard University Press, 1977.

James, William. "The Moral Equivalent of War." Lecture. San Francisco, 1906.

Jarman v. Patterson. 23 Ky. 644 (1828).

Jefferson, Thomas. *Jefferson: Writings*. Ed. Merrill D. Peterson. New York: Library of America, 1984.

Jeffries, John C., Jr. *Justice Lewis F. Powell, Jr.* New York: Fordham University Press, 2001.

Johnson, Lyndon. Great Society speech. May 22, 1964.

———. Speech before Congress on voting rights. Mar. 15, 1965.

Johnson, Samuel. *Taxation No Tyranny: An Answer to the Resolutions of the American Congress*. London: T. Cadell, 1775.

Kahan, Dan M. "The Logic of Reciprocity: Trust, Collective Action, and Law." In *Moral Sentiments and Material Interests: On the Foundations of Cooperation in Economic Life*. Ed. Herbert Gintis et al. Cambridge, MA: MIT University Press, 2005.

Keller, Morton. *Regulating a New Economy: Public Policy and Economic Change in America, 1900–1933*. Cambridge, MA: Harvard University Press, 1990.

———. *Regulating a New Society*. Cambridge, MA: Harvard University Press, 1994.

King, Martin Luther, Jr. "I Have a Dream" speech. Washington, DC, Aug. 28, 1963.

Kohut, Andrew, and Bruce Stokes. *Two Americas, One American*. Washington, DC: Pew Research Center, June 6, 2006.

Kramer, Larry. *The People Themselves: Popular Constitutionalism and Judicial Review*. Oxford: Oxford University Press, 2004.

Lawrence v. Texas. 539 U.S. 558 (2003).

Leggett, William. "True Functions of Government." In *The American Intellectual Tradition*, ed. David A. Hollinger and Charles Capper. Oxford University Press, 1977.

Lessig, Lawrence. *Free Culture: How Big Media Uses Technology and the Law to Lock Down Culture and Control Creativity*. New York: Penguin, 2004.

Lincoln, Abraham. Address to the Wisconsin State Agricultural Society. Sept. 30, 1859.

———. Gettysburg Address speech. Gettysburg, PA. Nov. 19, 1863.

———. Speech to the 140th Indiana Regiment. Mar. 17, 1865.

Lind, John. *An Answer to the Declaration of the American Congress.* London: T. Cadell, 1776.

Lochner v. New York. 198 U.S. 45 (1905).

Mayhew, Jonathan. "A Discourse Concerning Unlimited Submission and Non-Resistance to the Higher Powers." Boston, 1750. http://www.lawandliberty.org/mayhew.htm.

McCabe, Kevin, et al. "A Functional Imaging Study of Cooperation in Two-Person Reciprocal Exchange." *Proceedings of the National Academies of Science* 98, no. 20 (Sept. 25, 2001).

McCorkle, Samuel E. *The Work of God for the French Republic and Then Her Reformation or Ruin.* Salisbury, NC: Francis Coupee, 1798.

McCoy, Drew R. *The Elusive Republic: Political Economy in Jeffersonian America.* New York: Norton, 1980.

McCurdy, Charles W. "The 'Liberty of Contract' Regime in American Law." In *The State and Freedom of Contract,* ed. Harry N. Scheiber. Stanford, CA: Stanford University Press, 1998.

Mickelthwait, John, and Adrian Wooldridge. *The Right Nation: Conservative Power in America.* New York: Penguin, 2004.

Muller v. Oregon. 208 U.S. 412 (1908).

Murray, Charles. *What It Means to Be a Libertarian.* New York: Broadway, 1997.

Noll, Mark A. *America's God: From Jonathan Edwards to Abraham Lincoln.* Oxford: Oxford University Press, 2002.

Oakes, James. *The Radical and the Republican.* New York: Norton, 2007.

Oakeshott, Michael. "On Being Conservative." In *Rationalism in Politics and Other Essays.* Indianapolis: Liberty Press, 1991.

O'Brien, Conor Cruise. *The Great Melody: A Thematic Biography of Edmund Burke.* Chicago: University of Chicago Press, 1992.

Olson, Mancur, and Satu Kahkonen. *A Not-So Dismal Science: A Broader View of Economies and Societies.* Oxford: Oxford University Press, 2000.

Paul, Ellen Frankel, et al., eds. *Ethics and Economics.* Oxford: Blackwell Publishers, 1985.

Pettit, Philip. *Republicanism: A Theory of Freedom and Government.* Oxford: Oxford University Press, 1999.

Purcell, Edward A. *The Crisis of Democratic Theory: Scientific Naturalism and the Problem of Value.* Lexington: University Press of Kentucky, 1975.

Purdy, Jedediah. "A Freedom-Promoting Approach to Property: A Renewed Tradition for New Debates," 72 *Univ. of Chicago Law Review* 1237 (2005).

Putnam, Robert D. "*E Pluribus Unum:* Diversity and Community in the Twenty-First Century." The 2006 Johann Skytte Prize Lecture. 30.2 *Scandinavian Political Studies* 137 (2007).

Rawls, John. *A Theory of Justice.* Cambridge, MA: Harvard University Press, 1971.

Reagan, Ronald. "A Time for Choosing." Television address. Oct. 27, 1964.

Reid, John Philip. *The Ancient Constitution and the Origins of Anglo-American Liberty.* De Kalb: Northern Illinois University Press, 2005.

———. *The Concept of Liberty in the Age of the American Revolution.* Chicago: University of Chicago Press, 1988.

Rilling, James K., et al. "A Neural Basis for Social Cooperation." *Neuron* 35 no. 2 (2002).

Robbins, Lionel. *An Essay on the Nature and Significance of Economic Science.* 2d ed. London: Macmillan, 1945.

Rodgers, Daniel T. *Atlantic Crossings: Social Politics in a Progressive Age.* Cambridge, MA: Harvard University Press, 1998.

Roosevelt, Franklin. Address to the Commonwealth Club of San Francisco. Sept. 23, 1932.

Roosevelt, Theodore. "The Strenuous Life." Speech. Chicago, Apr. 10, 1899.

Rothschild, Emma. *Economic Sentiments: Adam Smith, Condorcet, and the Enlightenment.* Cambridge, MA: Harvard University Press, 2001.

Ryan, Frank X. *Darwin's Impact: Social Evolution in America, 1880–1920.* Bristol: Thoemmes Press, 2001.

Sandel, Michael. "The Case Against Perfection." *Atlantic Monthly.* Apr. 2004.

———. *Democracy's Discontent: America in Search of a Public Philosophy.* Cambridge, MA: Harvard University Press, 1996.

Sanfey, Alan G., et al. "The Neural Basis of Economic Decision-Making in the Ultimatum Game." 300 *Science* 1755 (2003).

Schumpeter, Joseph A. *Capitalism, Socialism and Democracy.* New York: Harper Perennial, 1950.

Scott, William Robert. *Francis Hutcheson: His Life, Teaching, and Position in the History of Philosophy.* Cambridge: Cambridge University Press, 1900.

Sen, Amartya. *Development as Freedom.* New York: Knopf, 1999.

———. *Rationality and Freedom.* Cambridge, MA: Harvard University Press, 2002.

Shiller, Robert. *The New Financial Order.* Princeton, NJ: Princeton University Press, 2003.

Siegel, Stephen A. "The Revision Thickens." 20 *Law and History Review* 631 (2002).

Smith, Adam. *An Inquiry into the Nature and Causes of the Wealth of Nations.* 2 vols. Ed. R. H. Campbell and A. S. Skinner. Indianapolis: Liberty Fund, 1981.

———. *Lectures on Jurisprudence.* Ed. R. L. Meek et al. Oxford: Oxford University Press, 1978.

———. *The Theory of Moral Sentiments.* Amherst, NY: Prometheus, 2000.

Smith, Vernon L. "Constructivist and Ecological Rationality in Economics." 93 *American Economic Review* 465 (2003).

Spooner, Lysander. *The Unconstitutionality of Slavery.* Boston: Bela Marsh, 1845.

State v. Jones. 1 Miss. 83, 85 (1820).

State v. Mann. 13 N.C. 263 (1829).

Steinfeld, Robert J. *Coercion, Contract, and Free Labor in the Nineteenth Century.* Cambridge: Cambridge University Press, 2001.

Stout, Harry N. *The New England Soul: Preaching and Religious Culture in Colonial New England.* Oxford: Oxford University Press, 1986.

Sumner, William Graham. "The Absurd Effort to Make the World Over." In *Darwin's Impact: Social Evolution in America, 1880–1920,* ed. Frank X. Ryan. Bristol: Thoemmes Press, 2001.

Sundquist, Eric, ed. *Frederick Douglass: New Literary and Historical Essays.* Cambridge: Cambridge University Press, 1990.

Sunstein, Cass R. *Worst-Case Scenarios.* Cambridge, MA: Harvard University Press, 2007.

Taylor, Charles. *A Secular Age.* Cambridge, MA: Harvard University Press, 2007.

———. *Sources of the Self: The Making of the Modern Identity.* Cambridge, MA.: Harvard University Press, 1989.

———. "The Politics of Recognition." In *Philosophical Arguments.* Cambridge, MA: Harvard University Press, 1997.

Tocqueville, Alexis de. *Democracy in America.* Ed. J. P. Mayer. Trans. George Lawrence, New York: Perennial, 1969.

Tulis, Jeffrey K. *The Rhetorical Presidency.* Princeton, NJ: Princeton University Press, 1987.

Tushnet, Mark V. *Slave Law in the American South:* State v. Mann *in History and Literature.* Lawrence: Kansas University Press, 2003.

United States v. Amy. 24 F. Cas. 792, 810 (C.C.D. Va. 1859).

Warren, Rick. *The Purpose-Driven Life: What on Earth Am I Here For?* Grand Rapids, MI: Zondervan, 2002.

Wesley, John. *The Works of the Rev. John Wesley, A.M.* Vol. 6. Ed. John Emory. New York: J. Collord, 1839.

West Coast Hotel v. Parrish. 300 U.S. 379 (1937).

Whitman, Walt. *The Portable Walt Whitman.* Ed. Mark Van Doren. New York: Penguin, 1973.

Wilentz, Sean. *The Rise of American Democracy: Jefferson to Lincoln.* New York: Norton, 2005.

Wills, Garry. *Inventing America: Jefferson's Declaration of Independence.* New York: Doubleday, 1977.

Wilson, Woodrow. *The New Freedom.* New York: Doubleday, 1913.

Winthrop, John. "A City Set upon a Hill." In *The Penguin Book of Historic Speeches,* ed. Brian MacArthur. 65–67. New York: Penguin, 1995.

Witt, John Fabian. *The Accidental Republic: Crippled Workingmen, Destitute Widows, and the Remaking of American Law.* Cambridge, MA: Harvard University Press, 2004.

Wolfe, Alan. *One Nation After All.* New York: Penguin, 1998.

Wolfe, Tom. *The Bonfire of the Vanities.* New York: Farrar, Straus, & Giroux, 1987.

Wood, Gordon S. *The Creation of the American Republic.* Chapel Hill: University of North Carolina Press, 1998.

———. *The Radicalism of the American Revolution.* New York: Knopf, 1992.

Index